THE DYNAMICS OF HUMAN COMMUNICATION

A LABORATORY APPROACH

SIXTH EDITION

Gail E. Myers
Consultant
Applied Communication

Michele Tolela Myers
President
Denison University

McGraw-Hill, Inc.
New York St. Louis San Francisco Auckland Bogotá
Caracas Lisbon London Madrid Mexico City Milan
Montreal New Delhi San Juan Singapore
Sydney Tokyo Toronto

THE
DYNAMICS
OF
HUMAN
COMMUNICATION
A Laboratory Approach

4 5 6 7 8 9 0   DOC   DOC   9 0 9 8 7 6 5

ISBN 0-07-044231-2

This book was set in Souvenir by Ruttle, Shaw & Wetherill, Inc.
The editors were Hilary Jackson, Lyn Beamesderfer, and Scott Amerman;
the production supervisor was Janelle S. Travers.
The photo editor was Inge King.
Drawings were done by Fine Line Illustrations, Inc.
R. R. Donnelley & Sons Company was printer and binder.

Cover photos: Background, J. Whitmer/H. Armstrong Roberts; inset,
Jeff Lowenthal/Woodfin Camp & Associates.

This book is printed on acid-free paper.

Library of Congress Cataloging-in-Publication Data

Myers, Gail E., (date).
The dynamics of human communication: a laboratory approach / Gail
E. Myers, Michele Tolela Myers.—6th ed.
p.   cm.
Includes bibliographical references and index.
ISBN 0-07-044231-2
1. Interpersonal communication.   2. Interpersonal communication—
Problems, exercises, etc.   I. Myers, Michele Tolela, (date).
II. Title.
BF637.C45M9   1992
153.6—dc20   91-17784

THE DYNAMICS OF HUMAN COMMUNICATION

A LABORATORY APPROACH

ABOUT THE AUTHORS

Since 1972, Michele and Gail Myers have published three communication textbooks with McGraw-Hill: *Communicating When We Speak, Managing by Communication,* and this book, *The Dynamics of Human Communication,* now in its sixth edition.

Translated into French, *Dynamics of Human Communication* has recently been issued in its second French-language edition and is available in Europe as well as in Canada.

Managing by Communication has been translated into Spanish for students in Mexico and Latin America, and has been published by McGraw-Hill Tokyo in a Far East edition.

Gail E. Myers now heads up his own organizational communication consulting service, Applied Communication. While teaching recently both graduate and undergraduate courses at Temple University (including interviewing, interpersonal, and business communication) he was also the director of that Speech Department's graduate program in applied communication. He joined the Temple faculty after leaving a professorship at Trinity University (Texas) where he had earlier been Dean of the College of Arts and Sciences and of Communication and the Arts. His teaching appointment as full professor at Trinity was in both the Speech Department, teaching interpersonal, organizational, and group courses, and the Communications Department, where he taught public relations, mass media in society, and the aesthetics of sight, sound, and motion. His administrative career also includes positions as alumni and publications director at the University of Northern Iowa (Cedar Falls), technical editor at the Colorado School of Mines, vice president and then president of Monticello College (Illinois), and founding president of Lewis and Clark Community College (Illinois). In addition to part-time teaching during his administrative assignments he has taught full-time at the University of Denver and at Trinity University. He has a B.A. and an M.A. in journalism from the State University of Iowa, where he was editor of *The Daily Iowan,* and his Ph.D. is from the University of Denver in communication methodology. His dissertation involved a sociometric study of the channels of communication used by Spanish-surnamed residents of Denver.

Gail and Michele have two children, Erika, born in 1972, and David, born in 1977, and have dedicated all the editions of their books to them.

Michele Tolela Myers is the first woman president of Denison University in Granville, Ohio. A native of Paris, France, she graduated from the Institute of Political Science at the University of Paris before coming to the United States to study communication at the University of Denver. She earned an M.A. and a Ph.D. at Denver, later adding an M.A. in clinical psychology from Trinity University in Texas. Her dissertation was in the field of group dynamics and was directed by Alvin Goldberg. Before her appointment as president at Denison, she was Dean of the Undergraduate College at Bryn Mawr, and earlier was Associate Vice President for Academic Affairs at Trinity. She was an American Council of Education fellow in administration at Northwestern and at Trinity; in addition she taught at the University of Denver, Manchester College (Indiana), Monticello College (Illinois), and Trinity University (Texas) before moving into academic administration. She had a private practice in family and group psychology, and helped establish networks for women in the professions. She and her husband have been very active in communication and organizational behavior consulting for many different business organizations, professional groups, health care institutions, and governmental agencies.

To Erika and David

CONTENTS

PREFACE

The first edition of this textbook grew out of a need to combine the essential *practice of communication* with the rapidly growing *knowledge about communication*. The first edition of *Dynamics of Human Communication* was a pioneer in the field, as it put theories to work with the skills of applying them to human interaction.

Feedback from students and teachers who have used this book has influenced each new edition—the content, the writing style, the kinds and sources of exercises, and the organization of the manuscript material. New theoretical developments, new ways of looking at human relationships, new emphases on discourse and transactions all have meant changes in what this textbook covers. New ways of viewing the human communicative condition gave rise to new research directions, new nomenclatures, and new scholars whose work deserves inclusion in the updated texts in this discipline. To update a textbook it is necessary to review the writing and research about human communication reported in many journals both outside the discipline (for example, in publications of the social and behavioral sciences) and in the communication field in such works as *Human Communication Research, Quarterly Journal of Speech, Journal*

xix

of Communication, Communication Education, and *Communication Monographs,* as well as the regional journals in the field. You will still, however, find many references to classical research and theorists in human communication dating back many years; these must be included to help you gain a historical perspective on communication studies. These references also pay tribute to the earliest scholars, thinkers, and leaders in the field of interpersonal and speech communication.

Wide acceptance not only of this textbook but of the principle of "laboratory learning" has meant a significant change in the way many communication courses are taught. Invention of the Interpersonal Communication Laboratory by Elwood Murray at the University of Denver marked a new beginning in speech teaching—adopting as he did the laboratory principles from the physical sciences. Nobody up to that time seems to have questioned the need to apply chemical principles in a chemistry lab, or the idea that students develop a greater understanding of energy or motion in a physics lab. But it seemed a bit revolutionary fifty years ago when Dr. Murray took that next logical step in developing a social science laboratory where communication theory can be brought to first-person experience in a safe and controlled learning environment.

Organization of This Book

The Laboratory Manual—The feature which has consistently made *Dynamics* both student-centered and unique is the laboratory manual section, located at the end of the book. The participative function of the manual relates the student directly to the text material, chapter by chapter. This is truly "laboratory learning," as the assignments, activities, and experiences link a world of theory with the world of communicative action. There are cases to solve or discuss or role-play. There are topics for lively discussion. There are questions about communicative behavior which stimulate both thought and interaction. There are games and problems. All are designed to give you more insights into the principles and theories introduced in the first part of the book. It is not likely you will have the opportunity in class to use all the incidents or activities, but students may want to read the items or answer for themselves some of the suggested discussion questions; or they may want to do additional assignments beyond what is covered in the course.

New to This Edition—Because *Dynamics* enjoyed such a leading and pioneering role in the teaching of interpersonal communication, we are challenged to reflect the current needs of teachers and the changing responses by students. Thanks to generously informal and rigorously formal reviews and suggestions, we can take advantage of thoughtful feedback in making this Sixth Edition a joint effort to serve yet another generation of learners and teachers. These efforts include:

- Pulling "listening" from a later and subordinated position to recognize its growing centrality of communication focus.
- Developing for the first time a "four-stage" construct for understanding listening; suggesting this exciting new taxonomy to help clarify the complexities of listening behavior.
- Adding more cross references between text and the important activities and exercises in the Lab Manual.
- Moving the "language and meaning" materials later in the book better to reflect an implicit order of problem-solution in the content.
- Deleting, adding, editing relevant communication examples and triggers for discussion to represent changing demographics and curiosities of the readers.
- Assembling fresh visual support for the text data—photos, diagrams, charts, etc.—which enrich the students' interactions with the text.
- Expanding our discussion of feedforward (also referred to as "candidate answers" or "trial balloons") as an adjunct to the clearly prescriptive use of feedback.
- Moving citations to a position of end-notes; continuing the balance of classic references in relation to notations of very current literature; and emphasizing new ranges of references which will be both interesting and available to further library search.

The Text—The eleven chapters in the text portion of the book progress from an overview of human communication, through the complexities of interpersonal relationships, to the specifics of managing interpersonal tensions.

Chapter 1 introduces some of the more popular, interesting, and useful theories about how people communicate with one another and with what effect. A brief historical review helps place this study in perspective.

Chapter 2 includes theories of perception, with many familiar and descriptive illustrations of how communication is affected by how you perceive. We propose a process view of the world rather than a static one.

Chapters 3 and 4 involve the development and maintenance of self-concept. We explore the ways in which people respond to others' opinions, and focus on how a choice of communicative style (especially assertiveness) can be employed as a means of managing your self-esteem as well as interpersonal relationships.

Chapter 5 relates to needs, attitudes, values, and beliefs and explains how they support or inhibit your interpersonal communication. Again, an historical perspective traces the origin of today's theories and demonstrates how their current implications affect communication.

Chapter 6 provides an original treatment of listening as a special case of communicative behavior. It addresses the limits of our listening habits and the consequences, as well as some suggestions which have been made about assessing and overcoming listening problems. Unique to this book is the classification of four listening types, which make a significant argument for taking a fresh look at listening behaviors.

Chapters 7, 8, and 9 explore how communication relates to language, meaning, and the fascinating nonlanguage systems we refer to as nonverbal and silences. Recognizing the powers of language to build or destroy, we propose several ways of looking at the use of language. This analysis will help us detect the unhealthy use of language when it occurs, and, in turn, help us make our own use of language more effective.

Relationships, trust, and the roles we play in their development and maintenance are treated in Chapter 10. While our most personal relationships are important, the study of relations goes much further because "interpersonal" is not a synonym for "intimate." For this reason we will study relations in the family, in friendships, in work and study contacts, and in intercultural and international affairs, as well as in our casual everyday associations with strangers.

Chapter 11 offers new ways of looking at conflict, and at negotiation as one means of managing various types of conflict. Use of feedback and feedforward and self-disclosure are related to management of the tensions that inevitably arise during your communication transactions.

Learning Aids in the Chapters—Each chapter has End Notes that refer to the sources from which material in this book has been derived and offers further reading opportunity. In addition, there are figures and "boxes" of related items to trigger critical thinking and discussion about the text material. Objectives at the start of each chapter indicate what can be expected, while the summary at the end gives a brief review of the data contained in the chapter.

Acknowledgments

Previous editions of this textbook, as well as our own personal and professional lives, were deeply influenced by Dr. Elwood Murray, a creative scholar and an innovative teacher. In this preface we have already mentioned that Dr. Murray pioneered the interpersonal laboratory, and that is simply one of his accomplishments which has actually changed the way speech communication is taught today. At least three decades before the rest of the discipline had accepted the human transactional view of communication, Dr. Murray was writing, campaigning, arguing, and probing this set of then-revolutionary formulations. His students, and *their* students in turn, have had a continuing effect on the field of interpersonal communication. In her excellent book on interpersonal communication, Kathleen Reardon credits Dr. Murray with substantial contributions to this field, including founding the International Communication Association (founded as the National Society for the Study of Communication) and positing the "important connection between personality and interpersonal relationships."[1] In this new edition of a textbook which comes directly from Dr. Murray's life and work, we want to simply add our most sincere and public acknowledgment to those many other accolades he has received, most recently Dr. Reardon's insightful recognition of Elwood Murray's significant place in the communication discipline.

This sixth edition is very substantially changed from previous editions, both in the text matter and in the arrangement of the chapters. Critical and highly qualified reviewers have provided excellent advice on how to make the book more effective. All have used or are presently using this text, and their comments come from experience with previous editions of *Dynamics* as well as knowledge about other textbooks. We also seek and use student reactions to help us make crucial improvements in the text and the lab manual. We especially made grateful use of the careful and thoughtful comments from Anita Pomerantz and her graduate assistants at Temple University. Collegial encouragement from former Temple U. associates Joe Folger, Bob Craig, Karen Tracy, Tom Rosteck, Herb Simon, et al., has helped broaden our approach and clarify the presentation of this book.

For the following seven reviewers selected by McGraw-Hill, we are appreciative, as their comments meant much in the revision of the order and content of this sixth edition: John Anglin, East Central College; Nelson da Costa, University of Kansas; Allan Frank, SUNY–Brockport; Colan T. Hanson, North Dakota State University; Anita Pomerantz, Temple University; Linda Reese, College of Staten Island; and Dick Stine, Johnson County Community College.

To the McGraw-Hill team of publishers, editors, artists, and production people we want to express our appreciation for their work as well as their confidence in this new revised edition. Specifically we are grateful to Hilary Jackson, Lyn Beamesderfer, Scott Amerman, Janelle Travers, and Chuck Carson as professionals in the difficult role of bringing ideas from an author into a classroom.

Gail E. Myers
Michele Tolela Myers

---

[1] Kathleen K. Reardon, *Interpersonal Communication: Where Minds Meet*, Belmont, Calif., Wadsworth Publishing Company, 1987, p. 33.

THE
DYNAMICS
OF
HUMAN
COMMUNICATION

A LABORATORY APPROACH

(© Richard Pasley/Stock, Boston)

CHAPTER

1

YOU AND YOUR COMMUNICATION

After completing this chapter you should be able to:

1. List six reasons we communicate, and give examples from your own experience.
2. Compare and contrast intrapersonal, interpersonal, group, and mass communication.
3. Explain the use of models in relation to emphasis, clarification, simplification, and expression of a point of view.
4. Draw and label a model of human communication including the most important factors.
5. Explain the ''bull's-eye'' view and the Ping-Pong view of communicating and why each may be inadequate to describe the dynamics of communication.
6. Define and list two major assumptions of the transactional view.
7. Defend with examples the argument that you cannot not communicate.
8. Discuss the relationship of ''predictability'' to human communication.

9. Distinguish between the content level and relationship level of communication, and list uses of each.

10. Define and give examples of complementary and symmetrical relations and how they relate to our communication.

INTRODUCTION

You live in a world of communication. You speak to the student next to you in class. You phone someone. You watch a soap opera or a news show on television. You go to a church service or a political rally. You read a news magazine account of violence in the Middle East. You shop for a new pair of shoes. You compare feelings with a friend about a movie you saw. You buy groceries. You attend a club meeting and elect officers. You sit with friends in a coffee shop and watch people go by. You go to a lecture. You put on earphones and tune in FM on your portable radio. You wave at a friend driving by.

Each of these activities involves communication. In each of your communication contacts you make choices on how to behave. The choices you make are not random—even if you are not conscious about why you are communicating in that way. What we are saying is that your communication has purpose. The question that follows, then, is what are the purposes of communication?

WHY COMMUNICATE?

Purpose A—You communicate to learn more about yourself, to discover who you are. You also communicate to figure out who you should be in relation to others. Many writers on communication have expressed the idea that each of us is the most important subject of our interpersonal communication, but none so eloquently as Wendell Johnson when he titled one of his books *Your Most Enchanted Listener.*[1] The message is that you are, and you ought to be—and should not be ashamed to be—a primary focus of your own communication.

Purpose B—You communicate to learn more about others, to reduce uncertainty about your relations with those around you. Much of what other people do and say influences you; you tend to behave in relation to how you see others behaving. You can choose to be like them or unlike them, but much of the time people communicate to find out how others are "doing it" or what they feel or think. How does it feel to be 6 feet tall and female? Are left-handed people different from right-handed people? What's it like to be the only one in a dorm or a neighborhood with a different color skin? How many in the class got lower or higher grades than you did on a test, and what does that mean to them. . . . to you? Who are some others who may have the same (or strongly opposite) problems, ideals, and outlook on the world as you do?

Purpose C—You communicate to learn about the world around you. You can discover your world as it is now, as it was, and as it will be, because you have that uniquely human ability to use symbols—mainly language—for your effective communication. Not only do you find out about current happenings and ideas (as trivial as an order of catsup for your french fries, or as complex as international terrorism), but you have available to you information and arguments about events and beliefs that happened centuries ago or occurred thousands of miles away from you. When you travel, read, do scholarly investigations, or have informal discussions with fellow students or family, you are discovering your world.

Purpose D—You communicate to share that world with others and to help others. When we wrote earlier that you are your most important object of communication, we implied that you get information about yourself from others. Whether it is linking yourself to a family, to friends, to groups, to community, or to causes, another important communication purpose you can recognize is establishing and maintaining contact with others—to be recognized, to be paid attention to, to love and to be loved. You set up important human relationships when you talk with others about themselves, when you show interest and affection to others. Even though we are concentrating on you as an individual, many professions have this purpose of sharing with others. Teachers, nurses, doctors, lawyers, public servants, counselors, and hundreds of other professionals dedicate themselves to *communication about the good of* clients, subjects, patients, or pupils, as well as to the more evident purposes of caring for their more material needs.

You communicate to learn about your world and to share it with others. (© *Richard Wood/The Picture Cube*)

Purpose E—You communicate to persuade or influence others or to test and resist influence on you. Whether you are trying to convince a friend to go to a movie with you instead of to the library, or whether the President of the United States is promoting new trade policies with another nation, communication is clearly at the center of the activity. In your own family, your very early childhood was characterized by your being ordered around, and only later did the communication pattern perhaps change to one of persuasion and influence instead of power. A boss or parent, as a center of authority, not only must have the power to manage others, but also gets and maintains influence by communicating to others what will happen if they don't perform as directed. *Communicating about* rewards and punishments may be the strongest ancillary to power in keeping others in line. Teachers, administrators, parents, politicians, salespeople, and religious leaders are only a few of the people whose communication purpose is regularly devoted to influencing or to changing how others act or believe.

Purpose F—You communicate to have fun, to play, to relax from the rigors of the other kinds of communication we have listed above. When you joke with others, you may affect your relations even though your main purpose is simply amusement. Attending concerts, shows, movies, and stage performances may have a number of purposes, one of which is to provide you with a way of engaging in less serious communication as a break from what you may feel are the stresses and responsibilities in your life. "What do you do for relaxation?" is a question often asked in interviews with the busiest public figures. While answers to that common question may range from activities that are physical ("I jog," "I play tennis," "I take kids biking," "I work out") to those that are intellectual ("I read," "I travel," "I play cards," "I attend concerts"), most of the activities will involve communicating, whether in participating in competition or in associating with others in some interactive pursuits—all of which are premised on and dependent on some kinds of communication.

SCOPE OF COMMUNICATION STUDY

It is not unusual to look at communication according to (1) where it happens (inside people as compared with over broadcast airwaves) or (2) how many people are involved at a time (just yourself, or small groups, or masses of people).

Intrapersonal Communication

You will read a lot in this book and in other textbooks about what goes on inside people as they think, feel, value, react, imagine, dream, etc. A dimension known as "intrapersonal" has been the subject of psychological and cognitive studies which attempt to learn how people respond to symbols and how they make decisions or store and retrieve data in their

---

BOX 1-1. Intrapersonal Processes

In his book *Meaning and Mind*, author Leonard Shedletsky includes a list of what goes on inside a person in the process of communicating. He believes that *intrapersonal* communication includes people's

Perceptions
Memories
Experiences
Feelings
Interpretations
Inferences
Evaluations
Attitudes
Opinions
Ideas
Strategies
Images
States of consciousness*

* L. Shedletsky, *Meaning and the Mind*, Indiana University/Speech Communication Association, Bloomington, IN, 1989.

---

brains. How do people's biases, loves, hates, and even apathies affect their interactions? Managing information and processing data about your world goes on inside your head, but effects of those processes show up in your behaviors.

In developing a theory of meaning, some writers refer to "coordinated management of meaning," which necessarily starts inside everyone's symbol-processing centers—*intra*personally.

The locus of meaning is intrapersonal, while the locus of action is interpersonal.[2]

It is not possible to study one without the other. Even if there is no chapter in this book specifically called "Intrapersonal," the influence of inside-the-head communication is clear in the sections dealing with perception, values, self-concept, styles, general semantics, language, meaning, etc.

Interpersonal Communication

You will read later in this chapter about definitions and models. You will find that we emphasize a definition of interpersonal communication as a *transaction* between people and their environment, which of course in-

Interpersonal communication includes interaction between strangers as well as between intimates. (© *Spencer Grant/ Stock, Boston*)

cludes other people such as friends, family, children, coworkers, and even strangers.

As we have written above, the behaviors of people are the most evident parts of interpersonal communication. You need to pay attention to people's habits of relating to each other as well as to the words they use. People tend to make up their reality about each other, and then communicate in relation to that internal perception.[3]

Group Communication

Defining small group communication is not easy. Not all theorists agree on such items as how many people make up a group, what differences there are between dyads and other numbers of people in communication, etc. A field called *group dynamics* represents an interesting and special case of communication. It involves theories of group discussion, leadership, management, and decision making.

We will not attempt to cover thoroughly the complex field of group process in this textbook. You should notice, however, that many examples in this book and many exercises and activities involve groups in interaction. There is no way you can avoid groups, nor should you ignore the

Interactive systems of communication include computers that link people with data in a wide variety of ways. (© *Mimi Forsyth/ Monkmeyer*)

principles of group interaction as you analyze and learn about communication.

Mass Communication

A very popular area of study today is the *mass media*. We will refer only indirectly to the mass communication systems of the society, although much of what we know about the world and how we react to one another is influenced by the mass media. Mediated communications, whether radio, television, newspapers, or magazines, still have an effect on people.

There are many links between interpersonal communication and mass communication. As the mechanical and technological limits to communicating disappear, there will still remain the human limits—different meanings in different people with different needs and desires and levels of understanding. Interactive systems now becoming more and more familiar in the mass media include computers linked by modems, teletext news and information systems, banking and shopping by television-supported devices, fax machines, public access to cable television outlets, and a wide variety of ways in which people can "talk back" to a mass communication source or sender. One-way transmission over mass media is no longer the only way to look at information and entertainment access. As the influence of "interactive" (or two-way) media communication grows, those working in mass communication will have to take into account the theories and principles of interpersonal communication. As mass media develop "two-step flow" and "multistep flow" analyses of human behavior, there will continue to be a merging of the fields of mass media and interpersonal communication studies.

MODELS AND DEFINITIONS

Scholars and researchers from the beginning of their serious study of this complex subject of human communication have offered definitions and have made models of their theories and ideas. Looking back on the ways "communication" has been defined over the years brings us to a not-too-startling conclusion that people define communication pretty much in relation to what they themselves decide to look at. In this way, models and definitions let others know what you want to emphasize, what you think is important to pay attention to; models and definitions help clarify and simplify complicated ideas, and explain the point of view from which you are approaching a subject.

Models and Definitions Focus Attention

Mass media researchers may define communication in terms of either technological advancements or the influences of the press on publics. One of the classic ways of looking at communication is the "source, message, channel, receiver" mathematical model of Shannon and Weaver which served the telephone industry so well in setting up additional models for phone technologies. Social science researchers quite naturally include the intentions of the senders of messages, and the impact of those messages on the recipients—ranging from dyads to social movements of large populations. Management theorists have concentrated on sending clear messages to workers to get the job done. A speech therapist may focus a definition on the act of receiving messages orally. Scientific views of communication have a very special and clear mission:

FIGURE 1-1
Model developed by Shannon and Weaver which focuses on information theory. This mechanistic system reflected the needs of the Bell Laboratories in studying how an information *source* can get a *message* to a *destination* with a minimum of distortion in spite of interference from the *noise* source and a further consideration that the intrapersonal or internal elements in the source may be different from those in the destination or receiver.

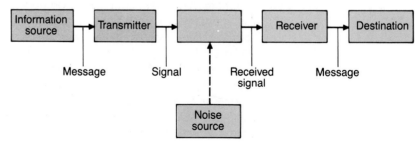

The science of communication has to deal with the physical transmission of information over thousands of miles, but if the information is to end up in the human brain, there is always this final biological step to consider—the transmission between the sense organ on the surface of the body and the brain inside the head.[4]

Psychologists who work with interpersonal communication tend to focus on the complexities of both internal and external relations, personalities, motives, and drives of the people doing the communicating. Other scholars may study the origins or meanings of the words. McLuhan believed that study of communication was distorted by too much attention to senders-messages-receivers. He claimed that such attention excluded the most essential focus on the *medium* and argued for his own emphasis in his book *Understanding Media*.[5]

Katz and Lazarsfeld[6] questioned the idea that the public was influenced directly by messages from media—they asserted that the interpersonal contacts by people, especially opinion leaders talking to nonleaders, were more likely to influence attitudes than were the mechanical media messages just by themselves. Their idea, which they called ''two-step flow'' of information, is very important to students and teachers of interpersonal communication as well as to those studying mass communication.

Models and Definitions Simplify the Complex

When you want to talk about or understand something which is complex, it helps if you can look at its individual parts before trying to understand the whole. That is one of the uses of models and definitions: to simplify a complicated activity by looking at the separate parts one at a time. It is imperative, however, that you realize that the parts may add up to much more than their simple sum when the whole is considered; this principle is called *synergy*. For example, you can consider each player on a football team, assess every player's skills, and look at every player's statistical record of tackles or yards gained, but it will not tell you, except in a general way, how the *team* will perform after the kickoff. If you learned to play chess, the first step was to understand the move of each piece— but you never believed that the game was just one piece all by itself; you knew that the game consisted of the total interaction of all the different pieces and their accumulated positions and respective moves. But until you understood the parts, the action of the game didn't make much sense.

It also helps, if the concept is an action or a process such as communication, to be able to *stop it* in its flow so that you can see what is going on at any moment. When a model maker draws a picture of communication with boxes attached by arrows, it is a very static representation of the dynamics involved when people communicate. Again,

Example of "synergy": a basketball team equals more than just the sum of five athletes acting as individuals. (© *Bob Daemmrich/Stock, Boston*)

you must remember that the diagram lacks the motion and the kinetic forces and behaviors of real-life communication.

Models and Definitions Represent Your Point of View

As far back as Aristotle, teachers, scholars, and other professionals have looked at human communication as consisting, at the very least, of a process in which (1) someone sends, (2) someone receives, and (3) in between there is a message. If it is your intention to study human communication based on sender-message-receiver, then that model is sufficient for you. Remember that we mentioned above that such a model did not adequately fit McLuhan's point of view, and so he chose to emphasize the *medium*. There have been many views (it may not be proper to call them "theories") of communication which historically have been used to describe and define the complex activity. Bull's-eye and Ping-Pong views are described here, together with some discussion of why they are limited or even, in many respects, inaccurate in their description of the dynamics of human communication.

The bull's-eye view

Some rhetorical traditions and earlier information theory share the view that communication consists of a one-way act like shooting an arrow into a target. You hit the bull's-eye. You got close in one of the colored rings. You missed. The activity of communication was centered on doing something to someone. How good you were depended on how well you shot the arrow, or how well you made your point. Emphasis was on the *sender* and his or her encoding skills. The key question was what should the speaker do in order to persuade, tell, sell, help, or just "get the message across." If the receiver did not understand, what had the sender done wrong?

There are several problems with this view. One error is in a person's thinking that he or she had control over the situation—could aim a straight arrow and hit the target if only the eye and arm were coordinated. This leaves the receiver—the target—defined as passive and receptive.

A second error is to look only at the sender (or arrow shooter) to find out what went wrong. If you as the speaker are skillful enough, you will hit the target. This view is promoted and widely believed today by those who are buying and selling instant "speaking success" systems or training programs to make you an overnight power in influencing others (hitting the bull's-eye).

This view also gives rise to another kind of attitude which paradoxically changes who gets the blame when there is "missed communication." (Equivalent of this blaming view in the arrow-shooting analogy is the excuse that "the target moved.") It happens when a person yells at you, "How come you don't understand plain English?" Or when the boss says, "How come they don't know what I said? I told them." Or a lecturer complains, "My message was really very clear, so I can't believe they missed what I said."

The Ping-Pong view

Another favorite, if incomplete, way to look at communication is to compare it with taking turns at a table tennis match. You say something; I reply. You say more; so do I. You serve; I return. We take turns at being sender and receiver under a set of rules which takes into account more than the bull's-eye view but is still limited to a linear, single-cause–effect relationship. The weakness of this view is that communication, when practiced interpersonally by humans, is not divided into ping and pong, stimulus and response, shot and return, action and reaction in a simple turn-taking process.

Developing a better model

For some occasions, the sender-message-receiver model may be quite adequate, even though it describes poorly the actual interactions of human

---

BOX 1-2.   Lasswell Model

Who
says What
through What Channels
to Whom
with What Effect

---

communication. As we learn more about what happens between people who communicate, we modify our definitions and develop new models or alter the previous ones. Also, when we begin to concentrate on new activities or behaviors, it is necessary to modify the former models, even those which serve us well under some traditional circumstances.

Lasswell's model/definition[7] (see Box 1-2), while not yet a "transactional" view, follows along the bull's-eye or Ping-Pong pattern, except that he includes a *channel,* and very importantly adds an *effect.* When Schutz proposed his "three dimensional theory of interpersonal behavior," he particularly paid attention to interpersonal *needs* and specifically excluded computers or other technological actors but stressed attention of people to each other:

> The term "interpersonal" refers to relations that occur between people as opposed to relations in which at least one participant is inanimate. . . . An interpersonal situation is one involving two or more persons, in which these individuals take account of each other for some purpose. . . .[8]

A transactional view   Modern views of the transactional nature of communication have developed from much research and writing. An early assertion of transactional communication comes from Barnlund's model and discussion:

> . . . [communication] is not a reaction to something, nor an interaction with something, but a transaction in which man invents and attributes meanings to realize his purposes. . . .[9]

Transaction implies, then, a purposeful relationship much more complex than we have built our models or definitions to cover in the past. It can be predicted also that as we know more about the interactions of human communication, the models may grow even more complex in the future. There are already, as you can see from the discussions above, many ways of looking at communication. As we learn more about conversation, nonverbal systems, cross-cultural systems, persuasion, and individual and mass effects of communication, the process becomes even more difficult to talk or write about completely. What we say today may be modified tomorrow with some new research data.

Miller and Sunnafrank argue that the earlier "situational" definitions were not sufficiently dynamic to describe communication, and so have proposed a "developmental" model based on two assumptions—which are the main assumptions we include in our transactional approach in this textbook:[10]

> *Our first major assumption is that the basic function of all communication is to control the environment so as to realize certain physical, economic, or social rewards from it. . . . The second fundamental assumption stems directly from the centrality of control to our conceptual perspective. . . . We assume that whenever people communicate with others, they make predictions about the probable consequences, or outcomes, of their messages. . . . Typically, communicators remain blissfully unaware of the predictions they are making until such predictions are disconfirmed.*[11]

Wilbur Schramm, one of the pioneering leaders in communication study over the years, offered his current view of the transactional definition:

> *Communication is now seen as a transaction in which both parties are active. The parties are not necessarily equally active—that is more likely in the case of interpersonal communication, but less so in the case of mass media and their audiences—but to both parties the transaction is in some way functional. It meets a need or provides a gratification. To a greater or lesser degree information flows both ways.*[12]

A DEFINITION OF INTERPERSONAL COMMUNICATION

You will notice that we have titled this section "A Definition" and not called it "*The* Definition." Use of the article "A" will indicate to you that this is not the only definition you may encounter in your studies—there are many ways to slice the pie of communicative experience and that includes how you define the terms. It should also indicate to you that this, or any definition, will not hold still forever, but will perhaps be modified as new ways are developed for looking at interpersonal communication. The definition which follows, therefore, is a summary of selected ways of looking at this activity and will serve as our "contract" with each other for how we are using the term:

> *Interpersonal communication is an ever-present, continuous, predictable, multilevel, dynamic sharing of meaning for the purpose of managing our lives more effectively.*

FIGURE 1-2
Intrapersonal transactional model: The intrapersonal model demonstrates the internal processing of data coming to the organism (you) from the environment. You select some cues from the outside to pay attention to. You compare with older memory; you organize the incoming data by some personal system; and then you begin to formulate a response—or an output using your symbolizing system of language. In this diagram we are using a wave-generating model because most everyone is familiar with the ripples in a pond when a stone is dropped into it. Such moving waves make an interesting analogy to the ripples of our outputs—speaking, for example—as some hit a "far shore" and come rolling back.

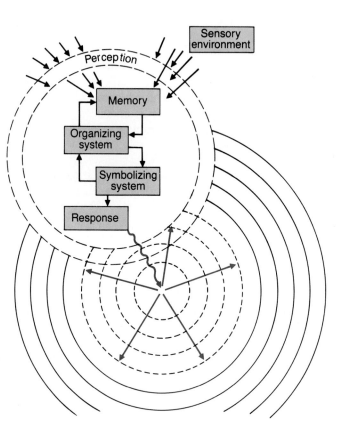

In following up on developing that definition from transactional models and theories, several principles about communicating are important to list and discuss. Sometimes called axioms or postulates or rules, these principles relate to the definition we proposed above and are subject to the same difficulties of word meaning that you will find as you take apart our suggested definition.

A SET OF TRANSACTIONAL PRINCIPLES

The transactional view emphasizes that in our communication we are all in it together, trying to get something to happen, improving our ability to predict or guess at the outcomes, and in some measure affecting how things turn out for us. As we already stated, models and definitions simplify complex ideas, help focus our attention, and announce to others our points of view. Now we can propose a set of rules or principles about the transactional view which can be used in this book as the basic definition of human communication.

FIGURE 1-3
Interpersonal transactional
model: This combination of
two interacting systems
shows you and another
person in communication—a
brief, stop-action moment.
An identified sender (or
source) goes through an
intrapersonal process to emit
a message to a receiver.
Receiver will become sender
if you start at the other side,
so you must remember that
as long as there is more than
one of us in the other's
environment, we may operate
as both sender and receiver
and neither of us can avoid
communicating. If you don't
want to be either a sender or
receiver, you'd better get out
of the other person's
attention and environment.
Who is sending and who is
receiving is largely defined by
where you want to focus your
attention and how you will
punctuate this complex
transaction.

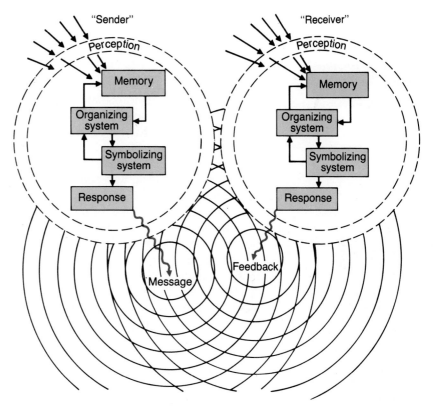

First Principle: You Cannot Not Communicate

Communication truly does not have an opposite. There is no way for human beings *not* to behave, and all behaviors have possible communicative value. Whether you speak or are silent, whether you act or do not act, in some way you will affect others. They in turn cannot *not* interact with you, if only to not respond, which in itself is communication. Someone sits next to you in the library and you stick your nose deeper in your book, very clearly indicating you do not want to be disturbed. Usually your neighbor gets the message and leaves you alone. Did you ever wait at a store counter while some clerks busied themselves behind the counter with paperwork? You waited in silence, probably, at least for a short while, indicating you had received the message. At some time, you may give a message that you want help. They cannot not respond—even if only to make you more upset by further ignoring you.

Many people do not think of silence as communicating. They assume that if there is no noise going on between people, there is no communication. But communication does not take place only when it is planned, conscious, or successful. You communicate many things which you may not intend to communicate. You may not be aware of what you actually communicated—nor can you be sure that what you intended was what was heard and understood.

Communication is not random

During your day you will speak, be spoken to, write, read, and respond to thousands of cues to communicate. You will be in touch with many people who will tell you things, ask you to remember some others, and ask you to do still others. If you walk to work or to class, you move past people and manage to avoid running into them. You have a radarlike system of communication which tells you which way to dodge when you come close to colliding with someone. These moves, like all your communication, are not random. In those events, as in all others, you are capable of giving off clues to your intentions. Even when you are not completely conscious of your motives or of your actions, they are acting out your messages to others.

As you try to interpret actions of others, you "attribute" meaning to those behaviors. An extensive area of study in interpersonal communication involves "attribution" of motives and intentions, and how people assess them. Obviously, when you try to figure out why people act the way they do, it can have a major effect on your relations with them. So you watch and listen to others, receiving messages that may or may not have been intended; and you send messages back. Because you choose what and how to communicate, and because you choose to see and interpret the communicative behaviors of others, we say that communication is purposive, not random.

Moves of people on a city street are not random, and you can understand them by "attributing" purpose to individuals. (© *Barbara Rios/ Photo Researchers*)

Communication is everywhere and is inevitable

You may feel satisfied or dissatisfied with your day in relation to how successful you feel your communication has been: Did you ignore someone you wished you had spoken to? Did you miss seeing and talking with a friend or not get the telephone call you expected? Did you get confused in class? Out of an entire day of communicating possibilities, you have selected certain things to do and not do; like tuning a radio, you tune in and tune out parts of your environment.

You make choices because you cannot attend to all the possible communication at once. Do you listen to a radio, watch television, talk on the telephone? These are extensions of your personal contact with people. An advertiser on radio will tell thousands of you at once where to get a bargain in short-term loans, hoping some of you need money and will respond—this advertiser has paid a broadcaster on the assumption that the communication will reach someone.

You can find out from newspapers, magazines, or new media reports what has happened in New York, Washington, Moscow, London, Chicago, or Podunk, even though you were not there. A commentator is ready to report to you every hour the big news stories of worlds you may not even know and people you have never met.

Mechanical and electronic means of communication have increased far beyond your ability to pay attention to all their potential messages. You listen to only one radio station at a time, although there may be hundreds within reach of the instrument you tune in. You may read only one or two newspapers or news magazines out of the hundreds of printed opportunities you have. You may see only a few selected television programs, although there may be many stations available all day and most of the night. A friend telephones you, or you call someone to seek information or perhaps just to keep your personal contact with others.

Your day may start with the communication from an alarm clock or someone calling you to get up. Getting dressed and ready to go out are largely the accumulated habits of previous communication. You were not born with a great urge to brush your teeth or wash your face—if these have become part of your behavior patterns, it is because you learned them. Such learning probably occurred as a result of a very effective communication system that we refer to as "child rearing." Even the cereal you eat for breakfast, the kind of coffee you drink, the clothes you choose to wear, and the way you comb your hair are all the result of conditioning from your ever-present communication environment.

Second Principle: Communication Is Predictable

You have read several times now our claim that communication is not random. Why is it then that sometimes someone's communicative behaviors don't seem to make sense to you? The problem is not the amount or content of the material that is communicated; it is how you organize it

---

BOX 1-3.   Intercultural in the School

Recent emphasis on ethnic diversity and study of cross-cultural influences on society has an important relation to study of communication. How people interact is based on their assumptions about themselves and others, much of which is historically based. The following quotation suggests a very widespread need for intercultural, interracial, and international understanding.

> The intercultural approach is an important step for all Americans to undertake as they look at their school systems and programs. We are Americans all, immigrants all. . . . A valuable approach is adopted in a first reader in Brazil, a nation of white and color peoples, which states that there are three mothers in Brazil, one white or European, a second red or Indian, and one black or African, and the book then describes how the Brazilian people have developed not only from three sources but from still others. Our youth could have similar approaches rather than the direct or indirect implication that Americans are tall, white, and blond, and that this was and is the ideal of American beauty. Since a contrary view is closer to reality, readers should be given more complete pictures of American life in history.*

*C. H. Wesley, "The Treatment of the Negro-American in the Study and Teaching of United States History," in R. L. Hill, *Rhetoric of Racial Hope*, McDaniel Press, Brockport, NY, 1976, p. 318.

---

that counts. In the earlier quotation from Miller and Sunnafrank, they state that you try to predict the behavior of others from observing their communication and pay most attention when your predictions don't fit. The point of your continued communication with others often is to make better predictions of outcomes—the more you talk with people, the better guesses you can make about how they will behave.

In a book on family communication, Galvin and Brommel make the point clear that communication patterns are predictable, that you can learn to improve predictability, and also that you depend on transactional communication to share meaning:

> When we talk about communication, we are dealing with symbolic acts to which we assign meaning through our transactions with the people around us. The meanings emerge through the use of symbolic acts as our interactions give us information on how to interpret the symbols. After each encounter with a person or object, we become better able to deal with similar situations, and our behavior takes on certain patterns. The greater the repetition, the greater the probability of the assigned meaning.[13]

In this textbook we will attempt to provide you with the means of understanding more about your communication, and in that way help you better predict the outcomes of your communication. Many years of research have led communication scholars to believe that outcomes generally can be predicted when a particular kind of message comes from a particular kind of source and reaches a particular kind of audience.[14]

With all the built-in uncertainties of human association, some by accident and some on purpose,[15] you still can make your sending and receiving of messages consistently more accurate if you know more about the process of interpersonal communication. To repeat, communication is not random, and only *seems to be* random when you do not understand the parts of the process and how these parts are organized and related to each other.

Political candidates use opinion polls to help guide their campaigns; they will test reactions to certain approaches and then modify the appeals to potential voters based on "what the polls say." You may do much the same type of "poll taking" when you talk to others and sensitively watch the feedback you get—when you "play back the tapes" of your experiences by recalling how others responded to your communication behaviors in the past. On the basis of your assessment of your past performance, you try to make things come out better next time.

You can become more effective as you know more about what goes on in your interpersonal communication. Adapting to reduce uncertainty in your communication is a constant challenge to you. You want things to work well for you, and whatever you can do to make things happen in your communication you will try. An interesting insight into adult behavior springs from watching the development of very predictable interpersonal communication behaviors in children:

> As children become competent communicators, they learn . . . how to comfort a good friend, how to refuse someone a ride on their Big Wheel, and how to join a game of frisbee. Children learn to adapt their communication strategies to the particular situation. . . . Just because children are small does not mean that they are powerless with each other or with adults. Just as adults assume dominant and submissive roles in their communication, children also communicate in equal and unequal status conversations. . . . Children must acquire a flexibility to alternate between dominance, equality, and submissiveness. With time and plenty of experience with family members and peers, children develop skills in communicating effectively in different communication contexts.[16]

Third Principle: Communication Is a "Chicken and Egg" Process

It has been suggested that for any generation of people, history for them began when they were born. We have traditionally developed what can be termed a "linear" outlook at our world. That means that we tend to look at all our experiences and interactions in relation to a "starting" and

Children develop effective communication skills in different contexts. (© Bob Daemmrich/The Image Works)

a "stopping" sequence, or as having very clear beginnings and endings. We have been trained to look for cause and effect, for stimulus and response, for action and reaction, for sender and receiver, for beginnings and endings. The process of putting incidents or behaviors together to make sense of them has also been called "chunking," a simple way to divide up experiences in easy-to-understand bunches or packages.

Looking at communication in a linear fashion may be misleading. Your communication comes from someplace in the past, and you make a decision on when that communication began. It is like starting a new sentence with a capital letter—in fact, the term for this practice of putting a beginning and end on our communication sequences is called "punctuation." The teacher who says he has to stand over students while they do their work so that they will not make mistakes punctuates the interaction differently from the students. Students say that they make mistakes because the teacher is standing over them. You tell your friend that you were late for the appointment because your friend is never punctual; and your friend claims that she is never on time because you are always late.

BOX 1-4. Punctuation

A hen is only an egg's way of making another egg.
                                                  Samuel Butler, Life and Habit

---

Those differences in perception depend on when you think the process began—how you punctuate the interaction.

Human communication, as a dynamic process, is best understood as a system where senders are simultaneously receivers and receivers are simultaneously senders. Who starts the process is an irrelevant question since processes have no discrete beginning or ending, except as we may stop them to look at the component parts. In a transactional view of communication you are both cause and effect, stimulus and response, sender and receiver. To isolate a communicative act is to fix an arbitrary beginning and an arbitrary end to what is essentially a continuous process. Although both you and your friend will "chunk" your experiences by habit, you may not do them the same way—was it your jealousy that caused your friend to flirt with others, or your friend's flirting that caused your jealousy? Settling an argument or fight between children (of any age), you will customarily say, "Okay—how did this start?" Then you will likely get different answers, each side blaming the other for "starting it" because they punctuate the events for their own best interests.

Your daily communication is a flowing, dynamic part of your life—changing as your environment changes, as you change, and as others change. Your communicative needs are never static and therefore require some adjustment based on your previous experiences and predictability (that term "predictable" again) about the future. While there is no way to avoid punctuation differences, you can at least recognize this common way of looking at communication as a possible danger. You can try to anticipate how others punctuate relationships as well as study your own ways of determining if the chicken came before the egg.

Fourth Principle: Communication Occurs at Two Levels

"Communication not only conveys information, but . . . at the same time . . . imposes behavior."[17] Information conveyed through communication is usually the *content level* of communication and refers to *what* is said. However, more than conveying content, communication of any kind always implies a relationship between communicators, and contains information about how to interpret the content of that communication.

This *relationship level* refers to how the message or content is to be taken, and how the relationship between people is defined. When you say "I was only joking" or "I really meant that" or "This is an order," you are giving actual verbal examples of relationship. You are telling the other person how to interpret your message, aside from giving the message itself.

Relationship need not be expressed in words; in fact, very often it is expressed nonverbally. I can tell you, by using nonverbal and contextual clues, that this is a serious conversation, or a joking one, or a friendly exchange, or an angry reprimand, or a put-down, or sarcasm. As I give you content, I also give you clues on the relationship level about the way I expect you to respond.

It may bother you if your teacher or your parents speak to you in a different way than they speak to their peers when they want something done. Galvin and Brommel refer to these as "report" and "command" factors,[18] asserting that you respond both to the content of the message ("you do the dishes"; "turn in the assignment on Tuesday") and to the relationship ("I can boss you around"). When parent or teacher messages sound too authoritarian, the message may make you feel that you are still being treated as a child. Resentment may result if you are not spoken to in a way that is consistent with how both you and the other person see your relationship.

Confusion can be another result if relation messages (1) are not clear or (2) do not match the content messages. While shopping, have you ever asked for help from a person who looked like a store clerk, but who turned out to be another customer like yourself? Something about the person's clothing or demeanor made you think "that person works here." On the other hand, when you want to be waited on in a store, you usually find the correct person to ask, not because salespeople keep saying "May I wait on you?" but because you look for name tags, uniforms, or simply people who "look helpful." A relationship is established where you are in need of help, and others can provide that help.

Fifth Principle: Transactions Are between Equals or Up-and-Down

As we discussed above and will write more about in Chapter 10, you can relate to people as equals or as nonequals. A typical example of nonequal relationships is that of the mother-infant pair. Mother clearly takes care of baby, and baby is clearly taken care of. The two cannot exist without each other, and that is not simply a biological truism; it is a comment on relationships. Like trying to clap one hand, there can be *no taking care of* if there is *no one to take care of.* Nonequal relationships include two different positions: one communicator is in the superior, or one-up, position, while the other is in the one-down, or inferior position.

Please do not equate the words "up" and "down" with judgmental terms as "good," "bad," "strong," or "weak." Nonequal relationships are

Transactions may occur among equals in age, culture, interests, gender, authority, and so on. *(© Joel Gordon)*

often set by social or cultural factors as in the examples of doctor-patient, student-teacher, clerk-customer, and parent-child transactions. It is usual for one-up persons to define the nature of the relationship, while the one-down persons accept and may go along with the definition, or resist it.

That relationship of one person serving the needs of another has been called "complementary," while relationships between equals or peers have been referred to as "symmetrical" transactions,[19] since the behavior or communication of one person will produce a similar or corresponding behavior or communication in the other. As you "reflect" the other person's behaviors, you are said to be behaving like a mirror, a favorite way of describing balanced symmetrical actions.

Your behavior in symmetrical communication means you and others exchange the same kind of behavior as near as you can identify what is going on. You attempt to keep differences to a minimum, and strive for similarity in your actions with the others. Mutual respect and a feeling of partnership may exist. Friends, peers, teammates, and colleagues are usual examples of relationships among equals.

Some potential problems

Problem communication behaviors may occur in either of these transactional types. One kind of *complementary* problem we mentioned earlier is offspring whose parents treat them as children long past the age or experience when such treatment is appropriate. Students often complain that they feel quite grown-up and independent at college, but when they go home for holidays or even later as young marrieds, their parents still

---

BOX 1-5.   From One Stereotype to Another . . .

Authority is sometimes "bestowed" on a class or group of people by popular convention or persistent stereotypes. This can occur when some men consider all women to be less capable of "logical" reasoning, or some women believe all men to be incapable of any emotion. Relations can be seriously affected by unspoken and even unrecognized biases about gender, age, religion, ethnicity, nationality, economic status, height, weight, beards, hair color, and almost any identifying features or implied characteristics.

---

want to treat them as children. Children may resent too much bossing from parents, and parents may resent too much asserting of independent actions by their children.

This same problem may exist in a work setting when a particularly bossy superior insists on dictating every move of the subordinates—and there are subordinates who will rebel at being given instructions or directives from anyone.

On the other hand, a person in a position of authority expects subordinate behavior from others—the doctor does not want the patient to argue about prescribed treatment; judges won't permit lawyers to openly question their legal rulings during a trial; teachers may not like students to argue points of information given in a lecture; an arresting officer does not tolerate much back talk from a suspect. If you violate an agreed-upon complementary relationship, it makes interaction difficult and may have bad consequences for you.

In any of these instances, it is important to clarify the mutual relationships. You do that by considering each person's expectations—how each *wants to be* treated as well as how to treat the other. Perceptions of the traditional roles of who is equal or nonequal are not always clearly expressed, but will influence interactions.

In *symmetrical,* or between equals, transactions there are also some potential problems when each person may try to outdo the other. Have you ever been in the spot of holding a door for someone to go through and the other person urged you to go through first? Each trying to be more polite than the other, until neither one of you can move. (As often as not, this silliness ends with both of you jamming into the door at the same time.) Two people giving increasingly lavish gifts trying to top each other is another possible difficulty in a symmetrical relationship. On the other end of a continuum are the equals who, reflecting minor irritation, grow more angry back and forth, getting progressively irate at each other to a final violent outburst.

BOX 1-6. Sharing to Communicate

It is illuminating to think of communication as a relationship built around the exchange of information. . . . For example, recall how important a goodnight hug can be to a parent-child relationship, or how a good-morning greeting can improve a neighborhood or a workplace relationship, or how the satisfaction of seeing one's candidate do well in a debate or a television appearance can reinforce one's party relationship.

Source: W. Schramm, "The Unique Perspective of Communication: A Retrospective View," *Journal of Communication,* vol. 33, Summer 1983, p. 14.

Sixth Principle: Communication Is a Sharing of Meaning

In describing communication we have already emphasized that it has a purpose. Although most communication scholars agree that communication is related to symbol manipulation, there is not always agreement on the actual aims of communication. Some may view communication as designed to transmit information and to transfer ideas (using a simple linear model or the bull's-eye view) as if there were a pipeline over which meaning was pumped from one person to the other. For this textbook, our principle involves the sharing or creation of meaning, which is discussed at length in Chapter 8.

Yours is a world of booming and buzzing confusion in which you are assailed from all directions with messages and stimuli. Yet this world becomes understandable to you, full of beauty or of ugliness, because you assign meaning and significance to what you perceive. Imagine that you were in a vast supermarket of noise and sights without any organization pattern. From your own experience, then you begin to sort things out, as you would in a grocery supermarket. The vegetables are there, the canned goods are over there, meats are over there, and so on—and you can find your way to whatever conclusions you want by understanding the organizational systems.

In the supermarket you get help from a classification system known to you from your past experience and from the arrangement of clues of signs and aisles. You don't expect to find fresh string beans next to canned string beans because they are also beans. Would you expect to find milk with the other drinks such as colas, coffee, or tea? Classifications used by most supermarkets are not the only way of arranging the grocery world; but they reflect a need to display and preserve goods—which is why fresh vegetables are not found near the canned ones, and why milk is in the dairy cooler with butter and eggs.

Barnlund concluded: "Communication, then, is an 'effort at meaning,'

Meaning comes from knowing how things are classified and understanding predictable organizational systems. (© *Hazel Hankin/ Stock, Boston*)

a creative act initiated by man in which he seeks to discriminate and organize cues so as to orient himself in his environment and satisfy his changing needs.''[20] To communicate is to process stimuli from raw data into meaningful information. This creative act of generating meaning performs the function of *reducing uncertainty.* The cues you select out of your internal, physical, and social environment all serve to clarify what is going on so that you can adapt to it.

Meaning may not be the same in any two individuals because they may select different items to pay attention to, they may have different classification systems, and they have had different experiences or come from different cultures, gender, geography, religion, age groups. Communication is an attempt to call up inside yourself a meaning which has a close relationship to what is going on around you. You also try to share your meanings with others by providing them with words or cues to which they will assign meaning, and you hope that those will be similar to yours.

SUMMARY

This chapter developed six reasons why you communicate—to learn more about yourself; to learn about others; to learn about the world around you; to share that world with others; to persuade or influence others; and to have fun, or play, or relax, or enjoy yourself. Study of communication may involve (1) what goes on inside you (intrapersonal) and (2) your relations with others (interpersonal)—on a one-to-one basis, in small face-to-face gatherings or meetings (groups), or in a larger group (mass communication).

Models and definitions are used to focus attention on details or some aspects of an idea, to simplify the complex, and to represent your point of view. This book approaches communication from a transactional point of view.

The six principles of transactional communication are related to our definition of communication as an *ever-present, continuous, predictable, multilevel, dynamic sharing of meaning.* Each principle has some relation to our suggested definition.

First principle: "You cannot not communicate" relates to the idea that communication is going on whenever you are in the presence of others, whether or not you intend it to. In that respect, communication is inevitable. Communication is also not random; you do it for some purposes even if you are not always completely conscious of your intentions.

Second principle: Communication is predictable if you just know the organizing principles used by yourself and others. One major aim in most communication is to increase predictability of message effects and behaviors around you, and thus to reduce the ambiguity of your world.

Third principle: Communication is a "chicken and egg" process in which you decide how to "punctuate" the interactions of yourself and others. Although communication comes from somewhere and goes somewhere, you take out a small slice to pay attention to, and how you slice that experience will help determine what sense you make out of behaviors and events. You divide things up into "chunks" of a size you can manage.

Fourth principle: You must watch both the messages of *content* and messages of *relationships* if you are to manage your interactions effectively. You need to know what is being said. You also need information about how you should take the messages and what relationships with the others give them authority to tell you what to do, or give you the authority to tell them what to do.

Fifth principle: Communication is between equals (as peers), or it is between unequals (as those depending on each other), or it is between people who see each other as like or as different based on diversity of gender, race, culture, ethnicity, age, etc. How you decide to interact relates to how you see your relationships with others. *Symmetry* and *complementarity* are the two terms used by many transactionalists to describe relations of "mirror," or equal status, and of dependency.

Sixth principle: Meaning is shared. It is generated inside the people who use communication. Meaning, as we discuss further in Chapter 8, is in people, not in words. The system for sharing meaning is not a pipeline carrying meanings like some commodity from one place to another. Meaning can be described as a calculated guess within you as you organize a systematic response to what you hear or see.

END NOTES

[1] W. Johnson, *Your Most Enchanted Listener,* Harper & Brothers, New York, 1956; also published as a Collier Books paperback retitled *Verbal Man: The Enchantment of Words,* 1979.

[2] V. E. Cronen, W. B. Pearce, and L. Harris, "The Coordinated Management of Meaning: A Theory of Communication," in F. E. X. Dance (ed.), *Human Communication Theory,* Harper & Row, New York, 1982, p. 71.

[3] For two studies about the effect of intimate communication relationships see A. Sillars and M. D. Scott, "Interpersonal Perception between Intimates," *Human Communication Research,* vol. 10, Fall 1983, pp. 153–176; and S. Ting-Toomey, "An Analysis of Verbal Communication Patterns in High and Low Marital Adjustment Groups," *Human Communication Research,* vol. 9, Summer 1983, pp. 306–319.

[4] E. H. Adrian, "The Human Receiving System," in Grenada Lectures of the British Association for the Advancement of Science, *The Languages of Science,* Basic Books, New York, 1963, chap. 6.

[5] H. M. McLuhan, *Understanding Media,* McGraw-Hill, New York, 1964, p. 13.

[6] E. Katz and P. F. Lazarsfeld, *Personal Influence,* Free Press, New York, 1964.

[7] H. D. Lasswell, "The Structure and Function of Communication in Society," in Wilbur Schramm (ed.), *Mass Communication,* University of Illinois Press, Urbana, 1960, p. 117.

[8] W. C. Schutz, *The Interpersonal Underworld,* Science and Behavior Books, Palo Alto, CA, 1966, p. 14.

[9] D. C. Barnlund, "A Transactional Model of Communication," in J. Akin, A. Goldberg, G. Myers, and J. Stewart (eds.), *Language Behavior,* Mouton Press, The Hague, 1970, p. 47.

[10] G. R. Miller and M. J. Sunnafrank, "All Is One but One Is Not for All: A Conceptual Perspective of Interpersonal Communication," in F. E. X. Dance (ed.), *Human Communication Theory,* Harper & Row, New York, 1982, pp. 224–233.

[11] Ibid., selected from pp. 233 and 224.

[12] W. Schramm, "The Unique Perspective of Communication: A Retrospective View," *Journal of Communication,* vol. 33, Summer 1983, p. 14.

[13] K. M. Galvin and B. J. Brommel, *Family Communication,* 2d ed., Scott, Foresman, Glenview, IL, 1986, p. 12.

[14] See C. I. Hovland, I. Janis, and H. Kelley, *Communication and Persuasion,* Greenwood Press, Westport, SCT, 1982. See also E. Bettinghaus, *Persuasive Communication,* Holt, Rinehart and Winston, New York, 1980.

[15] For a discussion of "strategically ambiguous" messages and an interesting possibility that *clarity* in communication may not always be most effective, see Chapter 8; especially writings by Eric Eisenberg.

[16] B. S. Wood and R. Gardner, "How Children Get Their Way: Directives in Communication," *Communication Education,* vol. 29, July 1980, pp. 264, 265.

[17] P. Watzlawick, J. Beavin, and D. Jackson, *Pragmatics of Human Communication,* W. W. Norton, New York, 1967, p. 51.

[18] Galvin and Brommel, op. cit., p. 128.

[19] Watzlawick, Beavin, and Jackson, op. cit.

[20] D. C. Barnlund, *Interpersonal Communication: Survey and Studies,* Houghton Mifflin, Boston, 1968, p. 6.

CHAPTER
2

PERCEPTION: THE EYE OF THE BEHOLDER

OBJECTIVES

After studying this chapter you should be able to:

1. Distinguish between the physiological limits and the psychological limits to perceptions.
2. Describe in sequence and give original examples for the process of
   a. selecting
   b. organizing
   c. interpreting sensory data from your environment
3. Define the term "context," and identify its role in your communication.
4. Predict the ability of one person to understand another by comparing their respective perceptions of an event or incident or person.
5. Compare a "process view" of the world with other ways of looking at human experience.
6. Explain how the study of sensory perceptions relates to your communication.

INTRODUCTION

"Hey, did you see that King horror movie? It was great; I really like the scary way he writes."

"Yeah. I saw it. Hated it. Except for special effects it was dumb; King's a hack writer."

"I saw the photo exhibit at the art museum—it's outstanding."

"You mean that porno stuff they put up and call art?"

"Well, I talked to the prof, and he said I could leave early. He's a great person and a wonderful teacher."

"You can't mean Jones? Not Jones! He's such a creep!"

"How about that football game Sunday—the Bears are really putting it together this year."

"Football? Who watches it? The Met had a great performance in simulcast stereo."

Do those sound like conversations you have heard before? All these exchanges demonstrate that some of us see things differently—that you can go to watch football and like it, and a friend doesn't; you can see art and call it trash when someone else thinks it is beautiful; you can have a perception of a teacher very different from a classmate's opinion.

Why is it that two people looking at what seems to be the same thing come up with different reactions? Who is right about the painting or the photograph, and is the "right" or "wrong" to be found somewhere in the painting or the photograph itself? Which of us knows the "real" Professor Jones, and so which of us is right about him? Do we see things as they "really are," or as we would like them to be?

Do you see things as *they* are, or as *you* are?

WHAT YOU PERCEIVE

In Chapter 1 we introduced the idea of "scope" by saying that according to one way of looking at communication it begins inside us and is called *intrapersonal*. Intrapersonal communication is defined to include the processes of perceiving, creating meaning, and determining symbolic interactions. *Interpersonal* refers to the processes which take place when two or more people trade the currency of language with each other, or interact nonverbally.

Although this distinction has been convenient to use, it has some limitations and sometimes appears arbitrary. Because of the transactional nature of communication it is difficult to separate what is internal to the individual from what belongs or originates in the environment. For example, perception may be considered an internal process because certain things happen inside our heads when we perceive. At the same time, however, our perceiving is conditioned by our interactions—past and present—with the sociocultural climate we live in.

Is self-perception—how you see yourself—strictly an internal affair?

Or should we treat self-concept as an interpersonal and transactional process, since you learn who you are by watching others responding to you? We will try to focus in this book on the transactional and meaning nature of your communication rather than on the dichotomy of intrapersonal versus interpersonal communication.[1]

Referring again to the examples above, did the King movie have a quality of story which operated aside from how you respond to the special effects? Does the photograph you and I disagree about possess the quality of "liking" or "appreciating" or "admiring," or does that happen inside you and me? In other words, are you and I responsible for making King a writer or giving the photograph some value by our perception of it? The beauty of nature, if you can believe Alfred North Whitehead's comments in Box 2-1, is largely what you do to it; not what is out there.

You and Your Senses

You rely on your senses to tell you what is happening in the world around you. You see things, people, situations, happenings. You hear noises and words. You taste food and drink. You smell odors and scents. You feel and touch objects and surfaces. You are generally excited by something outside your skin and react to this stimulation by becoming aware of something you were not aware of before. Then you say you perceived something—a sound, a taste, a sight, a touch.

What is recorded in your brain is no more the real happening "out there" than the cowboy on your television set is real. When you look at the world, those objects toward which you turn your eyes reflect light to you—you take in those reflections through your optical system. Cells of the retina react and send nerve impulses to optical nerves which send them on as electrical impulses to the brain. Then the pattern of intensities and durations is reconstructed as a picture in your head of what you "saw" out there. Vision alone cannot account for the picture you get of your world—you depend on very complex patterns of mental processes of selecting and remembering and organizing.[2]

Studies in *sensory deprivation* report that if you are cut off from sound, sight, and touch, you have such a need for stimulation that you

---

BOX 2-1.   Nature Is Dull without You

Nature gets credit which should be in truth reserved for ourselves; the rose for its scent, the nightingale for his song, and the sun for its radiance. The poets are entirely mistaken [because] nature is a dull affair, soundless, scentless, colorless; merely the hurrying of material, endlessly, meaninglessly.

Alfred North Whitehead

make things up. In some classic experiments[3] subjects have been blind-folded, with soundproofing muffs placed over their ears and heavy wrap-pings placed over their primary tactile centers, the hands; they are in as much of a vacuum as a laboratory can provide. Cut off this way from outside stimuli, the subjects report that they begin to hallucinate—to think they see flashes of light and sense other unaccountable responses. Other studies suggest that if you do not use your senses, it is possible to become less competent in using them.[4]

Because you do not live in a vacuum, you are constantly being bombarded by sensations. You are surrounded by things, people, odors, tastes, happenings, noises, and lights. There are sights to be seen and words to be heard. Asleep or awake, you are the center of noises, smells, and a multitude of stimulations.

If you are that prepared, as a communicating human, to have things going on in your world, it is no wonder that you may enjoy a multitude of sensations coming to you at the same time: reading, listening to the radio, watching television, talking on the phone, doing homework, listen-ing for the arrival of a friend, smelling dinner cooking, feeling a draft from an open window, and so on. A problem arises, however, when there is

The attending to a variety of stimuli and sensations at the same time is a very common pattern of behavior. (© *Spencer Grant/The Picture Cube*)

much more happening than you can effectively attend to. Psychological studies have indicated that you have ways to protect yourself from sensations you don't want to take in, and also, in the same way, ways to resist perceiving threatening events or behaviors.

Who Is in Charge of Your Perceptions?

People have a tendency to believe that they are the passive receivers of all this stimulation that comes from the world "out there," or the "empirical world." How do you imagine yourself related to all the things which may "just happen" to you? Do you believe that all you have noticed just sort of drifted into your world and there you were to get hit by it? Do you think that you were the passive receiver of the material that came your way?

You are probably convinced that the world is full of things, objects, and people who are separate from you. You know what they are like, what they do, and what you can do with them. You also do not expect people or things to change suddenly or even disappear into thin air as if a magician had control of your environment. It is most valuable for you to have a knowledge of what things "are," their certain identity, and their implicit permanence. That gives you a feeling of security and also allows you to react to events and people's behaviors quickly if you can predict what might happen. A friend who suddenly becomes loud, boisterous, and overbearing in contrast to that friend's former behaviors will make you feel very uneasy. As long as you accurately predict what will happen—and how your friends will behave—you have a sense of being in control.[5]

Do You and I See Alike?

How you experience the world is in some ways an experience that is unique to you and in other ways an experience that is commonly shared. If you believe that all those behaviors and events are going on "out there" beyond your influence, you would be quite helpless. It is important to understand that perception is not something which randomly happens to you. You are never the passive receiver of information. You are not a nonparticipating, zombielike recipient of unselected stimulations. In fact, you are a major force in the perceiving process—and hence in human interactions—and a very active partner in what is happening around you. In many ways, you quite literally create what you see. A common example is the motion picture, which is only a set of still pictures run past you. With your eyes' *persistence of vision* you connect the stills together to make them appear to move. A patterned light across the television screen makes the picture you see seem as if it were a replica of the world. Does your heart pound in real fear when you suddenly see a strange shadow on your nighttime wall? In your personal relations, do you "see" a friend differently after you have heard some damaging gossip about him or her?[6]

Communication is essentially a process of making up your own reality through perception and symbolization. How you do this also influences the information you will select. This in turn shapes your own ideas and

---

BOX 2-2. Language Habits and Perception

Even comparatively simple acts of perception are very much more at the mercy of the social patterns called words than we might suppose. If one draws some dozen lines, for instance, of different shapes, one perceives them as divisible into such categories as "straight," "crooked," "zigzag" because of the classificatory suggestiveness of the linguistic terms themselves. We see and hear and otherwise experience very largely as we do because the language habits of our community predispose certain choices of interpretation.

Source: E. Sapir, *Culture and Personality* (E. Mandelbaum, ed.), University of California Press, Berkeley, 1985, p. 69.

---

image of what the world is like generally. Thus you begin a cycle of paying attention to things which interest you, and enjoying the things which you favor, and then making up your own behaviors and comments based on those selections.

To put it another way, your image of the world guides what you prefer to pay attention to, and then those items become part of your experience and further guide your perceptions of reality. For example, if I like to read Agatha Christie mysteries, I will talk to others about them and get reinforcement that they are good to read. I will probably read more of them, and then as I see movies and television plays based on Agatha Christie's writing (ones by other authors are not part of my world), they influence my experience and I expect mystery writing to conform to that style; as a result, I may cut myself off from reading mysteries written by Erle Stanley Gardner or Harold Adams.

Carl Sandburg (see Box 2-3) makes[5] this same point in the conversations with newcomers. Most people are not as aware as this poet is about how much of our relationships are projections from inside us on the outside world. Many people assume that the world is an experience apart from their own involvement; it just happens, and you have to take what it gives you.

Your relationships with others are related to perception in this three-step, "logical" system: (1) "If I see something it must be there," (2) "If I see a person behave in a certain way, it is what that person is like," and (3) "Everybody sees everyone else and everything else the same way I do."

Perceptions Lead to Behaviors

Although you will never know whether your perceptions of red and E-flat are the same as mine, *you can and do act on the assumption* that most people see colors and hear tones very much alike. You assume that others

---

BOX 2-3. What Kind of People?

Drove up a newcomer in a covered wagon: "What kind of folks live around here?" "Well, stranger, what kind of folks was there in the country you come from?" "Well, they was mostly a lowdown, lying, gossiping, backbiting lot of people." "Well, I guess, stranger, that's about the kind of folks you'll find around here." And the dusty grey stranger had just about blended into the dusty grey cotton-woods in a clump on the horizon when another newcomer drove up. "What kind of folks live around here?" "Well, stranger, what kind of folks was there in the country you come from?" "Well, they was mostly a decent, hardworking, law abiding, friendly lot of people." "Well, I guess, stranger, that's about the kind of people you'll find around here." And the second wagon moved off and blended with the dusty grey. . . .

Source: C. Sandburg, *The People, Yes,* Harcourt Brace Jovanovich, New York, 1964. Reprinted by permission of Harcourt Brace Jovanovich, Inc.

---

create a world out there similar to your world. Fortunately, this is often close to true. But you must not forget that your perceptions are no more than guesses about what the world is like, and there are other people making guesses also.

In the poem by John Godfrey Saxe (Box 2-4) the six blind men each made selective assessments of the elephant and came up with six different conclusions. The moral in this case is not only the one stated in the last part of the poem—that each was partly right and each partly wrong. Consider an additional moral: *no amount of arguing will make an elephant something that it is not.* No amount of reporting, arguing, or discussing your *perceptions* will change the nature of the world or the people in it.

Much of the time your guesses, or theories, about reality work well enough to get others to generally agree. However, when someone challenges your view of the world, a great sense of uneasiness and dissonance is created. You may experience a sense of anxiety when you discover not everyone sees people, objects, and events exactly as you do. Such experiences will be more or less unsettling depending on who challenges you and whether those perceptions are particularly important to you. Discovering that there is no Santa Claus is often a very traumatic experience for little children, who must then realign their whole sense of what is real and what is fantasy. Discovering that you have been deceived by a close friend can also be a shattering experience and may result in your taking a very different view of people in general as well as the former friend—once burned, you vow never to trust anybody again about anything.

BOX 2-4. The Blind Men and the Elephant

It was six men of Indostan
To learning much inclined,
Who went to see the Elephant
(Though all of them were blind),
That each by observation
Might satisfy his mind.
The First approached the Elephant,
And happening to fall
Against his broad and sturdy side,
At once began to bawl:
"God bless me! but the Elephant
Is very like a wall!"
The Second, feeling of the tusk,
Cried, "Ho! what have we here
So very round and smooth and
   sharp?
To me 'tis mighty clear
This wonder of an Elephant
Is very like a spear!"
The Third approached the animal,
And happening to take
The squirming trunk within his hands,
Thus boldly up he spake:
"I see," quoth he, "the Elephant
Is very like a snake!"
The Fourth reached out an eager
   hand,

And felt about the knee
"What most this wondrous beast is
   like
Is mighty plain," quoth he;
"'Tis clear enough the Elephant
Is very like a tree!"
The Fifth who chanced to touch the
   ear,
Said: "E'en the blindest man
Can tell what this resembles most;
Deny the fact who can,
This marvel of an Elephant
Is very like a fan!"
The Sixth no sooner had begun
About the beast to grope,
Then seizing on the swinging tail
That fell within his scope,
"I see," quoth he, "the Elephant
Is very like a rope!"
And so these men of Indostan
Disputed loud and long,
Each in his own opinion
Exceeding stiff and strong,
Though each was partly in the right,
And all were in the wrong!

John Godfrey Saxe

HOW YOU PERCEIVE

Now that we have discussed *what* it is you perceive, let us turn to *how* you perceive and how the mental processes work that account for your vision of the world.

You Select

At any given moment you pay attention to—notice, are aware of, perceive—only very little of what is going on around you. When you pay attention to something, it means that you are not paying attention to something else. Why you select what you do is usually the product of several factors, some environmental, some internal.

Environmental factors

The environmental factors include influences such as intensity, size, contrast, repetition, motion, and familiarity and novelty.

INTENSITY

The more intense a stimulation, the more likely you will perceive it. A loud noise in a silent room, or a very bright light in a dark street, usually

You pay attention to objects in relation to their size, repetition, contrast, intensity, and so on. (© *Bill Anderson/ Monkmeyer*)

commands your attention. Advertisers capitalize on this when they use particularly bright packaging or television commercials slightly louder than regular programming. The army sergeant shouts commands, and many a teacher finds himself or herself yelling at an unruly class to get the students' attention.

SIZE
The principle of size is quite simple. The larger something is, the more likely it will capture your attention. A full-page newspaper spread is more catchy than the fine print of the classified ads. Toys are often packaged in large boxes containing a lot of cardboard fillers to give children the impression that the actual toy is bigger than it really is. Although toy manufacturers are now obligated to print the actual dimensions of the toy on its box, few children notice the fine print and most are lured by the sheer size of the box. To most of us, bigger is better.

CONTRAST
Things that stand out against a highly contrasting background are usually quite noticeable. Safety signs with black lettering against a yellow background, or white lettering against red, catch your attention. A woman manager stands out in an all-male executive meeting.

REPETITION
A repeated stimulus is more attention-getting than a single one. This is particularly true in dull contexts where your attention may be waning. An interesting story may be remembered after one telling, while nonsense

words or just dull material needs to be repeated several times to be remembered. Advertisers know well that a repeated short message is more effective than a longer message with a one-time exposure.

MOTION

You will pay more attention to a moving object in your field of vision than to the same object when it is stationary. Again, advertisers use this principle when they incorporate moving parts into otherwise still signs. The flashing or rotating lights of the police cars or of ambulances are designed to command attention.

FAMILIARITY AND NOVELTY

The principle of familiarity and novelty may simply be an extension of the contrast principle. New objects in familiar surroundings are likely to draw your attention, just as familiar things in an unfamiliar environment will stand out. Going to shop at a new store may be interesting even if they display the same merchandise, but in a different setting. If you change the way you cut your hair, you may attract attention to yourself in new ways. In business, flextime and job rotation are based partly on the idea that a worker's productivity may be enhanced by a change in routine of prescribed hours or boring tasks.

The environmental factors we have just described represent only a small part of what goes into selective perception. Internal factors of a physiological and psychological nature are extremely powerful in determining not only what you do perceive and how you perceive it but also what you cannot perceive.

Internal factors

PHYSIOLOGICAL FACTORS—HOW YOU ARE BUILT

As you probably know, you are stimulated by what is going on outside of you through your five senses. You see, hear, smell, taste, and feel. However, these five senses are not all-powerful. Human beings are built in such a way that there are sights you cannot see, sounds you cannot hear, tastes you cannot distinguish, smells you do not sense. Your sense of touch does not give you much information if you do not use your eyes to help you determine what you are touching. Many animals have much sharper senses, which enable them to see better, hear better, and smell better than humans can. Most other animals, of course, rely more on their senses than you do and have thus developed them more than you have. It's a little bit like the blind, who cannot rely on their eyes to find out what's going on and develop their sense of touch and hearing to compensate for their lack of sight.

Most of you cannot distinguish between fine differences in delicate taste sensations. Part of your food selection is thus made for you. You do not pay attention to certain things simply because you are not built to perceive them.

BOX 2-5. Your Limited Senses

Most of your communication data come to you from your senses of sight and hearing. You hear sounds, however, only within a certain range of from about 20 cycles per second up to 20,000 cycles per second even if your hi-fi set has capabilities to exceed that range. Your dog, as we know from experience with high-pitched dog whistles, has the ability to hear frequencies above those heard by humans.

Vision has similar limitations for humans. You do not see all the waves available to you—ultraviolet rays are too short (from 0.00003 to 0.000001 centimeters), as are x-rays, gamma rays, and cosmic rays. On the other end of the light spectrum, infrared rays (with a wavelength of 0.00008 to 0.32 centimeters) are not seen, nor are the longer heat waves, radar, or long radio waves. The visible spectrum for humans is quite narrow in relation to all the wave transmissions occurring all around us. What would it be like if you had the x-ray vision which some comic strip characters have developed, or if you could hear the extra-high-frequency sounds emitted by some creatures?

Sensory limitations are shared by every human being (see Box 2-5). In addition to our limitations as a species, there are individual physiological differences which affect what each of you can and does perceive. Not everyone has 20/20 vision, and not everyone hears perfectly well. The finely tuned ear of professional musicians permits them to hear tones in a much more discriminating manner than nonmusicians. The wine connoisseur distinguishes extremely fine variations in taste that most people could not begin to experience.

PSYCHOLOGICAL FACTORS

Motivation.   All of you differ in terms of your needs, motives, interests, desires, etc.; and each of you will tend to perceive what is in accord with your needs, motives, and interests. If you are hungry, you will notice restaurant signs and you will detect food smells which might otherwise go unnoticed. In this culture, visual stimulations dealing with sex are powerful attention-getters. Here again, advertisers, who make it their business to get your attention, know that if they play on your needs, particularly basic sexual and social needs, they will succeed. It may be hard to get your attention about toothpaste, but when toothpaste is linked with sex appeal, the task of getting your attention becomes easier.

You tend to pay attention to what interests you. Sometimes you distort things so that they will fit what you want. You see what you want to see,

Perception involves being "programmed" to see or hear certain stimuli, paying special attention to what interests you most. *(© Arlene Collins/Monkmeyer)*

and sometimes you hear what you want to hear. To a person who feels very threatened or insecure, everything will appear to be a potential source of danger. If you are in a house alone at night and suddenly you feel uncomfortable or nervous, every little noise will reinforce your fear, although the same noises in broad daylight would sound perfectly normal and harmless if you paid any attention at all.

Past experience and past learning—Perceptual set. People are more likely to pay attention to aspects of their environment they anticipate or expect than to those they do not anticipate or expect. And people tend to expect or anticipate what they are familiar with. You may, for example, vaguely hear people talking behind you without really identifying anything they are saying until they mention your name. You will usually hear your name distinctly. That word will stand out from all other words they were saying because you are familiar with it.

Look at Figures 2-1 and 2-2. These are good examples of how you are likely to see only what you expect to see.

If you counted three F's and read "Paris in the spring time," "once in a lifetime," and "bird in the hand," you are wrong. There are six F's in Figure 2-1. Because the F in "of" sounds like a V, it seems to disappear; most people will count only three F's in the sentence. Read again the sentences in the three triangles. Perhaps you need to read them aloud to realize that in two of them the word "the" was repeated and in one of them the word "a" was repeated. Habit makes us fail to perceive things

FINISHED FILES ARE THE RE-
SULT OF YEARS OF SCIENTIF-
IC STUDY COMBINED WITH THE
EXPERIENCE OF MANY YEARS

FIGURE 2-1
Count the F's in the
statement in the box.

as they really are, and learning affects your perceptual set by creating expectations to perceive in a particular way. You see what you expect to see. Have you ever bought a car only to find that the whole world seems to be driving the same kind of car? It is not that the sales of these cars have dramatically increased overnight. You were simply cued to noticing this type of car; it is familiar to you. Also, you were unconsciously looking for it in the street in an attempt to reinforce your buying decision. Much of the time you look not just "at" but "for."

Your particular training has a great deal to do with what you perceive. Education is at best a process of differentiation, of learning to make discriminations. What to the untrained eye looks all the same is full of significant differences to the specialist.

A jeweler will perceive the differences between two seemingly identical diamonds. A physician will notice the differences between seemingly identical symptoms. An English professor will perceive differences between two student essays which to others would seem very much alike. You see what you are trained to see, and you bring to any perception a lifetime of past learnings and experiences: your perceptual set.

You report on you

If you were given the task of reporting on the size of the fish in a local river and had a 2-inch-mesh net, your report might include the statement,

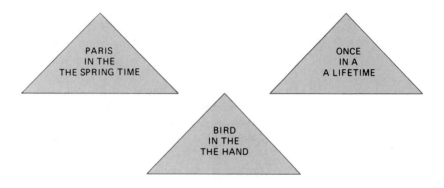

FIGURE 2-2
Read aloud the phrases in
the triangle.

"The fish are 2 inches or bigger." If you repeated the task with a 4-inch-mesh net, your report might read, "The fish are 4 inches or bigger." Remember, you are reporting on the same fish in the same river. Which report is accurate? Each? Neither? What are you reporting on? The size of the fish? *No.* You are reporting on the size of the net you used. The size of the net determines the size of the fish you catch.

In a way, you all have nets in your heads. These nets of course are made not of threads but of all the things that make each of you a unique person: your physiological makeup, your motivations, aspirations, needs, interests, fears, desires, past learning, past experiences, training, etc. These nets act as a filter. The stimulations from your environment have to pass through that filter before they are perceived. Each of you has your own filter. Even though you may share the same environment with others, chances are that you will filter different aspects of that environment and perceive a somewhat different reality than the others do.

Some people have defective filters—filters that are so clogged up that they see very little of what is going on. Some people have filters that distort the stimuli which come to them from the environment. To the extent that your filters are similar to those of other people, you will select out of your environment pretty much the same kinds of things they do.

It is important to remember that *whenever you make a comment about something, you are describing not the thing but rather your net, your filter.* When you report that Sam Jones is a conscientious fellow, you are commenting not so much on Sam Jones as on yourself and your value system. This is not a trivial point. Much of the trouble people experience in communicating with one another stems from two misguided assumptions: (1) What they see is what everyone else sees. (2) They have direct access to reality. Access to reality is at best indirect, filtered by your own observations and your built-in physiological and psychological limitations.

Uncertainty in science

Furthermore, the physicist Werner K. Heisenberg in his famous "principle of uncertainty" (reported in 1927) removed hope for determining the "real" nature of the microcosm. There is a basic indeterminacy about the atomic universe which no refinement of measurements and observation can ever dispel. Heisenberg demonstrated that determination of the position and speed of an electron is impossible, for the very act of observing its position changes its speed. This demonstration shook traditional science, which was based on causality and determinism. "Probabilities" replaced the previously held notion that nature exhibits a determined sequence of cause and effect between events. Another tremendous implication of the Heisenberg principle is that whenever you attempt to observe the "real" objective world, you change it and distort it by the very process of your observation.

FIGURE 2-3
Which do you see—the
goblet or the famous twins?

When we talk about selecting among the stimuli in your environment, we refer not only to the various kinds of sounds and sights you select from. Much of the time you are also selecting from among the different sensory stimuli, so that you ignore sights to pick up sounds, etc. You develop habits of watching or listening or touching, and so your selecting process is actively sorting out a whole barrage of sounds; but it is also flitting back and forth between seeing intently and listening acutely. Selecting not only is always part of your communication habits, but is a combination of physical choices and psychological preferences all woven together.[7]

You Organize

Once you have "selected" what to perceive, you usually organize it in some fashion. Even the most simple experience requires that you impose order on a series of disconnected elements. The way you order or organize what you perceive is neither random nor arbitrary; you follow certain "rules." According to gestalt psychologists, these rules are innate. Behavioral psychologists, however, claim that these rules are learned through social experience. There is evidence to support both views, and we will not try to settle this argument here. What is clear, though, is that these rules have important effects on how you perceive.

Look at Figures 2-3, 2-4, and 2-5. What do you see? Perhaps at first just some white and black shapes. Perhaps one shape will stand out. In that case you have organized the shapes into a picture by visually putting some of the shapes in the background and some in the foreground. Of course, you may not organize shapes in the same way everyone else does. Some of you fail to organize certain visual stimuli into some coherent

FIGURE 2-4
Describe the woman you see
in this drawing. How old is
she? Is she attractive? What
kind of covering is on her
head? Etc.

FIGURE 2-5
In these patches of black and
white, do you see the face of
Christ?

FIGURE 2-6
This collection of twenty
discrete blotches is a picture
of a dog.

picture. Many people do not see the face of Christ in Figure 2-5. Some cannot see the old woman or the young woman in Figure 2-4. Yet every line or shape you need to organize the particular configurations is in the picture. Organization of the lines and shapes into a specific design depends solely on the perceiver.

You usually organize by giving priority to what is striking or outstanding. In figure-ground relationships you tend to identify figures by their usually more dominant color. When there is not enough contrast between figure and ground, it is more difficult to decode which is which, as in the picture of Christ.

You also tend to organize what you perceive into whole figures. If what you look at is incomplete, you fill in the gaps, a process called "closure." Look at Figure 2-6. You see a dog, not twenty different spots. Look at Figure 2-7. You see a completed square even though the lines do not touch.

Sometimes we tend to organize what we perceive in misleading ways, as the optical illusions in Figures 2-8 through 2-10 prove.

FIGURE 2-7
Even though the corners are missing here, our imaginations can still fill them in to make a square.

You Interpret

What you look at or hear is often ambiguous. Sometimes you may not see distinctly because a room is dimly lighted or because you are looking at something that goes by very quickly. "Now you see it, now you don't," says the magician, who capitalizes on distraction and speed of movement to create visual illusions. But even when what you look at is very clearly delineated, there is no automatic conclusion about what the object is.

FIGURE 2-8
Are the long lines in this drawing parallel?

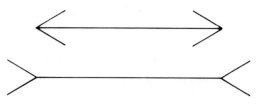

FIGURE 2-9
Are both of these lines the
same length?

Even the simplest objects can produce a variety of visual stimuli (for example, a cup and saucer seen at different angles), and different objects can produce the same stimuli (for example, an orchestra and a 12-inch high-fidelity speaker). Consequently, it is necessary to interpret what object the thing you are looking at actually represents. This interpretation is not always easy, and it is rarely conscious. The greater the ambiguity of the object, the more room there is for interpretation. This is the theory behind what psychologists call "projective tests," such as the test in which you look at an inkblot like the one in Figure 2-11 and tell what you see. Usually what you see reveals what you project into it, and this comes from your personal experiences, motives, needs, interests, etc.

Context

You usually interpret what you see by looking at the context of the object. For example, the shape 13 will be read as the letter B if it is preceded by the letter A. However, if it is preceded by the number 12, then it will be perceived as the number 13 (see Figure 2-12). It is often not the facts

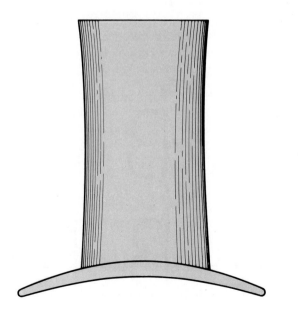

FIGURE 2-10
Is the hat higher than it is
wide?

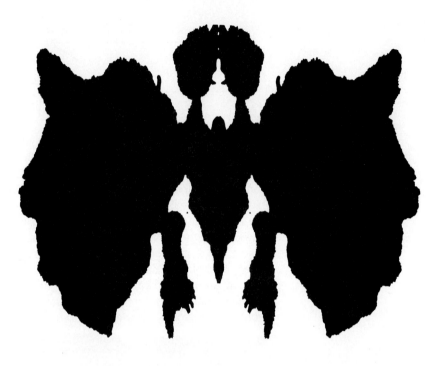

FIGURE 2-11
The inkblot projective test
assists our minds to shape
meaning.

themselves that are the basis for different perceptions of the same event. Rather, it is the interpretation of those facts in the light of differing contexts which creates most of the communication difficulties in interpersonal encounters.[8]

Another very important factor which affects how we perceive things in context is age, or maturity. Just as we learn how the world works by experience in it, and just as we learn our language by a special imitative developmental process, we also develop habits of perception of the en-

$$ A \quad B \quad C $$

$$ 12 \quad 13 \quad 14 $$

FIGURE 2-12
An example of the effect of
context. The middle figure
can be either the letter B or
the number 13, depending on
what kind of sequence it
appears in.

vironment. Television advertisers of products appealing to young children are conscious of the effects of showing toys, prizes, or candy "blown up" to make them look larger than they actually are. Some adults also can be fooled by camera tricks and by distortions of perspective. A study by Acker and Tiemens that compared "preoperational" children with older children and adults determined that younger children responded differently to images of a candy bar shown "normal size" and in close-up.[9] The younger children believed that the candy bar actually had "more candy in it" when the image was larger. Most older children and adults perceived a trick of the camera rather than a candy bar that was "growing."

You Create Your World

What we have been saying all along in this section is that your world, the environment in which you live, is uniquely yours. Your view of the world belongs to you because you created and constructed it as you selected, organized, and interpreted bits and pieces of stimulations which originated outside of you. How you do this selection, organization, and interpretation is largely based on how you have done it in the past, and in a very real sense, you are the product of your past perceptions. Much of what you perceive stands against the backdrop of a lifetime of previous experiences which have permitted you to develop expectations about how the world goes around. Your "frame of reference," as psychologists call it—or your "nets and filters," as we have referred to it—permits you to make sense out of all the stimulations you experience. A person who grew up in the center of a large city does not respond to the outdoors the same way a rural person does.

A PROCESS VIEW OF THE WORLD

Ours are the days of relativity and uncertainty. Since Max Planck, Albert Einstein, and Werner K. Heisenberg, a new era of scientific thought has begun—one much less in agreement with your everyday perceptions of the world based on imperfect instruments such as your senses and moderately powerful microscopes. "The certainty that science can explain *how* things happen began to dim about twenty years ago," Lincoln Barnett wrote originally in 1948, "and right now it is a question whether scientific man is in touch with 'reality' at all—or can ever hope to be."[10]

Much of what is talked about, even by scientists, is only guesswork. Even aided by powerful electron microscopes, scientists cannot view the subatomic functioning or our world so perfectly that they can conclusively say what is going on so far below the threshold of our ability to perceive directly. It is a humbling thought that even with the training, the instruments, and the rigor of the scientific world, there are problems of accuracy and meaning. Think, then, what you face in the majority of communicative situations when you think and talk about events and people that are not amenable to the scientific method.

What modern science tells you about the world is that it is an ever-changing, dynamic, moving pattern of radiations or energy transformations; that what appears solid and unchanging to the naked eye is merely a construct of your brain. You cannot know reality as it is, since your act of observing it changes it. By dealing with happenings in the world in terms of probabilities, you abandon the idea that nature exhibits an inexorable sequence of cause and effect among individual happenings.

An important comment on this subject comes from Rogers and Kincaid in their book *Communication Networks:* "Most past discussions of communication have not stressed: (1) that the creation of information occurs at a physical level of reality, (2) that interpretation occurs at the psychological level, and (3) that perception bridges the physical and psychological levels of reality."[11] Their term "interpretation" also includes the organizing function we referred to earlier. Perceiving provides the link between us and the ongoing buzz of events, noises, sights, smells, and other stimuli of the world around us. It is a dynamic process, subject to change as we change, subject to personal whim and individual tendencies and habits.

Checking Perceptions

In practice, then, how do you go about checking perceptions to try to get along better in the world? One way you test your ideas about relationships is by finding out if others see events and your friends the same way you

The checking of perceptions with people who are authorities is an effective means of "consensual validation." (© J. Berndt/ Stock, Boston)

do. When you get support from others, you feel more confident that what you see is accurate. You depend on others to help you sort out what is real and what is not. If enough people agree with you about a given perception, you tend to trust that perception. This process is known as *consensual validation,* which simply means that other people agree with you that they see what you say you see.

You also tend to trust a perception which you *experience repeatedly.* If it happens over and over again, it builds your confidence. Your bus or train may be consistently five minutes late, and pretty soon you plan your trips on that schedule. A friend says he or she will phone you, and then forgets. After a series of such broken promises, you change your perception of this person's reliability—at least in terms of using a telephone.

Still another way, slightly different from repetitions, is to check your perceptions by *comparisons.* You compare what you have known in the past, or under some similar conditions, with the new items or behaviors you see now. If you have known, in another time or place, some artists, some bald-headed men, some blonde women, some crabby teachers, some dishonest car salespeople, some helpful police—you have stored up data to make some comparisons with the new artist, bald head, blonde, or teacher you encounter. You should be warned, however, that there may be as many differences in the new relationship as there are similarities. As Wendell Johnson wrote: "To a mouse, cheese is cheese. That's why mousetraps work."[12] The mouse, by focusing on the similarities it perceives—cheese is cheese—fails to notice a very significant difference in its environment, the mousetrap. You may behave toward a friend as if you were still teenage buddies, and be disappointed to find more differences than similarities in how you see things today. Parents expect to have their children return from college with ideas, values, and even manners of dress that are very similar to what they went away with, and judge them on that expectation.

Both the repetition process and the comparison process are based on your ability to store up and classify information. They differ, however, in that repetition depends on duplication of like experiences and behaviors; comparison is based on perceived similarities past and present.

Perception and Diversity

There can be some dangers in relying on the validation systems mentioned above. For one thing, in using *consensual* validation, if you check your perceptions with only those whose "filters" or biases agree with yours, you may not get much closer to an objective truth about a person or an event. In fact, we sometimes seek out another person to agree with us when something we want to do or some opinion of ourselves requires validation—our Uncle Ben went to four different doctors before he could find one who would prescribe a martini before dinner as a suitable way to lower his blood pressure; a student we know phoned six people before getting one who would validate her low opinion of the professor who gave her a failing grade on a test.

For another thing, you can be fooled by people who want to trick you or who may be deluded themselves. How would you react if close friends (either as a joke or because they really believed it) told you that communists had infiltrated the whole sociology department, or that all seniors had to take regular drug tests twice during their last semester before graduating, or that the town government was broke and there would be no more garbage pickup or other city services?

Selectively remembering certain incidents or behaviors (called "selective recall") can also be misleading if you are determined to love or hate. When you find yourself attracted to another person, you tend to pay attention only to the most positive qualities and behaviors—just as when you are intent on hating a person, a cause, or an event, you will select only those negative items to pay attention to, and remember only the "downside" for comparisons or validation.

If, as we wrote earlier, even great scientific minds have some limits in perceiving, given the care with which we think scientists look at their world, imagine the trouble most of us scientifically untrained observers have in handling our perceptions. In this chapter we have suggested many times that *how people look at their world will determine how they act in it.* No clearer picture of that can be drawn in what has come to be called "intercultural communication."

Actually encompassing more than different "cultures"—in fact, involving race, gender, age, ethnicity, religion, economics, language, and so on—the study of what we refer to as intercultural communication begins with our ways of thinking about others who are different from ourselves. We obtain and verify our stereotypes and our biases and our beliefs from parents, peers, the media, and all kinds of contacts both interpersonal

---

BOX 2-6. Persistence of Perception

Bigotry is never a pleasant subject so you didn't bring it up but you stuck by your guns anyway. Indians were drunks, Jews were thieves, and the colored were shiftless. Where you got this, I don't know, because there were none of them around, but you believed it more absolutely for the utter lack of evidence. Everyone knew about those people. It was common sense.

Source: From *Lake Wobegon Days* by Garrison Keillor. Copyright © 1985 by Garrison Keillor. Reprinted by permission of the publisher, Viking Penguin, a division of Penguin Books USA, Inc.

and public. We may hold tightly to our hates and fears, and we behave in abusive ways by oppressing or discriminating against others.

Much used current words like ''diversity'' and ''pluralism'' remind us that the society we live in is composed of many different kinds of people. Differences in people may give healthy variety and strength to the world, so everybody does not have to be just like everybody else. In the concept of ''diversity'' the idea is to accept those people who are different from us; to encourage perceptions and social behavior which foster tolerance, respect, empowerment, mercy, and love instead of bigotry, bias, provincialism, parochialism, derision, racism, sexism, oppression, and hate.

Perception of diversity requires insights into your own biases and ''presets'' about people and events. As important, you should pay attention to the statements and behaviors of others to consider what perceptions—known and unknown—motivate and guide their words and actions.

What Does This Have to Do with You?

What does all this have to do with you? Here are a few comments which should point out what this discussion of perception has to do with the way you communicate and relate to other people.

There are many ways to experience ''reality.'' No two people experience it in exactly the same way. To the extent that many perceptions are common to most people, their ''reality''—that is, their theories about reality—will be common, and they are likely to understand each other when they communicate. To the extent that your perceptions of reality are different, because each of you is unique, you may have difficulty sharing them with others.

Although absolute certainty and absolute objectivity are impossible, some people's predictions about the world are more often correct than other people's. Although all people are biased, some are more biased than others, and some may not even be aware that they are biased.

To increase the probability that your perceptions will yield accurate information about your world, (1) you must become aware of the part you play in perceiving, (2) you must realize that you have biases and that your filters shape, limit, and distort the information you take in, (3) you must interpret your perceptions in light of your biases and correct for them whenever you can, and (4) you must realize that simply perceiving something does not give you, or anybody else, a corner on the truth of the matter.

SUMMARY

What you perceive is exclusively yours as you work it out inside yourself. Your perceptions may or may not be shared by others.

You get your perceptions by *selecting* from all the things that are going on around you, based on your senses and your internal state. Then you *organize* this material into some kind of understandable order. After that, you *interpret* what you have seen in relation to its context and your past experiences and what you know and believe.

By that process of selecting, organizing, and interpreting, you begin to make sense out of the busy, hurrying, complicated *process world* around you. Reality for you may be simply a combination of your guesses, the guesses of others who seem to confirm yours, and the fact that you happen to agree. In spite of the fact that you may make careful guesses, and get them validated by *checking with others,* by *repetition,* and by *comparisons,* what you perceive is largely made up by your own creative mind.

END NOTES

[1] For a definitive discussion on the use of intrapersonal and interpersonal nomenclature see Gerald Miller, "The Current Status of Theory and Research in Interpersonal Communication," *Human Communication Research,* vol. 4, no. 2, 1978, pp. 164–178.

[2] B. Bower, "Subliminal Deceptions," *Science News,* vol. 138, Aug. 25, 1990, p. 124; and see "Subliminal Learning: A Fraud?" *USA Today,* vol. 118, September 1989.

[3] W. Heron, "Cognitive and Physiological Effects of Perceptual Isolation," in P. Solomon et al. (eds.), *Sensory Deprivation,* proceedings of a symposium at the Harvard Medical School, Harvard University Press, Cambridge, MA, 1961, pp. 6–33.

[4] P. E. Kubzansky and P. H. Leiderman, "Sensory Deprivation: An Overview," in P. Solomon et al. (eds.), ibid., pp. 221–238. And see also S. M. Schanberg and T. M. Field, "Sensory Deprivation Stress," part of a special section on psychobiological studies in stress and coping, *Child Development,* vol. 50, December 1987, p. 1431.

[5] P. Chance, "Seeing Is Believing: Even Though What You See Is Not Necessarily What You Get," *Psychology Today,* vol. 23, January–February 1989, p. 26.

[6] D. B. Fedor, M. R. Buckley, and R. W. Eder, "Measuring Subordinate Perceptions of Supervisor Feedback Intentions: Some Unsettling Results," *Educational and Psychological Measurement,* vol. 50, Spring 1990, p. 73. R. A. Gordon, R. M. Roselle, and J. C. Baxter, "The Effect of Applicant Age, Job Level, and Accountability on Perceptions of Female Job Applicants," *The Journal of Psychology,* vol. 123, January 1989, p. 59.

[7] W. R. Dickinson, W. Bains, and F. Pansera, "The Great Fireworks Illusion," *Nature,* vol. 343, Jan. 25, 1990, p. 320.

[8] J. Walker, column titled "The Café-Wall Illusion, in Which Rows of Tiles Tilt That Should Not Tilt At All," *Scientific American,* vol. 259, November 1989, p. 138.

[9] S. R. Acker and R. K. Tiemens, "Children's Perceptions of Changes in Size of

Televized Images," *Human Communication Research,* vol. 7, Summer, 1981, pp. 340–346.

[10] L. Barnett, *The Universe and Dr. Einstein,* Time, New York, 1962, p. 6.

[11] E. M. Rogers and L. D. Kincaid, *Communication Networks,* Free Press, New York, 1981, p. 52.

[12] W. Johnson, *People in Quandaries,* International Society for General Semantics, San Francisco, 1980.

CHAPTER
3

SELF-CONCEPT: WHO AM I?

OBJECTIVES

After studying this chapter you should be able to do the following:

1. Describe the process by which you develop a self-concept from earliest childhood.
2. Explain the terms "looking-glass self" and "generalized other," and identify the theorists associated with them.
3. Contrast and give original examples of confirming behaviors and disconfirming behaviors.
4. Give examples of how the self-concept is maintained through interpersonal communication.
5. Explain the terms "self-fulfilling prophecy" and "Pygmalion effect," and give original examples.
6. List at least four ways the low-self-esteem characteristics are different from high-self-esteem characteristics.
7. Distinguish between the verbal pattern tendencies of low self-concept and high self-concept.
8. Distinguish among the *physical*, the *role*, and the *introspective* ranges of self-concept.

9. Explain what is meant by behaviors, and cite reasons for distinguishing between a *person* and that person's *behaviors*.

INTRODUCTION

In Chapter 2 we discussed how you develop your view of reality, your perceptions of what the world is like, and the meanings you attach to your experiences. In this chapter we will look at the primary feature of your filter system that you use to make sense out of the world—that is, your perception of yourself.

AN INTRODUCTION TO YOURSELF

You live in a world of other people, many of whom have a part in shaping what you know and how you feel about it. You need others to help you conduct the business of living. Not surprisingly, you look to them to find out things about yourself.

In your study of interpersonal communication you must first explore the most important agent in the process—you. Who you "really" are, how you see yourself, how others see you, what roles you play for the various audiences in your life, all are significant to you. Because you are the only one who can do something about your communication, it is very important for you to look carefully at how you communicate and how you can do it effectively.

Do other people affect you? If you want to be seen as a "bright student" by your teacher, you will study the assignments and turn in good work. How you behave will be determined by how you want to be evaluated. If you decide to be known as a friendly person, you will act in an open, cheerful way around others. They may respond in the same way to you, which reinforces your feelings that you are a "friendly person."

Accumulations of past experiences influence your behaviors today; but more than that, those past experiences had very personal meanings and feelings attached to them. So what you do is not just a function of what happens from the outside. It is very much a function of how you

---

BOX 3-1. Who Am I?

"Who am I?" is a question you may have asked yourself at some time. How you answer that question will determine not only how you feel about yourself, but also how you relate to other people. The question "Who am I?" is not just an adolescent or metaphysical query. It is a question which all of you face daily and which takes on greater significance as you go through life crises and make important decisions.

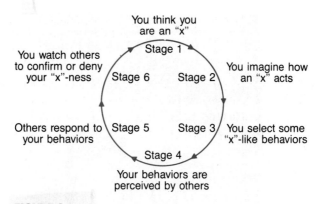

FIGURE 3-1

Self-concept transactions: This circular diagram illustrates the continuous nature of self-concept. All parts are connected, as a change in one place (for example, how you behave) has an effect on other stages (reactions of others, your own ideas and conclusions). You may also enter any stage—like suddenly being seen in a specific role by others (stage 4).

At stage 1, you see yourself as a "serious student"; at stage 2 you imagine that serious students read books, take notes in class, write term papers, study hard for and take tests, go to the library, listen attentively to the professor, etc. At stage 3, you adopt behaviors consistent with those ideas and you actually perform those activities, and at stage 4, you are seen by others, the professor, and your fellow students as behaving in those ways. Then at stages 5 and 6, you get good grades and interpret that as the professor likes what you are doing better than your fellow students do (who would like you to spend more time with them than in the library and not be an "average raiser" in class). You are back at the start where you can continue to define yourself as a "serious student," but now you have more data on how you are being seen by others. You can select a change in any place—by deciding serious students don't do all those things (stage 2), by behaving a little differently (stage 3), by trying to hide your actions from your peers (stage 4), or by selectively ignoring responses from others (stage 6).

feel about yourself on the inside. That means you will make choices of behaviors today by remembering what went on yesterday; and probably more importantly by remembering how you felt about those incidents and reactions. Figure 3-1 shows the circular nature of how our self-concept is developed and maintained. The rest of this chapter discusses ways in which transactions become images, and ways in which images affect the transactions.[1]

HOW YOUR SELF-CONCEPT DEVELOPS

How the self and the self-concept develop has been the subject of much speculation and research. What psychologists and sociologists tell us basically revolves around the key assumptions that the self-concept is learned, maintained, and changed through interpersonal communication processes. Let us look at how this process works.

"Looking-glass self" describes what you learn about yourself by "looking in a mirror" that is, establishing an image of yourself by analyzing other people's reactions to you. (© *Joel Gordon*)

You Learn Your Self-Concept through Interpersonal Communication

How you come to see yourself is a result of how you see others seeing you. The process is a lot like looking in a mirror to find out if your hair is arranged, your tie is straight, or your face is clean. In fact, the term "looking-glass self" has been used for many years as a description of the way you develop a self concept.[2] Most of you don't depend solely on your own image of yourselves, made up without checking with others about what they see in you. You look at others looking at you and try to figure out what they see. You very early develop an ability to see a situation as you imagine other people would see it, including, of course, your own person.[3] The way you think you are is to a great extent shaped by how people treated you when you were growing up.

When you were born you did not have a sense of self. The way you were treated began to lay the foundations upon which you developed feelings and thoughts about what kind of person you were. If you were lucky, you received messages of warmth and love, you were fed when you were hungry, you got attention when you cried, you were cuddled and held, and you learned that you were cared for—the roots of a basic sense of worth. Some children are not so lucky and go ignored and untouched for long periods of time. The tragedy of such children is that

> ### BOX 3-2. Parenting and Self-Esteem
>
> While it is beyond the scope of this book to report on all the various theories of self-esteem acquisition, there seem to be three primary conditions encouraged by parents for developing self-esteem. It must be noted, young people's self-esteem is affected by whoever performs the role of parents, as well as a few significant others, including peers as an important source of self-concept.
>
> Three conditions often listed as developing positive self-esteem in early adolescents include (1) attitude of acceptance by parents about their children, (2) clearly defined and enforced limits, and (3) respect and latitude for individual action within the defined limits.
>
> On the other hand, it is believed that rejection, dominance, and severe or brutalizing punishment tend to foster low self-esteem. All these factors involve communication transactions between human participants, primarily at an early age and interpersonally as well as in groups.*
>
> * R. B. Nelson and M. A. Zielinski, "Children's Self-Esteem and Parental Support," *Journal of Marriage and the Family,* vol. 51, August 1989, pp. 727–729. J. P. Comer, "Encouraging Self-Esteem, 11 through 13," *Parents Magazine,* vol. 62, February 1987, p. 162. S. Coopersmith, *The Antecedents of Self-Esteem,* W. H. Freeman, San Francisco, 1967, pp. 236 and 249. M. Rosenberg, *Society and the Adolescent Self-Image,* Princeton University Press, Princeton, NJ, 1965, pp. 12–15, p. 243 et seq.

they learn at a most impressionable stage of their lives that they do not matter, that no one cares for them, and consequently that they must be no good.

Language shapes you

Beyond the first months of your life, language begins to introduce some degree of permanence into the objects around you. How people talk about you and to you makes a great impression and literally shapes the way you begin to feel about yourself. You may learn traditional role expectations, such as "Big boys don't cry," "Little girls should mind," "Boys don't play with dolls," "Girls help their mommies in the kitchen." The way you begin to view yourself is a function of how other people want you to be and how well they reinforce your learned identity.[4]

Imitation

From the time you are about 10 months old to about 18 months, you go through a phase of simple *imitating* without understanding the actions and words of the people around you. Some of these behaviors and words will be reinforced and will remain in your repertoire of roles and in your developing vocabulary. As you get a little older, you go through a phase

From a very early age, language shapes the way you feel about yourself. (© *Susan Lapides/Design Conceptions*)

of *role playing,* which simply consists of trying on roles that you are familiar with, patterns of behaviors that you have observed around you and that you now associate with specific meanings. Watch a 3-year-old playing house. A child is extremely skillful in imitating the role of the father or mother with a doll or another child. Eavesdropping on little kids can be a revelation for many parents, allowing them to see themselves as they come across to their children.

Role-taking practice   Between the ages of 3 and 5, children begin to understand the dimensions of the roles they play. This role-playing ability is directly related to the degree of language development achieved by the child. As they role-play, children develop the capacity to imagine how others behave in certain situations. When the little girl plays mommy, she is in effect imagining how her mother would act in a given situation. This is a most crucial skill, which ultimately permits children to imagine their own behavior in relation to other people. If a little girl can imagine what her mother will do in a given situation, she can then develop expectations about her mother's behavior in relation to her should that situation arise. Interpersonal trans-actions are based upon your ability to imagine what other people think

Role-taking behavior becomes important to children aged 3 to 5 as they begin to imagine how others act. (© Rita Nannini/Photo Researchers)

and expect of you in a given situation, how they are likely to respond to your behavior.

Role-taking symbolically

Finally, you reach a phase when you no longer need to actually play the role of another person to figure how that person might respond to you. You simply go through the process symbolically, in your head. The process of *symbolic role taking,* as Berlo describes it, permits you to behave on the basis of what you believe other people think of you.[5] You become accustomed to classical questions like "What will people say?" or "What would Daddy think about that?"

As you grow up, you have more experiences to test your role-taking ability, and you know many more people to think about. You no longer think in terms of just one person—like mother, or teacher, or good friend—when you wonder what people expect of you. You begin to think of other people *in general,* so that existence of "generalized others" in some ways adds to the individual "significant others" whom you expect to evaluate your role-taking.[6] As an adult you behave in a given situation not just on the basis of how you see the situation, but most often on the basis of how you *imagine other people in general expect you to act.*

The generalized other is very much related to your self-concept. How you view yourself affects how you think others will react to you. If you think you are a good tennis player or a warm, friendly person, you will expect others to see you that way. If you think you are too short or a poor conversationalist, you will expect others to see those qualities and act accordingly toward you. The important thing to remember is that you act in both cases on the basis of *how you think other people view you,* and not necessarily on the basis of *how they actually view you.*

The Self-Concept Is Maintained or Changed through Interpersonal Communication

The view that you hold of who you are is by no means static. Because the self-concept develops through interpersonal communication, it also is maintained and changed through interpersonal communication. Each new person and each new experience may confirm, but may also change, how you view the world, other people, and yourself. The impact of new people and experiences in your life may be tremendous and obvious at times, but more often it is quite subtle and may go unnoticed for a while. Yet, as you experience new behaviors in new environments and as you meet people whose response to you is different from what you expect, your sense of self and identity may change.

The Pygmalion effect and self-fulfilling prophecy

The "Pygmalion effect," a well-known case of "self-fulfilling prophecy," describes an outcome of a research study in which pupils appeared to be evaluated on the basis of how they were labeled rather than totally on ability. Teachers were told that certain pupils were likely to be better performers than others even though they were selected at random from the entire class. Experimenters discovered that teachers evaluated those selected students as "bright," judged their performances in the same way, and encouraged them to perform better. Being labeled as "bright," and being treated as if they were "bright," resulted in the pupils' performing at that level—at least in their own perceptions and the perceptions of the teachers.[7]

Language belongs to everyone. Audrey Hepburn, as a streetwise flower seller, has her life changed by the linguistics professor played by Rex Harrison in *My Fair Lady.* (© *The Museum of Modern Art/Film Stills Archive)*

BOX 3-3. Galatea to My Fair Lady

The Pygmalion story has been around since Greek mythology, when the sculptor of that name carved a beautiful ivory woman and fell in love with the statue. The gods granted life to the statue (and named her Galatea) because of the devotion of the sculptor. British playwright George Bernard Shaw created a stage play which he called *Pygmalion* about a slovenly flower peddler, Eliza Doolittle, who became a lady because she was treated like one and given appropriate clothing, manners, and speech patterns. The musical *My Fair Lady* was based on Shaw's play.

Self-fulfilling prophecy is an excellent example of the transactional nature of communication. One set of beliefs feeds on another and produces a reciprocal result. For example, Jason is a shy young man who feels inadequate around others, particularly women. He anticipates being rejected by others and will not ask a woman for a date. This retreating into his own shell gives others the impression he is not interested in social communication. This means that few people will invite him to parties or seek him out to talk to. As he remains a social isolate, he is more sure than ever that he is inadequate and unattractive. "No one pays any attention to me. I am unattractive. I knew it all along." He is not misreading the reactions of others; they are actually avoiding him. But where did it begin?

Had Jason been willing to act in an outgoing manner—talk to others and even risk asking for a date—he might have had more favorable responses from others. One or two positive reactions from others and he would have begun to feel more confident—"maybe other people could get to accept and like me." On that basis he begins to act more outgoing and discovers he can handle himself socially. That would be a positive self-fulfilling prophecy, one that acts in his favor.

In summary, a self-fulfilling prophecy is a cycle of your expectations of how others perceive you. Their perceptions encourage you to act in such a way that ultimately you help develop in others the kind of perceptions you thought they had in the first place. Then you find their overt behavior toward you the final proof that you were right all along.[8]

Confirmation and disconfirmation

Your image of who you are needs verification and support from other people, and much of your communication will in many indirect ways contain subtle demands to have your image confirmed. Just about every message you send includes a request: "Validate me." You seek confirmation not only of the way you view yourself but also of the way you view others and the way you experience the world around you. The

Winning is direct validation. Florence Griffith Joyner wears Olympic medals which represent an external validation of her outstanding achievements. (© Durand/Giansanti/Perrin/Sygma)

process of confirmation and disconfirmation has been described by several authors. Sieburg writes:

> Communication with others is a basic human need, for it is through communication that relationships are formed, maintained, and expressed. It was theorized that in attempting to establish relationships, individuals engage in behavior which involves the formulation of messages with the expectation of a response. If this expectation is met—if response is direct, open, clear, congruous, and relevant to the prior communicative attempt, the persons involved are likely to experience the benefits of genuine dialogue as well as the advantages of "therapeutic interpersonal communication." . . . If response is absent, tangential, unclear, ambiguous, or otherwise inadequate, the participants are likely to feel confused, dissatisfied, misunderstood, and alienated.[9]

Further clarification of confirming and disconfirming responses is provided by the following examples.

CONFIRMING RESPONSES

Confirming responses include: (1) *direct acknowledgment,* when you respond directly to another person's message and thus indicate that you heard what was said and acknowledge both the person and the message, (2) *agreement about content,* when you reinforce or support the opinions and ideas expressed by another person, (3) *supportive response,* when you give assurances, express understanding, or somehow attempt to make the other person feel better or encouraged, (4) *clarifying response,* when you try to get the other person to express more, to describe more feelings or information, to seek repetition or make past remarks clearer, and (5) *expression of positive feelings,* when you share positive feelings about what the other person has done or said.

DISCONFIRMING RESPONSES

Disconfirming responses include the following: (1) *impervious response,* when you ignore or do not acknowledge what was said, when you give no indication that something has been said; (2) *interrupting response,* when you interrupt or cut off something that is being said, or begin a new thought while the first person is still speaking; (3) *irrelevant response,* when you introduce a new train of thought or a new topic, or in some way indicate that what the first speaker said is so inconsequential that it is not worth commenting upon; (4) *tangential response,* when you make a slight attempt to relate a new thought to what was said previously, but when in fact you take the discussion in a new direction (the "yes, . . . but" ploy is often the mark of a tangential response; and so is "by the way, this reminds me of . . ." when the subsequent story has little relationship to the previous discussion); (5) *impersonal response,* when you use generalizations, clichés, pronouncements, and intellectualizations abundantly; (6) *incoherent response,* when you ramble, when you use words in special idiosyncratic ways that are unclear to your listeners, when you leave sentences uncompleted, or when you reword and rephrase so much that your main idea gets lost; and (7) *incongruous response,* when your nonverbal communication is completely at odds with your verbal statements (for example, when you are red in the face, bang your first on the table, and shout, "I am not angry!").

BOX 3-4. Self-Esteem Has Consequences

Self-esteem appears to have ramifying consequences that affect the manner in which an individual responds to himself and the outside world.

Stanley Coopersmith

WHY STUDY SELF-CONCEPT?

Who you think you are is confirmed or denied by the responses others make to your communication with them. Unless you get clear and supportive messages, you are not likely to have effective communication experiences. Early in your lives you learn how to give each other many different kinds of responses, and you should recognize that what you do to each other has an effect on your feelings of worth, on your self-esteem, and also on how well you can get the job done.

BOX 3-5. Self-Esteem Goes Public*

Since John Vasconcellos, a California assemblyman, in 1984 sponsored a bill to set up a task force on statewide self-esteem, the efforts seem to be spreading. Volunteers staff the *California Task Force to Promote Self-Esteem and Personal and Social Responsibility,* which asserts that higher self-esteem results in more productive workers, decrease in crime, less welfare, and wider financial self-sufficiency.

Interpreting how self-esteem may be taught are scores of companies, trainers, consultants, and hundreds of books all claiming to improve the self-esteem of persons involved in seminars, short courses, readings, conferences, or other training and self-help programs.

The *New York Times* reported in its March 28, 1990, edition (page B1) on widespread activities linked to attempts to raise self-esteem including grading in a San Antonio, Texas, school to include honesty, kindness, courage, and conviction as well as content; techniques to reduce stress and depression in Philadelphia drug and alcohol abusers; classes in self-esteem for welfare mothers in Cumberland County, New Jersey; incarceration goals for prisoners in a California penal center; and many skill-development courses such as those at Apollo High School in Simi Valley, California.

Success of this public effort has not been evaluated except anecdotally. Some detractors of the program suggest that it may glorify white American middle-class values and have questionable relevance to minorities such as blacks or Hispanics. Other opponents suggest that the effects of subjects' continued association with people who fostered or contribute to their low self-image may prevent much positive widespread enhancement of self-esteem. You're not likely to change much, they say, if you don't change your circumstances, the people around you, and your role models.

* "Task Force Feelgood: California's Group to Promote Self-Esteem," *Time,* vol. 129, Feb. 23, 1987; "Pondering Self-Esteem," *Newsweek,* vol. 109, Mar. 2, 1987, p. 70; "Boopsie's Task Force: Report on Self-Esteem in California," *The Economist,* vol. 314, Jan. 20, 1990, p. 26; "Learning Self-Esteem," *Time,* vol. 135, Jan. 29, 1990, p. 29.

The reason we have gone into this lengthy discussion of the formation of the self-concept and of the ways it is maintained and changed through interpersonal communication processes is that self-perception is a major filter mechanism. As such, it plays a significant part in how you generally perceive the world and hence how you behave.

Much of the development and maintenance of your self-concept is intimately related to your work and the roles you learn in the formal organizations you participate in. Much of your sense of inner worth comes from performing the roles that society provides. You learn to see yourself as a college student, a parent, a lawyer, an engineer, a professor, a secretary, a coal miner, an accountant; and you learn the expected behaviors of a "good" college student, parent, lawyer, engineer, professor, secretary, coal miner, or accountant. When what you do matches the standards you have learned to accept, you feel good, competent, and worthwhile. And you often know that you have achieved those standards when other people give you confirmation. "Good job on that report, Jones," an A+ on a paper, a promotion, inclusion in a highly select

---

Box 3-6. Defining Self-Esteem

Among the characteristics usually defined as high and low self-esteem consider the following:*

High-self-esteem tendencies in people who:
1. Respect themselves
2. Consider themselves worthy
3. Do not consider themselves perfect or better than others, but also do not think they are worse
4. Recognize realistically their personal limitations
5. Although satisfied, expect to be able to grow and improve

Low-self-esteem tendencies in people who:
1. Seem to verbally and actively reject themselves
2. Are dissatisfied with themselves
3. May even hold themselves in contempt
4. Do not like the selves they see in relation to others
5. Find this picture of themselves disagreeable and wish it were different, but may not have confidence in making any changes

* See Box 4-2 in the next chapter relating to IFD disease. Also M. Rosenberg, *Society and the Adolescent Self-Image*, op. cit., pp. 30–31. R. L. Duran and L. Kelly, "The Influence of Communicative Competence on Perceived Task, Social, and Physical Attraction," *Communication Quarterly*, vol. 36, Winter 1988, p. 41.

group—these are examples of the messages which confirm your sense of adequacy.

The anxiety you experience when beginning a new job or when meeting new people is closely related to the fact that you do not know whether you will measure up. The situation is ambiguous. You may be a top student in your class, but will you cut it in your first job? Will you be able to perform as you think you should or as you think others think you should? If not, the risk is not simply that you may lose your job but— more important—that you will lose some degree of self-esteem.

SELF-ACCEPTANCE AND SELF-ESTEEM

In the process of developing a self-image, you develop feelings about who you think you are, and you tend to look to other people for confirmation of those feelings. That confirmation, when you get it, makes you feel that you are entitled to have your image of yourself. Let us look at how we build a sense of self-esteem.

Building Self-Esteem

Self-esteem is the feeling you get when *what* you do matches *your self-image* and when that particular image approximates an *idealized version* of what you wish you were like. For example, you might see yourself as an "outdoor type" (self-image). You may imagine yourself as a successful forestry engineer (idealized self-image). You may go and register in a forestry school (action). That action matches your self-image and your idealized self-image. If you are accepted in the school and subsequently earn high grades, you are confirmed by others (peers and professors), and this confirmation will validate your feelings of self-worth and your self-esteem.[10]

Maintaining Self-Esteem

Maintenance of self-esteem is complex. Many times your attempts at maintaining positive feelings about yourself are successful. Yet some of your attempts are self-defeating.

You sometimes try to hide parts of yourself from others, fearing that if they knew these parts they might reject you. In his excellent book *Why Am I Afraid to Tell You Who I Am?* John Powell relates a poignant and real answer to that question: "I am afraid to tell you who I am because if I tell you who I am, you may not like who I am, and it's all I have."[11]

You hide parts of yourself, for example, when you cover up feelings. You store up anger or frustration and keep a cool facade. Half the time you don't really deceive others because your nonverbal behavior gives you away. But when you succeed in hiding, you tend to "gunnysack," that is, to collect angry feelings inside you until the time when a trivial incident will "make you" explode—the straw that breaks the camel's back.

Sometimes you try to put on masks to appear something you are not. You give off false cues to the people around you and erect walls of

Maintaining self-esteem is complex. You look for confirmation of what you are like from those close to you, matching your feelings about yourself with statements that others make. (© *Blair Seitz/ Photo Researchers*)

intended impressions. This little game, a full-time job for many people, consumes much energy and concentration; to pay off, it must be carried off well. Most of you, however, are not professional actors, and thus your masks, deceptive as they may be for a while, are usually seen through by others. The more you pretend to be what you are not, the more you tend to believe the phony verbal world you hope to create and to lose touch with the real world and your own reality.

VERBAL PATTERNS AND SELF-CONCEPT

A study of the verbal patterns of persons with low self-concept and high self-concept shows some characteristic tendencies. In looking at tendencies, let's not classify people or decide that a person who acts one way will always act that same way. Self-concept may vary with the situation or topic, and the relations of the others with whom a person is communicating. Highly verbal students in the dormitory may be tongue-tied in the classroom because they feel that they get along fine with their friends in a social setting but are lousy students. A boy or girl who is deeply sensitive in serious talk with others may become a giggling wreck in the presence of the opposite sex. A youngster may take advice and instruction from a teacher and not be able to listen at all when a parent tries to advise or explain the same items. The way people see themselves in relation to others has a great effect on the changing patterns of communication.

We want to emphasize that this list is partial and that it does not necessarily describe a person. It describes some verbal patterns which may, in some circumstances or if found persistently, indicate low or high self-esteem for that particular relationship. We would discourage your taking this list and analyzing your friends. We would, on the other hand, encourage your looking seriously at your own verbal outputs in light of these possibilities to find out how often you may act in these ways. Do not then conclude that you *are* one or the other. You may conclude that in some situations you *act* in a certain way. These actions may be changed if you feel like it. Also, you may—and again, only if you feel like it—ask someone who knows you well to tell you if you operate in one way or another (1) never, (2) seldom, (3) sometimes, or (4) frequently. We have left off "(5) always," because no one (including yourself) knows you that well.

Low Self-Concept

The following are some verbal patterns which may characterize low self-concept:

Frequent use of cliché phrases or a few words ("you know," "like," "young people are like that," etc.), which are used not so much because they help identify something in common with others, but because the person with a low self-concept does not trust his or her ability to be original.

A need to talk about self in terms of criticism, weaknesses ("all thumbs"), and difficult experiences which help explain why he or she is not better.

An inability to accept praise gracefully, often expressed by a superficially worded disclaimer which invites additional proof.

A defensiveness about blame to the degree that the person may be more anxious about who gets credit or blame in a project than about actually getting the project accomplished.

A cynicism about accomplishments or possessions; a hypercritical attitude about those of others.

A persistently whining or sneering tone of voice or posture assumed in relation to one's own or others' successes, as if to dismiss as luck or special privilege any accomplishments by anyone.

A pessimistic attitude expressed about competition. (In the game of Monopoly "I always get the cheap properties and end up in jail.")

High Self-Concept

On the other hand, here are some verbal patterns which may characterize a high self-concept.

Use of original expressions, a rich vocabulary used in appropriate settings, an ability to "find the right word" or to use the balanced correct forms of address with others (Mister, Miss, first names, or nicknames, for example).

A tendency to talk about the self less frequently and to talk about others easily in terms of their accomplishments; an apparent ability to get along without constant reassurance of personal worth.

The ability to accept praise or blame gracefully; in working on projects, taking risks and verbalizing positions other than the "correct" ones; not spending much time figuring out the "safe" way of approaching problems in order to avoid blame.

A willingness to look at accomplishments with a balance of credit to ability and to circumstances and to give credit to others for their part in what is done.

A confident tone of voice; avoidance of a condescending tone or attitude; ability to say "I don't know" or "I was wrong."

Admission of a wide range of feelings and empathy for others whether or not these are popular.

An optimistic attitude about competition; willingness to try new games, to enter discussions about new topics with questions (to risk displaying ignorance in an effort to learn more).

Lack of dogmatism about beliefs; little tendency to be biased, to stereotype others, or to classify events too broadly.

RANGE OF SELF-CONCEPT

What have variously been called "modes," "categories," "classes," "dimensions," "groups," or "types" of self-concept, we want to refer to as "ranges." How you see yourself is complex. You are a living, breathing, functioning human being, and you have a physical presence in the world which others as well as you can recognize on sight. You also have a great number of roles you play in relation to others and the world around you. There are many ways you behave in public or by yourself, many ways you carry on the business of acting like "you." You are even more complicated than that; internally there is a thinking, feeling, reacting, believing you—a sort of mental-emotional-spiritual-metaphysical creature.

The dynamic process of adjusting your self-image means that you have some control over your behaviors, and how they are seen. You can decide which of the ranges you will emphasize in any situation. You can choose which "you" is the most significant one as you move through your life. It is important for you to understand that you are not frozen into one set of responses but can adapt as you feel the need to show a different self or to take another look at yourself in relation to events or people around you.

Your adaptive self will therefore concern itself with the three broad and overlapping ranges described above: first the "physical" range, second the "role" range, and third the "introspective" range, which includes your intrapersonal workings such as intellect, emotions, fears, beliefs, and perceptual sets.

Physical Range

First is the *physical* range: your age, height, weight, hair color, and other such observable and functional attributes which make up your person. Items such as your sex may overlap into the other attributes; and for this reason we prefer to call these dimensions "ranges," to indicate that they are not always clear-cut classifications but may merge and shift back and forth. For example, your physical self-concept may affect the roles you play—if you consider yourself a physical weakling, then you will not attempt the role of athlete or bully. A very significant part of the physical range is the dimension of beauty or attractiveness. Plastic surgeons report that their work in changing the features of a patient improves the person's self-concept more than the actual physical appearance. Maxwell Maltz's popular books tell many stories about minor cosmetic changes in patients' appearances which resulted in major emotional improvements based largely on the way the patients saw themselves before and after surgery.[12]

Role Range

Your *role* range, as described in Box 3-7, in many ways says that what you are results from what you do—a common judgment in our society. Stereotypes of teaching, police work, medicine, law, and other occupations tend to restrict the behaviors of people in those fields. Roles, however, are much more than what people do for a living. Roles include your relationships with others in the environment. You may be a son to a parent, a friend to someone, a student in a university course, a patient in

---

BOX 3-7.   Ranges of the Self-Concept

Range	What you say to yourself	What others may say to you (for good or bad . . .)
Physical	I am quite handsome. I have pretty hair. I dance (swim, run) well. This jacket is expensive.	You are strong for your size. I like that dress. You played that shot well. Don't spill the milk again.
Role	I am a student. I am a lawyer. I am a pedestrian. I'm your friend.	Do you read a lot? You seem to work very hard. Boys don't cry. What grade are you in?
Introspective	I am sensitive to others. I have deep convictions. I'm a natural optimist. I cry at sad movies.	You look as if you are worried. Thanks for your concern. You always seem so happy. Do you really believe that?

a dentist's chair, a musician in a band, or a pedestrian on a busy city street. Think of the different ways you act as you move from one of these roles to another. (In Chapter 10 we will discuss roles further.) Most of you know what you should do when you interact with parents, sit in a dentist's chair, play an instrument in a band, or walk down a street. What do you think that you look like when you do these things? Are you satisfied with the way you handle yourself in such situations, or would you like to do something differently? You spend much of your time checking to see if you are acting properly in the role as you have defined it. Others give you feedback which helps direct your future role behaviors. Or if you cannot get feedback from others, you make a guess about how you are doing and tell yourself whether to continue or to adapt. [13]

Introspective Range

Within you are the *introspective* ranges. As you search for the "real you" within your head and heart, you watch others and assume certain attitudes and emotions from what they do. You begin to develop a set of your own private cognitions, emotions, and biases which you then may share with others. Sharing such personal ideas is not easy. When you ask a friend, "How did it go today?" you will likely get an answer about what the person did and where he or she was, etc. Less often do you find out how other people feel deep down about the things that went on in their day: feelings of guilt for not helping a homeless person, feelings of nostalgia on hearing an evocative melody, feelings of reverence in passing an open church door, or patriotic emotion on seeing a flag or a parade.

Sometimes you can share your deep feelings of faith with others, or

You generally will not discuss with others such introspective feelings as guilt for not helping a person in need. (© *Barbara Rios/Photo Researchers*)

you can talk about your anxieties or phobias. Those are all based on dimensions of your introspective self. Giving others your inner ideas will expose your introspective self, and as if looking in a mirror you will get responses from others which will add to your ability to understand and adapt your introspections. How much to disclose to others becomes an important part of the relations you develop and will have a direct effect on your self-concept.

Range Behaviors

Knowing that you are made up of a complex relationship of these factors, can you determine how your self-concept is conveyed? Do you tend to spend most of your time worrying about how you appear to people (physical range)? Is the job you hold a great source of pride or shame to you (role range)? Do you see yourself as a deeply religious person in relation to others (introspective range)? Which of the ranges seems to be one you would worry about and try to make very significant improvements in? Would you like most to be a physically attractive person, or does emotional stability or intellectual power appeal to you?

Before you decide that you can be only one of these, consider the idea that a range exists in each general grouping, and that the ranges overlap to some extent. Even more important, consider that you can adapt to the special circumstances in each range.[14] For example, when playing tennis you may want to see and check how others see your physical self, while in a class recitation your introspective range would become dominant. Before you decide once and for all that you "are" some set of qualities, remember that you (1) are a complex of many facets which make up the total person, (2) can adapt to the different ranges represented in your self-concept, (3) have developed your self-concept over a long period of time, and (4) have considerable control of how you see yourself.

BEHAVIORS AND SELF-CONCEPT

In this textbook we have been careful to distinguish between the person (as a total entity) and his or her behaviors. This is an important distinction. If you are to treat people appropriately, you need to recognize that you never see *all* that any person is, and that any person will change as experiences accumulate. In other words, it is inaccurate to label a person as dishonest, selfish, bigoted, smart, kind, etc. You will be more accurate if you *describe behaviors* which the person has exhibited and limit your judgment to those.

Behaviors and You

The question of whether or not to disclose information about yourself may not be a real question. You disclose with your behaviors constantly—sometimes intentionally, sometimes not. However you may try to hide certain things about yourself, there is always a chance that your behaviors will give you away. There is also a strong chance that you will not know the effects of these behaviors unless you remain open to (1) an under-

---

BOX 3-8. What You Do/Who You Are

Books on parenting as well as teacher training now stress the idea that you should separate the *actions* of a youngster from the child himself or herself. To do this the parent (or teacher, or other person in an authority position) tells the person being corrected or reprimanded: "You are still okay; but what you *did* was not okay." In this kind of appraisal, emphasis is on changing *behaviors*, which most everyone can do, not on trying to become a *different person*, a nearly impossible challenge.

Giving "one-minute reprimands" to workers, as recommended in a popular book on management,* has two stages. The first is to cover the content of what someone did wrong, being specific. The second is to tell that person you still think well of him or her as a person but not the behavior which led up to the reprimand.

* K. Blanchard and S. Johnson, *The One Minute Manager,* William Morrow, New York, 1982, p. 59.

---

standing of the nature of behavior as a part of self and (2) a willingness to adjust behaviors in relation to the feedback you receive. In this way, behaviors help people train each other.[15]

Your behaviors grow out of what you feel about yourself (your self-concept) and which role you elect to play in any circumstance. If you adopt a habitual orientation to your world, it is likely you will exhibit some typical behaviors. It is from this pattern of behaviors that others will judge your "personality." Without some interaction, there is little chance that anyone can develop a picture of you—right or wrong—in terms of behaviors. It is from the established pattern of typical behaviors that you begin to categorize one another and begin to make predictions on how the other will behave. It is then that you boast that you "know" someone. In a game of chess it may be more useful to know the other person's style of play than all the strategies of the game. If you can predict which moves the other is likely to make in response to your moves, you will play more effectively.

In human interaction you are often caught in a dilemma. On the one hand, society places such high value on dependability, steadfastness, and reliability that it would seem that you should strive to be predictable in your communicative behaviors. On the other hand, novelty, imagination, creativity, and spontaneity are also prized highly, and so you might therefore want to establish yourself as less predictable.

Changing Behaviors

To resolve this apparent conflict you should remember that not only are your behaviors a source of judgment from others, but they are also a testing ground for yourself. If you do not develop some patterns of behavior, you have very little to test; yet if you do not add some novelty to your behaviors, you cannot learn new things about yourself. The answer, then, seems to be to do both—to try to select wisely those events and circumstances in which to make familiar and typical moves and those in which to try some new behaviors. In all this discussion, it is imperative that you remember that your behaviors will not necessarily be "consistent" in all the roles you play, and are therefore not the total you when taken in by any one group you have interacted with.

SUMMARY

This chapter emphasizes how much you depend on others to (1) develop, (2) maintain, or (3) change your self-concept. It has been said many times that you find out who you are by checking how others react to you.

In addition, who you *think you are* will determine in many ways how you behave, whether you see yourself as a success or failure, and how you live up to those expectations you have of yourself and others have for you.

A range of self-concepts may be demonstrated in some ways by how you speak and by how you address your relations with others in the physical range, the role range, and the introspective range.

Your behaviors toward others appear to be directly related to how you see yourself. How others take your actions and then respond to you gives you both data about yourself and some choices of how to proceed. Before you decide that others are misinterpreting your behaviors, you need to make sure that you are giving the messages you want to and that you are taking responsibility for them.

END NOTES

[1] M. Rosenberg, "Self-Concept Research: A Historical Overview," *Social Forces,* vol. 68, Summer 1989, pp. 34–44. P. S. Nurves, "The Self-Concept: A Social-Cognitive Update," *Social Casework,* vol. 75, May 1989, pp. 285–294.

[2] C. H. Cooley, *Human Nature and the Social Order,* Transaction Books, New Brunswick, NJ, 1983.

[3] A. H. Baumgardner, "To Know Oneself Is to Like Oneself: Self-Certainty and Self-Affect," *Journal of Personality and Social Psychology,* vol. 58, June 1990, p. 1062. G. H. Mead, *Mind, Self, and Society,* University of Chicago Press, Chicago, 1967.

[4] M. Rosenberg, C. Schooler, and C. Schoenbach, "Self-Esteem and Adolescent Problems: Modeling Reciprocal Effects," *American Sociological Review,* vol. 54, December 1989, p. 1004.

[5] D. K. Berlo, *The Process of Communication,* Holt, Rinehart and Winston, New York, 1960.

[6] A. M. Juhosz, "Significant Others and Self-Esteem: Methods for Determining Who and Why," *Adolescence,* vol. 24, Fall 1989, pp. 581–594. For a discussion of the "generalized other" see G. H. Mead, op. cit.

[7] R. Rosenthal, "The Pygmalion Effect Lives," *Psychology Today,* vol. 7, 1973, pp. 56–63.

[8] E. M. Skaalvik and K. A. Hagtvet, "Academic Achievement and Self-Concept: An Analysis of Causal Predominance," *Journal of Personality and Social Psychology,* vol. 58, February 1990, p. 292. H. B. Braiker, "The Power of Self-Talk," *Psychology Today,* vol. 23, December 1989, p. 26. D. H. Demo and M. Hughes, "Self-Perception of Black Americans: Self-Esteem and Personal Efficacy," *The American Journal of Sociology,* vol. 95, July 1989, p. 132. M. H. Kernia, B. S. Frankel, and J. Brockner, "Self-Esteem and Reactions to Failure," *Journal of Personality and Social Psychology,* vol. 57, October 1989, p. 707.

[9] For the pioneering study of confirmation-disconfirmation see E. Sieburg, "Dysfunctional Communication and Interpersonal Responsiveness in Small Groups," unpublished dissertation, University of Denver, 1969. L. Jussim and others, "Reactions to Interpersonal Feedback," *Journal of Applied Social Psychology,* vol. 19, July 1989, pp. 581–594.

[10] P. Englander-Golden et al., "Communicative Skills and Self-Esteem in Prevention of Destructive Behaviors," *Adolescence,* vol. 24, Summer 1989, pp. 481–502. P. King, "To Know You Is to Love You," *Psychology Today,* vol. 23, January 1989, p. 73.

[11] J. Powell, *Why Am I Afraid to Tell You Who I Am?,* Argus Communications, Chicago, 1969, p. 12.

[12] M. Maltz, *Psycho-Cybernetics,* Pocket Books, New York, 1983, and by the same author, *Magic Power of Self-Image Psychology,* Prentice-Hall, Englewood Cliffs, NJ, 1989.

[13] L. J. Alpert-Gillis and J. P. Connell, "Gender and Sex-Role Influences on Children's Self-Esteem," *Journal of Personality,* vol. 57, March 1989, p. 97. J. L. Orlofsky and C. A. O'Heron, "Stereotypic and Nonstereotypic Sex Role Trait and Behavior Orientation," *Journal of Personality and Social Psychology,* vol. 52, May 1987, p. 1034.

[14] H. W. Marsh, J. K. Antill, and J. U. Cunningham, "Masculinity, Femininity, and Androgyny: Relations to Self-Esteem and Social Desirability," *Journal of Personality,* vol. 55, December 1987, p. 861. W. Gildea, "Winning at Any Age: Self-Esteem and Athletic Performance," *Readers Digest,* February 1990, p. 149.

[15] W. A. Faunce, "Occupational Status-Assignment Systems: The Effect of Status on Self-Esteem," *The American Journal of Sociology,* vol. 95, September 1989, p. 378. R. D. Granger, "How to Feel Good about Being You," *American Journal of Nursing,* vol. 90, April 1990, p. 14.

(© Michael Hayman/Stock, Boston)

CHAPTER
4

ASSERTION: WHO CAN I BE?

OBJECTIVES

When you have completed this chapter you should be able to:

1. Explain how the "fraction formula" of William James relates to changes in self-esteem.
2. List four premises of the study of behavior modification.
3. List and explain five communication styles and the communication characteristics of each.
4. List four characteristics of assertive people.
5. Explain how assertive behavior may be used in
   a. Giving and receiving compliments
   b. Caring for others' feelings
   c. Helping others
   d. Tolerating annoyances
6. List several consequences of assertiveness, favorable or unfavorable.
7. Describe and predict some responses for at least three categories of behavior which are likely to provoke defensiveness.

INTRODUCTION

Just as you learn self-esteem by communicating in your interpersonal world, you learn how to cope with others by communicating. In the last chapter we wrote about your feelings of worth—where they come from, how they get reinforced or torn down, how you depend on communication to find out who you are. In this chapter we will develop the idea that you can choose who you want to be, within reason, of course. Gravity will not permit you to leap unaided twenty feet in the air; and there are social, physical, cultural, intellectual, and interpersonal limits on some of your achievements. We argue, however, that few people actually live up to their interpersonal potential. They settle for less than they can be.

We will also argue that limits you place on yourself may not be inborn, natural, or permanent. They may be limits of language and self-esteem. Also, they may reflect the *situations* you are in more than some personality characteristics you decide you own.

MANAGING YOUR SELF-ESTEEM

Writing more than a century ago, the psychologist William James[1] set up a fraction to examine what he called "self-feeling" as a ratio of "our actualities to our supposed potentialities." It looked something like Figure 4-1 and he asserted that in this equation the value of the self-esteem can be changed, like any fraction, either by making the numerator (success or achievement) greater, or by reducing the denominator (pretensions, or expectations).

Following James by about half a century, Wendell Johnson[2] described people's maladjustment as their attempts to live up to some impossible goals for their performances, not realizing that the goals they set might be the problem rather than their own low achievement. His argument was that "success" is a word which we can define any way we want; and we usually define it in a way which makes us fail. Both James and Johnson, writing a half-century apart, argued that failure seems to be determined by how we talk about it.[3] Both stated that people make their own failures by how they set themselves up with impossible expectations or "pretensions."

Johnson described a basic pattern of personal maladjustment running from Idealization to Frustration to Demoralization to which he gave the acronym of "IFD disease." This pattern begins with *ideals* which are (1) vaguely defined to the point of your not being able to state them clearly or operationally ("success," "happiness," "love," are examples), (2) highly

FIGURE 4-1
Model of fraction equation adapted from William James (1890).

$$\text{Self-esteem} = \frac{\text{Success or accomplishment}}{\text{Pretensions or expectations}}$$

BOX 4-1. Paradox of Pretensions

I, who for the time have staked my all on being a psychologist, am mortified if others know much more psychology than I. But I am contented to wallow in the grossest ignorance of Greek. My deficiencies there give me no sense of personal humiliation at all. Had I "pretensions" to be a linguist, it would have been just the reverse. So we have the paradox of a man shamed to death because he is only the second pugilist or oarsman in the world. That he is able to beat the whole population of the globe minus one is nothing; he has pitted himself to beat that one; and as long as he doesn't do that nothing else counts. He is to his own regard as if he were not, indeed he is not.

William James

---

valued because you or other voices which speak for you (ventriloquize) like parents, peers, authority, tradition, religion, etc., are very strongly committed to accomplishing those unclear ideals, and (3) unrealistic insofar as you are not able to define them adequately or know definitely when they are accomplished or not.

Failing to attain those fuzzily stated ideals, you become *frustrated* as your words identify your "failure" of accomplishment.

That leads you to a feeling of inferiority in some degree and then anger, aggression, worthlessness, to the stage which Johnson calls *demoralization.*

This unhealthy sequence begins and continues because of the way we "talk about things" and not because of the "way things are" in the world of action. IFD is a language-induced pathology. (Effects of language and verbal definitions are explored more fully in Chapter 8.)

More recently, books related to self-esteem make much the same

---

BOX 4-2. Self-Esteem Is More Than Skin Deep

Plastic surgeon Dr. Maxwell Maltz reports that his work in restorative surgery usually results in dramatic changes in patients' inner selves as well as physical changes. He confirms others' views of the origin of self-esteem by this statement: "Self-respect, then, is basically something that you manufacture for yourself in your mind."*

* M. Maltz, *The Search for Self-Respect,* Grosset & Dunlap, New York, 1973, p. 10.

argument: that it is possible to change both our behaviors and our beliefs about ourselves.[4]

ASSERTIVENESS AS BEHAVIOR

Attention to human rights in the recent past has emphasized assertiveness, or assertion, in people's relations. While there are many definitions of assertiveness, most are based on the simple principle of taking control of your personal rights. Box 4-3 provides a summary of what many trainers

---

BOX 4-3.   Capsule of Behavior Choices

The most familiar terms used in training programs, self-help books, and both scholarly and popular articles are ''aggression,'' ''assertion,'' and ''nonassertion.'' People are encouraged to select whichever behaviors they find most rewarding to themselves. Everyone should understand that all behaviors have purposes and consequences, generally summarized as follows:

Aggression means you:

1. Stand up for your rights in such a strong way you violate the rights of others
2. Ignore and dismiss the beliefs, needs, opinions, feelings, desires, emotions, attitudes, data, information, or involvement of others
3. Express or demand attention to your own opinions, needs, or feelings in an inappropriate way

Assertion means you:

1. Stand up for your own rights in a way that does not violate rights of others or threaten them
2. Take into account the feelings and beliefs of others as part of your interaction with them
3. Express your own feelings and beliefs in an open, direct, honest, and appropriate way

Nonassertion means you:

1. Neglect your own rights, fail to stand up for yourself, give others permission or encouragement to disregard your rights
2. Apologize or otherwise put down your own ideas, feelings, attitudes, beliefs, or information
3. Avoid expressing your own feelings or needs in situations where you would like to be heard or included

---

and students of assertiveness believe are the characteristics of assertive behavior.

Although much of the current research and popular writings about assertion appears to be centered on women's rights, the actual focus is much broader than that. In library or bookstores you may find assertive behavior books specifically published for the elderly,[5] for childbearing women and/or couples,[6] for educational administrators and teachers at all levels,[7] for bus drivers,[8] for librarians,[9] for nurses,[10] for Christians,[11] and for managers,[12] and many more titles relating to assertiveness in general that don't target specific audiences.[13]

Self-help books on assertiveness seem to stress the advantages of acting in an assertive way, with improved personal outcomes at least some of the time. Most writers admit that you will not always win or get your way using assertion. However, they do predict that you will feel better about yourself from having made an effort to stand up for your rights.[14]

Assertiveness Is for Anyone

In spite of the recent concentration on assertiveness behaviors among women and minorities,[15] it is clear that most people can benefit from a new look at their behaviors when they went to "declare themselves"[16] without whining or pouting or apologizing and also without clobbering or blasting others. A familiar suggested "checkpoint" is to evaluate the ultimate effectiveness of assertive behavior by asking yourself: "Did that behavior increase my self-respect, even a little?"

If you are curious about how assertiveness can be effective for everyone, put yourself in some of the following situations. These are common occurrences which can happen to everyone. They do not begin to exhaust the possibilities for selecting assertive behaviors over some more aggressive or self-effacing ones, but they do represent conditions and events which may be very familiar to all of us.

Responding to compliments

Giving and receiving compliments can be one of the difficult encounters people have. From our earliest years we are told not to boast and act better than anybody else, to be modest and always give others credit, and that "pride goeth before a fall." There is a norm in society which says nice people don't brag or act proud of their own accomplishments. To call someone else "conceited" is a damaging term; and giving criticism of others is easier than giving praise. When we do not want to appear conceited we may respond to compliments with denial or with disclaimers. "You like this suit? It's just what I could find on the rack." "I got an A? Guess I lucked out." "A good shot? Not like you could do, really."

We also have difficulty giving compliments because we don't want to sound insincere or too effusive. Many compliments are given negatively, in the form of a joke or a denigrating comparison to ourselves, or with carefully worded disclaimers. "How come you always get A's in everything—just smart or do you study hard?" "That shirt really looks good

> **BOX 4-4.   Characteristics of Assertive People**
>
> **1.** They feel free to express themselves, to reveal their feelings.
> **2.** They can communicate with people on all levels—strangers, family, and friends—and communication is open, direct, honest, and appropriate for the situation.
> **3.** They have an active orientation toward life; they take charge of events and situations, and seek new experiences.
> **4.** They act in a way which shows respect for themselves; they accept the limitations of their behaviors but still try to achieve their goals and thus maintain self-esteem from having "given it their best shot."

on you; I never can wear anything as colorful as that." "I'm really not after anything, but I think you did a great job on that report."

It would be more assertive to be able to give a simple, direct compliment which comments specifically on another's behavior or possessions. You may want to phrase compliments in terms of your feelings: "I'm glad for you that you got all A's this term." "Your shirt is beautiful. I like that color." "Your report was very clear to me and well presented."

Watching out for others' feelings

You have been taught not to hurt others' feelings, to be careful what you say or it will bother or embarrass someone. It may happen that you will have to tiptoe around an issue so you don't hurt someone's feelings. No question that deliberately hurting someone else is not acceptable. There are times, however, when issues come up on which you have strong feelings. How far should you go in denying your own beliefs; how much should you suppress of your own opinions? You will have to decide at what point you will simply be phony or dishonest when you do not assert your ideas. If you accidentally hurt someone, and do not do it out of meanness, you will likely be forgiven, or at least understood. But at some time you will have to assert your right to have an opinion, and to express it. You cannot run your life in fear of occasionally hurting someone. You also have to be aware that some people have been known to use "hurt" to manipulate others, or may be unreasonably sensitive.

Helping until it hurts

Some people have been trained since childhood to help everybody else even if it imposes on their own time and resources. Sacrificing for others, being a martyr for a cause, putting others first, are ways of expressing this behavior. In his lectures, John Narcisco, coauthor of the book *Declare Yourself,* demonstrates this principle of putting others first by asking for several volunteers from the audience to come to the front of the room. Then he asks them to do the behavior of "putting others first . . ." These

---

BOX 4-5.   Women in Public Life

Self-esteem and assertion are linked in this writing from an English author concerning public service by women:

The major problem for women entering public life is a general lack of confidence. But this lack is not simply due to inexperience, or lack of practice at the skills required in the public domain. For many, many, women it is part and parcel of their lack of self-esteem, and consequent inability to make positive choices about their needs or even to feel they have the right to exercise choice over their own lives. *

* S. Slipman, *Helping Ourselves to Power*, Pergamon Press, Oxford, England, and Elmsford, New York, 1986, p. 19.

---

people keep switching around, each trying to get behind the other in order to put others first. Result is an impossible free-for-all which demonstrates what happens in a society dedicated to putting others first.

Demands are quite different from requests and should be used sparingly. A demand leaves no option but for the other person to comply or refuse. A request preserves the dignity of both parties—the asker and the asked—to be able to say "yes," to say "no," or to negotiate a compromise. If others impose on you for your books, for your time, to run errands, to borrow clothes or lecture notes, and you reach a place where you feel imposed on, how do you act? Do you make excuses like you are too busy, like you do not have the notes or books they need, or do you simply say you do not want to lend the book, run the errand, or spend that time? Assertiveness trainers tell us that you have a right to refuse the requests of other people, and you also have a right not to accede to others' demands when they impose on you. You have a right not to suffer in silence when you are being abused.

Tolerating the little annoyances

Getting angry is not an acceptable behavior in most of society. It gets drummed into you that you should not be angry—or show anger. Putting up with small annoyances is simply the price you pay for being around other people. How do you tell someone who finishes your sentences for you that it is annoying? How do you ask noisy people behind you in the movie to be quiet? How do you let a waiter know there is something wrong with the food or service? Most important, do you have any right to speak out when seemingly trivial events become bothersome enough to make you seethe inside?

Assertion proponents say you have every right not to have to tolerate actions or events which make you angry enough. It is up to you to decide

Putting up with little annoyances is simply the price you pay for being around other people. (Drawing by R. Chast/© 1987, The New Yorker Magazine, Inc.)

when the value of asserting yourself is worth the possibility of relieving the annoyance. Effective assertion involves what has been referred to as "I messages" where you take responsibility for the feelings—you talk about your reactions instead of what the others are doing. Instead of saying, "You are very rude to finish my sentences for me . . ." you might say, "I'm bothered when you finish my sentences for me . . ." In the case of people talking in a movie, don't get them angry by telling them how boorish they are acting, but report on your own inability to hear. If you accuse a waiter of incompetence, it will not be as effective as telling him specifically what bothered you, from your viewpoint: "We waited too long for a menu and had to ask several times for a glass of water. . ." Such rhetorical devices not only put the responsibility for feelings where they belong—in your insides—but also tell the other person where you stand, not what a bad person he or she is, and so soften the tone of the accusation.

Consequences of Assertiveness

Assertiveness has consequences you may or may not like. Besides the outcomes described in the examples above—outcomes involving asserting or not asserting—you may grow to predict accurately what happens when you respond in any one of the styles suggested earlier. As you put yourself and others on notice that your old ways of acting are not going to persist, you begin to pay more attention to how you are behaving. You may find, if you employ the suggested assertive behaviors, that others will respond differently to you. Your relations with others are likely to change; you may end up with different friends, or in different situations. As your behaviors change, so may your attitudes and your values about who you choose to spend time with, and what you spend time doing.

Some positive outcomes

Earlier we noted some ways that assertiveness improves your behaviors. It makes it easier for you to give and receive compliments. You get your rights respected just as fully as you respect the rights of others. You can avoid being victimized by others who may demand unreasonable help. You can cope with small aggravations and prevent their becoming major confrontations. You can be a thoughtfully independent person in charge of your own feelings, time, and resources. You can develop a new respect for yourself as a person, a new confidence in what you are capable of, and higher regard from others.

Some negative outcomes

Life for an assertive person does not always run smoothly. You must be conscious of the potentially *negative perception* of your assertiveness by others. When evasiveness and indirection are so widely used in public behaviors, the assertive person may be seen as abrupt, curt, or impolite. Even moderate firmness can appear aggressive or abrasive to people who are used to pushing others around. How you sound when you declare yourself may be misconstrued as pushy, overbearing, or demanding, when in fact you may be simply or precisely stating your position. If you can avoid the trap of neglecting your own rights, just as you resist violating the rights of others, you can develop honestly assertive behaviors.

The choices are yours, and you should take charge of your communication, knowing about your behavioral options and their consequences.

COMMUNICATION STYLES

No two people behave in exactly the same manner, and the same person does not act the same way all the time. However, there are regularities in human communication. Although most people are quite capable of communicating in a variety of ways, they often choose to fall back on familiar patterns of handling their communication with others. Such characteristic ways of dealing with interpersonal situations are called "styles." People develop their own styles for communicating; and while it is possible to use many different styles, each person tends to repeat a preferred style in certain situations.

Before we identify some common styles of communicating, let us emphasize three important points:

1. A range of styles is available to all of you. There are many different ways to respond to interpersonal situations, and you use them all, at one time or another.
2. Each style is effective in some specific situations.

A range of communication styles is available to all of us in our interactions with others. *(© Richard Hutchings/Photo Researchers)*

3. It is the habitual use of one style, indiscriminately, for all situations, which creates interpersonal problems.

The following description of communication styles is based on Virginia Satir's discussion of patterns of communication.[17] The five basic communication styles she describes are (1) the blaming or aggressive style, (2) the placating or nonassertive style, (3) the computing or intellectual style, (4) the distracting or manipulative style, and (5) the leveling or assertive style.

The Blaming or Aggressive Style

The person using the blaming or aggressive style tends to act in a demanding fashion with others. Blamers are fault-finders and come on rather critically with others. Blamers often act in a superior fashion and are often described as very bossy people. Carried to extremes, blamers become tyrannical and loud and get their way at the expense of other people's rights and feelings. Blamers send messages which imply that everybody else is stupid for not believing as they do and that other people's wants and feelings simply do not count. The major goal for blamers in interpersonal relationships is to win and dominate, forcing the other person to lose. Winning is often ensured by humiliating, degrading, and overpowering other people so that they are too weak to express and defend their rights. Blaming and aggressive behavior, unfortunately, often works, and it provides emotional release and a sense of power for blamers. Blamers get what they want without direct negative reactions from others. A blaming boss who holds power over you may be feared and may scare you into doing what he or she wants. If you are overpowered, you probably will not take on the boss directly or openly.

In the long run, however, the consequences of the blaming style can be quite negative. Blamers usually fail to establish close relationships, and they feel that they have to be constantly on guard against other people's attacks and possible retaliation. They feel alienated from other people, misunderstood, and unloved. Blamers are usually lonely people.

The blaming style is not always dysfunctional. There are times when legitimate criticism and evaluation must be offered, when orders and directions must be given, when responsibility must be taken to fire or flunk someone, or when limits for acceptable behavior must be imposed. As we will see later, however, criticism and evaluation are usually much more effective when they are given in a leveling or assertive style.

The Placating or Nonassertive Style

Placaters always try to please and often attempt to ingratiate themselves. They often apologize, seldom disagree, and talk as though they could do almost nothing for and by themselves. They must always have someone else's approval. Placaters violate or simply ignore their own rights, needs, and feelings, and they are unable to express what they want in a direct and forthright manner. When they do express their feelings or thoughts, they do it in a very apologetic and self-effacing way that usually makes others disregard them. Placating (using a nonassertive style) says that the placater does not really count and can be taken advantage of. And indeed, placaters often are taken advantage of. Placaters show so little respect for themselves that they teach others not to respect them. The basic goals of the placater are to avoid conflict at all costs and to appease. Nonassertive superiors, for example, have great difficulty saying "no" to their employees' requests and end up trying to please everyone, which in the long run pleases no one. They are afraid of hurting people's feelings. They are worried that saying "no" or standing up for their own needs will cause other people to dislike them or to think them foolish, stupid, or selfish.

The Computing or Intellectual Style

People who use the computing style rely on intellectualizations to deal with interpersonal situations. The style requires an outward appearance of being calm, cool, and collected. Feelings are not allowed to show. A person using this style believes that emotions are best kept hidden inside, since they basically distract from the work at hand. The intellectual style requires emphasis on logic and rationality. People relying on this style are very distrustful of feelings and personal emotions. "If people were only reasonable and used their heads, there would not be so many problems around here" is their motto. Intellectualizers often feel quite vulnerable and deal with their fears of inadequacy by presenting a distant and aloof front so that no one can really get too close to them. Because they consider people to be unpredictable and irrational, they may choose professions which do not put them in contact with other people. They prefer professions in which their status and authority will keep them at a distance from others.

The Distracting or Manipulative Style

The distracting style is based on not being involved with interpersonal situations. "Avoid threatening situations" is the motto. People using this style have developed all kinds of strategies to manipulate unpleasant communication encounters. When encounters cannot be avoided, their style for dealing with people is characterized by distracting maneuvers, or by manipulating other people's feelings. Anger, hurt, and guilt are often used as ways to get to others. A boss may get employees to work overtime by appealing to their potential guilt feelings by using verbal ploys like "How could you let me down after all I've done for you?" A parent will use the same strategy by calling children "ungrateful" or "mean to your mother."

The Leveling or Assertive Style

Levelers are able to stand up for their rights and express feelings, thoughts, and needs in a direct, honest, straightforward manner. Tone of voice, gestures, eye contact, and stance all fit the words that are spoken. Actions also match words, and assertive people follow through on what they say they will do.

If you are being assertive, you never stand up for your rights at the expense of another person's rights. You have respect for yourself but also respect for others, and you are open to compromise or negotiation. The basic message of leveling is "This is what I think about the situation" and does not imply domination or humiliation of the other people who may not happen to think or see things the same way. Leveling involves respect, not blind deference. The goal of leveling is better communication and mutual problem solving. Whenever conflicts of rights or needs arise, the attempt is to solve them by working together with the other people involved.

Although leveling and communicating assertively do not guarantee that you will get your way, this style can have positive consequences. It usually increases your self-respect and helps you to develop greater self-confidence. You will feel good about being able to say what you believe without fear. Whether others agree with you or whether they do what you want almost becomes incidental. For example, you may not get a raise after asking for it. But if you ask your boss in a leveling way and explain honestly and directly the reasons you are entitled to a raise, you will feel good to have expressed yourself and to have stood up for what you believed. If the boss gives you the raise, so much the better. If not, at least you will have the satisfaction of going directly to the issue. You didn't act like the placater who would never ask for a raise for fear of being turned down. You didn't play the role of the manipulator who constantly complains to others about the unfairness of management. You didn't copy the aggressive person who yells and screams in useless and heated loud arguments with the boss. In any of those styles, besides getting or not getting a raise, you may develop very strong feelings of resentment and anger.

Many books are now available for those of you who wish to read more on the assertive style of communication. The basic point about assertive communication is that it is the style most likely to foster trust, self-respect, and respect from others. Those are all vital ingredients for effective interpersonal communication.

Summary of Styles

Communication styles show up not only in such important actions as buying a car, selecting a college, and asking for a raise, but also in common, everyday communication. When you talk with friends about plans for meeting at a coffee break, you can see the styles used by different people: "The only place I will go is . . ." (aggressive statement, no compromise, or discussion permitted). "I'll meet any place; my schedule is not very important, and I don't want to put anyone else out" (placating statement; "I'm not worth worrying about, so I'll do whatever anyone else wants to"). "If we have five minutes for each of us to get to a central place, then we should . . ." (intellectual, logical, analyzing statement; any decision is based on factors or forces outside the people themselves). "It's going to be tough to find time to get together; I'm not sure coffee is worth the effort" (manipulative statement; an attempt to get control by suggesting that the meeting is not worth much). "For my schedule, the snack bar works out fine, and I like the doughnuts there. What do the rest of you think?" (assertive statement; says how the speaker feels and still leaves the situation open for discussion).

For another example of these communication styles and what they might mean see Table 4-1, which deals with a similar question.

CHANGING BEHAVIORS

Variously called "behavior modification," "behavior therapy," or a number of other names, the process of changing how you act has become a common subject in psychological research, clinical reports, popular literature, and the media.

Behavior modification is based roughly on these premises: (1) people can change their attitudes and beliefs, (2) people can change how they behave, (3) there are systems or techniques available to accomplish change in people, (4) much of the time a change in people's attitudes or beliefs follows change in behaviors and not the other way around, in spite of the efficacy of "brainwashing" techniques in altering attitudes in some subjects. (See Chapter 5 for more discussion on attitudes, beliefs, and values.)

There is also evidence that behaviors may not reflect a person's "traits" or "personality" so much as they reflect the situations in which

Table 4-1.
Communication Styles

In this table, the question content could be almost anything. You could be working out how to ask for a raise, how to talk to another person about buying a car together, how to decide to go on a vacation or trip with another person, or any other small or large decision. Assume, for this example, that the question is: "What movie should we go to see?"

Style	Statement	Translation (What is really being said)
Aggressive	"Only one movie in town is any good; we'll go to that one."	"My way or nothing."
Placating	"Whatever movie you want to see is fine with me. I never know what's good or bad."	"Poor dumb me; I'm really helpless."
Intellectual	"Reviews say that the new French film is directed, acted, and filmed well, and is a 'must.' "	"I have no feelings about it myself, only the intellectual advice from others."
Manipulative	"I'm not sure I want to go to a movie."	"Coax me: I want to be in a position of deciding by playing hard-to-get."
Assertive	"I'm most interested in the new Robert Redford movie. How about you?"	"Here's what I want. What do you want?"

people find themselves. In other words, few people are so consistent in their actions that they "always" behave in a certain way; their actions may change quite dramatically from one circumstance to another. Is your friend, Julia, just naturally shy and reticent because you see her being quiet in class, or is she "really" a very gregarious person because she is always talking and leading highly articulate arguments at the coffee break? Because you see people habitually acting in a certain way, you may erroneously assume that what they do is the result of some character trait they have inside themselves, instead of a reaction to the temporary occurrences or conditions confronting them.

DEFENDING YOURSELF

Much of your interpersonal communication depends on how you define the situation in which you find yourself. You appraise the threatening or nonthreatening quality of your interactions with others in terms of your self-esteem. Much of your communication with others involves some kind of risk, since communication means presenting to others a definition of yourself, your role, and the situation—a definition they may reject. What the communication climate is like and how you can change it are an

Behavior modification: "Now relax. . . . Just like last week, I'm going to hold the cape up for the count of 10. . . . When you start getting angry, I'll put it down."
(THE FAR SIDE © 1987 Universal Press Syndicate)

important part of your guesses about how much risk is involved for you in a given situation. You behave on the basis of how safe you think you are. If you do not feel safe, you are likely to use defensive strategies to protect yourself. Perhaps you have been in a classroom situation in which the teacher insists that students participate and discuss issues openly. Then the teacher shoots down student comments or ridicules them. You learn quickly that the climate is not safe, and your communication will probably be characterized by defensive strategies designed to protect yourself.

The Reduction of Defensive Climates

The professor-student relationship is not all that different from any other dyadic relationship. People always figure out whether they are safe or not, and their communication and behavior will rest on that assessment. Defensive strategies are simply an indication that a person does not feel secure in some way, at some level.

Why do you feel insulted or have your feelings hurt? "An insult is a valuation of the individual by others which does not agree with his valuation of himself," according to Lecky,[18] who goes on to discuss how people deal with such contradictions. Other writers have asserted that the basic reason for defending yourself in interpersonal situations is related to your unmet needs for reinforcement from others.[19] Both these ideas seem to say that when you think about yourself in one way, you would like others to agree with that opinion. If you see yourself as smart, you'd like others to see you that way too and not discover ways in which you are not smart. If you like to be considered a good musician, you are anxious to be supported in that evaluation by the things people see you do and what they say to you and about you. Each of you has a self-image to maintain. Each of you also values opinions and support from some persons more than others. Some of your friends are more important to impress than others; some of the people in the world are more significant than others in how you pay attention to what they think (or say) of you. The degree to which you need reinforcement (positive feedback) from others and the degree to which that need is not met will determine how defensively you may act in your communication. You also encounter social situations which are stressful in the sense that you are afraid a blow will be struck at your self-image if you do not behave as you think others expect you to behave. You can also damage your self-image if you do not live up to your own expectations just as much as you can by not living up to the expectations of others. For those situations you may employ defensive strategies designed to protect yourself from negative feedback, from embarrassment, from losing face. You look in each other's eyes to find yourselves, but sometimes you are afraid to look.

Defensive strategies   How then do you defend yourself? Your defensive strategies when you respond to an *actual* threat are somewhat different from your defensive strategies when you respond to a *potential* threat. In the first case, you adjust; in the second, you avoid.

ADJUSTMENT

The best defense is a good offense, according to many coaches. In your verbal games, you tend to follow that advice when you verbally attack any persons who may be a threat to you. If it is too risky or too rude to attack directly—to tell your boss to go jump in the lake may cost you your job—you can attack indirectly. You may use sarcasm or ridicule, by questioning the other person's motives or competence (thereby becoming a threat to the other person). You may put the other person down. You may exclude others from your conversation through use of specially selected jargon words, the latest slang, private jokes, private references, or topics known to be of great discomfort to the other persons.

Besides this *verbal aggression*, some other common adjustment strategies are *rationalization, denial, fantasy,* and *projection.*

When you acknowledge that a threat is present, but tell yourself that you can handle it without loss of face or embarrassment, or that it is really not that important to begin with, then you engage in *rationalization.*

Saying that a threat does not exist, or, when another person has threatened your self-concept, telling yourself that it wasn't meant that way, that you misinterpreted, that "she would never do such a thing," is moving from rationalization to *denial.*

If you really want to make the situation appear brighter than it is, and believe the best, and overcome the threat by replacing it with a more pleasant situation, you can call up your imagination and convince yourself by *fantasy* that another thing is happening instead of the threatening one.

In *projection,* you make use of the technique of assuming that others are thinking, feeling, or saying things out of an anxiety which they are trying to cover up. You can say the other person is acting aggressively toward you only to cover up his or her own problems of anxiety or aggressiveness, a reflection of *your* feeling of anxiety in the face of the threat, which you project onto the other person.

AVOIDANCE

If you see a threat coming, you may use strategies which are different from those you use after you have experienced the distressing situation. One way to avoid threats to your self-image and communicative personality is simply to get out of the way, or not to put yourself into situations where you have to communicate with others in potentially embarrassing situations. If you want to sign up for a course in college and have no idea how to do it, you will delay until somehow the ambiguity of the situation is reduced so that you can safely risk making errors. The young man trying to get up enough nerve to ask a woman for a date is a classic example. He is afraid of being turned down, and so he solves the problem by not asking for the date.

Besides the kind of *physical avoidance* we discussed above, another form is *retreat* as the threatening occasion comes closer. A child will have to go to the bathroom to get out of performing in front of the class. A person who has difficulty getting a vending machine to work may retreat quickly to get out of a public confrontation with a machine that is likely to win anyway.

Verbally you can avoid situations by two simple strategies, *invoking taboos* and *controlling information.* In the former, you avoid certain topics for fear that you might say or do things you will feel embarrassed about or hear things which might make you feel uncomfortable. Telling Polish jokes in front of your friend Kobos may embarrass both of you. Referring to the insensitivity of university administrators when talking to a dean may not be worthwhile conversation. If you are sensitive about one of your physical features (nose, hair, chin, ears, etc.), you will not usually steer the conversation to those topics. Talking about divorce in front of children whose parents are recently separated is sometimes considered taboo. In such situations as these you may invoke a strategy to change the subject—you interrupt by calling attention to an activity or person nearby; you distract a speaker by moving away; you verbally intrude when the talk

---

BOX 4-6. I'd Rather Go Hungry . . .

In her book *Reporting,** Lillian Ross describes the behavior of a group of
high school boys from a small midwestern town on a senior trip to New
York who refused to eat in restaurants. They made up all kinds of excuses
to avoid eating out, they were even content to go hungry. None of their
excuses made sense to their chaperones. It turned out that the boys
simply wanted to avoid the eating out situation because they did not
know how to order from a menu—so they behaved to avoid risk to their
self-esteem. When it was discovered that the restaurant placed them in
a situation in which they might be found inadequate and which might
prove embarrassing, their refusal to eat out made more sense and could
be handled.

* L. Ross, *Reporting,* Dodd Mead, New York, 1981.

---

approaches a dangerous area. You may also use very ambiguous remarks
to get away from sensitive areas; or you can say directly that you do not
want to talk about it. One such comment can be used in almost every
conversational situation: "I'm not sure that would apply in all cases." A
variation can be most useful in turning from a taboo topic: "You must
need a lot of information (or experience or knowledge) to go into that
subject."

INFORMATION POWER
Information is power. People who control information often control their
environment and how people can interact. The person who can strategically withhold or dispense information can tightly control interpersonal
situations. In work situations, the person "in the know" is sought after
and generally believed. Deciding how much is good for others to know
is a significant power in a communicating relationship. Office traffic will
flow around the person who receives the confidential memos on what is
happening or who gets the telephone calls from supervisors outlining
projects or programs. By controlling the information which others may
need, you can operate your interpersonal relationships on your own terms;
you can avoid threats by being in charge of the basic raw materials of
interaction, the content of messages.

SOME COMMON ELEMENTS OF DEFENSIVE STRATEGIES
Defensive strategies have several elements in common which have been
investigated by many researchers.[20] One common element is that defensive strategies encourage a *ritualistic* approach to your interpersonal com-

munication and thus discourage freedom and spontaneity. In that way you rely on "cookbook" techniques to get by in your world and try to force each situation into a "recipe" you have memorized rather than responding naturally or openly.

Another element is your tendency to hide some facet of your behavior which you feel will not be accepted by others, to minimize some feature of yourself. An opposite of this is to exaggerate some feature when you pretend, unrealistically, that you can do no wrong; that nothing should be unacceptable to others in any situation. Either of these two reactions displays a rigidity to the situations which is not appropriate—you should recognize that different behaviors are useful in different situations and are never always right or always wrong.

If you value open, free, honest, direct, and trusting communication, what can you do to help build a climate that will increase the likelihood of developing such communication transactions? Again, let us emphasize that whether someone feels safe ultimately depends on his or her perception of the situation. Although you cannot control how people perceive, you can control to some extent the stimulus for their perceptions. You may present yourself in a nonthreatening way. It is up to them to perceive you as nonthreatening.

Defenses provoked and reduced

Researchers have isolated several categories of behavior which are likely to provoke defensiveness and other categories of behaviors which are likely to help reduce defensiveness.

EVALUATION VERSUS DESCRIPTION

Communication which appears evaluative, judgmental, or blaming tends to increase defensiveness. If you feel that people are judging you, criticizing you, or even evaluating you positively, you are likely to feel threatened. If you watch the way people respond to compliments or praise, you will note that they invariably seem to react with discomfort, uneasiness, and defensiveness. Their response is often a vague denial of the compliment or even a self-derogation:

"I really can't take credit for it. . . . "
"Well, it's nothing, really. . . . "
"You look nice, too. . . . "
"You did well, too. . . . "
"Oh, you're just saying that. . . . "
"Uh, that's OK. . . . "

These statements are all defensive statements, indicating that the situation was perceived as a difficult one. Often people get so flustered when they receive compliments that their discomfort is apparent through their nonverbal behavior. They squirm; they look away; they become flushed; they make denial gestures. Part of the reason for the discomfort is that evaluation, even if positive, is still evaluation. Unless you have built a relationship you trust with the person giving the compliment, you may suspect that person's motives. "What does this person want from me?" is often the nonexpressed thought of someone who is receiving a compliment. It is also possible to predict that a negative item will follow a positive one; when you hear a compliment, you wait for the other shoe to fall because you are used to the "sandwich technique." Briefly, this technique consists of praising someone about something, then following up with a criticism, then returning to something nice. It goes something like this (from a parent to a child):

> *Honey, this is a beautiful picture (praise), but you are so messy. You shouldn't smear paint all over the place (criticism). Well, go ahead, honey, and show your pretty picture to Daddy (praise).*

No wonder you don't know how to respond. In this way, you get schooled in waiting for the reprimand when you hear the compliment.

Sometimes a question sounds as though it is information-seeking when in fact it is evaluative or accusative. You hear it between parents and children, teachers and students, husbands and wives. It is "Why did you do that?" when asked with a tone of voice which clearly reveals an accusatory reaction. To avoid as much as possible either making or reacting to evaluations, describe rather than evaluate; make unvalued statements rather than critical ones; ask questions which are relevant and information-seeking rather than rhetorically evaluative.

CONTROL VERSUS PROBLEM APPROACH

Communication used to control others is likely to be resisted. The degree of defensiveness aroused depends on the degree of suspicion you have about the controller's motives. If you suspect ulterior motives, you get defensive. You have grown suspicious in a culture where control is often sugarcoated. "You don't want to stay up late and get all tired, do you, honey?" is a devious way of saying "I want you to go to bed now." "What do doctors recommend?" is a question which sets up the answer that you should buy a product recommended by doctors but sold by that advertiser. Whether the message is personal, political, or commercial, it carries an implicit attempt to control a person who needs to be changed and is inadequate—and that makes it a threatening message. A preventative against control strategy is to address our communication to problems rather than to people, to issues rather than to personalities. In political campaigns there is much voter attention being given to the "smear" or the "mudslinging" approach as an unethical attack on a person rather than dealing with issues.

STRATAGEMS VERSUS SPONTANEITY

If you would like your motive not to be known, you employ stratagems, or devious measures, tricks, devices, or games with each other. When you suspect that a stratagem is being used on you, you resent it and become defensive. Most people have an aversion to deceit in any form. You do not like to be manipulated. You especially resent the idea that others might think you are foolish enough to fall for their tricks. By avoiding obvious "sales" tricks of the big hand clasp and overdone compliments, you will develop spontaneity in your relations with others. Staying flexible and being yourself, you can avoid triggering defensive behaviors induced by your obvious or obscure stratagems.

LACK OF CONCERN VERSUS INVOLVEMENT

Any behavior which openly conveys lack of feeling, caring, or warmth says to others that you are not concerned. A detached and aloof attitude

Showing concern means becoming involved with others' ideas, issues, abilities, behaviors, and so on. (© *Rhoda Sidney/The Image Works*)

often gives the impression of rejection. Even by appearing neutral you can make another person feel unwanted. Defensiveness based on rejection or even the possibility of rejection is common. Overcoming this tendency can be described as becoming involved with others, showing empathy, and finding a level of honest concern for the ideas, the issues, the constraints, the abilities, and the behaviors of another person. As we describe it in Chapter 6, an attitude of caring and involvement can be communicated by actively listening to others.

SUPERIOR ATTITUDE VERSUS SHARING

When a person conveys to you a feeling of superiority over you, it brings out your defenses. Arrogance, distance, aloofness, haughtiness, and condescension all send you a signal that the other person is not willing or ready to develop a shared or equal relationship. You have difficulty communicating in that situation. Equality is sharing of similarities and differences without having to rank each other on every item or idea, without having to compete for "first place" in every exchange of ideas or messages.

DOGMATIC ATTITUDES VERSUS FLEXIBILITY

People who come on as all-knowing, who appear to need to be right and to win arguments rather than to solve problems, and who tend to impose their views as the only right ones are classic generators of defensiveness in others. For one thing, it is hard to communicate with such people unless you happen to agree exactly with their ideas. So dogmatic are they that you must agree entirely or you will be put down and judged negatively for holding the "wrong" ideas. People who have a provisional idea of what is going on, who act as if there were some other ideas to be heard, and who believe that truth does not necessarily always reside in their own insides can reduce defensiveness in communication. Being right does not mean that every other idea is wrong and must be stomped on; there are provisions for some error even in the best answers.

IN SUMMARY: PROVOKING VERSUS REDUCING DEFENSIVENESS

It is crucial to recognize that behaviors which provoke defensiveness are serious obstacles to effective interpersonal communication. People who communicate judgmentally and dogmatically, who need to control and manipulate others, who appear unwilling to develop a shared relationship based on mutual trust, make interpersonal communication particularly difficult. Once defensiveness is aroused, people tend to resort to shallow rituals and protective behavior. Ritualistic behavior, in turn, is likely to strengthen the motivation of the initial communicator for behaving the way he or she started to behave. Both sender and receiver are caught in

the web of self-fulfilling prophecies. Their behaviors feed e~
person's behavior arousing additional defensiveness in the o.
no way out of a contest of attack-defend-protect. It is unlike
encounter will prove satisfying for either person, because behavi   ..ich
provoke defensiveness in the first place are likely to be attacks on the
self-esteem of others.

SUMMARY

Study of self-esteem is not new. As early as a century ago William James wrote a prescription for maintaining self-esteem which has been echoed by many outstanding writers and researchers. Very similar to James's prescription for adjustment to goals and attainment is the IFD formulation of Wendell Johnson. He asserts that success and failure are linguistic artifacts and need to be put in perspective by people who use those evaluative terms.

Behaviors can be modified and changing includes consideration of attitudes, behaviors, techniques, and the sequence of change attempts. Evidence is growing that attitude change follows changed behaviors, and that people's behaviors are a result of external circumstances more than of inbred personality traits.

Relating to others, you develop certain patterns of communicating which have been referred to as "styles." A range of styles is available to anyone. Each style has some communication uses, but it is the habitual, unselective, inconsiderate selection of one single style for all situations that can cause you trouble.

Assertiveness, which gained popularity relevant to the movement for women's and minority rights, is a useful and widely available style appropriate for anyone who is not satisfied with his or her communicative relationships. It improves self-esteem and reflects self-determination without abusing others. Assertive people appear to be (1) free to express themselves, (2) able to communicate easily with all kinds of others, (3) active in their orientation toward others and new experiences, and (4) able to act in a way which demonstrates they respect themselves even if their efforts may not always work out. Several kinds of circumstances in which assertion may be effectively tried include (1) exchanging compliments, (2) sharing feelings, (3) giving and receiving help, and (4) handling annoyance and anger. Employing assertive behavior can have both positive and negative consequences for communication and should be used in full recognition of potential outcomes.

Defensive behaviors come as a natural response to situations in which you feel threatened or frustrated. Just as there are different styles of communication available, there are ways to reduce defensiveness in your efforts to achieve mutually rewarding relationships.

END NOTES

[1] William James, *Principles of Psychology,* vol. I, Henry Holt, New York, 1890, pp. 310 et seq.

[2] Wendell Johnson, *People in Quandaries,* Harper & Row, New York, 1946, pp. 10 et seq.

[3] James, op cit., p. 310; Johnson, ibid., p. 12.

[4] Check any bookstore which has a section on "self-help"; in addition, references similar to the following may be found shelved under "Psychology" and you will find books with titles and subject matter like these: N. Brandon, *How to Raise Your Self-Esteem,* Bantam Books, New York, 1989; L. T. Sanford and M. E. Donovan, *Women and Self-Esteem,* Penguin Books, New York, 1985; J. O'Connor and J. Seymour, *Introducing Neuro-Linguistic Programming,* Hartnolls, Bodwin, Cornwall, 1990; D. Burkett and J. Narcisco, *Declare Yourself,* Prentice-Hall, Englewood Cliffs, NJ, 1975; M. Maltz, *Psycho Cybernetics,* Pocket Books, New York, 1983; and *Magic Power of Self-Image Psychology,* Prentice-Hall, Englewood Cliffs, NJ, 1989.

[5] D. W. Hudson, *Assertive Training for the Elderly Client,* American University Studies, Washington, D.C., 1983.

[6] S. McKay, *Assertive Approach to Childbirth,* International Childbirth Association, New York, 1986.

[7] L. Canter and others, titles include *A Take-Charge Approach for Today's Educator* (1976), *Administrator Guide* (1986), *Assertive Discipline Awards for Reinforcing Behavior: Primary Educators* (1987), *Assertive Discipline Award for Reinforcing Behavior: Secondary School Educators* (1989), *Assertive Discipline for Paraprofessionals* (1987), all published by Lee Canter Associates, Santa Monica, CA.

[8] L. Canter (ed.), *Assertive Discipline for Bus Drivers,* Lee Canter & Associates, Santa Monica, CA, 1987.

[9] J. S. Caputo, *Assertive Librarian,* Oryx Press, Phoenix, AZ, 1984.

[10] C. C. Clark, *Assertive Skills for Nurses,* Aspen Publishers, Rodiville, MD, 1978.

[11] M. Frost, *Assertive Christian* (M. Emmons and D. Richardson, eds.), Harper & Row, New York, 1981.

[12] D. Cawood, *Assertiveness for Managers: Learning Effective Skills for Managing People,* ISC Press, Bethlehem, PA, 1989. E. Zuker, *Assertive Manager: Positive Skills at Work for You,* American Association of Management (AMACOM), New York, 1989.

[13] R. F. Rakos, *Assertive Behavior,* Routledge Chapman and Hall, New York, 1990. M. Linchan and K. Egan, *Asserting Yourself,* Facts on File (Checkmark), New York, 1986. H. Virkler, *Assertiveness,* Zondervan, Grand Rapids, MI, 1989. A. D. Russo, *Assertiveness Is,* Publications Twenty First, Tolland, CT, 1985. H. B. Forkey, *Assertiveness Training: Some Reflections, and Considerations,* New Dynamics Publications, Laconia, NH, 1980. P. Jablonski and A. J. Lange, *Assertive Option: Your Rights and Responsibilities,* Research Press, Champaign, IL, 1978. C. W. Brandon, *Learning to Say No,* Health Communications, Inc., Deerfield Beach, FL, 1990. A trio of books by S. Helmstetter, *Choice,* Pocket Books, New York, 1989; *The Self-Talk Solution,* Pocket Books, New York, 1987; and *What*

to Say When You Talk to Yourself, Pocket Books, New York, 1982. Books by W. W. Dyer such as *You'll See It When You Believe It,* Dell Books, New York, 1990. R. E. Alberti and M. L. Emmons, *Your Perfect Right: A Guide to Assertive Living,* Impact Publications, San Luis Obispo, CA, 1990; and by the same authors, *Stand Up, Speak Out, Talk Back,* Pocket Books, New York, 1989.

[14] M. J. Smith, *When I Say No I Feel Guilty,* Bantam Books, New York, 1985. H. Fensterheim and J. Baer, *Don't Say Yes When You Want To Say No,* Dell Books, New York, 1975; and by those same authors, *Making Life Right When It Feels All Wrong,* Dell Books, New York, 1989. In addition, see any widely used handbooks for assertion trainers, such as L. G. Manis, *Assertion Training Workshop: Leader's Guide,* Learning Publications, New York, 1984, or A. J. Lange and P. Jakubowski, *Responsible Assertive Behavior: Cognitive/Behavioral Procedures for Trainers,* Research Press, Chicago, 1976.

[15] S. Phelps and N. Austin, *Assertive Woman: A New Look,* Impact Publications, San Luis Obispo, CA, 1987. M. Drake, *Assertive Woman and Other Anomalies,* Bethany House, New York, 1989. A. Walker, *You Can't Keep a Good Woman Down,* Harcourt Brace Jovanovich, San Diego, CA, 1981. C. Gilligan, *In a Different Voice,* Harvard University Press, Cambridge, MA, 1982. L. Z. Bloom, K. Coburn, and J. Pearlman, *The New Assertive Woman,* Delacorte Press, New York, 1987.

[16] A term used by Burkett and Narcisco in *Declare Yourself,* op. cit.

[17] V. Satir, *New Peoplemaking,* Science Behavior Books, Mountain View, CA, 1988, and her earlier *Peoplemaking,* Hazelden Foundation, Center City, MN, 1976.

[18] P. Lecky, *Self-Consistency: A Theory of Personality,* Island Press, Fort Myers, FL, 1982.

[19] F. Heider, *The Psychology of Interpersonal Relations,* John Wiley & Sons, New York, 1982.

[20] W. Bennis et al., *Interpersonal Dynamics: Essays and Readings in Human Interaction,* Dorsay Press, Homewood, IL, 1979, pp. 211–212. J. Gibb, "Defensive Communication," *Journal of Communication,* vol. 11, September 1961, pp. 141–148.

CHAPTER
5

NEEDS, ATTITUDES, BELIEFS, VALUES: HOW DID I GET THIS WAY?

OBJECTIVES

When you complete this chapter, you should be able to do the following:

1. Explain two theories of human needs and relate them to their authors.
2. Define the terms "beliefs," "attitudes," and "values," and distinguish among them.
3. Define and give examples of reference groups and cite their influence on communicative behavior.
4. Explain a classical theory of dissonance and dissonance reduction.
5. Explain a classical theory of consistency.
6. In relation to attitudes, define and give examples relating to the terms "direction," "intensity," and "salience."
7. Describe the range of beliefs which most people seem to hold and give examples.

INTRODUCTION

In the previous chapters you have read about communication in general (Chapter 1), about how you perceive the world (Chapter 2), and about how you see yourself in relation to others (Chapters 3 and 4).

You will, in this chapter, begin to look more intensely at the relation between what happens inside you—your needs, attitudes, values, and beliefs—and what goes on in the world outside. That outside contact, of course, includes your behaviors toward others. From those ways you behave, others will decide what kind of person you are, not always accurately or fairly, but they will evaluate you on the basis of what they see you do and hear you say.

The world places many demands on you. How you meet those demands is the subject of this part of the book.

You also want people to behave in a certain way, and you want events to come out the way you expect them to. If that doesn't happen, you would like to know (1) why things came out that way, and (2) what you might be able to do about it. Understanding your own needs and motivations can help you understand how others act, which in turn may help you adapt to the relationships which will inevitably develop as you try to meet your interpersonal needs.

MOTIVATION

Human motivation is a complicated matter. It is also generally hidden from others and often from ourselves. It is also subject to analysis from many points of view. For example, psychologists study motivation to determine something about human cognitive or personality adjustments and drives; businesspeople study motivation to find out how to get more loyal or productive workers; politicians study motivation to figure out how to move a population to vote for them; advertisers study motivation to develop sales campaigns to move products or services; media analysts study motivation to understand how to make people pay attention to messages. Many adults believe if they knew what motivated youngsters in general they would become better parents to their own children.

While most behavioral scientists might agree that people are motivated by the desire to satisfy many needs, not all agree about (1) how to describe or define what those needs are, (2) which needs are most important (salient) to people in any given time or situation, and (3) how much effort people will exert to satisfy their needs.

Maslow and the Hierarchy of Needs

Abraham Maslow identified five basic needs which have become widely accepted by behavioral scientists, and are often referred to both in scholarly and in popular literature. He also claims these needs are arranged in an order, or hierarchy, based on these two assumptions:[1]

1. Only when the first basic level of needs is satisfied can people seek satisfaction of the needs on the next level.
2. Once a need is satisfied, it no longer acts as a motivator.

From the bottom of the hierarchy to the top, Maslow's five needs are:

Social needs are related to desires for companionship, belonging, acceptance, friendship, and love. (© Jerry Howard/Stock, Boston)

Physiological needs

Maslow's most basic need includes the most elemental necessities which sustain and perpetuate life—the needs for air, water, food, sleep, sex.

Safety needs

The second level of needs in Maslow's hierarchy he refers to as "safety," or the desire for protection from danger, threat, or deprivation. People may look to their homes often as a safe place to be, and also look to others to protect them from danger as a way of meeting this need.

Social needs

These are related to people's desire for companionship, for belonging, acceptance, friendship, and love. "Roots" and family reunions are familiar attempts to meet this need, as are people's joining social and professional clubs or organizations.

Esteem needs

This "higher-order need" relates to this book's discussion in the past two chapters as it consists of (1) the need for *self-esteem* which is characterized by feelings of self-confidence, self-respect, and competence, and (2) the need for *esteem from others* which includes recognition, status, appreciation, and prestige.

Self-actualization needs

Maslow's fifth need level is described as the need for self-fulfillment, creative expression, and a sense of realization of your potential. Partly because this is the most ambiguous of the needs to pin down, many popular self-help books have borrowed from this concept to persuade people to lift themselves to new creative, psychological, or personal levels. "Peak experiences" has sometimes been used to describe ways this need is met. This implies that self-actualization may be such an amorphous and high-level need that many people are not aware of it and are hence not motivated to achieve it.

Needs as Motivators

A need is a motivator only if it is felt as a frustrated need by the persons themselves. Only you know whether you are hungry, need friends, or would like a pat on the back. Furthermore, only you know the relative importance of a given need for you at a given time. Sometimes you may forgo the satisfaction of a need, even a basic one, for the fulfillment of another, higher-level need. You may choose to deprive yourself of sleep and social activities for great periods of time in order to have the satisfaction of achieving professional goals which require a great deal of commitment and work. The student who works long hours to get through school and has little social life is motivated essentially by *esteem* needs (or perhaps *self-actualization*) at the expense of meeting "lower" needs such as *social* or *physiological,* including sleep.

Not all students will make this choice, of course, and ultimately motivation is a very personal matter. Knowing that *generally* all people have five basic needs does not provide a specific answer to the question "What should I do to motivate Susie to work harder?"

Herzberg: motivating for production

While Maslow's hierarchy of needs provided a classical base for studying how people are motivated, it was inevitable that managers and industrial leaders would also be interested in ways to improve employee motivation. Frederick Herzberg[2] suggested that there are "hygiene factors" which keep employees "well" but do not motivate and these are items such as salary, working conditions, benefits, and supervision. Beyond those, he asserts, are the effective, and intrinsic motivators such as meaningful tasks, opportunities for promotion or creative expression, responsibility, and feelings of achievement. Adequate salary is a necessary part of a working person's life, but not sufficient to truly motivate the way the intrinsic motivators do.

Current professional literature and popular writings in management continually pose the question "How can we motivate the modern workers[3] and managers in order to compete with production in such places as Japan?"

There are no more simple answers to managerial motivation[4] than there are in the interpersonal arena, but any study of motivation can be helped by a deeper understanding of human needs and—most important—how people communicate about them.

Needs as Transactions

Satisfying basic needs directly involves interpersonal communication. It is through transactional communication that people let each other know what is important to them. Even with good listening and careful feedback

BOX 5-1.   Motivation by Discontent

Studies of motivation most often involve (1) how to get students to learn, or (2) how to get employees to work better. The similarity of research approaches between educational motivation and business is that they rely on understanding of human needs as motivators.

In this respect, it is possible for teachers and managers alike to appeal to the highest unmet needs in their students or employees.* They may do this by making sure the student/employee is not content with doing things the same old way, but should be actually dissatisfied with things the way they are—in the classroom or the workplace. It is important to provide the "hygiene" or basic needs first, such as learning and working conditions, acceptable safety and security, salary, or other rewards. Then the student/employee can be stimulated to look for fulfillment of higher-order needs such as psychological growth, achievement, and recognition.**

* E. Jantzen, "An Approach to Overcoming Student Passivity," *Education Digest,* vol. 53, January 1988, p. 33; S. G. Save, "Holding on to Student Enthusiasm," *Education Digest,* vol. 52, March 1987, p. 28; J. Brophy, "Synthesis of Research on Strategies for Motivating Students to Learn," *Educational Leadership,* vol. 45, October 1987, p. 40.
** B. S. Gooch and B. J. McDowell, "Use Anxiety to Motivate," *Personnel Journal,* vol. 67, April 1988, p. 50; R. M. Ryan and E. L. Deci, "Bridging the Research Traditions of Task-Ego Involvement and Intrinsic-Extrinsic Motivation," *Journal of Educational Psychology,* vol. 81, June 1989, p. 265.

you can go wrong, since needs are more often inferred than they are openly stated.

Verbally and nonverbally you try to let others know about your needs. Through your own sensitivity and attention to messages you get from others you may be able to determine (1) what their needs are, (2) what needs are important to them at a particular moment, and (3) whether or not they perceive accurately your attempts to satisfy their needs. You may be doing all the "right" things, but if other people do not perceive what you do in the spirit in which you intended it, they may interpret your actions in a counterproductive way.

Interpersonal communication is satisfying to you when you manage to satisfy your needs. In the case of interpersonal needs, you depend on others primarily. If others give you the recognition you seek, or give you a chance to exert influence when you wish, or provide you with a satisfactorily close, intimate atmosphere, you feel satisfied and you will again seek out those people for more interpersonal situations. On the other hand you avoid, when you can, interpersonal communication situations in which your needs are generally denied, unmet, or thwarted.

Schutz and the Theory of Interpersonal Needs

Based on now-classic research and extensive and current evaluations and norming, FIRO testing—the initials stand for Fundamental Interpersonal Relations Orientation—was developed by William Schutz.[5] Schutz identifies three basic interpersonal needs which underlie most of your behavior around other people.[6] These needs can be best represented as dimensions or continuums along which most people can be placed. Schutz calls these interpersonal needs the "need for inclusion," the "need for control," and the "need for affection."

Inclusion

According to Schutz, the need for inclusion is the need to be recognized as an individual distinct from others. A person with a very high need for inclusion needs recognition and attention from others—someone who likes to be in the spotlight, to be singled out, to be noticed. At one of the extremes of the continuum, we find the prima donna, or the obnoxious little kid who does anything simply to attract some attention, even if it results in punishment. To be punished is better than to be ignored. On the other end, a person with a low inclusion need prefers not to stand out, would rather not receive too much attention, does not like to be prominent in the public eye.

People at both extremes are motivated essentially by the same fear of not being recognized as individuals. The people high on the inclusion need will combat the fear by forcing others to pay attention to them. Those low on the inclusion need have convinced themselves that they will not get any attention, but that it is just the way they want it. Your needs for inclusion may change as the people you associate with differ, and as situations change. You may want very little recognition from a professor when you have not done an assignment and do not wish to be called upon, while in the same class you may have a strong need for attention from the person sitting next to you, whom you are interested in getting to know better.

Control

The need for control involves a striving for power, for being in charge, for running things, and for influencing one's environment. The need for control is not necessarily related to the need for inclusion. Some people enjoy being in charge of things even if no one is aware that they are running the show. These people are high on control while low on inclusion—power-behind-the-throne types. It is not always easy to determine whether a person's behavior is influenced by one need or the other. You should be careful not to play "analyst" with your friends and summarily peg them into one or the other category.

Naturally, some people are quite low on the need for control and are not interested at all in taking initiative, in assuming responsibilities, in making decisions, or in leading a group. As is true for the inclusion need, a mixed group composed of highs and lows on the control dimension has a better chance of getting things done.

Affection

The need for affection has to do with how close people want to be to one another. Some people like to be very intimate and enjoy warm relationships, even with relatively casual acquaintances. They enjoy telling about themselves on a personal level and expect similar behavior on the part of others. They want and need to be liked. Sometimes people high on the need for affection are perceived by others as being too friendly or coming on too strong.

Other people prefer to keep an interpersonal distance. They do not like to become too friendly too rapidly. They may have a strong distaste for closeness and intimacy except with carefully selected people. These people are usually perceived as aloof, cold, or "superior."

In the case of affection, a mixed group is not the best combination for productive interpersonal relationships. Cold people and warm people do not mix well. Each type of person makes the other uncomfortable, and they find it hard to figure each other out. Neither is able to satisfy the other's needs.

Dimensions of Interpersonal Needs

Interpersonal needs as described by Schutz and subsequent writers generally follow the pattern of transactions. The two essential dimensions on any scale can measure how you like to act toward others, and how you like to be treated. Clearly, the way you behave toward others may not

Need for affection relates to how close people like to be to each other. (© *Judy Gelles/Stock, Boston*)

always be the same, nor do you always get the same behavior from others.

Persistence of patterns

Interpersonal orientations are so deeply rooted, and have been part of a person's behaviors for so long, that there is every reason to expect adults to behave very much the ways they did as children.[7] Interpersonal relations among adults are similar to those in children, and in his discussion of relations, Schutz makes reference to child and adult behaviors which were forerunners to the child-parent-adult descriptions of transactional analysis.[8] Choices you make, friends you choose, the job you may seek, the amusements and sports you pick, the clubs and organizations you join, are all related to fulfilling needs on the scales of control, affection, and inclusion. However, there is some question about whether you are attracted to a particular profession or lifestyle because of your needs, or if needs are affected by the situation or profession you select.[9]

Universality of patterns

Fulfilling needs goes well beyond interpersonal relations and must include more global relations as well. Some attempts have been made to probe the need orientations of various cultures, usually making comparisons with American-related needs. Dean Barnlund, a long-time student of Japanese communication behaviors, developed a scale of interpersonal relations and applied it to a comparison of American and Japanese behaviors. He found, for example, that intimacy (affection) proved important to both cultures: "Both countries show evidence that intimate relationships are highly valued and maintained for equally long periods of time."[10] As in other situations, however, the means of fulfilling the need for intimacy or affection may be quite different.[11]

An ongoing study of graduating college students by the authors and a French human resources research firm makes cross-national comparisons between the expressed desires for what is most important in the first job out of college.[12] Preliminary data indicate much similarity in basic needs for control and affection, with less agreement on the strength of the inclusion need. Again, while the basic needs may be very similar across national boundaries, the means of attaining them and their relative importance may be very different because of situations and the attitudes and cultural values of participants. (See the section on attitudes, beliefs, and values, which follows.)

Compatibility

In discussions of interpersonal relationships the term "compatibility" occurs frequently. There is a tendency to think of compatibility as part of "affection" or liking. It should, however, be more closely linked to the dimension of "inclusion" and must be defined as an ability to work together.[13] You know of many examples of people who can work very successfully together on a task, and who may not particularly like each other. On the other hand, you may know people who have a strong affection for one another but who can't seem to accomplish anything when they work together.

In this way, "liking" may not be the most significant measure of effective cooperation or coordinated relations. Where "incompatibility" is stated as a basis for divorce, it is likely that the marriage did not suffer so much from lack of affection as it did from lack of inclusion or a battle for control.

In Summary: Why Study Needs?

An understanding of interpersonal needs is essential, not only in facilitating your insights into group processes, but in helping you predict the situations that will be more or less satisfying and productive for you.

Many problems in today's world can be better understood—and perhaps solved—by an increased understanding of the issue of human needs. For example, the changes in family life (which some observers claim are the cause of many social ills) can be managed more effectively with increased knowledge and acceptance of the changing needs of family members in relation to their community, religion, work, school, and friendships. Widespread frustration across the world over unmet needs is likely at the root of many global human problems. Poor or enslaved nations with few resources and many unmet needs cannot make innovative or creative contributions until starvation and personal deprivation are overcome. Our expectations as well as our social consciousness of human interactions, from family life to international affairs, will be enhanced as we learn more about needs and how people behave to meet them.

BELIEFS, ATTITUDES, AND VALUES

You may often feel that your personal world is unique, peculiar to you, unshared by anyone. You have great difficulties explaining to someone else a feeling or an experience. Even when you manage to describe the feeling or the experience with words, you doubt that others know it as you do.

However, people are peculiar. At the same time that you intuitively believe in your uniqueness, you also assume that you live in the same world others do. You assume that what you see is what others see. Despite your feeling of uniqueness, your daily life is usually spent in a world you assume is shared as much as unique.

This may be the vital function of communication. Were it not for human communication or human contact, you would live alone, exclusively in your world of uniqueness, without getting confirmation of your experiences.

Confirmation of your experiences (or disclosing) not only involves the physical world—checking your perceptions with others to test their reliability. It also involves the social world—comparing your ideas about religion, politics, morals, etc., with others to test their validity.

Because human beings are symbol-using creatures, they can create for themselves rules of conduct which go beyond the mere survival needs of the species. When a female animal raises her young, she does so because she is programmed to do so in order for the young to survive and for the species to continue to exist. When human parents raise their children, considerably more is involved—feelings, societal expectations, laws, duty, etc. Human beings create value systems, form beliefs about the nature of their world, and, as a result, learn to respond to their environment in some ways more than in others.

A Few Definitions

Beliefs

Beliefs represent the way people view their environment. Beliefs are characterized by a true-false continuum and a probability scale. The existence of ghosts, for example, may be closer to the "false" end of the continuum for some people than for others. That humans evolved from apes is still debated by many who place Darwin's theory of evolution closer to the "false" end of the continuum and place the story of Genesis closer to the "true" end of the continuum. Beliefs represent what you agree with and what you usually think is true. Some things you believe to be absolutely true, some you believe to be probably true, some you are not sure about, and some you think are false, probably or absolutely.

You cannot observe a belief. You can only observe a person's behavior and assume that it came about because of a particular belief. Beliefs are not necessarily logical. They are largely determined by what you want to believe, by what you are able to believe, by what you have been conditioned to believe, and by basic needs which may influence you to have a certain belief in order to satisfy those needs.

CENTRAL BELIEFS

Some beliefs are more central than others, which means they are connected to more other beliefs and are very likely to resist change. They are important for you because any change in them would have great consequences. Marrying someone from another faith may cause a series of changes in your religious beliefs and practices, as well as altered relations with your friends or family. Being unemployed may have serious personal as well as financial consequences to the person with a strong central belief in work as an ethical imperative.

Everett Rogers[14] and others have studied how beliefs are changed in a population and many of the same principles apply to change in an individual's beliefs, particularly the role of communication in change.[15]

Centrality of beliefs has been shown to depend on where you got them (the importance of your source: family, peers, authorities, religious leaders, etc.), how dependent you are on them for your daily survival, and the intensity with which you want to hang on to them in relation to the rewards you get from holding to them compared with the punishment you might get for changing. Any change in a very central belief means changes in a larger number of other related or closely connected beliefs.

RANGES OF BELIEFS

Your belief system includes some which are very important to you and for which you might fight or die, and ranges all the way to inconsequential beliefs which you can change with little or no encouragement or effort or consequence. At one end of the scale are the very evident beliefs like the sun rises in the east and will do that every morning. You also have beliefs involving religion, politics, racial issues, national pride, which are supported by seeking concurrence from others, and which are very resistant to change. Some of your beliefs are given you by authority figures, and may change as you mature or become involved with other authority beliefs—you do not persist in a belief in Santa Claus even if your parents once told you he existed, and your beliefs were probably changed by peers, another group you listen to in developing beliefs.

The least important beliefs to you are those which include matters of taste or personal choice. You may change them as you switch brands of cereal when new data emerges about cholesterol or fiber. You may change them as styles or fads come and go. This does not mean you are not strong in our desire to wear the right length skirt or the correct width of necktie; it means that your belief in that skirt length or necktie is based on another more basic need—to be in fashion or vogue—and you can change that belief to meet an expediency of acceptance.

You have beliefs involving issues of morality, religion, politics, race, environment, and so on. (© *Joel Gordon*)

Attitudes

Attitudes are relatively lasting *organizations of beliefs* which made you tend to respond to things in particular ways. Attitudes are never seen directly; you infer their existence from what people do. Attitudes include positive or negative evaluations, emotional feelings, and certain positive or negative tendencies in relation to objects, people, and events.

Attitudes are human responses and can be examined along three dimensions: their direction, their intensity, and their salience.

DIRECTION

"Direction" of an attitude refers simply to how favorable, unfavorable, or neutral one tends to be in relation to an object, person, or situation. It refers to whether one is attracted to, repulsed by, or simply indifferent to a particular course of action; whether one evaluates a thing positively or negatively. You like someone, or you do not, or you do not much care. You approve of birth control, or you do not, or you are ambivalent about it, oscillating between one direction and the other. You have attitudes on just about everything you know about. When you do not know much about something, and thus have no particular attitude about it, what people communicate to you will usually help you form one.

INTENSITY

"Intensity" of an attitude refers to how strong it is—to how much you like or dislike someone or something. You may not like science courses

---

BOX 5-2. Attitudes, Values, and Car Ownership

In Lake Wobegon, car ownership is a matter of faith. Lutherans drive Fords, bought from Bunsen Motors, the Lutheran car dealer, and Catholics drive Chevies from Main Garage, owned by the Kruegers. . . . Years ago, John Tollerud was tempted by Chevyship until Pastor Tommerdahl took John aside and told him it was his (Pastor Tommerdahl's) responsibility to point out that Fords get better gas mileage and have a better trade-in value. And he knew for a fact that Kruegers spent a share of the Chevy profits to purchase Asian babies and make them Catholics. So John got a new Ford Falcon. It turned out to be a dud. The transmission went out after ten thousand miles and the car tended to pull to the left. In a town where car ownership is by faith, however, a person doesn't complain about those things, and John figured there must be a good reason for his car trouble, which perhaps he would understand more fully someday.

Source: From *Lake Wobegon Days* by Garrison Keillor, Copyright © 1985 by Garrison Keillor. Reprinted by permission of the publisher, Viking Penguin, a division of Penguin Books, USA Inc., p. 112.

very much, but your dislike of mathematics may be stronger than your dislike of biology. You may like all members of your family, but your feelings about your older brother may not be as intense as for your younger sister.

SALIENCE
"Salience" refers to how important the attitude is to the person holding it. As mentioned earlier, you have attitudes on just about everything you know about. However, you do not attach the same importance to everything you know about. There are things in your life that are much more important than others. Salience and intensity should not be confused. For example, you may be convinced of the merits of a certain toothpaste and buy only one brand—a strong attitude—yet toothpastes in general do not represent what is most important (salient) in your life. There are other things that are more salient, such as your attitudes toward freedom, individual rights, or pollution.

Values

Values are fairly enduring conceptions of the nature of good and bad, of the *relative worth* you attribute to the things, people, and events of your lives. Values are usually embodied in complex moral or religious systems that are found in all cultures and societies. Values indicate to those who share them what is desirable, to what degree it is desirable, and therefore what one should strive for. They also provide people with a guidance system which is supposed to enable them to choose the "right" alternative when several courses of action are possible.

Values are fairly enduring and resistant to change because they are tied to fundamental human needs and because they are learned very early in life in a somewhat absolutistic way. Thou shalt, and thou shalt not. However, many values that are held by a given group of people can be, and often are, conflicting. In order to act, people must decide which of the conflicting values is more important or more basic, which takes precedence over the other. (For example: Thou shalt not kill; yet is it all right to kill the "enemy" in war?)

Values grow out of a complex interaction between basic needs and the specificity of a given environment. For example, all humans need to eat in order to survive, but they do not all value the same foods. In America beef is commonly eaten, while in India the sacred cow must not be touched. What is valued in a particular area, region, or country is partly determined by the availability of certain foods. Values thus differ from place to place or time to time because of the variety of ways specific needs can be fulfilled. The indictment of "materialism" directed at the generation who lived through the great depression in the United States, by a generation who lived mostly in post-World War II affluence, may reflect a change of need levels.

Words you use in making your value judgments, such as "bad," "good," "moral," "immoral," do not stand for any quality of the object or people you apply them to. Value judgments are applied by human beings to objects; they are not "in" the objects. Something is good to a particular individual or group only because it is defined as good.

Communication is what makes our system of values possible. Judgments about beauty or ugliness are in the same category as those about goodness or badness. It has been said that beauty lies in the eye of the beholder. You cannot discover beauty—you can only discover how people define it. It is a dimension created by human beings.

Formation of Beliefs, Attitudes, and Values

The point we wish to emphasize strongly here is that beliefs, attitudes, and values are *learned*. People are not born anti-Semites, conservatives, atheists, or football fans. They are not born fearing God and valuing freedom and human dignity; nor are they born convinced that a steady use of mouthwash will make them social successes.

All beliefs, attitudes, and values are learned from the people with whom you live and associate. Because they are learned, they can be unlearned—that is, changed—although change may often be resisted (as we will see later in this chapter).

It is primarily through interpersonal communication that people develop prejudices, assumptions, and outlooks on what life is like or ought to be like. Your beliefs, attitudes, and values were formed through the various human groups you were and are exposed to, which "indoctrinated" or "socialized" you—and still do—in those beliefs, attitudes, and values they hold dear.

To communicate with others is to influence them and to be influenced by them, because any time that you have human contact with others, their behavior and what they tell you affect you. Any time you learn something new, you change and become a little more like those who taught you. This is what makes society possible. Interpersonal communication thus fosters the minimum uniformity necessary for people to live and work together. Sometimes the indoctrination is successful, and there is evidence that children tend to be like their parents socially and politically. Sometimes it has a reverse effect; the child of an ultraconservative parent becomes a radical. This common phenomenon may be explained in terms of what social psychologists call "reference group theory."

Reference groups

No one is an island. Most of your ties, commitments, aspirations, and goals are related to other people in one way or another. You identify yourself with a lot of different groups of people—your family, your friends, organizations you join, etc. Some of these groups matter more than others in your life. Some may influence you more than others because you have a higher desire to belong, or have an especially great admiration for members you want to emulate. Reference groups are those groups to which you relate yourself as a member, or with which you identify, or to

It is important to identify with, to aspire to be like, and to belong to reference groups so that support can be given for goals, aspirations, standards, and achievements. (© Reuters/Bettmann)

which you aspire to belong, or to which you attach yourself either physically or psychologically.

Reference groups are the source of your goals, aspirations, standards, and criteria for judging how you are doing. You use them to check on yourself and to evaluate your successes and failures.

In our complex society, in your busy life, you have many reference groups—not just one—and in each you have a special role to follow. Later, in Chapter 7, you will meet Jackson, the man in the middle. He is a father, a husband, an employee, a boss, a golf partner, a member of a church committee, and many other things. In only some of these reference groups does he play the same kinds of roles.

Although not all the reference groups to which you belong or with which you identify will demand that you change how you act, there are often conflicting demands as you move from one reference group to another, paying attention to how you are to perform in each group. The multiple values of your multiple memberships may sometimes be incompatible. Usually the group with whom you most deeply identify will be the most successful in shaping your values and in influencing your behaviors.

Role models

A commonly used term to describe people from whom others get their attitudes and values is "role model." What this implies is that the roles you take in your interpersonal transactions are patterned after others you have seen behaving or speaking in certain ways. You watch these others—people whom you perceive to be like yourself, or people you admire or

Role models are often chosen from public figures. *(© Rafael Macia/Photo Researchers)*

want to be like. What they wear, you want to wear. How they talk, you will talk. What they seem to believe in, you will believe in. What they dislike, you will also want to dislike. You may take for your role models such persons as teachers, parents, friends, stars in show business, or leaders in business or government. Sports and entertainment figures are role models for many young people, not just in how to play a sport or perform on stage, but in the way they conduct their lives. Much attention is given to the influence on young men and women when a prominent athlete or entertainer uses drugs or speaks out against drug abuse, or adopts a nontraditional lifestyle.

Stabilization

Once an attitude is formed, several factors are influential in keeping it stabilized. Many of you resist change and expose yourselves only selectively to new information (for example, when you read a paper which reflects your political, social, and economic views or listen to a political candidate you like and plan to vote for).

People actively seek reinforcement and get involved in those situations which they consciously or unconsciously believe will reinforce their beliefs, attitudes, and values. This has important implications for your interpersonal communication. You tend to seek people whom you think hold beliefs, attitudes, and values similar to yours. You choose to stay away from those people whom you think differ too much from you.

If you cannot avoid exposure to opposing views, you listen only selectively and thus hear only those things which confirm beliefs you already have; sometimes you may not even become aware that opposing views are being stated. If you pay attention to information from your world in relation to your predispositions—your presets, or your ways of looking at the world—and if you tend to avoid uncomfortable situations which attack your attitudes, then perhaps your selection of television programs is a significant factor in your continued drive for support for your attitudes, values, and beliefs.

Related Theories

As we pointed out earlier, a person can hold many different attitudes, beliefs, and values, and it is quite common for some of them to be in conflict with each other. A group of classical psychological theories[16] called the "consistency theories" (or "balance theory," "dissonance theory," and "congruity theory") deal with this phenomenon. These theories say (1) that people need consistency among their values, beliefs, and attitudes, (2) that the awareness of inconsistencies will produce tensions, and (3) that they will usually do something to reduce the tensions.

In his theory of cognitive dissonance, Leon Festinger refers to the same ideas when he states that (1) the existence of dissonance (inconsistency) will motivate people to attempt to reduce it to reestablish consonance (consistency) and that (2) when dissonance is present, people will, in addition to reducing it, actively avoid situations or information likely to increase it.[17] According to Festinger, two major factors account for the occurrrence of dissonance: (1) new events or information may create dissonance between what a person does and what a person "knows" or believes, or between two opposite beliefs, and (2) few things are black-and-white and clear-cut, and so most opinions or behaviors are likely to be to some extent a mixture of contradictions.

An example of a dissonance-producing situation is finding out that a close friend whose opinion you respect is politically engaged in a cause you despise. The two facts clash: the person is a close friend whose opinion you respect, yet your friend is supporting a despicable (in your eyes) cause. The clash will probably arouse some tension in you which you will try to reduce in some way. Dissonance might also occur when you get a low grade from a professor you admire and for whom you worked very hard or when you buy a stereo and find out later that it was considerably cheaper in another store.

Reduction of dissonance

You seek to reduce the tension generated by dissonant situations by use of several "strategies." If you hold two conflicting values or beliefs, you will tend to reduce the dissonance created by conflicting information by changing one of the two beliefs, generally the less salient belief or the one with less intensity. Let us say, for example, that you believe that cigarette smoking is really not harmful and you read a very convincing medical document giving ample evidence to the contrary. If your initial belief in the harmlessness of smoking is very strong, chances are you will reject the medical document.

This rejection may take several forms. You may (1) belittle the source (they don't know what they are talking about; they don't really have enough evidence), (2) accuse the source of dishonesty or bias (that's just propaganda), (3) find new information which fits the belief you do not want to change (I read another report that said just the opposite), or (4) escape psychologically or physically (when you realize that the report goes against what you believe in, you do not finish it, or you skim it in such a way that not much of it will create an impression).

Take the example of your highly respected friend whom you found supporting a political cause you despise. To reduce dissonance you can use one of several strategies. You can mentally change one or the other of the two conflicting elements, the friend or the political cause. If you choose to change the friend, you may decide that this person was really not respectable and admirable after all, and you were pretty dumb to have been fooled, and you no longer wish to be friends. Consonance is then reestablished. You now have a person you do not care for working for a cause you do not care for.

Most of these strategies are based on *rationalizations*. People have, unfortunately, a great capacity to fool themselves, willingly or unwillingly. You very often believe what you tell yourself simply because you want to believe it so badly. No harm is done when you tell yourself accurate things. Rationalization, however, always involves an element of self-deception. When you depend on this strategy too often, you run the risk of not being very much in phase with reality.

Resistance to change   Reduction of dissonance does not always involve rationalization strategies. There are times when you will simply change the behavior. For example, if you smoke and find out that smoking is dangerous and may lead to severe health problems, you may simply reduce the dissonance by quitting smoking.

However, it is never easy to change a behavior, an attitude, a belief, or a value. You tend to resist change because change is always difficult. You often regard change with mixed emotions. You usually feel more confident toward something you know well because you know how to perform. You also know what rewards you can get and how to avoid unpleasantness. Change occurs each time a new situation presents itself: it may be starting a new job, moving, going to a new school, joining a new organization, meeting new people, or being exposed to new ideas.

Change *does* have many positive aspects: doing new things is exciting. It is a relief from boredom, an adventure, an opportunity to make new dreams. However, the risks are great because change always represents the unknown. You fear what you do not know well and tend to hang on to the familiar.

Social judgment theory

In discussing attitude change, Sherif and others claim that your attitudes are best represented by a three-part continuum, or a range of responses divided roughly into three kinds.[18] The first range is your *latitude of acceptance,* which includes the various positions or ideas about an issue you are ready to accept or agree with. Along the continuum, the next area would be your *latitude of noncommitment,* which includes the range of positions about the same issue on which you are either undecided or neutral. Finally, at the other end of the continuum is your *latitude of rejection,* which includes all those known positions on the same issue which you find unacceptable. For any idea or issue you may confront, the continuum would look something like Figure 5-1.

According to this theory,[19] if you hear a communication message which falls within or slightly out of your latitude of acceptance, you will tend to perceive it as closer to your own position than it really is. This is called the *assimilation effect* (Figure 5-2). As a result of assimilation, your latitude of acceptance expands a little.

On the other hand, if you hear a message which falls in your area of rejection, you will tend to experience it even further from your position than it really is. This *contrast effect* (Figure 5-3) might even lead to a *boomerang effect,* which consists of shrinking your acceptance area in such a way that positions which might have been acceptable or tolerated before will be definitely rejected.

How these effects operate in our communicative lives can be illustrated by a person who is, say, a Presbyterian. The rituals and the dogma of the Presbyterian church are a strong part of this person's acceptance area (latitude of acceptance). Other Protestant denominations are likely to be in this person's latitude of noncommitment. In this person's latitude of rejection are likely to be Islam, possibly Roman Catholicism, and certainly atheism. If this person hears something about another Protestant church activity, it will probably be considered positively because such denominations are close to Presbyterianism (demonstrating the assimilation effect). On the other hand, a message about atheism will pull the reaction further away from any neutral possibility, demonstrating the contrast effect. This person is likely to think more positively about other Protestant messages (assimilation) and more negatively about atheistic messages (contrast) than the messages really deserve.

Another example might involve two persons with distinctly different attitudes about marijuana—one in favor of it, the other opposed. They both read the same research report on the effects of smoking marijuana.

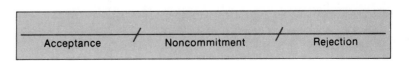

FIGURE 5-1
Attitude continuum.

FIGURE 5-2
Assimilation effect: A communication message falls in the "latitude of noncommitment" near the "acceptance" area; the "latitude of acceptance" moves over to take in the new material and enlarges the "latitude of acceptance" on this issue.

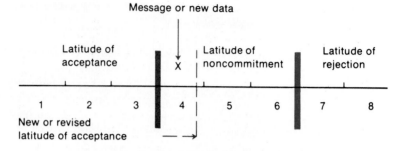

In the report are tentative findings that dangers may exist with prolonged use, and other findings that occasional use has not been demonstrated to be immediately harmful by itself. Each of the readers will tend to perceive these messages in terms of what he or she already believes, as we have discovered in earlier chapters. The readers also will have their attitudes involved either by assimilation (reading the mildly supportive messages as being more strongly supportive to either argument) or by contrast (reading the messages as being more divergent from original beliefs when they mildly disagree with the original positions held). What happens in many cases like this is that the person who starts reading an article will end up with previously held beliefs soundly reinforced because the reader can either exaggerate the strength of the supporting messages or downgrade the effects of the disagreeing ones.

Implications for Communication

Who you think you are is largely determined by the reactions you get from other people to what you do. Your choices to do or not to do certain things, as well as other people's reactions, are heavily influenced by how you define social situations which you encounter. These definitions in turn come from the values and beliefs you share with people and develop through interpersonal communication.

So you come full circle. It is by interacting and communicating with others that you make decisions about what is good and bad, about what

FIGURE 5-3
Contrast effect (boomerang effect as a "latitude of acceptance" shrinks): A communication message falls in "latitude of rejection." It is perceived as more discrepant—more different—from the original ideas held and may under some circumstances actually narrow the person's "latitude of acceptance" on that issue if the message is threatening or strong enough.

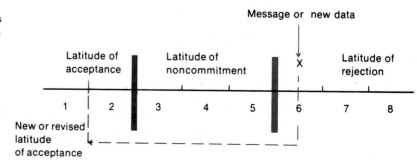

> **BOX 5-3. The Power of Tradition**
>
> A young bride cooked a ham for the first time and cut off both ends before putting it in the pan. Her husband was surprised but said nothing. When she served ham a second time and both ends of the ham were cut off again, he asked why she did this and she answered that her mother always did it that way. The next time he saw his mother-in-law, the young man asked her why she cut off both ends of the ham before cooking it. She answered that she did not know, but *her* mother always did it that way. When the grandmother was asked why she cut the ends off the ham, she answered plainly, "Oh, because my pan was too small."
>
> And so it is with many of your uninspected values and beliefs. You believe certain things and act a certain way simply because your mothers, or fathers, or teachers, or friends believe and act that way. Perhaps they have a realistic reason to act the way they do, as the grandmother did when her pan was not big enough. But when life situations change and old beliefs and values are kept indiscriminately, you may end up cutting off the ends of a ham for no good reason at all.

is beautiful and ugly, about what type of toothpaste is best for preventing cavities. In turn, these value decisions affect how you define social situations, what you expect from other people, what you think they expect of you, and finally how you choose to act.

Your attitudes, values, and beliefs need to be inspected often, since they affect so much of what you do and so much of what you are.

It is important for you to know what you value and believe in, how you came to hold these values and beliefs, whether they are adequate for your life situations now, and how congruent they are with what you say and what you do.

SUMMARY

People are motivated by a variety of needs. Although these needs—as well as your beliefs, attitudes, and values—cannot be seen or touched, they are often displayed by your actions or behaviors. From a set of needs you figure out what system or sequence of activities will satisfy them. Then your inner motivations are clarified and organized in your system of beliefs, attitudes, and values, which are largely developed through your interpersonal communication.

Beliefs represent how you view your world, what you think is true, what you agree with. Attitudes reflect your tendencies to respond to things in certain ways, a tendency to act on your beliefs. Your values are your conceptions of the relative worth that you attribute to things, events, or people in your world and their goodness and badness.

You learn your beliefs, attitudes, and values from others, particularly your "reference groups." Such reference groups consist of people whom you admire, like, and identify with, and whom you use as your source or models for your goals and aspirations, and ultimately your behaviors.

You may experience situations when one set of your beliefs or attitudes or values may be challenged by competing ideas. You experience dissonance, or the disquieting feeling that you have to choose between opposites. You may cope with such discomfort by rationalizing strategies or by changing your beliefs or your attitudes or values to make them fit new situations. Change is very difficult, however, and there seem to be more forces acting to make us stay the same than to help us change.

Transactions are where your needs, as well as your beliefs, attitudes, and values, are demonstrated. You are involved in transactions (1) when you take each other into account, (2) when you differentiate your role relationships, and (3) when you conduct your interactions by rules and a continuing awareness of others. Roles are made up of collections of relationships or transactions and are defined by your responses to the situation around you, to others, and to your own needs.

END NOTES

[1] Abraham Maslow, *Motivation and Personality,* Harper & Brothers, New York, 1970.

[2] Frederick Herzberg, *Work and the Nature of Man,* Collins, New York, 1966. And by the same author, "One More Time: How Do You Motivate Employees?", *Harvard Business Review,* vol. 46, 1968, pp. 53–62. *The Managerial Choice,* Olympus Publishing, Salt Lake City, UT, 1982; and with others, *The Motivation to Work,* 2d ed., Books on Demand, Ann Arbor, MI, University Microfilm International.

[3] S. C. Lundin, L. C. Lancaster, and J. W. Gardner, "The Importance of Followership," *The Futurist,* vol. 24, May–June 1990, p. 18.

[4] H. L. Petri, *Motivation: Theory and Research,* Wadsworth, Belmont, CA, 1986.

[5] William Schutz and Marilyn Wood, *FIRO-B Test,* is currently available from Consulting Psychologists Press, 577 College Ave., Palo Alto, CA, 94306. This and other versions of FIRO have tests for ages 4–8, 9–16, and adults and have extensive normative data.

[6] William Schutz, *The Interpersonal Underworld,* Science Behavior Books, Palo Alto, CA, 1966; originally published as *FIRO, A Three-Dimensional Theory of Interpersonal Behavior,* by Holt, Rinehart and Winston, New York, 1960. See also by the same author, *Joy: Expanded Human Awareness,* Irvington, New York, 1981; *Joy: Twenty Years Later,* Ten Speed Press, Berkeley, CA, 1989; *Elements of Encounter,* Irvington, New York, 1982; *Here Comes Everybody,* Irvington, New York, 1982.

[7] Schutz, *The Interpersonal Underworld,* p. 66.

[8] Ibid., p. 82.

[9] Ibid., p. 73.

[10] Dean Barnlund, *Communicative Styles of Japanese and Americans: Images and Realities,* Wadsworth, Belmont, CA, 1989, p. 83.

[11] Barlund, p. 115.

[12] Preliminary research conducted under the auspices of Institut de la Dominance, Paris, France, 1990.

[13] Schutz, *The Interpersonal Underworld,* pp. 15, 106.

[14] Everett M. Rogers, *Diffusion of Innovation,* 3d ed., Free Press, New York, 1983.

[15] ———, *Social Change in Rural Societies,* Prentice-Hall, Englewood Cliffs, NJ, 1988.

[16] F. Heider, *The Psychology of Interpersonal Relations,* John Wiley & Sons, New York, 1982. T. M. Newcomb, "An Approach to the Study of Communicative Acts," *Psychological Review,* vol. 60, 1953, pp. 394–404. P. Lecky, *Self-Consistency: A Theory of Personality,* Shoe String Press, New York, 1961. C. Osgood and P. H. Tannenbaum, "The Principle of Congruity in the Prediction of Attitude Change," *Psychological Review,* vol. 62, 1955, pp. 42–56.

[17] L. Festinger, *A Theory of Cognitive Dissonance,* Row, Peterson, Evanston, IL, 1967. See also, D. O'Keefe, *Persuasion,* Sage Publications, Newbury Park, CA, 1990, chap. 40.

[18] C. W. Sherif, *Attitude and Attitude Change,* Greenwood Press, Westport, CT, 1982.

[19] O'Keefe, op. cit., chap. 2.

CHAPTER
6

LISTENING: IS ANYBODY OUT THERE?

OBJECTIVES

When you have completed this chapter you should be able to:

1. Compare and contrast hearing and listening, citing at least three specific ways in which people may confuse the two.
2. State three myths about listening and indicate the ways people may behave which tend to perpetuate these myths.
3. List and explain at least four ways in which listening skills can be improved.
4. Define "attentiveness" in relation to listening behavior.
5. List and explain the four interpersonal types of listening described in this chapter.
6. Describe the relationship between assessment and training in listening skills.
7. Give examples of the factors for more effective listening in the categories of time, content, and psychology.
8. With practice in the use of listening exercises outlined in the Laboratory Manual's Chapter 6, demonstrate an understanding and skill in the process of active listening. (See page 381).

INTRODUCTION

When messages get misunderstood between people, whose fault is it—the speaker or the listener? The person speaking often will blame the person listening: "You didn't pay attention to what I told you"—while the listener argues, "You were not clear."

Have you ever missed an appointment, or bought the wrong item at the store for a friend, or arrived an hour early or an hour late, or not gotten an assignment in for a class—simply because you had not listened to some information you needed? All of us experience some problems with our listening communication, and if we are to believe parents, teachers, business executives, and well-intentioned friends, we really don't listen very well when they try to talk to us. So what's the big deal if almost everybody has trouble listening?

A noted mathematician, Norbert Wiener, bothered by the inefficiency of human communication and the wasted hours and resources, had this to say about interpersonal responsibility: "Speech is a joint game between the talker and the listener against the forces of confusion."[1]

In this chapter we will describe, analyze, and present some suggested antidotes for those "forces of confusion"; we'd like them to be minimized for the interpersonal listener.

THE CHALLENGE

Presenting clear data and giving accurate instructions are so strongly emphasized in our writing and speaking that we need to make a case for effective listening. Although listening may be one of the earliest forms of communication a baby develops, it is probably the last communication skill to be taught in any formal way. For the first sixteen years or so of your education, the communication skills of reading and writing were formally taught and strongly emphasized. Maybe during that time you had a course in speaking; but it is rare to find any students entering college today who have had as much as a single course in listening.

Because so much education depends on a teacher talking and a student's listening, it seems necessary to devote considerable attention to listening as a help in learning. According to Rebecca Rubin, "Too often students do not listen well enough to identify the main ideas in a class lecture or to understand the material presented in class. Too often students do not understand the directions for assignments given orally, let alone the expected performance standards."[2]

If that lack of ability to listen to directions or implied standards is important in classes, is it any less important in our personal contacts or on the job? Is listening for learning any more important than listening for working? We may be too late. Business organizations, industrial and public agencies, and many corporate groups are now emphasizing the need for listening skills in their employees and leaders. As they bemoan the fact that people cannot listen well, they also place most of the blame on the educational institutions where the skill and art of listening has historically been neglected if not ignored.

At least part of the problem comes from a very narrow definition of listening, in which people concern themselves with getting only data or content. Speakers, teachers, and order-givers assume that "anybody with two good ears can listen" and that the listener will then know all they hoped to convey with their words and inflections. Listening is a major ingredient in the communication process, and the unrecognized lack of skill in that area is primarily responsible for many of the problems you may experience in your interpersonal relations with others.

All of you want to be listened to and understood. Otherwise, you feel you are not worth much, since people don't even think enough of you to take the time to listen to you. What do you hear most people complain about? Not being listened to. "I can't talk to my parents; they never listen." Or, "I am quitting this job; my boss never listens to anything I say; it's as if I didn't exist." Or, "When we are together, I talk a lot but it seems you don't listen most of the time."

To listen actively to another human being may be the greatest gift you can give. The power to listen is a remarkably sensitive skill, perhaps the greatest talent of the human race. It is certainly the skill that makes interpersonal communication truly effective and rewarding for all participants.

The ways you choose to listen can influence others. How you listen may well determine how others will listen to you. For that reason, listening is truly a transactional process.

LIMITS OF LISTENING

A pioneering study by Paul Rankin[3] during the early years of listening research gave us some statistics which have been quoted and frequently retested with various but usually similar results. He reported that about 70 percent of your waking day is spent in communication and of that amount about 45 percent is spent listening. Another 30 percent is spent speaking, about 16 percent of your communication time is spent reading, and only about 9 percent of your time writing. (Various other studies show that we learn about 85 percent of all we know by listening.) Executives questioned about their time report consistently that they spend 80 percent of their working time in meetings, on the phone, or in face-to-face interactions; and most workers spend about 60 percent of their workday listening.[4] As future audio and oral technologies are enhanced or developed—miniature and more portable telephones, low-power radio, interactive cable and broadcast television, cellular telephones, laser tape cassettes, voice-activated computer systems for electronic mail—you may find yourself constantly decreasing the time you spend writing or reading.

How Bad Are We?

A few more statistics will give you an idea of the extent of our listening difficulties. For years Ralph Nichols and his associates[5] conducted many intensive studies at the University of Minnesota to test the ability of people to understand and remember what they hear. The listening ability of thousands of students and hundreds of business and professional people was examined. In each case the subjects listened to a short talk and were later tested on their grasp of the content. These studies led to the following conclusions:

1. Immediately after people have listened to someone talk, they tend to remember only about half of what they heard—no matter how hard they thought they were listening.
2. The University of Minnesota studies, confirmed by other classic studies at Florida State and Michigan State Universities,[6] showed that two months later people will remember only 25 percent of what was said. In fact, people tend to forget one-third to one-half of what they hear within eight hours.

What these data mean is that whenever you listen to someone talk, you are likely to miss about half of what a person tells you, and two months later you will remember only one-fourth of what was said. When you consider all the time you spend being talked to, and all the energy you spend trying to remember things you are told, it seems the whole thing is a pathetic waste of time.

However, before we give up on becoming effective listeners, we should (1) explore some reasons why the skill is so poorly developed, (2) develop a deeper understanding of some identifiable types of interpersonal listening, and finally, (3) come up with some ways to listen better.

Some Causes of Poor Listening

There are many complex reasons for poor listening. Often you deliberately tune someone out because you don't like the person, or because you are bored or simply tired. However, many times your poor performance as a

Listening as a job requirement: "I said, 'Are you a good listener?' "
(© Parade Magazine, 1991)

listener may be involuntary. To gain more insight into the reasons for poor listening, let's explore three myths which are quite generally known, are also generally in error, and which have obscured an understanding of the listening process.

Myth 1—Listening is a natural process

If you believe that listening occurs naturally, like breathing, then it follows that you never need to learn how to do it. Nobody had to teach you to breathe, so what's so special about listening? You did your breathing on your own, soon as you were born. You also heard noises and started making some sense out of them at a very early stage. Of course, if you want to excel as a singer or long-distance runner, your breathing could undergo some extra training, in spite of its being a "natural" process. But too often we simply take for granted that listening is a "natural" process and do not consider any ways we can make it better. You will never learn what you think you already know. If you believe something is inborn, natural, automatic, then there is not much you believe you can or want to do about it.

Myth 2—Listening is the same as hearing

Although the relationship between hearing and listening is a complex one, and despite the fact that it is sometimes difficult to distinguish between them, hearing and listening are generally two distinct processes. Too often you treat them as the same. You do this when you assume that just because you have uttered some words in front of someone else—made hearable noises—that the other person will know and remember what you said. The fact that the other person was awake and not deaf gives you extra confidence that he or she listened to what you said.

Look around a class during a lecture. Does the fact that the teacher makes noises that are in the proper language, at the proper loudness, in some sort of sequence, give any assurance that the lecture is being listened to and retained, even until the next exam? Hearing is a more natural process (see myth 1, above). Provided an undamaged auditory system is functioning, you cannot help attending to the sounds which come to you at certain frequencies and intensities. But you can avoid *listening* whenever you want to. You can tune out the speaker any time, at will. Listening is a higher cognitive process, under your control. If you are more interested in other classroom noises than a course lecture, you can select the lecture out. You can daydream. You can worry about a sick or absent friend. You can plan your weekend.

Part of the problem is simply the speed at which people can talk compared with the speed with which you can listen. The average rate of speech for the standard American has been estimated at about 125 words per minute. That is slow going for the human brain which can process, with its 13 billion cells, about 800 words per minute. The difference between speaking rate and thinking rate means your brain can handle hundreds of words in addition to those you are hearing. It means your

Lectures may not always be listened to and retained even until the next exam. (© *Susan Lapides/Design Conceptions)*

brain will continue to think in high speed while the spoken words arrive in slow motion. (It is like your impatient computer humming away thousands of bits faster than you can hunt-and-peck your way into a word processor.) You can listen and still have some spare time for your own thinking. Your use or misuse of that spare time holds the key to how well you listen.

Myth 3—*Listening is the same as "paying attention"*

It is not enough to just listen. You need to be perceived by others as listening to them in order to have effective interpersonal communication. In other words, the speaker needs some indications from you that you are actually listening.[7] On the other hand, pretending to pay attention while their mind drifts off is a highly developed skill in some people, and it misleads the speaker into thinking there is a communication transaction taking place. The quality of paying attention is referred to as "attentiveness" in an early analysis of communication style[8] which demonstrated how this factor adds to the effectiveness of a person as a communicator. At least it improves how you may be seen as a communicator. The possible danger is that you work so hard at being attentive that you may talk little in social situations, or at work, and that is a sign to many people that you are low in leadership potential or power. In general, however, the practice of "appearing to listen" may be as important as listening itself.

An attentive style of communication involves, obviously, both sending and receiving messages—you let the other person know, usually by talking and adding data or your own examples, that you are following actively.

An attentive style of
communication involves
letting the other person know
that you are following
actively. (© *Reuters/
Bettmann*)

(See the section on Feedback in Chapter 11.) In that way, attentiveness
is not only listening behavior in the strictest sense; it may involve actions,
nonverbal clues, and speaking as well. Attention or attentiveness need
not always be positive or supportive. You can listen critically, suspiciously,
negatively, unfeelingly, hostilely, or judgmentally, and still exhibit the qualities of attention.

DEFINING AND STUDYING LISTENING

As a relatively new subject for study, listening is beginning to have a strong
following of professionals whose business it is to research and instruct in
this field. Membership in listening professional groups is very diverse—
including such wide-ranging interests as academics, industrialists, counselors, public servants, and business leaders. Part of the diversity of interest
in listening is reflected in the difficulty of framing a very precise definition.
As we learn more about how listening occurs, we need to include more
considerations in whatever explicit definition we hope fits all the new
dynamics which seem to be involved.

BOX 6-1. Attentive Listening

Habits of working with other people clearly have led most of us to believe, even if it isn't always true, that if the other person is really paying attention, you will get agreement. When you don't get agreement, you may want to blame it on listening rather than on differences of opinion, bad arguments, competing resources, or other factors. The incidents below—both related to the principle of attentive listening sometimes being mistaken for tacit agreement—actually happened to one of the authors.

> *A student came to my office with a long list of reasons why he should not take the final exam. At the end of the discussion, I refused the request, although I made notes and could recite back each argument and his reasons. He later reported to a friend that I didn't listen to him. On the other side, I went to the office of a dean and asked for support for a project. In detail I described the advantages and the minimal costs involved. The dean, after going carefully over my proposal and spending an hour asking clear questions, said no. Later I caught myself in a conversation with another faculty member saying that I had an excellent proposal but the dean didn't listen.*

Some Background on Listening Study

Reseachers have been studying listening in a serious way for only a little more than half a century. Up until 1978 the federal educational guidelines for "basic skills" to be taught in the elementary and secondary schools listed only math, reading, and writing. The public law (P.L. 95-561) that year included speaking and listening for the first time. That did not mean any state was ordered to have such courses in its schools, but it did say such programs would be included for federal funding, and all states were encouraged to set their goals for teaching oral communication skills. One researcher[9] found that very few programs had been implemented and that even where there were good curricula developed in speaking and listening, these tended to be poorly handled in the classrooms.

In 1979 the International Listening Association was formed to bring together teachers at all school and college levels, businesspeople, consultants, counselors, and publishers—virtually any professional who had an interest in furthering listening teaching and research. The first issue of this organization's professional publication, *Journal of the International Listening Association,* appeared in March 1987.

Developing a Definition

Listening is generally considered to consist not only of hearing, but to include the added dimensions of understanding, paying overt attention, analyzing and evaluating the spoken messages, and possibly acting on the basis of what has been heard. The higher cognitive function (thinking) involved in listening is becoming more a subject of research as definitions have moved away from the overly simple mechanical signal-response ideas of the past.[10]

Developing *the final* definition of listening is likely to occur in the future,[11] although there are many working definitions which we use today. Here are two slightly different definitions which relate to both the semantic and interpersonal nature of listening behavior:

"[Listening is] the process by which spoken language is converted to meaning in the mind."[12]

"In a general sense, listening may be defined as *a receiver orientation to the communication process:* since communication involves *both* a source and a receiver, listening consists of the roles receivers play in the communication process."[13]

Those roles support the transactional view of communication as the interaction of words, meanings, intentions, motives, response, comes into play. The listener not only comprehends the meanings of the words, but may also infer the purposes of a speaker as well as the main points and details in the messages. Listening usually will include some consideration of the ability to retain, to report back, to summarize, if only by use of "short-term memory" for some information and longer-term memory for other. Understanding of complex ideas may not come to a listener without some delay or deliberation, or putting one set of ideas together with another—class lectures may be examples of such accumulated understanding as the students listen to explanations by a teacher and gradually come to a different level of awareness. A little-emphasized part of listening consists of spotting the hidden as well as obvious reasons a person is speaking, the persuasive devices used, and awareness of the relation between a speaker's motives and methods.

HOW WE DO IT: LISTENING TYPES

One of the problems in defining listening is that it is so variable, depending on purposes, needs, and motives of speakers and listeners; the communication setting; the dynamics of the changing situation; and the interaction of such qualities as age, gender,[14] cultural background,[15] self-concept, training, cognitive abilities, and physical and mental state.[16]

Some Listening Classification Options

It seems a reasonable approach to listening study that we look at the way listening happens as a communication transaction. It involves what is listened to, by whom, and for what purpose. Kinds of listening have been variously described, including one sample taxonomy which describes the following five different kinds: (1) appreciative listening, for enjoyment or some sensory impression, (2) discriminative listening, usually to analyze arguments and distinguish facts from opinion, (3) comprehensive listening to understand a message, (4) therapeutic listening, done formally to a

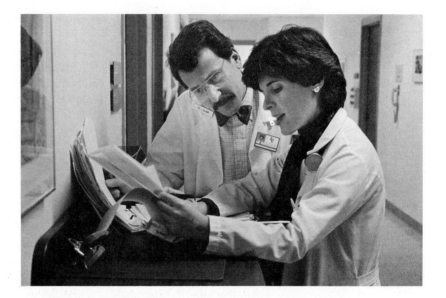

By listening discriminately, you can help to analyze arguments and distinguish between factual data and opinions. (© Ulrike Welsch/ Photo Researchers)

client or patient in counseling or informally to friends, (5) critical listening, in which you evaluate and then accept or reject a message.[17]

Cognitive processing

Still another way to classify listening is to focus on the mental processes used in listening, applying a model which includes three levels.[18] The first level, signal processing, involves being able to understand the language being spoken and hearing it in a reasonably clear manner. The next level, literal processing, involves your understanding of what the words mean that are being used—what is expected of you as a result of the message. The third level, reflective processing, involves both appreciative and critical listening when the listener draws conclusions about the message and about the speaker and his or her intentions and purposes and methods. While these levels engage different responses in a listener, they may be carried on simultaneously if you concentrate on different parts of the messages. Recognition of these levels will help you understand your own responses as you listen.

Memory or recall

An extension of cognitive processing involves remembering. "Most of us would agree that it makes little sense to hear, attend to, or comprehend oral discourse unless we remember it or use it in some way."[19] Listening effectiveness in classes, in personal relations, or in business has often been measured by how much you can remember of a message—either for immediate response (to act on instructions or orders like "phone Jim at 487-0580") or for longer-term recall as in class learning for later testing, or by how well you can interpret, or put together and recall, ideas you have heard at different times. Although there have been some indications that these kinds of memory tasks are related to intelligence, it is clear that there are additional important factors such as motivation, interest, selection, experience, habit, distractions, etc. to be considered.

Four Interpersonal Types of Listening

We will take an original approach in this book by looking at listening in relation to four types of internal/external responses to spoken messages. They range from very casual, almost accidental, responses, to very deliberative and purposive types of response. These are not stages to go through in some kind of order, nor are they sequences which must be followed. All or only a few of these types may occur within one set of listening transactions; or they may be skipped or types may be applied in any sequence. The emphasis in this typology is, of course, on interpersonal relations since that is the focus of this book and your present study.

Reflex listening (type I)

A very basic kind of listening involving little more than hearing and a recognition that some noise has come to you. A car honks behind you, and you jump out of the way. You are watching a television program and someone next to you comments on the program, something like "That was not very funny..." and you nod, without really being involved enough to agree or disagree. You hear the street noises as you study at night, and may notice without caring that a motor scooter putt-putted past. You are engaged in small talk at a party with someone you scarcely know, and from across the room a friend calls your name. A friend asks you to order pizza and recites the phone number which you then quickly dial without much worry about the content of the seven digits.

In some ways this type of reflex listening is almost subliminal, that is, below your present level of consciousness. Although you do have a recollection later that a motor scooter went by, that somebody commented on the television show, that you were doing party-talk with someone before your friend called you, and that you dialed a phone number as your friend read it off to you. When you put your listening on "automatic pilot," it does not mean nothing is happening—you may be engaging in an interpersonal transaction with others, but at a very low level of involvement.

Because you can listen faster than people can talk to you, as we mentioned earlier, it is possible to appear to be taking in the conversation while you simply fade in and out, getting enough cues so you can appear to be attentive. Reflex listening is very common in social settings, in classrooms, in public lectures, in concerts, and provides opportunity to daydream, build castles in the air, have reveries, all without being caught. In face-to-face conversation, however, it is considered less than helpful.[20] In summary, reflex listening involves primarily "guidance" noises where you can move out of danger, approach and engage prospective pleasant experiences, but stay tuned to hear other important messages should they occur.

Content listening (type II)

This type of listening is the one most frequently referred to when teachers and managers criticize "poor listening." Most research and training in listening has historically involved the reception of information and its retention, giving prizes for being able to recall data at some future time.

"Listening is the most basic communication skill and undergirds all learning processes because it is the primary channel of classroom instruction throughout all educational levels. . . . People can . . . develop listening skills in ways similar to learning mathematics, physical education, reading and writing. They can communicate more accurately, with positive attitudes, to gain useful information, and to improve understanding."[21]

Learning in school, receiving instructions on the job, getting information about what to do and how to run your life, are all involved in this content level. Emphasis in this type is on the acquisition and persistence of data. You listen to learn and to understand and to somehow retain information. You may be tested on it later.

An important dimension of content-type listening is an ability to detect which messages are accurate, useful, sound, truthful, reliable, and relevant. When a person is trying to convince you with content arguments or persuasion, it is well to listen carefully by putting the new data against what you already know or believe. It is never simply a matter of your processing the information given you. Consider how you put data into a computer. Even a computer has an operating system which will tell it if the incoming messages are reliable or appropriate for the purposes intended. In the case of your listening to messages, it is helpful to have your own "system" for deciding if the new information has qualities you can accept.[22]

Research has shown that children as well as adults can be taught to ask questions when information is incomplete ("I'm not sure I understood what you said" or "Can you tell me more about that?" or "I think I may have missed something; would you run that by me again, please?"). They also can learn to detect incomplete information and seek the additional data necessary for good listening habits.[23]

Relational listening (type III)

Listening is important not only in relation to getting the content of the message, called "deliberative listening" (which we refer to under type II above) but also in another dimension called "empathic listening."[24] This empathic dimension to listening, which we are calling "relational," includes what the psychotherapist Carl Rogers and his associates named "active listening."[25] It has also been called "therapeutic listening,"[26] as well as "listening with the third ear."[27] This dimension goes beyond the psychiatrist's field to permeate all areas of interpersonal interaction; it is more than a skill to improve understanding and information processing. "Active

Relational listening involves the dimension of empathy and the giving to others of a sense that what they say is important enough to be listened to. (© Spencer Grant/The Picture Cube)

listening" reflects a whole orientation to life and to people—one which implies that to listen is to have the creative power to imagine how it would make sense to say what the other person is saying. It says that the other person (the speaker) is fundamentally important and worth listening to, worth giving some of your attention, energy, and time.

How do you "do" active listening? Very simply, you do it by listening to a person without passing judgment on what is being said, and mirroring back what has been said to indicate that you understand the feelings the speaker was putting across. However, the implications of this apparently simple procedure are tremendous. By withholding judgment and by showing that you understand the feelings of another person, you encourage that other person to say more; you tell that person there is no risk of being judged or found stupid, wrong, or silly. You remove the threat to the other, diminish the need to raise personal defenses. Effective communication is free to happen when threats have been removed. By the mirroring process, the active listening proponents claim, you help build a climate in which you can be accepting, noncritical, and nonmoralizing. People then feel safer.

What do you do when your speaker says, "I hate this class. The assignments are so stupid"? You can either answer from your own insides, as: "I think so too." Or you can mirror to help the speaker get at the source of trouble, as: "You're really upset about the class, I guess." The speaker wants more than empty agreement.

When your speaker says, "I'm worried about not being promoted this year . . ." you can tell the person what you think, as: "Why worry?

You know you're good. You'll get promoted." But that only denies the speaker an opportunity to get at a worry. Instead of denying or arguing with the speaker's concerns, you might empathically focus on the speaker's feelings by reflecting, as: "Something happened at work that bothers you?"

Some practitioners have been criticized for the way they use active listening. Done badly, it can appear to be manipulative and not really in the best interests of the speaker who is led on by a counselor or friend to disclose more than is helpful. Other detractors say that the active listener may sometimes withhold helpful advice, honestly sought and needed by a speaker, in the listener's zeal for holding rigidly to only reflecting or mirroring the speaker's feelings.

Focus in type III is on helping the speakers work out their own problems by grasping as fully as possible the facts and feelings the listener hears, according to Rogers and Farson.[28] The purpose of active, empathic, or therapeutic listening is to help other people to express their true feelings and, consequently, to solve their own problems. It is listening that places strong demands on listeners, as they must strive to assume a helping attitude, acting as a sounding board for others.[29]

Introspective listening (type IV)

Focus in this type of listening is on having something happen to the *listener*, not to the speaker as in type III. It may be the inner enjoyment of hearing poetry or music or spoken endearments. You *experience* something when you listen introspectively. You may be listening to a very persuasive speaker advocating some cause which you have little or no interest in; gradually as you listen you come to change your mind and become converted. You listen to the interracial, intergenerational, international, or cross-cultural messages from excluded minorities or oppressed others with a highly developed attention to understand and react sensitively.

In type III active listening (above) you are concerned with helping another develop greater insights; however, in introspective listening you are inviting yourself to move beyond your own limits, to make new commitments, to involve yourself intellectually and emotionally. To do this is to risk being changed. To have an open mind while listening makes you vulnerable.

"Communication requires more than the successful performance of speech-acts; it requires, among other things, the capacity to be touched and moved by what one sees, and the capacity to listen carefully and with an open mind."[30]

Most of us have dearly held beliefs about such diverse things as morality, art, politics, religion, literature, culture, nutrition, or friendships. We tend to seek out messages and speakers to support—not to oppose— those beliefs. We seldom open up our listening when we are in the presence of opposing and threatening messages. We are more comfortable in familiar communicative territory.

We read news magazines whose politics agree with ours; we listen to music which has "meaning" to us and scoff at the "other" kind whether it is rock, rap, or classics. A national chain of convenience stores, bothered by teens loitering in large numbers in their parking lots and discouraging customers, decided to combat that congregating by loudly playing "elevator music" over loudspeakers. It worked, as the young people preferred to move out to mix where they did not have to listen to music they disliked.

Appreciation of any art form is a very personal matter, and attending art exhibits and listening to artists describe their work is much like attending political rallies or religious revivals: we most often go where we will hear beliefs or opinions that already agree with ours. In the *New York Times Book Review* a critic[31] wrote a review of three books of poetry, headlining the review with the plea "Will You Listen for a Minute?", and including a challenge to the potential readers: "All [these poets] take the reader aside for private communication, and who knows if the reader's life will be the same when they are done?"

"Consciousness raising" is a frequently used term to describe the possible experience of introspective listening. In campaigns against bigotry and attempts to develop wider social conscience in audiences, listeners are invited to open up their minds beyond their prior levels. The hope in such gatherings is that people will give themselves the chance to change their views and hence their behaviors. Neither listening for content (type II) nor listening for how the speakers are feeling (type III) has the dimension of self-involvement or personal commitment or conversion which is suggested by type IV listening.

As you approach listening with a very open mind, you also need to make judgments about which speakers make sense to you about how you want to run your life. Just as in type III listening you may help a speaker come to effective conclusions by mirroring back some messages, in type IV listening you should deliberately reflect back to yourself what your own needs and values are. Being introspective, therefore, does not mean being so pliant and agreeable that you will be taken in by every demagogue who makes an emotionally or intellectually persuasive speech to you. You don't have to fall for everything you hear just to prove you have an open mind.

"Just say 'no'" is a phrase in a campaign against drug use based on resistance to persuasive appeals, aimed at automatic rejection of the many arguments about belonging and peer pressure. By itself, that admonition may not be as effective as a very deep and self-centered understanding of the personal consequences of drug use.

Introspective listening, therefore, has the common quality of listening with a very open mind; but it also has the uncommon quality of your applying your own deep understanding of your personal commitments and of the persuasion process as you evaluate the speakers' messages.

LISTENING ASSESSMENT AND TRAINING

If listening is so important to our interpersonal communication, and so many people say we are not good at it, is there any way we can do it better? The answer is "Yes, you can do it better, but it takes work." It also takes a point of view on what it is you want to improve, and that calls for an interest in finding out where you are now with your listening. A limited amount of research has been conducted about success in school or on the job being related to listening ability. Teachers whose students do not seem to perform well in class may suspect that poor listening habits may be part of the problem; a study of organizational listening skills indicated that higher-level persons in the organizations were better listeners, and it is top management which seems to be most enthusiastic about teaching listening in corporations and other organizations.[32]

Assessment and Evaluation

A number of tests have been developed to test people's listening skills. Some are based on the need to pay attention in class or on the job, that is to help you listen-to-learn. Some are based on the idea that many factors interact in the listening process and the combination of those can be measured. Generally, however, the popular notion that people listen poorly has been given so much attention that both educational agencies and corporations have developed extensive training courses which do not specifically rely on testing to find out the listening shortcomings of participants. States which have tried to set up curricula on oral communication have found great difficulty in agreeing on assessment instruments—that is, they cannot seem to settle on how to define listening and therefore find out what listening problems there really are before they set out to correct them.[33] Even among listening scholars, there is not entire agreement on how to define the activity, so it is difficult to establish performance criteria for listening as a behavior. For that reason, it appears to be easier (and even quite acceptable) to set up programs to correct the implied poor listening habits than it is to actually measure the type and extent of the problem.

Training and Improvement of Listening

Concentration of listening training appears to be heavily both in education[34] and in business.[35] This is not surprising when you consider that the information delivery systems for both these areas is oral communication—lectures in classrooms at all academic levels, and orders, speeches, consultations, meetings, and "huddling" in the corporate and business settings. Among the many industrial applications of listening improvement, both Sperry and Xerox corporations have become associated with listening training for their personnel. You can subscribe to

training programs of all kinds which propose to help you list⟨
titles range from such straightforward names as "Listening Skil⟨
and Associates), "Cause for Listening" (Sperry Corporation), "⟨   ⟩gies
for Effective Listening" (Xerox Learning) to such titles as "Listening—The
Forgotten Skill," "How to Listen Powerfully," "Listening Made Easy,"
"Listening Your Way to Success."[36]

More Effective Listening

With or without training courses, the primary responsibility for improving
your listening is yours. No amount of reading and hearing about listening
will make you better, and simply taking a listening course is no guarantee
of listening success.

Listening is a skill, and as with any skill, practice is essential. Nobody
can do it for you. Listening well is hard work. Unless you are willing to
accept the difficult job of working at listening, your habits will not change.

What we can do in this following section is give you a composite of
the advice most often given in many of the resources we have cited
already. While each training program may have a slightly different approach, most of them consider three main categories of skills development:
(1) how to use your time more effectively while listening, (2) what to do
with the content and messages you listen to, and (3) what psychological
or personal barriers you put up for yourself.

Time factors

We earlier reminded you that you can listen much more rapidly than
speakers can talk. *Use your time more effectively:* Instead of going on
private sidetracks which have nothing to do with the topic being discussed,
think about what the other person is saying. *Think back:* What was said
before which did not seem to be clear to you and may need more data;
did you wait too long to ask for the speaker to explain something which
was confusing? *Think ahead:* Try to figure where the speaker is going and
what the next point will be. This may be easier with speakers who are
well organized and who present their points clearly. Most of us, though,
are not very precise and organized, and that makes more work for the
listener. So if you are really interested in what the person is telling you,
you may have to do a lot of the organizing yourself—and you have time
for it.

Content factors

Since so much of what we consider listening is a matter of getting information from one to another, the content of the messages becomes a very
important factor. *Focus on what the speaker is saying:* Most speakers,
particularly in informal conversations, tend to repeat themselves and often
go on tangents that may or may not be related to the topic. You must
focus on what is relevant, sift among the incidental material to get at the
main ideas. ("Do you mean . . . ?") Speakers may help by issuing voice
cues or by repetitions or nonverbal emphases, but you have to attend to
the total content as well as the distracting asides. *Summarize:* At times

you need to do an internal summary for yourself, sometimes even by interrupting to check where the speaker's information has taken you. ("Let me be sure I understand . . .") *Identify the speaker's evidence:* Ask yourself questions about the speaker's sources, their validity, where those ideas come from, how accurately you think this information is being reported. Do you find the speaker's evidence convincing, complete, accurate, honest, and believable? *Listen between the lines:* To listen effectively, you have to listen to two broadcasts at the same time. The first broadcast is the content of the discussion, the words the speaker is saying, and the topic itself. The second broadcast is the less obvious content of the nonverbal signals the speaker is sending while talking: tone of voice, gestures, posture, and facial expressions. Nonverbal content tells you about the speaker's feelings, and gives you a great deal of information on how to interpret what the speaker is saying. Listening between the lines is very difficult. It takes much sensitivity and patience because people have innumerable ways of setting up defenses and hiding behind them. Only careful attention and a willingness to spend energy deciphering the subtle dimensions of a person's communication will make you successful in your attempts to understand others.

Psychological factors   *Be aware that listening is affected by emotions:* Human beings are not machines. They have feelings, emotions, which play a fundamental part in their interpersonal communication. There are things you like and things you do not like, things you are afraid of or ashamed of, things you like to hear and things that are so threatening you would rather not hear them at all. As a result, quite unconsciously, you have a tendency to tune out what you do not want to hear and to listen better to what you agree with.

When you do not agree with a speaker, you have a great tendency to prepare a rebuttal while the other person is still talking. You hear the first few words or sentences, get an idea of what the speaker is saying, decide you don't agree, and here you go preparing your answer and waiting impatiently for your turn to speak. Sometimes, you don't even wait, and you interrupt the speaker, who never gets a chance to finish his or her thought. Unfortunately, when you do not hear a speaker out completely, you really do not know for sure what is being said.

People you do not agree with are often the most difficult people to listen to. Usually you have little difficulty listening to someone telling you how great you are or how smart you are, but listening to a professor who tells you your paper certainly did not deserve any better than a D is a lot more difficult.

Try to avoid being distracted: We know that children's spans of attention are very short. The younger the child, the shorter the span. In fact, most adults also have a short span of attention and have difficulty concentrating on the same thing for a long period of time. Naturally this varies with each individual, but think of the difficulty you have as a student listening to a fifty-minute lecture, even when the lecturer is an outstanding professor. Because it is hard to sustain attention for very long, you get distracted very easily. Distractions come from (1) within you, when you daydream, (2) the outside environment (outside noise, people passing by, someone waving, the temperature of the room, etc.), and (3) the speaker.

SUMMARY

Until quite recently, the skill of listening was relegated to the background; so little had been done in scholarly research, in working out how to measure it, in setting up training programs, in getting listening into school curricula, and in measuring its effect on lawmaking, media response, public affairs, corporate efficiency, marriage, and all interpersonal communication.

In making a case for the importance of listening, it is easy to figure out how many ways it can go wrong. Making it "go right" is not an easy task since it is a higher cognitive skill, depending on many complex factors for its mastery. As we begin to develop a broader, and hence a more accurate, definition of listening, we may be able to set up better means of assessing its levels of accomplishment and then to formulate more effective retraining programs for listeners everywhere.

Four interpersonal listening types are identified, ranging from the most casual almost subliminal type (reflex) to the most common and frequently referenced content type, to the more involved relational type including what has been called "active listening," and finally to type IV, introspective listening, which calls for an open commitment on the part of the listener to be involved with the messages as a potential peak experience, a conversion, a realization of the deepest meanings of the voices being heard.

Some very general recommendations on how to improve your listening—since you are the only one who can do anything about it—are included. They represent the time factors you can take advantage of, the content factors for you to be more deeply aware of, and the psychological factors which you must alert yourself to which can hold back your listening improvement.

END NOTES

[1] Norbert Wiener, *The Human Use of Human Beings*, Avon Books, New York, 1967.

[2] Rebecca B. Rubin, "Assessing Speaking and Listening Competence at the College Level," *Communication Education*, vol. 31, no. 1, January 1982, p. 19.

[3] Paul T. Rankin, "Measurement of the Ability to Understand the Spoken Language," unpublished Ph.D. dissertation, The University of Michigan, 1926.

[4] Leland Brown, *Communicating Facts and Ideas in Business*, 3rd ed., Prentice-Hall, Englewood Cliffs, NJ, 1982.

5 Ralph Nichols and Leonard Stevens, "Listening to People," *Harvard Business Review,* vol. 35, no. 5, 1957. See also by the same authors, *Are You Listening?* McGraw-Hill, New York, 1957.

6 J. J. Kramer and T. R. Lewis, "Comparison of Visual and Nonvisual Listening," *Journal of Communication,* 1951, p. 16.

7 S. Lodhi and R. D. Greer, "The Speaker as Listener," *Journal of the Experimental Analysis of Behavior,* vol. 51, May 1989, pp. 353–359.

8 Robert W. Norton and Lloyd S. Pettegrew, "Attentiveness as a Style of Communication," *Communication Monographs,* vol. 46, no. 1, March 1979, pp. 13 et seq.

9 D. L. Rubin, "Instruction in Speaking and Listening: Battles and Options," *Educational Leadership,* vol. 42, February 1985.

10 For a succinct summary of the problem of defining and assessing listening see R. N. Bostrom and E. S. Waldhart, "Memory Models and the Measurement of Listening," *Communication Education,* vol. 37, no. 1, January 1988, pp. 1–7.

11 A. D. Wolvin and C. G. Coakley, *Listening,* Wm. C. Brown, Dubuque, IA, 1982.

12 S. W. Lundsteen, *Listening,* ERIC Clearing House on Reading and Communication Skills, Urbana, IL, 1979.

13 J. J. Floyd, *Listening: A Practical Approach,* Scott, Foresman, Glenview, IL, 1985.

14 M. L. Devault, "Talking and Listening from Women's Standpoint: Feminine Strategies for Interviewing and Analysis," *Social Problems,* vol. 37, February 1990, pp. 99–116.

15 R. Hamel and T. Schreiner, "Speak English, Troops: As Immigrants Join the Work Force Accent Reduction Clinics Gain a New Market," *American Demographics,* vol. 11, January 1989, p. 22.

16 D. B. Strother, "On Listening," *Phi Delta Kappan,* April 1987.

17 Wolvin and Coakley, op. cit.

18 B. Goss, "Listening as Information Processing," *Communication Quarterly,* vol. 30, 1982, pp. 304–307.

19 Bostrum and Waldhart, op. cit., p. 4.

20 T. W. Harris, "Listen Carefully" *Nation's Business,* vol. 77, June 1989, p. 78.

21 J. C. Nixon and J. F. West, "Listening: Vital to Communication," *The Bulletin of the Association for Business Communication,* vol. 52, no. 2, June 1989, p. 16.

22 See the book *Teaching as a Subversive Activity,* Delacorte Press, New York, 1969, where authors Neil Postman and Charles Weingartner suggest very earthily that listeners need to know how to distinguish between accurate and spurious data in their Chapter 1, called "Crap Detecting," pp. 1–15.

23 F. Leverentz and D. Garman, "What Was That You Said? (The Art and Skill of Listening)," *Instructor,* vol. 96, April 1987, p. 66. E. J. Robinson and W. P. Robinson, "Knowing When You Don't Know: Children's Judgments about Ambiguous Information," *Cognition,* vol. 12, 1982, pp. 267–280. G. L. Revelle, H.

M. Wellman, and J. D. Karabenick, "Comprehension Monitoring in Preschool Children," *Child Development,* vol. 56, 1985, pp. 654–663.

24 C. M. Kelly, "Empathic Listening," in R. Cathcart and L. Samovar (eds.), *Small Group Communication,* Wm. C. Brown, Dubuque, IA, 1979, pp. 340–348.

25 C. R. Rogers, "Communication: Its Blocking and Facilitating," *Northwestern University Information,* vol. 20, 1952, pp. 9–15. C. R. Rogers and R. E. Farson, "Active Listening," in *Readings in Interpersonal and Organizational Communication,* R. C. Huseman et al. (eds.), Holbrook Press, Boston, 1969, pp. 480–496.

26 Wolvin and Coakley, op. cit.

27 T. Reik, *Listening with the Third Ear,* Farrar & Strauss, New York, 1949.

28 Op. cit.

29 Wolvin and Coakley, op. cit., p. 109.

30 David Michael Levin, *The Listening Self,* Routledge, London, 1989, p. 102. This philosophical treatise is a masterful development of what we are calling type IV listening; as the publishers write, it "offers an account of personal growth and self-fulfillment based on the development of our capacity for listening."

31 Stephen Dobyns, "Will You Listen for a Minute?" *The New York Times Book Review,* Sept. 2, 1990, p. 5.

32 B. D. Sypher, R. N. Bostrom, J. H. Seibert, "Listening, Communication Abilities, and Success at Work," *The Journal of Business Communication,* vol. 26, no. 4, Fall 1989, p. 293.

33 Strother, op. cit., p. 627.

34 H. D. Funk and G. D. Funk, "Guidelines for Developing Listening Skills," *The Reading Teacher,* vol. 42, May 1989, p. 660. A. A. Hinds and A. M. Pankake, "Listening: The Missing Side of School Communication," *The Clearing House,* vol. 60, February 1987, p. 281. R. B. Rubin and C. V. Roberts, "A Comparative Examination and Analysis of Three Listening Tests," *Communication Education,* vol. 38, April 1987, p. 142. A. V. Beale, "Assessing and Improving Your Listening Skills," *NAASP Bulletin,* vol. 74, March 1990, p. 88. H. R. Dalrymple, "Theatre as a Listening Laboratory," *Communication Education,* vol. 36, July 1987, p. 283.

35 R. G. Nichols, "Listening is a 10-Part Skill", *Nation's Business,* vol. 75, September 1987, p. 40. C. Hamilton and B. H. Kleiner, "Steps to Better Listening," *Personnel Journal,* vol. 66, February 1987, p. 20. W. Kiechel III, "Learn How to Listen," *Fortune,* vol. 116, August 17, 1987. *How Important It Is to Listen,* Sperry Corp., New York, 1983. *Your Personal Listening Profile,* Sperry Corp., New York, 1985. A. D. Wolvin and C. G. Coakley, "A Survey of the Status of Listening Training in Some Fortune 500 Corporations," *Communication Education,* vol. 40, April 1991, pp. 152–164.

36 Reported in Nixon and West, op. cit., p. 17.

CHAPTER
7

SYMBOL SYSTEMS: LOOKING AT YOUR LANGUAGE

OBJECTIVES

When you have completed this chapter, you should be able to:

1. List two reasons for the popular interest in the study of language.
2. Summarize the principle of language and thought as expressed by the Sapir-Whorf hypothesis.
3. Distinguish between "signs" and "symbols," and give an original example to illustrate the difference.
4. Discuss the way symbols are used as shortcuts to describe experiences.
5. Explain how language is responsible for linking the past and the future.
6. Discuss the problems you might encounter if you confuse the word with the thing it symbolizes.
7. Develop an original example of "differences that don't make a difference" based on the principle that language serves to classify items, people, and events in our environment.
8. Explain why stereotyping has been referred to as a shortcut to thinking.

9. Cite two examples of language being involved as an officially adopted medium of symbolic exchange.

10. Identify the ways in which a person who speaks only one dialect may have difficulties in situations where that dialect is considered to be inferior.

INTRODUCTION

Language is the medium through which you organize, talk about, and make sense out of your reality. Many people also believe that your language actually causes you to think about things a certain way, and therefore to behave in ways which reflect your language. When you understand the relationship between language (your symbolic world) and your environment (your empirical world), you can better adapt to changing relationships and uncertainties, which are inevitably part of your life. Study of language is really a study of your way of living, a study of your way of seeing your world.

What has come to be known as the "Sapir-Whorf linguistic hypothesis" asserts that language and thought are tied together in a very direct way—that every language both embodies and imposes on its culture and users a particular world view.

There is some distinction made among linguistic scholars as to whether

---

BOX 7-1.   Determinism or Nominalism?

The terms "linguistic relativity" and "linguistic determinism" have been applied to the hypothesis that language strongly affects your thought and actions. That idea is opposed by another way of looking at language called "nominalism." As a recent review of language theories reports:

> Linguistic relativity is a reaction against the nominalist position originating in Platonic and Aristotelian philosophy and popular through the 19th century, that knowledge of reality is not affected by language. The nominalist position regards language as an arbitrary outer form of thought, contending that any thought can be expressed in any language and that translatability is not a problem.*

* E. Rosch and B. B. Lloyd (eds.), *Cognition and Categorization,* Lawrence Erlbaum, Hillsdale, NJ, 1978. D. T. Slobin, *Psycholinguistics,* Scott, Foresman, Glenview, IL, 1979. B. J. Reilly and J. A. DiAngelo, "Communication: A Cultural System of Meaning and Value," *Human Relations,* vol. 43, February 1990, pp. 129–140. See also R. Wagner, *Symbols That Stand for Themselves,* University of Chicago Press, Chicago, 1986.

language structure actually *determines* the logic and thinking of its users ("strong" linguistic relativity, or sometimes referred to as "linguistic determinism"), or only *influences* user logic and thinking ("weak" linguistic relativity).[2]

Our view in this textbook is that language not only reflects the way you talk about your world, but also in many ways will determine what you look for, will affect how you perceive the world and people around you, and even how you think about your perceptions.

EVERYBODY LOVES LANGUAGE

Because it is all around, and because it is used so much, language is a very interesting topic for nearly everybody. You would like to know why you say the things you do and to be able to predict what will happen when you communicate. Scholarly studies and reports of historical and linguistic research give much organized evidence of how language came about, how it affects people, and how it changes or resists change. A television series on the English language produced for PBS, the public

Everybody loves language. Every culture has meanings which are symbolically expressible in language. (© *Martin Benjamin/Retna)*

broadcasting system, was extremely popular because it appealed to public fascination with language. The related book, *The Story of English,* in its "Introduction" explains its journalistic approach by pointing out that "hardly a week goes by without a news story, often on the front page, devoted to some aspect of English." The authors go on to assert that language belongs to "each one of us, to the flower seller as much as to the professor... everyone uses words, even if, at first, they don't stop to think about them. . . . We live in and by language. We all speak and we all listen. . . ."[3]

Popular interest in language and symbols is not limited only to the English language. "Flower sellers and professors" everywhere are also interested in relationships in any languages. Comparing one language with another in its application of the symbol systems helps us better understand the lives of the speakers of those languages. Some languages are noun-oriented and thus place high value on things and material objects; other languages are verb-oriented and place a high value on actions and movements.[4] But in spite of our pride in the English language, most scholars will agree that there are no "superior" languages in the world, and that any language is capable of handling the affairs of the culture it represents. As the sociologist Sapir writes:

> The content of every culture is expressible in its language and there are no linguistic materials whether as to content or form which are not felt to symbolize actual meanings, whatever may be the attitude of those who belong to other cultures.[5]

LANGUAGE AS THOUGHT

Language is your medium in which to think about and to talk about ideas as well as things. What you might call "knowledge" is language. What each one of you "knows" is a product of your language. In this way, language (or symbolization) is more than the mere naming of things you bump into in your life.

Language lets you dream about things that never were, and perhaps never will be. You can imagine a unicorn because you have a name to put on it, although there is doubt such an animal ever existed. If you see a picture of a handsomely beautiful person of the opposite sex, you can imagine or talk about meeting such a person in your future because you have language. Past and future can be part of your reality when you use language—just as much as pointing to an item and using the word for it is in the present.

"Language is a guide to social reality... it powerfully conditions all our thinking about social problems and processes." After writing that statement, Sapir goes on to argue that humans do not live in the world alone, but live at the mercy of the language which their own society or particular group uses.[6]

Language is not merely an incidental means of hashing over problems or talking about issues—it is the determining factor in how you think about and therefore deal with problems and issues.

No two languages are ever so precisely alike that speakers in those different languages think about the world in precisely the same way. The "real world" for people speaking Japanese or German or Polish is created for them out of their language habits. For that reason, those "worlds" become different worlds from those of people speaking English, not merely the same worlds with different labels attached to things. Even when we can translate a word like "dog" into several languages with some common understanding, we recognize that translating with understanding high-order words such as "liberty," "family," "trust," "equality," or "democracy" will be more difficult.

LANGUAGE AS SYMBOLS

A "symbol" is anything which we as thinking humans decide stands for something else. *Things* can be symbols when a ring is a symbol for marriage, a uniform a symbol for some occupation or rank, and a flag a symbol for a nation. A *person* can be a symbol when the President stands for the country, the minister or rabbi stands for a religious order, a police officer or a judge stands for the law. A *picture* is a symbol of the event or item that it depicts, and is not the item itself, however real the image may appear. *Gestures* like the clenched fist, or a facial expression like a smile or a frown, come to be symbols of attitudes or moods.

A *word*, spoken or written, is a symbol. The word "chair" is a symbol for that item of furniture you can sit on—although you would never be crazy enough to sit on just the word "chair," would you? The word to some so-called "primitive" people actually may become the event itself as when incantations are uttered and magic spells are cast. In our modern society we like to think that we do not engage in such silly word-event confusions, except perhaps in such instances as kissing the letter you received from a loved one, or during a baseball game not talking about the pitcher's potential no-hitter, or forbidding others to use your enemy's name in your presence . . . or?

> *A . . . psychological characteristic of language is the fact that while it may be looked upon as a symbolic system which reports or refers to or otherwise substitutes for direct experience, it does not as a matter of actual behavior stand apart from or run parallel to direct experience. . . . . it is generally difficult to make a complete divorce between objective reality and our linguistic symbols of reference to it; and things, qualities and events are on the*

"No fishing" nonverbal symbol is at the top. Below the English words are Spanish, Burmese, Thai, Vietnamese, and Laotian. What does this sign in San Diego tell us about the occupations of immigrants from Southeast Asia? (© *Mimi Forsyth/Monkmeyer*)

whole felt to be what they are called. For the normal person every experience, real or potential, is saturated with verbalism.[7]

Your Real World and Your Symbol World

If your experiences are "saturated with verbalism," as Sapir has asserted, then you can see yourself going around in two worlds at the same time. There is your real (or *empirical*) world, where you bump into things and view others and engage in all your daily activities. This empirical world is the world of firsthand experiences, of personal and real-time observations, of your seeing, touching, feeling, smelling, tasting—a world of objects outside your own skin.

Then there is your verbal (or *symbolic*) world, where you put words to those experiences outside your skin. You use language to name things, to think about things, to talk about ideas or other people or events, and to report to others about your internal reactions to the real world.

BOX 7-2.   Symbols or Signs?

A *sign* is something which stands for something else and bears a natural relationship to it—smoke is a sign of fire. A *symbol* stands for something because we agree to it, or have made up a relationship. Smoky the Bear is a symbol for fire prevention.

If your car's engine sputters and dies, it is a *sign* something is wrong with the car, although the car itself can be a *symbol* for status, for wealth, or for youth, because we believe it to be.

At the beach, scudding dark clouds may be a *sign* of an impending storm, while the storm flags the authorities may fly to warn bathers and sailors are *symbols* because they have no natural connection with a storm, but only what we have agreed to have them mean.

Symbols as shortcuts

Imagine what it would be like if you did not have the convenience of words or symbols to communicate with another person. Your conversation would be limited to the objects, or persons, or events, actually present in your empirical world at that moment in the conversation. Animals, and especially our pets, for all the wonderful personalities we can believe that they have, are very limited in this way as nonusers of symbols as sophisticated as those used by humans. Fortunately for the human race, our ancestors developed a symbol system for those people living together in which certain sounds or sequences of noises were adopted as shortcuts to refer to objects, persons, situations, or items around them not only in the present, but in the past and future as well.

Symbols link your past and future

These beginnings of oral language meant that humankind would step out beyond the limited boundaries of the immediate present. It meant that people could talk about food to eat at the present time, and also food tomorrow and food yesterday. If you believe that your dog has a human-like language ability to communicate, try to explain to Fido about "hamburger tomorrow."

Symbols make it possible for you to store experiences in your mind, record them in your memory, and later recall them to yourself and report them to others. Ability to communicate one's experience is essentially what made human civilization possible. Humankind was able to transmit its knowledge—the sum of stored experience in spoken or written form—to the next generation, and that generation to the next.

In this way the late-twentieth-century residents, like you, are a product of all the symbol-using generations which existed before you.

Although you needed to learn to read, write, and count, you did not have to invent an alphabet or number system. Although you have had to learn to type, probably to use word processing, you did not have to discover electricity or invent the computer.

The use of language in cultural accumulation and historical transmission is obvious and important. . . . Modern civilization as a whole, with its schools, its libraries, and its endless stores of knowledge, opinion, and sentiment stored up in verbalized form, would be unthinkable without language made eternal as document.[8]

Symbols are not the events they symbolize

What you can accomplish with symbols, then, is to translate your firsthand experiences from the empirical world into a communication version of those experiences. When you communicate to another person about what happened, you use a symbolic picture of the happening. This symbolic picture is *not* the experience itself. Words you use to refer to the objects, the persons, the events, the situations, and the sensations and feelings are of course not those actual objects, persons, events, situations, or sensations and feelings.

It is one thing to experience a toothache and quite another to comment "I have a toothache." Those words merely refer to your pain, and there is no way the other person can experience your own personal toothache.

Have you ever tried to experience something and not name it, even if you do it silently (which is called thinking)? Then when you want to describe or share an experience with others, you may choose to use spoken words, written words, or nonverbal gestures or expressions. In any case, you must necessarily use symbols.

LANGUAGE AS CLASSIFICATION

To talk is to classify. Language helps you organize the confusion of all those things you observe at a given time into some orderly sequence or categories. Any person or object can be classified in different categories depending on which of its characteristics you pay attention to. Classifications may not be right or wrong, but are personal choices and reflect what criteria you use to place things, events, and people in groups.

Similarities and Differences

Classifying lets you pick out certain qualities to pay attention to, usually by comparing similarities or differences. Take a book from the shelf and compare it with this book. Both have pages. Both have covers. Both have reading material or pictures. You can find a number of similarities which describe some qualities or "bookness," and so when when somebody asks you to go get a book, you know the general category asked for.

BOX 7-3. Power of Classifying

Questions of definition have to do with the *meaning* you attach to words. They have to do with the arbitrary agreement of how you classify something. Take the questions "Is photography art?" and "Is bullfighting a sport?" Whether photography and bullfighting fall into the categories provided by your definitions, the answers are essentially verbal, for the definitions are verbal. No amount of staring at a photograph will yield an answer. Those who reject the classifications or reject the values implied in your definition will probably disagree with your answer.

Louis Salomon gives some examples of classification questions in the legal world. The answers are important, although seemingly arbitrary, for the imposition of legal penalties or the granting of legal immunities hinge upon them.

1. Are peanuts nuts? (The Food and Drug Administration is responsible for enforcing accurate labeling of food products.)
2. Is an alligator farm a museum? (Liberal income tax deductions are allowed for contributions to museums.)
3. Is a coffeehouse a cabaret? (A cabaret license is expensive and often subject to special restrictions.)
4. Is a police slowdown in issuing parking summonses a strike? (There are laws penalizing public employees who strike.)
5. Is a ship that is registered in Panama but owned by a United States citizen or corporation an American vessel? (There is a legal minimum wage for crew members on American vessels.)
6. Is a man who has lost his job and refuses to take a new one that has been offered unemployed? (At issue is not only his unemployment compensation but the reliability of official statistics of "unemployment.")*

* L. Salomon, *Semantics and Common Sense,* Holt, Rinehart and Winston, New York, 1966, p. 91. (Reprinted with permission of the publisher.)

The classifying function of language is so important to you that when you are exposed to new events or new people you will ask yourself, automatically, what is this like that I already know about? In other words, what category can I put it in? This is a judgment based on how you pay attention to similarities and differences. Stereotyping is a direct result of classifying. You stereotype people as students, teachers, blacks, whites, radicals, activists, liberals, conservatives, Jews, Republicans, Democrats,

---

BOX 7-4.   Classification Determines Behaviors

In his classic book on language behavior, S. I. Hayakawa notes that *classifications* generally determine your attitudes and behavior toward the object or event (or, we must add, even persons) classified.* He writes that when lightning was classified as "evidence of divine wrath," no course of action other than prayer seemed to be available for anyone to prevent being struck by lightning. However, when it was classified as "electricity," Benjamin Franklin achieved a measure of control over it by his invention of the lightning rod. Also, relating to the field of medicine, there was a time when certain physical disorders were classified as "demonic possession," and so the indicated cure was to "drive the demons out" by whatever spells or incantations we could think of. The results, Hayakawa suggests, were uncertain. But when these disorders were classified as "bacillus infections," courses of action were prescribed that led to more predictable results.

* S. I. Hayakawa, *Language in Thought and Action*, Harcourt, Brace, New York, 1949, p. 217.

Communists, parents, etc. You imply that if they have some similarities with the category, they are all alike. If you see one penguin, you've seen them all.

Using Stereotypes

One problem with stereotyping is that it encourages a shortcut for thinking, and keeps you from finding out in what ways any individual of that stereotyped class is unique. Stereotyping permits you to set up neat, well-ordered, oversimplified categories of similarities into which you can slip your judgments of people, situations, or concepts.

Another problem with stereotyping is that the generalizations you make are based on your own special standards of judgment and are evaluative, not descriptive. Generalizations are not all bad, and you could not survive without some—there are some differences that don't make a difference in our world. A red traffic light may be a slightly different color in one city than in another, but for the purposes of traffic control, the different shades of red won't make a difference. You learn to enjoy books by a favorite author, concentrating on similarities among them and paying less attention to the differences from one story to another. But when you assert that your conclusions and values are right for everybody else to use, you ask others to submit to your own peculiar way of generalizing—

You tend to like people who are like you: "What'll it be, handsome?" *(Drawing by Ziegler; © 1988 The New Yorker Magazine, Inc.)*

your own specific way of organizing the similarities and ignoring differences.

It is not surprising that research has shown that you like people who are *like you* (the similarities are more attractive than the differences), and people even tend to marry people who are like their parents. The tendency to divide people into categories of "like us" and "not like us" is called *ethnocentrism,* which divides your world dangerously into the good side and the bad side without any careful thought to balancing similarities and differences.

Polarization: Real and False Opposites

Another shortcut in our language is to think—and therefore to speak—in terms of opposites. Black is opposite of white. Young is opposite of old. Happy is opposite of sad. Bad is opposite of good. Just as you overlook similarities, you tend to make the differences complete and absolute and divide the world into competing opposites. Our language is built on *polar terms.*

To give you an idea of how easily the polar terms are expressed in our language, look at the lists below. Can you fill in a middle point with a one-word term? Can you, in other words, find a simple and defined word exactly between the expressed opposites? Start with "gray" as the in-between term for black versus white—you may have even said sometime that "everything isn't either black or white, but there are shades of gray."

black	gray	white
success	———	failure
bad	———	good
stingy	———	generous
honest	———	dishonest
polite	———	rude

Little in our language supports that concept of midpoints, however, when you try to place a term between good and bad, or success and failure. Even though there must be instances of people who are good sometimes and bad sometimes, the language makes it difficult to talk that way, to act in the real world as if there was a third alternative between those poles. In this way, your language makes it hard for you to describe the important gradations, shadings, and subtle in-betweens of the empirical world.

Language Guides Your Observing

Related to the Sapir-Whorf hypothesis of language-thought links is a statement by Clyde Kluckhohn that language is a "special way of looking at the world and interpreting experience."[9] The structure of any language hides a whole set of unconscious assumptions about the world. Anthropologists and linguists have come to realize that the ideas people have about what happens in the world are not merely "given" by events themselves. Rather, you see what your language structure has made you sensitive to and has trained you to look for.

Many languages discriminate between those people close to you and strangers. French uses *tu* and *vous* to distinguish familiar address from

BOX 7-5. Violent Form of Address

While embarrassment may be one outcome of misuse of special forms of personal address, more dramatic incidents have been reported. On July 2, 1983, three seamen from the Korean freighter *Tokai Maru* entered a bar in Oakland, California, and began speaking in Korean to another patron at the bar. According to a report from the Associated Press, the bar patron took offense at the use of a familiar form of address used by one of the Korean sailors, pulled out a large-caliber pistol, and shot the three sailors, killing one of them.*

* San Antonio *Light*, July 3, 1983.

BOX 7-6.   Trash By Any Other Name . . .

In English, many different words can be used to describe "what we throw away because we don't want it anymore." We have words such as "litter," "garbage," "trash," "rubbish," "refuse," "junk," "debris," and "waste." As you know, our culture is one in which cleanliness is very important. So you know all the little differences among things that are usually dirty and that you want to get rid of. Of course, because you pay much attention to these things so that you can get rid of them, you learn to perceive differences among them. Garbage is not trash. Trash is not litter. Etc. As recycling has become important, an additional set of categories is emerging to describe what substances can be recycled. The more familiar you are with something, the more likely you are to perceive differences and to have a name to call these differences.

---

formal; Spanish uses *tu* and *usted* the same way. In the Navajo language, verbs can be richly conjugated to tell you if a statement, such as "it is raining," is a direct report by somebody who actually experienced the event (in this case, got wet in the rain). Another form can tell that you view the event as a spectator (inside looking out at the rain). A third form of the verb can indicate that somebody told you about it (but you did not see it yourself; it was hearsay). Even in English you can convey quite different ideas by choosing to say "I am reading a *book*," or "I am reading a *textbook*," or "I am reading the *Bible*."

"Each language," Kluckhohn wrote, "is an instrument which guides people in observing, in reacting, in expressing themselves in a special

---

BOX 7-7.   The Language of Buckle Up

At one time the devices to restrain automobile drivers and passengers were called "crash belts" and were generally worn by racing drivers and sporting types. In an attempt to widen their use, the devices were installed in passenger cars and were given a less ominous label, "safety belts." But that term was still not entirely acceptable, and the devices have more recently been labeled "seat belts" or "lap belts," much more neutral terms suggesting neither disaster ("crash belt") nor impending danger ("safety belt").

way. *The pie of experience can be sliced in many ways, and language is the principal directive force in the background"* (emphasis added).[10]

Again, language is a means of categorizing and classifying experiences and events and not just a handy tool for reporting them. Your linguistic filters permit some experiences to enter your consciousness, and others are stopped.

LANGUAGE AS POLITICAL AND SOCIAL POWER

Language has been, since recorded history, a force for maintaining power over others, for gaining economic, political, and social advantages. The spoken—and sometimes written—language of a nation is considered an integral part of that nation's heritage and its present impact on the world. One of the significant contributions made by the PBS television program *The Story of English* and its related book is to trace the relationships of English to historical conquest, to power from the earliest developments of the language to today's global communication ties. The authors contend that English is used by a fourth of the world today—350 million speakers as a first language and 400 million others as a second language.[11]

International Language Power

When some languages appear to be universal, in the sense that most of the literate world uses them, it indicates more about *power* than about simple information exchange. Studies of the numbers of world radio stations which broadcast in various languages provide more than just data about the statistical numbers of potential listeners—this is also a measure of how the world's people think, since the different languages will reflect the political, economic, and social norms of the nation whose language is being transmitted. Researchers find that even if the content of the radio broadcasts is not, by itself, political, the choice of which language to broadcast in is a clear political choice. In addition, religious and political messages are among the most frequent broadcasts worldwide.

Transnational broadcasters use shortwave broadcast bands, and the languages which dominate are English first (by a wide margin), French second, Arabic third, and Spanish fourth. German, Russian, and Portuguese follow in that order. On the other hand, the Voice of America broadcasts in thirty-six different languages (the BBC is close with thirty-four languages), while Radio Peking (broadcasting from the People's Republic of China) broadcasts in forty-three different languages and Radio Moscow airs a staggering total of seventy-two different languages.[12]

"Official" languages of the world

With so many languages in the world, it is not unusual for Americans to think of languages as properties of nations. For example, we assume that in the United States the language is English. We assume that everybody in Mexico speaks Spanish—although there are areas where Mayan, Nauhatl, or other Indian languages are used. We also have an oversimplified idea that a language starts and ends at a nation's borders.[13]

There are, however, countries within which several "official" languages exist. Linguistic minorities are present in many nations of the world. Hindi as a language in India is opposed by Tamil-speakers and others, who have expressed their opposition in bloody actions; and while it is the "official" language, it has been defaced on many signs and does not have nationwide support. You hear or read current news reports of the confrontations over language. Balance is difficult to achieve in language issues, as they involve not only economic and political concerns but very personal rights as expressed by linguistic minorities. "If, however, the minority became large, powerful, or compact enough, it might claim special language rights, ranging from local tolerance for limited purposes to universal and equal status for all purposes under the jurisdiction of the state. Afrikaans in Africa, Flemish in Belgium, French in Canada, and more recently Basque and Catalan in Spain are examples of languages whose speakers have obtained official status within bilingual states."[14]

A number of states in the United States (including Georgia, Illinois, Indiana, Kentucky, Nebraska, and Virginia) have passed laws to make English their official language. In 1986 the proponents of "English First," as they call themselves, won a very decisive victory for the elimination of languages other than English when a referendum in California (one of our most heavily populated states and with many different languages

Official language laws, such as Quebec mandates concerning French, give rise to strong partisan feelings as well as attempts to build national unity. (© Henri Cartier-Bresson/Magnum)

spoken) resulted in 73 percent of the electorate voting for English as the official state language. There also continue to be very persistent moves to bring forth a federal constitutional amendment and to pass other restrictive national laws making English the only official language in the United States. Puerto Rico has recently voted to enforce Spanish as its official language.

Language is not neutral

Language has also been a passionate point of contention in many other parts of the world, including south Asia, where millions of people in Pakistan and Sri Lanka have gone to war largely over language issues.

According to census figures, about 15 percent of the population of the United States does not speak English as a native language. Use of languages other than English is a controversial issue in many parts of the country; debate over bilingual education is only one part of the conflict. Use of languages other than English in work settings has become more than an issue over understanding the words; there have been cases of segregating workers by their language use; employers have resisted promoting non-English-speakers, and young and old find occasions to ridicule members of linguistic minorities. Cases involving defaced street signs and other bilingual indicators (for example, Korean signs in Philadelphia, and Spanish posters in Los Angeles) and other issues have had to be settled by the courts, which are more and more being called on to help determine which languages are appropriate and under what conditions. Laws enacted in Quebec concerning French as the official language are a classic study of a political nation-building mechanism of language planning and policy.

Dialects and Varieties

In any society it is possible to have languages within the primary language, symbolic codes within codes, communication systems which only certain groups are familiar with and can understand. English as it is spoken in the United States may have its origins in England, but most British speakers of English will hardly recognize what the "Colonies" have done to their language. Of course, the "original" English already was a mixture of several languages, and today there are many sub-Englishes spoken within the British Isles.[15]

It should not be surprising to anyone that Americans have made dialectal changes in the original symbol system—as English is spoken in the United States, it is really many varieties of languages, also. Professional dialectologists can identify as many as twenty-seven major dialects in America.[16] Many scholars call them "varieties" rather than "dialects" and identify the differences as arising from variations in pronunciation, inflections, accents, rate, stress, grammar, vocabulary, and idiom.

BOX 7-8. **"Speak That I May See Thee."**

In a book called *Class,* subtitled *A Painfully Accurate Guide through the American Status System,* author Paul Fussell describes the role of language in relation to social class:

> *Regardless of the money you've inherited, the danger of your job, the place you live, the way you look, the shape and surface of your driveway, the items on your front porch and in your living room, the sweetness of your drinks, the time you eat dinner, the stuff you buy from mail-order catalogs, the place you went to school and your reverence for it, and the materials you read— your social class is still most clearly visible when you say things.*
>
> *"One's speech is an unceasingly repeated public announcement about background and social standing," says John Brooks, translating into modern American Ben Jonson's observation, "Language most shows a man. Speak that I may see thee."**

* P. Fussell, *Class,* Ballantine Books, New York, 1983, p. 175.

What dialect is better?

Most linguistic authorities agree that no one dialect or variety of language should be considered "better" than any other so long as it communicates meaning so that the user can function effectively in situations where the dialect is used.[17]

Scientific judgment about dialects says that so long as a speech variation has an appropriate grammar, appropriate vocabulary, and a consistent phonology (if spoken) and orthograpy (if written), it meets the requirements to be classified as a language. *Social judgment* may, however, not take quite as objective a view, and many people believe that whatever dialect is used by them and their friends is the only acceptable one, or the most prestigious one.

Sapir wrote that "a common speech serves as a peculiarly potent symbol of the social solidarity of those who speak the language. . . . The extraordinary importance of minute linguistic difference . . . is intuitively felt by most people. 'He talks like us' is the equivalent of saying 'He is one of us.'"[18]

What we want to emphasize here is that "better" or "correct" language is not "better" or "correct" because of any inherent qualities in the language or in the people who speak it. Language is basically an arbitrary business; common usage and common agreement are generally what make it work. So in a complex, changing world, where many languages and dialects are spoken, it makes sense to have a repertoire of languages to fit appropriately the varied situations you will likely be in.

SUMMARY: LANGUAGE MAKES US HUMAN

No matter what language or dialect you speak, it is your key to making sense of your world and being in touch with others. All cultures have spoken language of sufficient complexity and sophistication to take care of the needs of the people of that culture. Without the organizing power of language—by helping you classify experience—you would be forced to live in the present, cut off from the other places and other times.

There are significant limits and weaknesses of language, such as the tendency to *polarize* experience into competing opposites, to oversimplify both events and people by *stereotyping,* and to *narrowly observe* only what your language points you to. Through language you have great power to describe the world, to think about it and analyze it, and to express your relations to that world and to others.

END NOTES

1 E. Sapir, *Culture, Language and Personality,* selected essays edited by D. Mandelbaum, University of California Press, Berkeley, 1964 (original work, 1933). B. Whorf, *Language, Thought and Reality,* John Wiley & Sons, New York, 1956. C. D. Hockett, "The Origin of Speech," *Scientific American,* vol. 203, no. 3, 1960, pp. 88–96.

2 T. M. Steinfatt, "Linguistic Relativity: Toward a Broader View," in S. Ting-Toomey and F. Korzenny (eds.), *Language, Communication, and Culture: Current Directions,* International and Intercultural Communication Annual, vol. xii, SCA-Sage Publications, Newbury Park, CA, 1989, p. 35.

3 R. McCrum, W. Cran, and R. MacNeil, *The Story of English (A Companion to the PBS Television Series),* Viking Penguin, New York, 1986, p. 14.

4 Whorf, op. cit. See also J. O'Connor and J. Seymour, *Introducing Neuro-Linguistic Programming,* Harkmolls, Bodmin, Cornwall, 1990.

5 Sapir, op. cit., p. 6.

6 Ibid., p. 68. See also "Unbreakable Language Barriers," concerning brain processes used to learn different languages, *Discover,* vol. 10, December 1989, p. 10.

7 Ibid. p. 8.

8 Ibid. p. 18.

9 C. Kluckhohn, *Mirror for Man,* Fawcett Publications, New York, 1963, p. 139.

10 Ibid., p. 140.

11 McCrum et al., op cit., p. 23.

12 The Spring 1979 issue of the *Journal of Communication,* vol. 29, no. 2, devotes a large section to the politics of language including R. E. Wood (pp. 112–123) on transnational radio broadcasting, A. Posada (pp. 84–92) on bilingual education,

A. d'Anglejan (pp. 54–63) on a study of the French in Quebec, and W. F. Mackey (cited below) on planning.

[13] "A Tongue-Twister for 1992" (referring to the language barriers confronting the European Economic Community), *The Economist,* vol. 308, July 1988, p. 43. S. Thiederman, "Overcoming Cultural and Language Barriers," *Public Management,* vol. 71, August 1989, pp. 19–21.

[14] W. F. Mackey, "Language Policy and Language Planning," *Journal of Communication,* vol. 29, no. 2, Spring 1979, p. 49.

[15] See McCrum et al., op cit., chap. 2.

[16] For an interesting treatment of dialects see R. Hendrickson, *American Talk: The Words and Ways of American Dialects,* Viking Press, New York, 1987.

[17] For a study of the positive effects of additional intercultural styles in an organization see A. K. Foeman and G. Pressley, "Ethnic Culture and Corporate Culture: Using Black Style in Organizations," *Communication Quarterly,* vol. 35, no. 4, Fall 1987, pp. 239–307.

[18] Sapir, op cit., pp. 16–17. See also H. Tarver, "Language and Politics in the 1980's: The Story of U.S. English," *Political Science,* vol. 17, June 1989, p. 225.

CHAPTER
8

LIVING WITH
YOUR LANGUAGE

OBJECTIVES

On completing this chapter you should be able to do the following:

1. Identify and explain three myths of language.
2. Draw, label, and discuss the "triangle of meaning" as proposed by Ogden and Richards.
3. Defend the argument that meanings are in people, not in the dictionaries.
4. Define "denotation" as it relates to meaning.
5. Define "connotation" as it relates to meaning.
6. Explain what is meant by a "Humpty Dumpty attitude" about meaning.
7. Take a stand on the issue of equivocation or strategic ambiguity in our dealings with others.
8. List the three factors generally contributing to any misunderstandings related to meaning.
9. Define the term "newspeak," and identify current examples.
10. Give two examples of "embellishment" as a communication device.

11. Diagram a continuum of language pollutions in their order of ethical purpose.
12. Distinguish among the statements about observation, inference, and judgment, giving original examples of each.

INTRODUCTION

Language is the tool you use for sharing experiences with others and for coping with your real world. You construct meaning for yourself by using symbols, and with language you can influence others for good or ill. What you call "meaning" involves what you select to pay attention to and how you share those perceptions with others. The more you know about how meaning happens, the more effective you may be as a communicator.

MYTHS ABOUT MEANING

Problems you may have about getting others to understand you may be partly caused by one or more of the myths many people have about language and meaning. Only part of human difficulties are caused by what people don't know—the rest are caused by what people think they know but is actually wrong.

Myth 1: Words Have Meaning

Meaning is sometimes thought to be contained in words in a more or less permanent, logical, obvious, natural, and predictable way. In that myth, meaning comes already attached to the words you use, and all you need to do is give someone your words and the meanings go right along with them.

Meaning, however, is the *relationship* which *you make* between a symbol and what that symbol stands for. Meaning is in people, not in words. The words are simply used to "call up" meanings in others and yourself when you see or hear them.

Symbols and referents

Relating a word to what that word stands for is done in the minds of the speakers-listeners. Since the meanings are made by people, the meanings are arbitrary. They change. Only when you have some agreement between people about what words "mean" can you achieve more accurate communication. Figure 8-1 helps support our contention that "words don't mean; people mean" where Ogden and Richards refer to the indirectness of the relation between words and things.[1] We have adapted the original Odgen and Richards diagram so that you may compare meaning to a baseless triangle in which three points are represented by an object in your world (in this case a drawing of a four-footed canine creature), a symbol which stands for that object (it could be a noise as well as squiggles on paper), and a human being. Any relationship between the object and the word can be made only through the human mind. This triangle has no base, because there is no necessary connection between the word "dog" and the beast running around. Calling the object by that particular

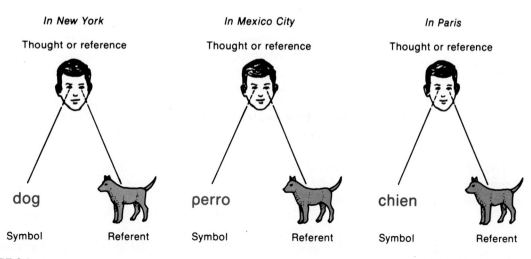

In New York — Thought or reference — dog (Symbol) — Referent

In Mexico City — Thought or reference — perro (Symbol) — Referent

In Paris — Thought or reference — chien (Symbol) — Referent

FIGURE 8-1
There is no direct relationship between the "referent" (the thing you are talking or writing about) and the "symbol" (the words you use). Only as these referents and symbols are related through the thoughts of a person (reference) do they have meaning. Meaning is not in the object or in the symbol but in the interaction of these through the human communicator.

name, that set of letters in that particular order, reflects only the fact that at some time people have agreed to do it that way. Thus the symbol came to "mean" the object in our mythology of language use.

Dictionaries and meaning

You might object to our statement that words don't have meanings. What about dictionaries? Aren't they the supreme authorities on meanings of words? Isn't that where you go when you want to look up the "meaning" of a word? That's another myth. What dictionaries give us is a *record* of what words have meant to speakers of that language, or how people in certain parts of the society have been using words up to the time the dictionary went to press.

Dictionaries also give you a list of various usages of words at different

---

BOX 8-1. How's That Again?

I know you believe you understand what you think I said, but I'm not sure that you realize that what you heard is not what I meant.

In this statement is contained the core of the many communication mishaps that plague your personal and professional life.

times, in different parts of the world. The trouble with this historical record, however, is that no dictionary can predict with any great assurance exactly how the next person you meet may be using the word in a message. Thus, although dictionaries are good for many purposes—for documenting how words have been used, for pronunciation preferences, for showing word origins, for settling bets about "meanings," and for looking up words for Scrabble—they do not provide you with a "true" meaning of words detached from the people using them.

Levels of meaning:
Denotation and
connotation

If meanings are inside people, what is the chance that two speakers will have close enough to the "same" meanings that they can communicate effectively? How can you be sure your words are understood the way you "meant" them? The answer is, you can't always be sure. You are more likely to be understood if you talk about objects which you can point to, or which have some width, height, weight, or color about them.

BOX 8-2.   Cocklebur and Lint Theory of Meaning

As a humorous demonstration in a workshop, this "theory" was developed by the authors to show how we acquire different meanings for words based on our personal experiences. It is a way of describing the difference between denotative meaning (the cocklebur) and connotative meaning (the lint).

We found a collection of cockleburs, those seed pods which a number of different plants produce. They were about half an inch long, were shaped like a small football, and had a number of sticky, thorny bristles.

Each participant in the workshop was given a cocklebur to carry for a week—in a pocket, purse, jacket, trousers—wherever there was a place for this prickly little seed pod. At the end of the week all participants were supposed to check what had happened to their own cockleburs and compare them with those carried by others.

Cockleburs pick up lint from pockets the same way they attach themselves to the fur of animals, which is nature's way of distributing the seeds of the original plant. In a week's time the original cocklebur is nearly covered with bits of lint, threads, dust, and other collected debris, so that one can barely make out the original bur.

As the workshop participants learned, everybody had some of his or her own special lint on the spines of the bur, just as we all pick up our own connotations for words. The original burs were very much alike—the denotative meaning—compared with the differences added to the original meaning by our association (lint)—the connotative meaning. The analogy was clear.

"Please pass the salt" will likely get you the saltshaker. "Please respect me" may not get you anything but a quizzical look. What's the difference?

The *objective* "salt" can be seen, pointed to, and acted on with some degree of assurance that it is what you are both talking about. Salt, in this case, has a *denotative* meaning, or one which can be pointed to, "out there." You and the other person can probably agree on that item from your common experience and from the label you put on it.

The *subjective* "respect," on the other hand, is pretty hard to point to ("give me two tablespoons of respect . . .") and has what we call a *connotative* meaning. There is no referent in the real world easily obtainable to both of you, and for that reason you must depend on the meaning of this word *to come solely out of the experiences you have had with it.* Different people want to have different things happen when they talk about "respect," and you may have trouble defining the term unless you and the others have had very much the same background and similar expectations of an outcome.[2]

Connotative meanings are more likely to be personal, private, complex, and hard-to-pin-down than are denotative meanings. But even the denotative meanings will depend to some extent on what similarities and differences we choose to pay attention to in the referent.

Myth 2: A Word Has Only One Meaning

Communication would be quite simple—and also quite limited—if each word had only one meaning and everybody could agree to it. It is possible for you to act as if a word has only one meaning, even if you are aware of this myth.[3] When you talk with others or about others, you may try to

---

BOX 8-3. Will You Run Out of Meanings?

Communication would be rather simple if each symbol could refer to only one unique unit of experience. You often are under the delusion that one word equals one usage—one way of using it. Take the word "run" as an example. You can

Run a 50-yard sprint
Run a business
Run your hose
Have a *runny* nose
Have a *run* of cards
Run your household the way you like
Run out of time
Run out of cereal
Run out on somebody
Run over someone with your car

impose your one-and-only meaning on such words as "honesty," "patriotism," "loyalty," "respect," "love," "cheating," "success," "hard work," "friendship," "expensive," "beautiful," "intelligent," or "crazy."

Making words mean what you want them to mean—like Humpty Dumpty in Box 8-4—is a kind of conceit which says that there is only one meaning for a word *and it is mine.* You should know, however, that only about 500 words are commonly used in the everyday conversation of Americans. Even more significant, however, is the fact that those 500 most commonly used words have some 14,000 different definitions (or "meanings"?) listed in the dictionary—an average of 28 different ways which somebody, at some time, has reportedly used each word.

Myth 3: Ambiguous Meanings Are Always Bad

Teachers, parents, counselors, and almost all people who work in communication spend much of their time trying to get everybody to communicate more clearly, more precisely, more accurately. In this quest for clarity, even this textbook will present in the forthcoming pages a discussion of "language pollution" which calls for an awareness of how language can mislead you and how you can be victimized by unreliable communication. Before we make a case for *clear communication,* however, let's

---

BOX 8-4. The Humpty Dumpty Attitude

For those of you who use jargon, or have ties to dialects, there is a message in the speaking patterns invented by Lewis Carroll which can show you how your language can be turned into "jabberwocky." The story of Alice in Wonderland has some remarkable commentaries about the semantic world you may invent and how you may try to make sense out of word foolishness. The following selection underscores the importance of meaning and the effect it has on communication:

> "I don't know what you mean by 'glory,'" Alice said.
> Humpty Dumpty smiled contemptuously. "Of course you don't—till I tell you. I mean 'there is a nice knockdown argument for you.'"
> "But glory does not mean 'a nice knockdown argument,'" Alice objected.
> "When I use a word," Humpty Dumpty said in a rather scornful tone, "it means just what I choose it to mean—neither more nor less."
> "The question is," said Alice, "whether you can make words mean so many different things."
> "The question is," said Humpty Dumpty, "who is to be master, that's all."*

* Lewis Carroll, *Alice's Adventures in Wonderland, Through the Looking Glass* and *The Hunting of the Snark,* Modern Library, Inc., New York, 1925, pp. 246–247.

explore the somewhat revolutionary idea that *under some circumstances it might be important to be ambiguous in your communication—to equivocate.*

Relationships are complex

Life is not simple. What you want to have happen in your relations with others may be complicated—in fact, one of your desired outcomes may be quite opposite from another. If you want to spend time with two different people but don't want to hurt either's feelings, how do you avoid making trouble with a communicatively clear statement such as "I'm going to date Jim (or Sally) tonight, but would enjoy seeing you on Friday." Advice to married couples from counselors sometimes suggests being ambiguous about responses to information demands from the partner.

Professional politicians have a reputation of being disarmingly vague, but we see the same behaviors in our everyday interpersonal transactions as well.

A politician facing a large crowd of voters has to decide which statements about a troublesome issue will best represent (1) the possibility of support from his friends, (2) the possibility of the least damage or alienation of neutrals or others, (3) what positions were stated in the past, (4) what positions are likely to be held in the future, and (5) the politician's own sense of integrity and honor. Equivocation may be the best solution, since no clear, unequivocal statement will begin to meet all those needs. One seasoned political figure had a favorite disarming answer when asked for his stand on what he knew to be a controversial issue: "You can count on me there, my friend. I'm all right on that one . . ."[4]

In daily relationships, faced with trying to figure out how someone will react to a request we want to make, or just to anticipate how to begin a conversation, we make ambiguous opening statements. Have you ever had a person come into your room while you are obviously studying and ask, "Hey, are you busy . . . ?" or "You got a minute?" Telephone open-

---

BOX 8-5.   Tragic Truth Telling

Little white lies, equivocation, or ambiguous answers are often considered socially acceptable forms of deception if feelings or sensibilities are spared. *Example:* After the very sudden death of his wife, a man we know approached the attending physician and in a tearful voice asked, "Doctor, was there anything I should have done that I didn't do?" The doctor proceeded to tell the bereaved husband that he should have brought his wife in for an examination many weeks earlier. Equivocation at that moment might have greatly softened the guilt felt by the grieving widower.

ings are designed to explore not the clarity of the connection, but the implicit interpersonal connection, as in the beginning question "Hi, what're you doin'?"[5]

Equivocation: Bad people or bad situations?

It is easy to say that some politicians are "slippery" or "evasive" or "speak with forked tongue" and blame equivocation on some kind of self-serving character flaw or evil personality trait, bordering on deliberate dishonest, misleading behavior. One popular notion is that equivocation and ambiguous behaviors come from some inner personal fault—a weakness of character, a lack of ethics, a dishonest tendency, an immoral attitude.

Based on their research, Bavelas et al. present the argument for a situational theory:[6]

> We propose that, although an individual equivocates, he or she is not the cause of equivocation. Rather, equivocation is the result of the individual's communicative situation. Equivocation is avoidance; it is the response chosen when all other communicative choices in the situation would lead to negative consequences.[7]

These researchers found, among other results, that people would choose direct messages where there was no communicative conflict, and "thus, situation determined the choice of message."[8]

A rich lexicon of words for "evasive actions" is included in this report, involved with metaphors for the act of being caught, such as "on the spot"; "in a bind" or "pinch" or "squeeze"; being "between a rock and a hard place," so as to make a person "straddle the fence," "skirt the issue," "dodge," "duck," "sidestep," "pussyfoot," "weasel," "vacillate," "beat around the bush," "waffle," or "back and fill."[9]

The great number of terms we have in our language relating to this activity of indirection or evasion could indicate that we must have a lot of it around—for the same reason the Eskimo has so many different words for snow.

Equivocation: The plus side

"Little white lies" permit you to tell your friends that their haircuts look great, that they are really not getting fat, that their term papers are really well written, or that it was really no bother for you to drive all the way across town to pick up the assignment.

Open communication in your relationships—personal or professional—may not be the only, or even sometimes the best, way to conduct your affairs. If you have multiple or competing goals to accomplish with your communication, it can be difficult for you to be unerringly clear and unambiguous as you speak or write to accomplish those goals.

Eric Eisenberg and others suggest the term "strategic ambiguity" to describe the effective activities of organizational communicators faced with "striking a balance between being understood, not offending others, and

Little white lies: "He's on a diet. Tell him he looks thin." *(Drawing by Modell; © 1984 The New Yorker Magazine, Inc.)*

maintaining one's own self-image."[10] The problems of trying to balance such competing needs as Eisenberg describes are, of course, not limited to communication in organizations. They may be present in your everyday behaviors with others in social settings, in marriage, in college classes, and in family interactions. Still another fertile field for ambiguous messages, the law, has been mentioned by Wendell Johnson, who himself dedicated his lifetime to helping people toward effective interpersonal communication:

> *The fact of ambiguity is not necessarily negative. Consider the writing of legislation, for example. Laws must have a certain vagueness fringe, a certain amount of ambiguity, if they are to have the most desirable effect for the greatest number of people. Yet if they are too ambiguous nobody will know how to apply or enforce them. And if they are too specific they won't be applicable in many situations. Ambiguity is fascinating.[11]*

USING LANGUAGE EFFECTIVELY

We are avoiding using the terms "good" and "bad" to refer to the ways in which people use language. Ethics in the use of language is of great importance to us, and we like to think that most communicators intend to do others no harm, and further intend their actions to fit the values and norms of the society they are communicating in.[12] Every society—every profession—has in it people who will abuse others by whatever means they can. Unfortunately, as we discuss later in this chapter, language is power and it is not really too difficult for people to use the power of language for unethical or immoral ends if they choose to do so.

BOX 8-6.   Nasty Names Will Hurt You

Language affects your behavior. You remember the old saying "Sticks and stones may break my bones, but names can never hurt me." If this were true, why would name-calling arouse so many violent feelings and reactions? If someone calls you a name you don't like, it will provoke some kind of reaction in you, which you may not show but which nonetheless affects you. Few people like to be called "chicken," "dummy," "goody-goody," "moron," "cheater," or "phony." Most of you can add your favorite insults to the list. Names do hurt you; words do affect you.

Language Relations in Three Parts

When an intended meaning is successfully selected by someone else from among the many possible meanings, you usually feel good; that communication has been "effective" or "successful." Too often, something is missing when meanings received are carefully compared with meanings sent. When misunderstandings occur, look to the three factors of (1) your own internal assumptions and symbol choices, (2) the assumptions and symbol interpretations by the other person, and (3) the language itself. That's a pretty simple model of communication, isn't it? You, the other person, and the language you use on each other. As you were told in the earlier chapters, however, the communication process is made complicated by people being complex accumulations of needs, interests, physical and psychological differences, and competing intentions.

Here we want to discuss the third part of communication potential: language itself. When language is used by people to say what they do not believe, when words are used (sometimes by accident and sometimes on purpose) to cover up rather than explain, to mislead rather than clarify, then we say a kind of "language pollution" is occurring.

In his book *1984*, George Orwell predicted that the official language "newspeak" would persuade the masses that "ignorance is strength" and "war is peace." Writing in 1949, Orwell believed that newspeak words would come to mean their opposites as in this sentence from *1984:* "The day to day falsification of the past carried out by the Ministry of Truth is as necessary to the stability of the regime as the work of repression and espionage carried out by the Ministry of Love." In America today the stationery of the Department of the Air Force, an arm of the Department of Defense, carries the motto "Peace Is Our Profession."

The Pentagon is a great originator of terminology which either obscures the grisly truth (as in the term for a population which survives several tons of bombs, which is "interdictional nonsuccumbers") or elevates common items all out of proportion to their reality (as in "wood interdental stimulator" for a toothpick, or "portable hand-held communicative inscriber" for a pencil).[13]

The *Quarterly Review of Doublespeak* is a publication which can keep you informed of the latest misuses of language; they were one of the first to call attention to the government's National Transportation

---

BOX 8-7. Language of Great Leaders

Language has long been known and respected as a force for moving people to believe or to act. Memorable language has been associated with the great leaders of history. During World War II, Winston Churchill was considered a great force in maintaining England's fighting strength and determination. His "prose" was so much like poetry that today a series of Churchillian phrases still demonstrate the most carefully constructed use of the language. For example: "We shall fight on the beaches, we shall fight on the landing grounds, we shall fight in the fields and in the streets. We shall fight in the hills. We shall never surrender."

A contemporary of Churchill, the United States' wartime president, Franklin D. Roosevelt, was a master at language use. One small story illustrates the dedication to the "right" phrase which made his rhetoric memorable. When the Japanese attacked Pearl Harbor on December 7, 1941, President Roosevelt went before Congress to ask for a declaration of war. Encouraged to use that time to develop a long discourse on the deterioration of Japanese-American relations, Roosevelt astutely said no. He would use his "fireside chat" on radio to the American people the next day to go into long details—but for his first dramatic message to Congress, as well as to the American people, he chose a six-minute

Martin Luther King, Jr. *(© UPI/Bettmann Newsphotos)*

address of remarkable power. He did not call his favorite speech writers of that time, Sherwood and Rosenman, but instead drafted this brief message himself. Most of us recognize the famous line "... a date which will live in infamy." Before he fine-tuned his own speech, Roosevelt had written that phrase as "*a date which will live in history.*" Roosevelt's choice of a little-used, obscure, but dynamic word made the message— as well as the word itself—memorable.

Martin Luther King's famous "*I have a dream . . .*" speech especially reflects the impact of well-chosen words which strike with power and leave lasting impressions on the listeners. Language from the minds and mouths of great leaders has moved nations and has caused changes of great importance in the world as far back as we have historical records.*

* For a discussion of rhetoric as poetry, see Helmut Geissner, "On Rhetoricity and Literacity," *Communication Education,* vol. 32, July 1983, pp. 275–284. An interesting account of Roosevelt's writing his famous "day of infamy" speech is in William Safire's *The New Language of Politics,* Random House, New York, 1968.

Safety Board euphemism for an airplane crash as "controlled flight into terrain."[14]

Jargon in a Specialized and High-Tech World

Some affectionate names have been given to words you might use to obscure information or to show you belong to a particular group with its own jargon and distinctive language. "Gobbledygook" is one such name and generally thought to come from the noise which turkeys make when they are just sounding off and making no sense. Often gobbledygook will be used to confuse a reader or listener and to make that person feel "one down" for not understanding the words. The originator of gobbledygook jargon also appears to be saying: "I know this stuff so well and you, stupid, can't belong to this same group." Have your computer-involved friends ever said something like "You really need more K to load Symphony, and if you have only 256 you won't boot up fast enough"? What would be your reaction if you were in the hospital and a nurse told you that you were ready to "pedangle"? Or announced you were "going to be prepped for an EMG"? Too often people in one profession believe that if they know something, it is known by everybody else, and also that everybody else knows the names for such things as "sitting on the edge of your bed and dangling your legs."

Another term for specialized language is "bafflegab," characterized by a deliberate desire to confuse rather than to clarify. William Safire suggests that these bafflegab terms are all ways of referring to economic conditions in a confusing, perhaps even deceptive, way: "healthy slow-down," "rolling readjustment," "high-level stagnation," and "mini-

Jargon in a specialized world. General Norman Schwartzkopf and other military briefing leaders used unfamiliar terms and acronyms. "Collateral damage" meant civilian casualties. "Smart bombs" may have included the enemy's missile that was named "SCUD" while our side had "Patriots" which sounds much better. (© Reuters/Bettmann)

slump."[15] An editor at the Princeton University Press, who normally spends his time translating technical language into plain English, has "reverse-engineered" the process and describes a cup of coffee as a "ceramic gravitational containment vessel containing psychoactive high-temperature botanical filtrate."[16]

Embellishment for Effect

Another form of word pollution you can find all around you is "embellishment." When you embellish a statement, you build on a simple statement to get a greater effect. "No, you can't go to Suzie's house" can be turned into martyrdom by paraphrasing it as "Mom says I have to stay home and that Suzie's house is off limits to me; probably forever." "I'll help if you want me to" can be reported later as "He said he would be delighted to help me in any way he could, and I only have to ask to get everything I need." The embellished form of "no comment," when used by news sources, can be reported in the papers or on television news specials (watch CBS's *60 Minutes* for examples) as "The official whose opinion was sought to get the other side of the story was not available for comment and refused to be interviewed for this broadcast." This is not a new device, however, as the press had a way of treating President Calvin Coolidge, famous for his communication brevity, to overcome that President's very tight-lipped style. When Coolidge would say, "I am not in favor of that legislation," the next day the newspapers would report: "President Coolidge, in a fighting mood, today served notice on Congress that he intended to combat with all the resources at his command. . . ."[17]

A Continuum of Polluted Language

Here are three dimensions or classes of language pollution which are not in the neat separations of individual categories we are printing them in— rather they should be seen as overlapping, shading from one to the other as general ranges of behaviors.

While we suggest some ways you can be alert to these sometimes questionable uses ("correctives"), we do not pass judgment on the people who use them or their intentions or ethics. In the same way we do not look with disdain at those people who are victims of these behaviors, or accuse them of being gullible. Table 8-1 is a statement about the language itself, as it is used by people who have needs to be met by their communication patterns which may fit some of these as listed. If these items represent symptoms of language disease, there is also the possibility that not all are fatal and that some may even be curable.

Confusion occurs most frequently when language is unfamiliar and when ideas are complex. Thus confusion results when you are faced with a foreign language, when you are presented with too much information when being given directions, when simple words are used in a way you are not accustomed to, or when you confront new or technical terminology. *Example:* (Instructions in a computer printer manual.) "For wiring the interface, be sure to use twisted-pair cable for each signal and never fail to complete connection on the Return side."

TABLE 8-1.
Common Classes of Language Pollution

Pollution type	Characteristics (how they show up in your communication)	Some communication correctives
Confusion (unknown meanings)	Foreign language Unfamiliar words Technical jargon Misused terminology	Ask for a translation. Ask for a definition of terms, or a restatement in other, more familiar terms, or a more direct statement.
Ambiguity (too many meanings)	Too many possible ways to define the words Vague references, hints Very general, imprecise statements or terms	Check to find out which meaning is really intended. Ask for more details. Seek examples, instances, clear cases.
Deception (obscured meanings)	Outright lies Distortions of data Incomplete data or careless reporting Nonanswers to direct questions	Confront with your own information. Seek some common or public data to check from. Ask for clarification, restatement. Rephrase questions if you don't get clear or adequate answers.

Ambiguity occurs mainly when your choices of what to do (or to understand) are far greater than what the "right" answer provides for. Words are equivocal, leaving you uncertain about how to respond or behave. *Example:* "When you go to the store, pick up something for supper" may mean meat, potatoes, salad, but you may not know what. "Y'all come over to see us some time" is so ambiguous as to not be an invitation at all.

Deception occurs most frequently when you don't want another person to know something. You may set out to trick the other person with language—to delude, divert, or defraud. Some deceptions like a magician's sleight of hand or plans for a surprise birthday party may be harmless. Deception is also used when you do not want to get into trouble, or want to protect yourself some way. *Example: "Did you do the dishes?"* You answer "I put them in the sink." *"What time did you get in last night?"* and you reply, "I didn't look at the clock." *"How much did that new sweater cost?"* and you answer, "I got it on sale." You notice in all these examples the answer was not a lie. You merely responded to some other question which had not been asked—"Did you put the dishes in the sink?" "Did you look at the clock last night?" "Did you get the sweater on sale?"

INFERENCE, OBSERVATION, AND JUDGMENT

Reports on what is going on around you are affected by what you see and what you think you see. You observe things and then begin making those observations fit what you know about your world. Inferences are what you add to your observations. They are the imagining and "certainties" you believe in. In the following examples can you trace the movement from one stage to another?

If you saw a woman you know driving a new car, what would you think? She bought it? She borrowed it? She was trying it out? She was driving it somewhere for someone? You observed her driving a new car and began immediately to make inferences that would explain the situation.

You see two people standing in the hall arguing. You begin to make some inferences on what is happening and what is going to happen.

A teacher asks one of the students to stay after class. The first-level observation includes the student and teacher talking, whereas the many-leveled inferences can be the source of all kinds of stories about it.

An office worker shows up late. Can the employer infer that the worker missed the bus, overslept, doesn't care, has bad attitudes about being on time, or got trapped for fifteen minutes in the elevator?

You can mislead yourself when you let your inferences go far beyond what you can observe. You begin to mislead others when what you tell them is based on what you thought about it (inferred), rather than on what you actually saw (observed). See the Laboratory Manual, page 410, for an excellent exercise in inference-observation confusion.

Statements about Facts and Statements about Inferences

In English two kinds of declarative statements are possible. You can look at a man and say, "He has on glasses." This is a *statement about a fact* because it corresponds closely to what you observed, and it can be verified by others through observation. Or you can say, "He bought the glasses." This is a statement about an inference which you make because the man is wearing the glasses, he looks honest, and few people would steal prescription glasses and wear them.

A statement about an inference is a guess about the unknown based on the known. The "known" may be an observation or a series of observations (the man is wearing glasses). Or sometimes the "known" may be only an inference or a series of inferences (the man looks honest, etc.). (Box 8-8 gives an amusing example of inferences.)

Some guesses, of course, are more easily and quickly verifiable than others. Some are more probable than others. For example, if you go to the post office to mail a package at 10 A.M. on Tuesday, you are saying to yourself, "The post office is open." This is a statement about inferences. You do not know for a fact that it is open. You have not observed it to be open. It is an inference which is (1) easily verifiable through observation (all you need to do is get there and observe whether it is open or not), (2) quickly verified (right away if you wish), and (3) highly probable (post offices are usually open on work days at 10 A.M., you have seen a sign telling what the post office hours are, you went there yesterday at 10 A.M. and it was open, and you went there last Tuesday and it was open).

Your decision to go and mail your package is thus based on a rather

---

BOX 8-8. The Kiss and the Slap

In a railroad compartment, an American grandmother, her young and attractive granddaughter, a Romanian officer, and a Nazi officer were the only occupants. The train was passing through a dark tunnel, and what was heard was a loud kiss and a vigorous slap. After the train emerged from the tunnel nobody spoke, but the grandmother was saying to herself: "What a fine girl I have raised. She will take care of herself. I am proud of her." The granddaughter was saying to herself: "Well, grandmother is old enough not to mind a little kiss. Besides, the fellows are nice. I am surprised what a hard wallop grandmother has." The Nazi officer was meditating, "How clever those Romanians are! They steal a kiss and have the other fellow slapped." The Romanian officer was chuckling to himself: "How smart I am! I kissed my own hand and slapped the Nazi!"*

* Alfred Korzybski, "The Role of Language on Perceptual Processes," in Robert R. Blake and Glenn V. Ramsey (eds.), *Perception—An Approach to Personality,* The Ronald Press Company, New York, 1951, pp. 170–171.

probable inference because the inference itself is based on past observation. Of course, something might have happened today that resulted in an unexpected closing. But that's a chance or a risk you have to take. In this case, however, because you were aware that you were making an inference, you assessed its probability; you figured out the odds, so to speak. You ran a risk, but this was a *calculated risk*. You based it on information and experience.

The need to distinguish between types of statements

If you look at statements about facts and statements about inferences on the basis of how certain or probable they are, you can construct a chart such as Figure 8-2.

A fact or an observation belongs to the "high probability" end of the curve in Figure 8-2. Why not absolute certainty? Because even observations cannot be fully trusted. Remember our discussion of perceptional distortions? However, if you observe something time after time, and if other people agree that they observe it too, you can approach certainty. But you never quite reach *absolute* certainty. Your feelings of certainty, however, come partly from the validity you attach to your senses and partly from the validation you get from other people. If you see something green, and everyone around tells you it's red, and you know they are not joking, you begin to wonder. Inferences, on the other hand, never reach this "may approach certainty" level. Inferences are in the realm of lower probability.

Why is it important to distinguish between statements about facts and

FIGURE 8-2
Probability of statements about fact and inferences.

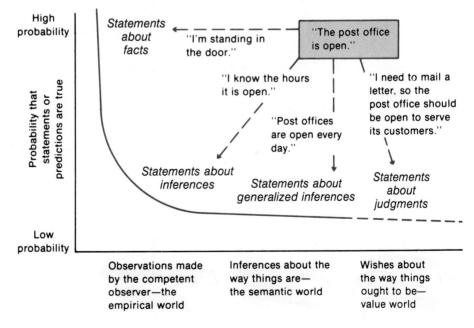

statements about inferences? If you do not know that you are making an inference, then you do not know that you are operating in the realm of probability, in the realm of guesses. If you do not know it, then you are not likely to figure the odds. If you make an inference and treat it *as if it were* an observation, then you will feel that it is almost certain and that you don't need to do any checking. In this case you run an *uncalculated risk*.

William Haney gives the following suggestions to distinguish statements about facts from statements about inferences:[18]

Statement about facts	Statements about inferences
1. Can be made only *after* observation	Can be made *anytime*
2. Must stay *within* what one observes and not go beyond	*Can go beyond;* are limited only by one's imagination
3. Can be made only by an *observer*	Can be made by *anyone*
4. *Approach certainty*	Deal only with *probability*
5. Can be made only to the extent of the observer's capabilities and competency	Can be made by the *incompetent*

It seems necessary to add the fifth qualification (not from Haney) because some people are better-trained observers than others (and, as we have written earlier in this chapter, more honest) and therefore their statements about what they observe are more reliable. If a totally incompetent person looks at your car engine and makes a statement such as "Your carburetor is full of dirt" and gets agreement from several other mechanically incompetent people, you do not have a statement about observations, because these people may not even know what a carburetor looks like.

How to verify an inference

When you hear statements about inferences, you should assess their probability. How can you do this? How do you figure out the odds? How do you calculate the risk? The first thing to do is to check the source of the inference. Is the inference based on one observation or many observations, on observations made by one person or many people? What kind of people made the inference: competent, incompetent, trustworthy, biased, prejudiced, or deceitful?

You can make for yourself a scale of probability and place on the scale the different possible sources of your information. For example, when you want to determine whether the post office is open, and you are not in a position to find out for yourself through observation, you will have to take somebody's word for it. One person's word will be more reliable than another person's. If you call the post office and one of its employees tells you it's open, then your inference is pretty reliable (although it is conceivable that the person could lie, or that between the time of the phone call and the time you get there something could happen to make the office close). If you ask someone who just went to the post office and that person tells you it is open, it is also quite probable the post office is open. If you ask someone who read the sign that indicates the hours the post office is open, the accuracy of the answer is a little more doubtful unless you can be pretty sure this person has a good memory. If you ask a stranger in town, then that answer may be less reliable. You should be cautious in evaluating the source of your inferences before you act on them.

Statements about Judgment

Some statements are neither statements about facts nor statements about inferences. They are called "statements about judgment" because they reflect a value held by the person making the judgment.

"The food in the cafeteria is terrible."

"The quarter system is better than the semester system."

"She is beautiful."

"He is really smart."

These statements are a reflection of personal values. They say very little about what is being talked about and a great deal about the person

Statement about judgment: "You are fair, compassionate, and intelligent, but you are perceived as biased, callous, and dumb." *(Drawing by Mankoff; © 1985 The New Yorker Magazine, Inc.)*

who does the talking. The boy in love who says that his girl is the most beautiful girl in the world is talking not about the girl, not about the world, but about himself. When you say the food is bad, you are talking about *your* tastes in food. When you say someone is smart, you are talking about *your* criteria for smartness. Agreement among people on these statements proves very little about the validity of the statements. People are agreeing on values and not on observation.

You can operate better in life if you can distinguish between a statement about what's going on "out there" (observation) and a statement about what's going on in somebody's head (inferences or judgment). Your communication will be helped if you can determine where speakers or writers got their information: did they get it by observing and then state only what they observed? Or did they make some inferences, and then report to you what they felt about the thing?

Statements about judgments come from somebody's insides and appeal to your own insides. It helps when you find others whose internal reactions seem to agree with yours, but it makes the judgment no more reliable—only more widely expressed.

It is true that standards of judgment or values are similar within a particular culture. Standards of beauty, right, wrong, good, bad, fashion, and pleasure are learned in the same way language is learned. To agree that long hair looks bad on men does not make it a fact. It simply means that those who agree have the same taste and value about hair.

If you believe that simply because other people agree with your judgments you must be absolutely right, this will reduce your tolerance of those people who do not agree with you. It will also increase your need to convert anyone to your position, since it is so "true and right." Both results diminish your chances of successful communication.

SUMMARY

Trying to understand—to make meaning out of—the events and behaviors around you is not always easy. You depend on other people speaking a language like yours, referring to things which you have some experience with, and putting the words together in an orderly and predictable way. If you go to another country where your own language is not spoken, you not only will have difficulty trying to translate the unfamiliar words, but also will lack some of the shared experiences in that culture to help make sense out of what is being said.

In summary, here are three major principles of meaning and language. *First, people have similar meanings only to the extent that they have similar experiences.* Connotations are private and developed with you all the years you have been seeing and doing things. No two people ever have identical experiences, and it is from those differences that you develop your nonidentical meanings.

Second, meanings are not fixed; they change as your experiences change. Heraclitus said that a person never steps in the same river twice; the person changes and the river flows.

Third, you always respond to your environment in relation to your own experiences. Whatever you say about the "world out there" is actually a report on your own way of looking at that world. An ability to see the world on someone else's terms is called "empathy," "sensitivity," "communication awareness," or "psychological adaptation." But when you talk about the world you know, you invariably end up talking about yourself.

END NOTES

1 C. K. Ogden and I. A. Richards, *The Meaning of Meaning,* Harcourt, Brace & World, New York, 1969, pp. 10–11.

2 T. P. McNamara and D. L. Miller, "Attributes of Theories of Meaning," *Psychological Bulletin,* vol. 105, November 1990, p. 355.

3 R. C. Anderson, "Inferences about Word Meanings," *The Psychology of Learning and Motivation,* vol. 25, 1990, Academic Press, San Diego, CA.

4 A. Glazer, "The Strategy of Candidate Ambiguity," *American Political Science Review,* vol. 84, March 1990, p. 237.

5 R. Hopper, "Sequential Ambiguity in Telephone Openings," *Communication Monographs,* vol. 56, September 1990, p. 240.

6 J. B. Bavelas, A. Black, N. Chovil, and J. Mullet, *Equivocal Communication,* Sage Series in Interpersonal Communication, Sage Publications, Newbury Park, CA, 1990; see chap. 3, "A Situational Theory."

7 Ibid., p. 54.

8 Ibid., p. 80.

9 Ibid., p. 60.

10 E. M. Eisenberg, "Ambiguity as Strategy in Organizational Communication," *Communication Monographs,* vol. 51, September 1984, p. 228.

11 W. Johnson and D. Moeller, *Living with Change: The Semantics of Coping,* Harper & Row, New York, 1972, p. 94.

12 For an insightful essay on the teaching of ethics in speech, see W. C. Redding, "Rocking Boats, Blowing Whistles, and Teaching Speech Communication," *Communication Education,* vol. 34, no. 3, July 1985, p. 245.

13 H. Bruce, "Language of the U.S. Military," *ETC: A Review of General Semantics,* vol. 44, Fall 1987, p. 295. (Originally published in *The Toronto Star.*)

14 Formerly printed as *Public Doublespeak Newsletter* by the National Council of Teachers of English Committee on Public Doublespeak, the *Quarterly Review of Doublespeak* may be addressed at 111 Kenyon Road, Urbana, IL.

15 William Safire, *The New Language of Politics,* Random House, New York, 1968, p. 26.

16 W. Tenner, *Tech Speak: An Advanced Post-Vernacular Discourse Modulation Protocol,* Crown Publishers, New York 1986.

17 Safire, op cit., p. 202.

18 W. Haney, *Communication and Organizational Behavior* (rev. ed.), Richard D. Irwin, Homewood, IL, 1967, p. 195. Reprinted by permission of the author and the publisher.

CHAPTER
9

NONVERBAL AND SILENCES: COMMUNICATING WITHOUT WORDS

OBJECTIVES

When you complete this chapter, you should be able to:

1. List eight different kinds of silences and suggest the occasions when each would be appropriate.
2. Distinguish between what can be identified as an "appropriate silence" and an "inappropriate silence."
3. Identify when people meeting for the first time begin to make judgments about each other, and describe the circumstances along with possible kinds of errors which can be made.
4. List four ways you can avoid careless or inappropriate use of nonverbal communication so that you may have a more realistic perspective on the strengths and weaknesses of analyzing nonverbal communication.
5. Define and give original examples of paralanguage, gestures, facial expression (including gaze behaviors), object language, and touching.
6. Discuss the intercultural nature of both time and space as textual features of nonverbal communication.
7. Discuss the reliability of perceived nonverbal communication in relation to verbal communication.

8. Explain and give an original example to show how nonverbal communication serves to establish relationships.

INTRODUCTION

Study of communication without words, or *nonverbal* as it has come to be called, is relatively recent. For a long time people felt that if words were not involved, there was no communication. This attitude was reinforced by a norm in our culture which places a strong emphasis on the virtues of speech. In spite of a few wise sayings to the contrary ("Silence is golden," "One picture is worth a thousand words," etc.), there is strong respect for a "gift of gab," and some grudging praise for one who has "kissed the Blarney stone" and thereby received a talent for talking. In groups and meetings, it is assumed that people who are silent are the least influential members and often the least capable or intelligent. Verbal spellbinders in our society can sell used cars, snake oil, and political beliefs.

This common attitude about silence—as the mere absence of verbalized noise—is rooted in a mistaken notion that communication can be turned on and off just by opening and closing your mouth. That's a misleading idea because, as we discussed in Chapter 1 and will continue here, you cannot *not* communicate. Your silences and other nonverbal behaviors are no more random than your words; they have much potential information value to another person.

The range of nonverbal communication is impressive; you will find entire volumes devoted to any one of the kinds of nonverbal used in your communication—books entirely on facial expression; books dealing only with gestures, or spatial relations, or time. We cannot, in this textbook, fully explore nonverbal implications or report on the enormous amount of study going on all the time about such a fascinating part of our interaction with others. In this chapter, however, we will touch on the following aspects of the nonverbal system: first, silences as communication, second, the process of sending and receiving nonverbal messages; third, the ways that contextual patterns of time and space influence communication; and fourth, a summary of the characteristics of nonverbal systems.

SILENCES

Silences Occur in Interpersonal Communication

You and your new date are driving on your way to a movie. After some time of idle chatting about the weather, where you go to school, where your date goes to school, what courses you are taking, and the kind of movies you like, you run out of things to say, and silence sets in—long, heavy, embarrassing silence. Your date just sits there, and you can't think of another thing to say. In desperation you turn on the radio.

You have just been introduced to a person sitting next to you at a dinner, and after the usual small talk neither of you finds a thing to say; the

BOX 9-1. Yogi Wisdom

Yogi Berra, former big league baseball catcher, is also known for some very curious philosophical statements about the world. He had this to say about nonverbal communication: "You can observe a lot by just watching."

(© AP/Wide World)

best you can do is stare at your napkin or appear very busy fiddling with the silverware.

These two examples are not unusual. They illustrate two principles about silence: (1) Silences are an integral part of interpersonal communication. They occur more often than you think. (2) Silences in many cases are perceived as embarrassing. You somehow feel they should not happen; and when they occur, you try desperately to fill the gaps they create. Silences, however, are not to be equated with the absence of communication.[1] Silences are a natural and fundamental aspect of communication, often ignored because misunderstood.

> As most students of social interaction are aware, lapses in conversation are so potentially embarrassing that participants will often resort to noisy "masking" behaviors to fill in the silence—coughing, clearing the throat, sighing,

whistling, yawning, drumming the fingertips; or they may utter meaningless "sociocentric sequences" such as "but ah," "so," and "anyway" in the hope of nudging a partner into taking a turn.[2]

Most studies of lapses (or "latencies," as they are sometimes called) in speaking exchanges have concluded that the person who cannot handle such gaps easily is considered a less competent communicator. The person thought to be more effective is the one who manages better the periodic silences which normally occur in much of our communication. Think about the people you know with whom it is "easy to talk." How do they handle the little lags in your speaking flow? How do you share the responsibility with them for "keeping the conversation going"? When lapses occur among your peers, or with your very close friends, do you react the same way as you do when lapses occur when you are in the presence of people you want desperately to impress?

Effective communication between people depends heavily on silences because people take turns at talking and at being silent when listening. Unless one is silent, one cannot fully listen. Unless you know that silences are a part of the gamut of communication, you will continue to be afraid of them and avoid them instead of making full use of them.

Silences Are Not Random

Perhaps you have noted that we use the word "silences" in its plural form. This is deliberate. We want to stress that there are many different types of silences, each with a meaning of its own and different implications and consequences for communication.[3] When you say you like silence or are afraid of it, you really fail to acknowledge the many differences between types of silences. To understand communication, you must differentiate between the many types of silences and meet them with an appropriate behavior.

For example: (1) Silence when you are terribly angry, frustrated, gritting your teeth, ready to blow up, yet tensing up so as not to let the steam out, is different from (2) silence which occurs when you are attentively listening to an important broadcast or a fascinating lecture or story. In both cases no word may be spoken, but what goes on inside you in terms of feelings, reactions, emotions, and thoughts is quite different. Not only does your silence stem from a different cause, but your actions, expressions, and movements reflect that difference.

(3) Silence when you listen but are bored is different from the preceding two silences. The silence of boredom expresses a withdrawal from the situation, a negative evaluation of what is going on; it implies an attitude of superiority which often offends those toward whom it is directed if they perceive it.

Earlier in this chapter we mentioned (4) the silence which occurs when you cannot think of a thing to say (on a date, at a dinner, or in any situation involving people you do not know well). During these social

BOX 9-2.   Cross-Cultural Silence

Many silences are of great importance to some cultures and to many religions. The "vow of silence," for some religious orders, and the meditative quiet for lay worshippers represent devotion, respect, depth of commitment, and focus of attention. Different parts of the world treat silence in different ways. One interesting difference involves the Japanese and the influence of the Zen Buddhism ideal of nothingness and incompleteness. The Japanese word *ma* signifies effective use of time and space intervals in which silences—absences of speech, musical tones, or other effects—are most important as they convey special significance.*
Silence is valued more than eloquence, so the Japanese adult tends to be more restrained and formal, less talkative or revealing, than an American adult, a habit which starts early in life according to Dean Barnlund.†

* N. Honna and B. Hoffer, *An English Dictionary of Japanese Culture,* Yuhikaku Publishing, Tokyo, 1986, p. 156.
† D. C. Barnlund, *Communicative Styles of Japanese and Americans: Images and Realities,* Wadsworth, Belmont, CA, 1989, p. 115.

encounters, talk is expected. Silence represents what is feared the most, and when it occurs, makes you feel terribly inadequate and self-conscious.

(5) Silence when you are thinking about a point made by a speaker is different from (6) silence which occurs when you do not understand what the speaker said. In the latter you may be so confused that you do not even know what to ask in order to get some clarification.

(7) Silence can be reverent, meditative, or contemplative. Perhaps you silently pray; or perhaps you take a walk and encounter something so beautiful that you are speechless and the sight stirs deep emotions in you.

(8) The silence of allness, the dogmatic "There is no more to be said on the matter; that's all there is to it" is quite different from (9) the silence of lovers or friends who may simply hold each other's hands and do not need to say anything at all to communicate their feelings. The latter is a comfortable silence, a silence you do not need to break, a silence you treasure because it reflects the depth of a relationship. A glance, an understanding smile, or a look is all that is necessary. Words are not needed.

(10) The silence of grief is another type of silence. "So they sat down with him upon the ground seven days and seven nights and no one spoke a word unto him. For they saw his grief was very great" (Book of Job 1:13). This is a difficult silence. You know intuitively that words don't

begin to express the sympathy or the concern you want to share with a person who grieves. Sometimes, just being silently there is enough.

(11) Silence can be a challenge, like the silence of the pouting child or the stubborn and angry friend, or the silence in a classroom toward the very last minutes of a period when the teacher asks, "Do you have any questions?" and students almost dare each other to say one word which might trigger the teacher to continue talking after the bell.

This list of silences is not exhaustive. There are many, many different types of silences which mean a lot of different things. What we are trying to establish here is an awareness that silences cannot be lumped all together. Each must be interpreted on its own. The reactions to each of these silences should be different because each means something different.

Using Your Silences Appropriately

A sensitivity to silences is imperative to two-way communication. This means sensitivity to your own silences and to the silences of others to whom you would speak. If you are silent because you are thinking about a point the speaker made, or if you are puzzled by what the speaker said, you should let him or her know. If people are silent when you speak, you must be able to read the cues that will tell you the reasons for their particular silence. Do they misunderstand you? Do they clam up because they are resisting what you are saying? Are they bored? Did you lose them?

There are many cues available which help you to understand people's

---

BOX 9-3. Rudeness of Silence

Irene Gunther, a resident of New York who writes frequently about New York issues, described a "new rudeness" in a column in the *New York Times*.* Gunther claims that *silence* has replaced other forms of rude interaction—nobody says anything to you in response to a question or a statement. People point, or otherwise interact by avoiding any words, carrying out your requests with an expressionless face, silently, and never looking at you. She used to be able to shout back at rude people, to verbally confront problem issues, to argue, but now, she says, "the silence—the cutting off of human contact—leaves me without a response." One of her ways of coping with wordlessly silent bank tellers who look past her and never utter a sound in response to questions or salutations is to use the money machines, which at least have polite instructions and a friendly "thank you."

* *New York Times*, Dec. 13, 1986, p. 27.

silences. The way they move, their gestures, and their facial expressions will tell you a great deal about the reasons for the silence. We will analyze these in detail in another section of this chapter.

Just as you may say the wrong thing at the wrong time, you may respond silently to a situation requiring talk, and not be silent when you should. A person who is engaged in serious thinking will probably not welcome the friend who comes barging in and talks a mile a minute about trivial things. When people are worshiping in church, they usually resent a loud intrusion by tourists exclaiming about the beauty of the ceiling, the organ, or the artwork.

On the other hand, in some social situations, you may be called a snob or someone may clap you on the shoulder and say, "Whassamatter? You're being awful quiet," when others think you should be talking. Conversation need not be about significant issues or weighty subjects, but silence may be perceived as an indicator that you do not approve of what's going on or that you would rather be someplace else. Even if this is true, you know that it is not polite to give that impression. So, usually, you chat away at the same level as the rest of the crowd. You talk about the weather, the decor of the room, or what you do for a living, and these simple exchanges set up avenues for further communication. Being silent in such situations seems to have very little virtue, as your social acceptability depends on your saying something, however inane it may be. Silence when the situation requires some form of verbal exchange makes you appear antisocial and drives people away from you. So when your neighbor hollers at you, "Nice day," you usually come back with an equally profound, "It sure is." Both of you have made contact and feel reassured that you are not isolated.

SENDING AND RECEIVING NONVERBAL COMMUNICATION

Your relationships with others depend very much on the nonverbal messages you send, and the way you interpret what you observe. You may have, even before a word is said, made up your mind about some person you are meeting. You suspect, also, that others somehow seem to judge you in advance of their finding out how smart, how witty, how charming, or how interesting a conversationalist you are.

In the first few minutes of meeting a new person, the two of you are sizing each other up. While you may be verbally saying safe and probably very shallow things to each other, it is likely that more meaningful messages about your likes and dislikes are being exchanged nonverbally. "Flabby handshake." "No wedding ring." "Tall: I'm nervous around tall people." "Southern drawl; or affected stage speech." "Hair needs shaping." "Looks like my best friend back home; nice person." "Gestures gracefully." "Awful necktie." "Stands too far back from me to talk easily; snob?"

Nonverbal messages are of course not used only on first meetings. In

Telephone styles are
expressive and often
exaggerated. (© *Walter S.
Silver/The Picture Cube*)

all your relationships you depend on nonverbal cues to send information
to others by tone of voice, gaze, gesture, touching, and so on. At the
same time you expect to have others give you clues to their meanings,
their moods, and their expectations not only with words but with nonverbal signals as well. Face-to-face communication can make use of the
visible nonverbal signals—facial expression, gestures, clothes, etc.—but
your telephone conversations limit your nonverbal signals to tone of voice
and choice of words. Notice, however, how your telephone style is usually
much more expressive and exaggerated than your normal face-to-face
speech. That's your attempt to make up for the loss of the other more
visual nonverbal cues no longer available. Radio announcers must use
more vocal expression than do television announcers, who have their
visual nonverbal capabilities for support of their messages.

Nonverbal as Popular Culture

Nonverbal communication has caught the attention of the public in the
same way that we have seen great popular interest in language (as mentioned in our earlier references to study of English and "American").
People want to know about how they can influence others by use of body
language or nonverbal systems. You may be curious about how the moves
you make, the way you say things, might tell the "truth" about you to
other people who can "read you like a book." This "Sunday supplement,"
popularized approach to nonverbal communication may be loosely based
on sound nonverbal analysis, but there is little chance you will either gain
powerful control over others or be completely victimized by them simply
because of nonverbal messages. Some cautions, or disclaimers, are nec-

essary to keep in perspective the power of nonverbal analysis or manip-ulation.

Caution 1: Consider the context

Just as words are spoken in the context of ongoing relationships, your nonverbal signals are related to your verbal ones, to your latest interactions with the other person, to what other messages you have given the person by the way you stand, touch, gaze, or provide clues to the total situation. Judging a person on the basis of one wink of an eye, one crossing of the arms, one detached stance, may be out of context—just as you would not likely get the full meaning of a conversation by hearing only one word spoken. You need a representative sample of words or of nonverbal signs to make a judgment about a person's meanings or attitudes or intentions. But too many popular how-to-do-it books and articles on nonverbal analysis ignore this important requirement that you must have a large number of messages to analyze, and they must be considered in an overall context or situation. Some experts even argue that the two systems—verbal and nonverbal—cannot and should not be studied or analyzed separately.

Caution 2: Was it really a message?

Did that person wink at me and therefore mean to flirt, or did he or she have something in the eye? Did your aunt cross her arms (a sign of rejection in some books) when you were talking to her because she felt a draft or because she hates you? Did your friend sit a little bit too far away from you at the game because of anger or because there was part of a milkshake spilled on the seat? The nonverbal messages may be, as many popular authors insist, a sign of some deep-seated psychological concerns—or they may simply reflect a natural response to some physical event or condition. Before you try to play psychologist with your friends, or overanalyze the messages you get, you might ask if this nonverbal signal is what it appears to be. The caution here is, in summary, don't overinterpret any single, isolated nonverbal fragment.

Caution 3: Don't expect too much

Maybe you have studied the theory and practice of nonverbal and hope to manipulate other people into doing what you want without their even knowing what happened to them. If you intend to control others by your use of nonverbal, you should know that there are many different inter-pretations that they can place on your moves; and some interpretations might not be accurate. Furthermore, even if you may work out a whole set of influential nonverbal acts, there is at least some chance nobody is paying close enough attention to be influenced by them.[4]

Caution 4: Everybody is not alike

Nonverbal behavior differs from person to person and especially from culture to culture—gestures in one society may mean something quite different in another. The spirited display of school spirit and loyalty in Texas of the upraised hand motion called "Hook 'em Horns" is a very

---

BOX 9-4. Nonverbal in International Affairs

In international affairs, meetings of heads of state are watched for their nonverbal signals as much as for the multilingual verbiage which can be subject to mistranslation.

Nonverbal may also be difficult to translate, as this report about a summit meeting between the U.S. President and the head of the Soviet Union shows.

A White House spokesman quoted the lead from two different stories sent out by Reuters news service about how the U.S. President looked and acted when the two heads of state got together—one version of the news story said the President was "still and impassive," and in the other version he was described as "relaxed and smiling." If you as a reader of these stories wondered how the meeting was going, would the description of nonverbal reactions give you a clue?

In addition, a news analyst for Cable News Network was called in to look at videotapes of the Presidential body language to try to get a reading on how the deliberations were going. The analyst reported: "The President shrugged; but it wasn't a negative shrug."*

* *New York Times,* Oct. 12, 1986, p. 12.

---

obscene gesture in Latin America. Facial display varies from one part of the world to another, and you should be careful to judge either a lack of expression or extreme showiness in relation to others' cultural norms, not just what you are used to in your part of the world. An American telling a joke to a Japanese business associate is encouraged by what the American perceives as a smile of appreciation, but what is more likely to be a normal (for that culture) expression of embarrassment on the face of the person from Japan, a sign that the American storyteller should quit. You grew up in a family, in a specific community, learning a personal set of nonverbal patterns just as you learned your own very characteristic speech patterns. Research has shown that men and women use nonverbal symbols differently, with women generally being more sensitive to cues than men.[5] Different people act differently when they lie as they differ in how they "leak" clues to their lying by expressions of tension and relaxation.[6]

NONVERBAL SYSTEMS

There is always a "what" and a "how" dimension to your communication relations. You say something (the what), and you say it in a particular way (the how). While the "what" is giving information or data about something, the "how" dimension gives clues about (1) *how your messages should be interpreted*—as serious, joking, important, in strict confi-

Gestures in one society may mean something else in another. "Hook 'em horns" does not mean the same thing in Latin America as it does at the University of Texas. (© Bob Daemmrich)

dence, etc.—and (2) *how you relate* to the person with whom you are communicating—as close friend, superior, subordinate, casual stranger, intimate, etc.

You expect the "what" to be carried by words primarily. You then can expect most of the "how" to be carried by closely related clues given in the nonverbal system.

Classifying Nonverbal

There are many ways of taking apart human behaviors to look at them, and the study of nonverbal communication is no exception. One of the problems with classifying is that writers and researchers tend to separate the inseparable, to divide the indivisible, and to freeze action which is fluid and free-moving. All that makes it easier to analyze and to understand the processes, but we must be continually aware of what we are doing—chopping up a dynamic process into smaller and static pieces so we can study it.

**Some traditional
systems**

One important way of analyzing nonverbal communication involves looking at facial expressions or gestures or body postures in terms of what qualities they show in relationships. For example, building on early claims that the face is used by people to show four categories of expression: pleasantness, control, intensity, and (much weaker) interest, Mehrabian's research followed with three categories of meaning in facial expression: evaluation, potency or status, and responsiveness. Considering gestures, Mehrabian asserted it was possible to make moves which show others that you like/dislike them, and to indicate if you were superior/subordinate to them. Body posture, another kind of nonverbal system, can indicate how close you feel to another person (immediacy), how much authority (power) you may have over them, and how much you are interested in what they are saying or doing (responsiveness).[7]

You can see how useful these categories are in studying human interaction beyond words. Tests are also available for you to take which evaluate your sensitivity to the nonverbal cues such as facial expressions. This, of course, suggests that with appropriate study or training you can learn to be a better judge of facial expressions, gestures, and postural cues.[8]

Kinesics

Special credit for developing techniques and taxonomies for studying human movement has been given to Ray Birdwhistell and his innovative kinesics system. He has described *kinesics* as ". . . groupings of movements which are of significance to the communication process and thus to the interactional systems of particular social groups."[9]

"Movement" in kinesics includes, very significantly, facial expressions as well as body movements (hands, arms, head, spine, etc.). Of importance also is Birdwhistell's insistence on two issues: first, that movements are interrelated and do not stand alone to "mean," and second, that behaviors are related to the cultures in which they occur.

> While body motion behavior is based on the physiological structure, the communicative aspects of this behavior are patterned by social and cultural experience. The meaning of such behavior is not so simple that it can be itemized in a glossary of gestures. . . . meaning . . . can be derived only from examination of the patterned structure of the system of body motion as a whole as it manifests itself in the particular social situation.[10]

**Nonverbal classes
and contexts**

In this chapter we will divide nonverbal phenomena into two basic groups. The *classes* of activities and behaviors themselves include (1) paralanguage, (2) facial expression, (3) gaze, (4) gestures, (5) body language, (6) touch, and (7) object language. The *contexts* surrounding nonverbal include (1) time and (2) space.

In each of these groups we will look at how the class or context is part of interpersonal communication, and give you some data and guidance on how you can participate in nonverbal as both (1) an *observer* of what others do to you, and (2) an *initiator,* or the person who does it.

Our developmental pattern for looking at the *classes* starts with the nearest class to verbal communication—paralanguage, or the overtones of your actual speaking—and moves generally farther from language until you are confronted with apparently detached "object language" or "artifactual" study which includes the outside items and material aspects of your self and surroundings.

Paralanguage

The spoken word is never neutral. It is always affected by the tone of voice, the emphasis or inflections given, the breaks in the sentence, the speed of delivery, the degree of loudness or softness, and the pitch of the voice. These nonverbal factors are called "paralanguage." As you know, a simple "yes" can express a lot of different feelings, such as anger, frustration, resignation, lack of interest, agreement, or challenge. A short sentence such as "I'll do it" may "mean" any of the following:

"I'll be really happy to do it."
"I'll do it, but it's the last time."
"You always make me do what you want."
"All right, you win."
"Don't worry, I'll take care of it."
"You're so dumb I'd better take care of it myself."

Which of the meanings is implied can usually be determined by the tone of voice, the inflection of the voice, the stress placed on each separate word, or the context. The meaning of the sentence lies not in the words alone but also in the vocal expressions, or paralanguage, always associated with the words.

In *everyday* life you naturally rely on words themselves *plus* their

---

BOX 9-5. A Paralinguistic Romance

A record titled "John and Marsha," popular some years ago, consisted of only two words repeated over and over—"John . . ." and "Marsha . . ." spoken in such a way as to tell a story of a romantic encounter. Meaning was carried completely by the use of paralanguage, or the intonations, inflections, pitch, etc., of the voices. That seven-minute production was the work of comedian-producer Stan Freberg, who spoke the parts of both John and Marsha and was able to successfully imitate both male and female voices.

BOX 9-6.   Pejorative Paralanguage

Minorities, outsiders, newcomers, are sensitive to the labels they are given, and particularly to the tone of voice used, as were the members of the Joad family in Steinbeck's *The Grapes of Wrath:**

> *Okie use'ta mean you was from Oklahoma. Now it means you're scum. Don't mean nothin' itself, it's the way they say it.*

* J. Steinbeck, *The Grapes of Wrath,* Penguin USA, New York, 1989.

---

paralanguage features to develop your meanings about what people are telling you. There are times, however, when you get distracted and miss the words themselves. If you have to respond and do not wish to admit you have not been paying close attention, you will rely on the paralanguage features alone to interpret what was said. This happens often at cocktail parties where people involved in small talk do not pay full attention to what is said and respond almost automatically. It may be pouring rain, but if someone says in a convincing tone, "It is really nice out, isn't it?" chances are the response will be an equally convincing "It sure is."

You the observer

You can get upset about how a person sounds more than for what is said. "He sounds so sure of himself and so arrogant, I want to prove him wrong." "She sounds like a little baby when she talks—so whiny and lispy." "He sounds like I'm his slave the way he talks to me in such a tone of voice." "She drawls out her words so slowly I get really impatient and want to finish her sentences for her . . ."

You respond to people in relation to these paralanguage features sometimes without realizing what you are really reacting to. If you can learn to pay attention to how you are responding to people's intonations, pitch, rate, stress, and emphases, you will better understand why you are attracted to some people and turned off by others.

You the initiator

Are you aware of the paralanguage features of your own speech? Maybe you do some of the same things which annoy you when you listen to others. If you find others finishing your sentences for you, are you speaking so slowly you annoy others? Why would someone accuse you of sounding cross or upset when you actually are in a friendly mood? Does someone accuse you of sounding bossy when you think you're being very accommodating and cooperative? It might be helpful for you to make a list for yourself of the things which "push your button" about paralanguage in others; then check to see if you do any of those things. You can also ask a close friend to monitor your speech patterns to see if you are sending the messages you think you are on the nonverbal level.

Facial Expression

Earlier in this section we described how different researchers have come up with different dimensions of facial expression. It is not certain that they are always measuring the same things. Tests have been developed for determining people's sensitivity to facial movements. There are also many varying estimates about how many different expressions the human face can convey. "Physiologists have estimated that the facial musculature is such that over twenty thousand different facial expressions are somatically possible."[11] Given that number, or even a vastly larger quoted figure of 250,000,[12] it is not surprising that the study of faces is a complex one.

Study is further complicated by these three factors: (1) the nearly infinite number of combinations of the muscles which move many parts from the eyebrows to the chin, so that the face is very fluid; (2) the fact that facial expressions can change instantly, "in the blink of an eye"; and (3) the fact that face-to-face interaction is the most basic and the busiest form of exchanging nonverbal interpersonal messages.[13]

Watching another person's face for cues is a common experience for all of you. When you hear a friend say something which can be taken several ways, do you quickly look at the friend's face to see how he or she "meant" it? Even at a public lecture when you are in the back row, you concentrate on the lecturer's nonverbal messages and usually wish you could see the speaker's face as well as the broad gestures.

Television has given us the advantage of close-up shots of a speaker or a narrator whose facial expressions then become a significant part of the total message. Researchers in media have studied the effects of nonverbal signals from commentators and reporters. One such study of potential bias by television news broadcasters, although inconclusive in its findings, did point out that news broadcasters showed different facial expressions when talking about different political candidates, and that even untrained observers could detect those different expressions. The study also mentioned that because many such broadcasters are professional performers, they have more control over their facial expressions than most people do.[14] Of course, tone of voice is very important in the television medium, but the fact is that facial expressions and other subtle gestures can add much to what the announcer says. Much more needs to be learned about how facial expressions affect others, not only in interpersonal relations, but also in public appearances where important social and political issues may be decided.

You the observer

Even with those complications, it should be possible (researchers tell us) for you to learn certain things from watching facial expressions. You can find out if someone feels friendly toward you or unfriendly—a quality of liking or disliking. You can find out if someone is interested in what you are saying or who you are, or is bored with you. You can find out others' degree of involvement with you—the intensity of their concern about you and what you might be saying. You can learn something about others' control over their facial expressions and perhaps infer something about their emotions, at least in the present situation. You can learn if the others understand what you are saying, or if they are confused.

You may not guess correctly all the time, but there are many facial expressions which are obvious, unambiguous, and commonly recognized. Even without additional training in facial observation, you should be able to move effectively in your world. If you find yourself persistently misjudging relations with others based on how you read their faces, then you can investigate the possibility of training.

You the initiator

Two problems often face those who want to give clear nonverbal messages by a facial expression channel. First, are you entirely sure what expression you should use to show another person how you feel—is this really the way most people show concern, or anger, or disgust, or pleasure? Second, what is the *span* and *clarity* of the nonverbal messages you send—do the expressions last long enough and facial elements fit together well enough to be "heard" by the other? In this regard, you've seen people who smile only with their lips, while their eyes or eyebrows seem uninvolved or angry. Mixed signals like that are not easy for another person to interpret. Check with a close friend when you think there is confusion or suspected misunderstandings coming from the "signals" you are sending from your face. At the card table it may be appropriate to wear a "poker face," but in most interpersonal settings you can practice giving more data to others so that your face supports, supplements, emphasizes, endorses, and confirms your spoken messages.

Eye Contact:
Gaze Behavior

Among the features of facial expression, the eyes deserve special attention. Poets may call the eyes "a window to the soul," and much mystery and mythology have been associated with eyes and how people look at each other—called "gaze behaviors."

"Look me in the eye and tell me the truth" is used in some situations, and in others you may demand: "Don't look at me in that belligerent way." To look or not to look? *How long* to look? *Where* is it permissible to look? Who can look at whom? All these relate to conventions or rules of gaze behavior which influence our relations with others.

Many aspects of gaze are carefully prescribed; many norms of eye contact are known to all of you, but never written down anywhere as rules of nonverbal behavior. Many norms are related to the culture you grew up in. Children in black or Hispanic cultures traditionally were taught not to look in the face of their elders (parents, for example), but the white middle-class culture demands it, particularly when the child is being reprimanded. Other norms are gender-related or age-related. Women tend

BOX 9-7. **Importance of Study of Gaze Behavior**

Even after researchers had begun to take nonverbal communication seriously, the study of gaze—looking at each other—had been somewhat neglected. Two British psychologists, Michael Argyle and Mark Cook, took to task the field of psychology for its evident neglect of this important area of behavioral study.

> Looking at others, and being looked at by them, is of central importance in social behaviour, for those who can see. We use our eyes to study the behaviour and appearance of others, and we look particularly in the region of their eyes. This is familiar and obvious, and has often been described by novelists and poets. Psychologists, however, failed to take any interest in these phenomena until very recently, and almost no research was done until the early 1960's. As a result the main theories of social behaviour—with the partial exception of the non-verbal communication model . . . take no account of gaze. . . . It follows that any account of social behaviour which fails to deal with the phenomena of gaze is quite inadequate.*

* M. Argyle and M. Cook, *Gaze and Mutual Gaze,* Cambridge University Press, Cambridge and London, 1976, p. ix.

to use eye contact more than do men, and under somewhat different conditions; and there are specific rules of gaze imposed between generations.[15]

There are also rules of *where* you may look. It is usually permissible to look at another person in the region above the neck and below the knees. Think about how you feel if you get caught looking at someone else in the region "in between." Or what do you think if you catch someone else looking at *your* middle area? You also spend a lot of your conversational time trying to look the other in the eye—particularly when you are speaking you try to engage the other person's eyes.[16] Eye contact is also used to signal that you want to take turns speaking.

You the observer

Since your gaze is both a "sending" channel and a "receiving" channel, it is difficult to separate out what signals are coming to you, and what signals you are offering the other person. Gaze is reciprocal in the sense that you must actually see others looking at you before it qualifies as a communication transaction. Does it make you uneasy when you turn around and find someone must have been staring at you for some time? You get uncomfortable if someone looks at you too long, and you might interpret that prolonged gaze as aggressive (who blinks first) or a sexual advance. You can accept longer gazes from someone you like than from others. The distance you are from others also determines how long they

Gaze behavior may suggest intimacy. (© Spencer Grant/ Photo Researchers)

can look at you without your being upset—intimates can look intently at you from close range, but other people within talking distance (see the section titled "Space" in this chapter) who look and do not speak will bother you more than if they are beyond normal conversational distance.

You the initiator

You may stare to express disapproval, or to signal to another person that you want to meet. With a close friend or spouse you may use prolonged eye contact to indicate that you think it is time to leave the party. Status differences also dictate who looks at whom and for how long—the person in a high-status position (parents, bosses, etc.) can look at those in low-status positions intensely and continuously. The low-status person generally accepts the norm of only glancing at the superior from time to time, but not sustaining a gaze contact. You risk appearing insubordinate if you look at the boss too long at a time.

There are rules for who can look, where, and for how long; and if you break those rules, both you and the others seem to know it intuitively.

Gestures

Gestures were probably one of the first means of communication that human beings developed, long before oral language appeared. All cultures have a system of meaningful gestures which either accompany spoken

CHART 9-1.
Factors Affecting Gaze Behavior

You will probably LOOK A LOT AT THE SPEAKER	DETERMINANT OR MEDIATING FACTORS	You will probably LOOK VERY LITTLE AT THE SPEAKER
If you are close together	DISTANCE APART	If you are far apart
If topics are intimate or difficult	TOPICS/CONTENT	If topics are impersonal or easy
If there is nothing else to look at	DISTRACTIONS	If there are relevant objects/items/persons in view
If you have high interest in the other	INTEREST LEVEL	If you have low interest in the other
If you like or love the other	PERSONAL FEELINGS	If you dislike the other
If your status is lower	STATUS/RANK	If you have higher status
If you are trying to dominate	POWER/DOMINATION	If power is even
If your culture is Latin/Arab/Mediterranean/etc.	CULTURAL NORMS	If your culture is Native American/Northern European/etc.
If you are extrovert/outgoing	PERSONALITY	If you are introvert/shy
If you are in the female cooperative state (more females present)	GENDER	If you are in the female competitive state (more males present)
When speaking	SPEAKING/LISTENING	When listening
When telling truth/facts	HONESTY/ETHICS	When lying/embarassed

Adapted from Argyle and Cook, *Gaze and Mutual Gaze,* Cambridge University Press, Cambridge and London, 1976, p. ix.

language or stand alone in conveying a particular message. You nod your head to say "yes" (but in some cultures, nodding means "no") and shake your head to say "no." The hitchhiker's hand gesture is recognizable in most automobile-using cultures. You extend your hand to shake someone else's as a greeting and not as a hostile gesture. The language of the deaf is probably one of the most sophisticated systems of exchanging messages by gesture.

You usually accompany your speech with a considerable number of hand gestures. If you've ever tried to give directions to someone over the telephone, you probably have caught yourself uselessly waving a hand in the air.[17]

Some cultures are known to be more expressive with the hands than others. The French, Spanish, and Italian, and other Mediterranean cultures, for instance, are quite effusive with their hand gestures. Sometimes certain gestures become automatic. Students are usually quick to recognize the familiar gestures of their professors. Impersonators of famous

---

BOX 9-8.   From Birdwhistell Back to Delsarte

Ray Birdwhistell, creator of the innovative "kinesics" study of nonverbal communication, was correct in his comment that "there is nothing new about the recognition that formalized gestures play a role in communication. . . ."* In nineteenth-century Europe, François Delsarte (1811–1871), famous for his highly formalized system of gestures to give needed impact to speaking, is credited with these arguments:

> *Gesture is more than speech. It is not what we say that persuades, but the manner of saying it. The mind can be interested by speech, but it must be persuaded by gesture. If the face bears no sign of persuasion, we do not persuade.†*

> *Speech is inferior to gesture, because it corresponds to the phenomena of mind; gesture is the agent of the heart; it is the persuasive agent.‡*

> *It is not ideas that move the masses; it is gestures.§*

> *The sign of the cross made at the opening of a sermon often has great effect upon good Catholics. Let a priest with his eyes concentric and introspective make deliberately the sign of the cross while solemnly uttering these words: "In—the—name—of—the—Father"; then let his glance sweep the audience. What do they think of him? This is no longer an ordinary man; he seems clothed with the majesty of God, whose orders he has just received and in whose name he brings them. The idea gives him strength and assurance, and his audience respect and docility.¶*

* R. L. Birdwhistell, *Kinesics and Context*, University of Pennsylvania Press, Philadelphia, 1970, p. 192.
† M. L'Abbe Delaumosne and Mme. A. Arnaud (pupils of Delsarte), *The Delsarte System of Oratory* (trans. F. A. Shaw), Edgar S. Werner publisher, Albany, NY, 1884, pp. 47–48.
‡ Ibid, p. 48.
§ Ibid, p. 49.
¶ Ibid, p. 50.

---

people rely on pose and gestures, in addition to their voice imitations, to create their characters. Gestures are often used to give emphasis to words and often to clarify meaning. Sometimes, the emphasis may be placed on the wrong word if the speaker's timing is bad, and you may misunderstand or get the impression that the message is not sincere.

Gestures are culture-bound. That is, they are learned within the society and culture in which you belong. Just as you learned to speak your native tongue, you learned a pattern of gestures to accompany your verbal language, and you learned how to interpret this pattern of gestures.

Can you interpret these gestures? What special experience or background do you
need to understand these nonverbal signals? *(Traffic hand signals: © Steve Goldberg/
Monkmeyer; kids cross fingers: © Dave Schaefer/The Picture Cube; baseball umpire:
© Reuters/Bettmann Newsphotos; Winston Churchill: © UPI/Bettmann Newsphotos)*

Here again, let us emphasize that no behavior, no gesture, has meaning of and by itself. Gestures contribute to the creation of meaning in interpersonal communication and point to certain attitudes or emotions. But gestures and their potential meanings seldom have a one-to-one correspondence. With the exception of *emblems* and *signs,* which are denotative gestures pointing to one commonly shared referent (the thumb of the hitchhiker, for example), gestures, like words, do not contain meaning but help create meaning.

Gestures help in many ways to interpret the content of communication. They help *define roles.* The way you greet others tells them whether the occasion is formal or social, friendly or distant. Large gestures are often attributed to authority and dominant figures while small gestures are often associated with meekness, discomfort, and lack of an authoritative stance. Gestures also *monitor* the flow of interaction. Scheflen defines "monitors" as actions which regulate or maintain order in interpersonal communication.[18] Shaking the index finger is a gesture frequently used by parents to tell a child that he or she is not behaving according to their expectations. A hand movement may indicate a desire to stop someone's flow of conversation, or a wish to have the other person slow down and give you a turn. Gestures are also used to establish the context of a relationship; some gestures are associated with courtship behavior, as touching or holding hands, and some with authoritative behavior, like shaking a finger or making threatening motions.

You the observer

Magicians use gestures to divert your attention from their "magic" so they can make use of distraction to pull their stunts. Some speakers also do that and intend to emphasize some weak arguments by big gestures. Are you aware of the power which gestures have to focus your attention, to distract you, to mislead you? On the other hand, as you watch a speaker are you easily distracted by some gestural habit such as continually slicing a hand through the air to punctuate ideas, or insecurely gripping the edge of a lectern? If you are not aware of your attention, you can soon concentrate on the deathlike grip on the edge of the speaking stand and forget to hear the spoken message. How many waves of a listener's hand does it take to get you to stop talking and give the other a chance? Gestures help you to understand the content of messages, and also help control the flow of information and define the speaker-listener relations.

You the initiator

Do you wave your arms too wildly when you are with people who are above you in rank or status? That's the time you are expected to use minimal gestures—subtle ones, tentative ones. On the other hand, if your gestures lack vitality when you are trying to dominate, win a point, or persuade others, they will not be effective. Do you have only one set of gestures—say, waving your right arm up and down—or do you use a variety of appropriate gestures indicating rejection when you dislike an idea, and approval when you want to be supportive? You should make your gestures actually support what you are trying to say, timed well and in proper proportion, and should avoid their calling attention to themselves so the listener watches your randomly flailing arms instead of listening to your argument. If you have a habit of shaking your finger at children, you may also inadvertently use that gesture inappropriately on other adults. In other words, you must manage to adapt your gestures appropriately to your audience and to the situation.

Body Language

You are seldom immobile or inert. Besides the gestures discussed above, other parts of your body give messages within the context of the situation you are in. How you stand or sit, how you lean or walk, how you pose yourself, all have meanings. Observe which movements a body makes, and also notice the shift, the frequency, and the rate of those movements.

Postures or body movements are reported by researchers[19] to show at least four types of meaning: (1) *agreement or disagreement*, depending on how much your posture is similar to that of another; (2) *immediacy*, which relates to how closely you allow yourself to interact physically with another; (3) *power or authority*, which is indicated by high body tension and aggressive, symmetrical stance or movement usually accompanying big gestures as mentioned above; (3) *responsiveness or alertness*, which is shown by the amount of change and the rate of your movements to assert interest or your willingness to be part of the interaction.

These classifications tend to overlap in your observations or your

Showing agreement can be demonstrated by how much your posture is similar to the other person's. (© *Tim Barnwell/Stock, Boston)*

initiation of them. For example, agreeing with someone may include your showing immediacy or responsiveness as well.

Each of the suggested "meaning classes" can have a negative as well as a supportive side to it—you can reject others with posture just as clearly as you can affiliate with them. Watch the behaviors of others when a boorish intruder joins a small group's conversation. What postural rejection signals do they present to the newcomer, and what affiliative signals do they give to each other to signify their disapproval of the intruder? That is a case of body movements being used for both negative and supportive messages by the same group of people in the same situation. In addition, as we will discuss in the section titled "Space" (page 228), how near or far people stand or sit is influenced by cultural norms and individual differences as well as a desire to send postural messages.

You the observer

Do you see the postural messages from others as a means of telling you "Get lost," "Tell me more," "I like you," "You must be stupid," "That's the same way I feel"? You must take into account other factors for body messages such as cultural differences, situational concerns, or the quickly changing sets of signals. When you see a friend approaching you very tensed up, are you prepared to interact on that person's terms or will you impose your own mood? Do you feel others are disinterested as they fidget with books, or keep shifting away from you? When you are in doubt, you should obtain clarification by asking the other person for an oral explanation of the observed nonverbal signals.

You the initiator

Are you aware of the signals you may be sending without consciously intending to? The way you walk or stand will show others that you feel well, are depressed, are tired, are angry, are happy, are sad, are friendly, or don't feel like interacting.

Besides telegraphing your moods and intentions, you show your perception of relationships and status by your postures. You relax more around people you like or who are of equal or lower status, and tense up around people you dislike or see as superior to you. If you want to show disrespect, dominance, or control to others, you can act more informally or casually in the way you stand, move your body in closely, use frequent and intrusive shifts of posture. To show respect or subservience, you may slouch more and hold yourself in a stance and at a distance which you think meets the status expectations of the others as you watch their cues.

Communication by Touch

Touch, or "haptemics," is one of the first modes of communication of the human being. Infants learn much about their environment by touching, feeling, cuddling, and tasting. Linus's security blanket in Charles Schulz's cartoons is a symbol of the objects children become attached to which they particularly like to touch, feel, or keep. We communicate a great deal by touching. Patting someone on the back, shaking a hand, or holding a hand can express more than a lengthy speech. Lovers know this. Mothers do too.

In American culture, except in a few well-defined situations, touching is linked with intimate interpersonal relationships, and is thus taboo for most other types of relationships. Many people thus refrain from touching others in more casual encounters for fear their behavior might be misconstrued or simply because they are afraid of or do not like physical contacts. When they must stand in line, Americans will usually form an orderly single line in which everyone waits patiently for a turn. In Arab countries, on the other hand, lines are almost unheard of; considerable pushing, shoving, and touching are involved in most gatherings, and such behavior is not considered distasteful. American children learn relatively young to kiss their relatives hello and good-bye. Spanish children frequently kiss not only their relatives but adult friends and acquaintances as well when they encounter them and depart from them.

Touching is a powerful communicative tool and serves to express a tremendous range of feelings, such as fear, love, anxiety, warmth, coldness. The importance of touch in your communication is evidenced by the number of common expressions in the English language which some-

---

BOX 9-9. Power of Touch

In their book *Speech and Man,* Brown and Van Riper recall an incident told by one of their students which dramatically illustrates the power of a touch.

A student was presenting to a class the view that verbal language, in the main, disguises the speaker, and that the real burden of a communication is sent in the nonverbal broadcast. This he illustrated with a story not to be forgotten. He said he was driving on a superhighway one morning at dawn, and an automobile approaching at a high speed began to sway crazily from one side of the road to the other. It eventually plunged off the road, crashed into a concrete pole which broke off and fell over the automobile, bringing it to a halt. The student stopped and ran to the man's aid. The victim was hanging out of his automobile, apparently dead, his face covered with broken windshield glass. The student began to lift the glass from the man's face and the man shook his head slowly. Without opening his eyes, he mumbled, "Give me your hand." The student took the man's hand and in a few minutes the man died. The student said, "In those moments I was told about death as no words will ever tell me."

* C. T. Brown and C. Van Riper, *Speech and Man,* Prentice-Hall, Englewood Cliffs, NJ, 1966, pp. 54–55. Reprinted by permission of the authors and the publisher.

how connote touching. Ashley Montagu lists a few of these figures of speech: rubbing people the wrong way, stroking, describing someone as a soft touch or as thick-skinned, getting in touch, making contact, handling people carefully, getting under someone's skin, being skin-deep, being touchy.[20]

Touching is so important in the healthy development of human life that infants who are not handled, cuddled, stroked, caressed, and touched get sick and sometimes die.[21] The touching dimension of interpersonal communication is a transactional process by which the self develops. By being handled and touched, a baby becomes aware of his or her body. Lack of adequate touching in early childhood can leave serious emotional scars which often affect the development of healthy intimate adult relationships.

You the observer

As you watch others involved in touching behavior you can learn a great deal about how they see their relationship. Two people holding hands or with their arms about each other are certainly seen as personally or romantically engaged. In any dealings you may have with others from another culture, can you accept their touch patterns, even if different from

Some cultures are comfortable with more touching and with closer contacts than others. *(© Hugh Rogers/Monkmeyer)*

yours? Interacting with some cultures (Latins, Mediterranean, Arab) you need to be prepared for more touching behavior, while others (Northern Europeans, Japanese, Native Americans) will not risk touching you. You need to assume also that people from different parts of the United States may exhibit different norms about touching, as is also true of different social levels. You can accept touching from good friends or from relatives, but you may resent it from strangers. What part of you is touched and how you are touched is also very important, as both aggressive, dominating behavior (pushing or shoving action, grasping your arm, etc.) and sexual implications (touching of gender–sensitive areas) are likely to make you uncomfortable.

You the initiator

How you touch will depend on how well you know the other person. How much do you know about that person's own touch-tolerance level as well as your own preferences and touch threshold? Tender gentle touching conveys positive and caring feelings, and rough abrupt touching seems aggressive and negative, unless you are in a situation which calls for rugged or violent activities as sports or horseplay. Where you touch someone is carefully prescribed by social and cultural norms, and in individual cases by the intimacy of your relationship. Arm-around-the-shoulder may be acceptable for same-sex touching and in some social settings, but may not be approved in casual or high-status and opposite-sex interactions. How often you touch others should be judged by their reciprocal touching with you, just as you need to watch for signals from others that your touching behavior is offensive.

Object Language

As most people do, you probably spend some time worrying and thinking about your physical appearance. Our culture places a lot of emphasis on physical attractiveness, however that may be defined from year to year and from fashion style to fashion style. Physical appearance is one of the major determinants in first impressions. What you look like and what you wear communicate something to others. As Dale Leathers notes, "You communicate your own identity by means of your visible self."[22] For most of you, the major medium of communication by appearance is clothing.

Clothes do serve many functions from a communication point of view. They can express emotions and feelings. Bright colors suggest youthful vitality, while grays and dark colors reflect a more sedate and subdued mood. Suggestive clothes, such as low-cut dresses, slit skirts, and tight slacks, carry sexual messages. Recently, books on "how to dress for success" have become popular and are used as a guide by both men and women to help them achieve the appropriate appearance. Your clothes have a great impact on your behavior as well as the behavior of the other people you associate with. Uniforms, for example, are rich in communicative value. Clothes also help differentiate among people. Young people do not dress the same way older people do.[23]

Clothes reflect socioeconomic differences as well as cultural and ethnic ones. In fact, a study by Gibbins revealed that people do make judgments about each other on the basis of the clothes they wear and that there is a good deal of agreement about the meaning conveyed by certain types of clothes.[24] Most of you choose the clothes you wear on the basis of how well you think other people will like them, not just for comfort or durability.

"Object language," then, refers to the meanings you attribute to objects with which you surround yourself. The clothes and jewelry you wear, your hairstyle, and the decorative objects in your house are all part of object language. They say something about you because they represent to some extent deliberate choices you make. Clothing and jewelry are particularly revealing. A wedding band or an engagement ring communicates something quite specific about a person. You usually dress differently for different occasions, and if you don't, you are still communicating something about yourself, about your attitudes toward others, your sense of appropriateness,, your upbringing, your values. Clothing is symbolic. Some young people's attire is rich in colorful symbols of their choice. Some people are so concerned about what they communicate with their clothes that they will buy them only in certain stores which guarantee the particular kind of status they seek, whether they be secondhand stores, army surplus stores, or fashionable boutiques.

You the observer

How do you react to others in terms of what they wear and what they own—and of course, what do those things mean to you? A woman wearing a police uniform has told us nonverbally a great deal, if not about herself personally, at least about the role she can be expected to play in certain situations. You notice people by their clothes and believe you can identify soldiers, sailors, salespersons, panhandlers, political candidates, executives, or students, by what they wear. All material objects and manifestations help you in making inferences about the people who display them. Do hairstyles, beards, and ornamentation (jewelry, headbands, Rolex watches, etc.), as well as room decorations, car or bicycle, or food choices, give you data about who these people "really are"? From what you see surrounding others, you make choices about whether or not you want to spend time with them. You probably will make more of an effort to know someone whose "object language" fits your own, than take the risk of associating with persons whose styles or artifacts you don't appreciate. You should be aware of how much of your interpersonal communication is involved in commonality of object language.

You the initiator

Would you like to have people ignore your object messages (how you dress, wear your hair, decorate your room) and decide they don't count? That is no more possible than deciding that your words don't count. You need to use your object language as directly and openly as you use speaking. Choice of what you wear is yours, just as choice of words is, and you will have to take responsibility for both and take the consequences of any misunderstandings generated. If you want to communicate effectively with others, you cannot behave as if what you own, wear, and surround yourself with are not part of the messages you send. This does not suggest you must conform to all the most common or traditional apparel and material norms—it simply acknowledges that you will be judged by others on those appearances and you will make the choices.

CONTEXTUAL PATTERNS FOR NONVERBAL MESSAGES

The anthropologist Edward T. Hall in his fascinating book *The Silent Language*[25] was one of the first scholars to probe into the contextual dimensions of interpersonal communication. Interpersonal communication does not occur in a vacuum. It takes place in a cultural context—that is, a system of norms and rules—which determines to a large degree the variables of the communication process. You are usually unaware of the cultural context which influences your communicative behavior because it is so familiar and "normal" to you. You sometimes see it when you contrast your cultural context with that of a foreign culture. The two most powerful factors which affect your interpersonal communication are time and space.

Time

Time is a form of interpersonal communication. In our culture, time is almost treated as a thing; you gain time, waste it, spend it, give it, and take it. Time is precious, a rare commodity in your rushed lives. Time speaks.

In American urban white culture, punctuality is valued, and tardiness is considered insulting. Being late for an appointment or in turning in an assignment may lead to unpleasant consequences. However, what is considered "late" varies not only with each individual and his or her personal sense of time but also with the situation, the other people involved, and the geographic area. For example, you may have a very important appointment with a person of higher status than yours—perhaps a job interview. Usually, you will try to be "on time," and this may mean about five minutes before the appointed time to five minutes after. If you arrive fifteen minutes after the appointed time, you will probably apologize and offer some explanation for your delay. The kind and extent of your apologies and explanations will vary according to how late you are. If you are only five minutes late, you may not have to say anything. If you are ten minutes late, you may feel that you have to apologize briefly but need not give any reason for the delay. If you are half an hour late, you will probably apologize profusely and need to explain thoroughly what kept you. If you are an hour late, you will not expect the other person to be still waiting for you. If the other person is still there, as when you meet your date at home and show up an hour late, you expect him or her to be very upset.

With a close friend the extent of tardiness may be increased without

---

BOX 9-10. Defining Time

In middle-class American business and interpersonal transactions, time is treated as a commodity—you can spend it, save it, waste it, or give somebody some of yours, and once it is used up, you never get it back. When you think that time is an item of exchange (like a sack of beans), you act differently about it than if you assume that time simply measures passing moments. It has also been suggested that the more frantic pace and careful attention to being prompt in the United States where a clock "runs" may be a linguistic difference to the stereotypically "mañana-paced" Mexico where the clock "walks."

---

drastic consequences; but here too, a scale will be established to determine whether you owe an apology or not, and, if so, the extent of that apology. Apologies are needed at some point, however, because extreme tardiness may be taken as an insult or a sign of irresponsibility.

In some cultures, tardiness may not be perceived as insulting, and one can go to a meeting hours after the appointed time without upsetting anyone. In Mexico, for example, it is not uncommon to arrive an hour and a half after the appointed time and still be considered on time. In the United States this would, of course, be considered very late and very rude. An American meeting a Mexican would feel insulted to have to wait so long and would probably expect a good story to account for such a delay. The American would be quite upset at hearing no story, for the Mexican would, in his or her eyes, be on time and thus would not feel the need to explain anything. Unless you know and understand another culture's sense of time, you may get very frustrated, and this naturally affects the way you communicate with members of that culture.

Arriving early at an appointment communicates as much as arriving late. In some circles where it is fashionable to be late to parties, the early arrival of a guest may throw the host and hostess into a panic, and they may be quite upset that their guest was not polite enough to arrive later.

Time communicates in other ways. A telephone call at 3 A.M. communicates a feeling of urgency and importance. People don't usually call you at that time of the night just to ask how you are and to say, "Gee, it's been a while since we've seen each other."

If you are two hours late coming home during the day, your family or friends may be quite worried and upset, but their fears will be less intense than what they would be if you were two hours late after midnight.

Space

The space in which your interpersonal communication takes place affects you in many subtle ways that you are not always aware of. Each of you has a "personal space," a sort of invisible bubble around you, which you feel is yours and which you do not like to see intruded upon without express permission. Although each of you sets his or her own personal boundaries, there are recognizable cultural patterns which regulate the handling of personal space and interpersonal distance.

Interpersonal distances

A classification made by Edward T. Hall[26] and updated by other researchers draws attention to the field of "proxemics," or interpersonal space. Hall believed that the human senses determine territoriality—oral, aural, touch, (kinesthesia), thermal receptors, smell (olfaction), and vision. In turn those same territorial boundaries can be considered as establishing relationships, so the categories of interpersonal distances are partly categories of relationships.[27]

Even though the distances in centimeters are not perfectly assignable to all cultures, conditions, communication content, or ethnic groups, Hall and others believe that this is still an appropriate basic system for drawing attention to the generalizations about proxemics.[28] In other words, even if the precise measurements differ from one person or one culture to another it is important to recognize that everyone seems to have territorial norms, values, behaviors, and expectations which affect communication.

The four distances are:[29]

1. *Intimate:* Ranging from as close as physical contact to 6 to 18 inches, where you may conduct your business in whispers and about very personal, secret things
2. *Personal:* Ranging from as close as 1.5 feet to 2.5 feet to as far as 2.5 to 4 feet, where you speak in a very soft, confidential voice about relatively private or sensitive matters
3. *Social:* Ranging from as close as 4 to 7 feet to as far as 7 to 12 feet, where you talk in a conversational, consultative voice about casual things
4. *Public:* Ranging from "close" at 12 to 25 feet to distances much greater than 25 feet, and your content is general, instructional, didactic, spoken in a formal style and a loud, or even amplified, voice.

When people violate the unspoken rules of interpersonal distance (get too close when they should be at a social distance or stand too far away when they are expected to be more intimate), you generally feel uncomfortable. When someone you did not invite comes too close to you, you tend to move away. Your territory is marked, and you may let others approach, but not too closely unless you specifically decide to let them. The uncomfortable feeling you get in a crowded room often comes from the fact that too many people are too close to one another. If someone crowds you at the library or at the cafeteria by sitting too close to you, you unconsciously move away by moving your books, tray, or chair away from the intruder. If for some reason the intruder moves closer, you try other avoidance behaviors. However, you rarely ask people in words to move away from you. If they do not respond appropriately by understanding your nonverbal avoidance moves, you usually change places in the library, or leave the cafeteria as soon as you can, feeling that your lunch was spoiled.

Interpersonal distance is one of the ways you have to express feelings. You tend to move closer to people you like and away from people you do not, if you have a choice. You sometimes take great precautions to avoid walking near someone you do not like.

Some general comments about our "life space," proxemics, or how close we tolerate others can be made based on the twin assumptions that (1) people have carefully drawn distances, based on many factors which they use when dealing with others, and (2) those distances are not always honored by other people. Scholars have developed a number of hypotheses based on previous research studies, and additional studies are being conducted on these and other hypotheses. Attractive people are more liked, more persuasive, and better understood if they come closer than the normal distance than if they are either at the expected distance or farther away. High-status people also are better liked, more persuasive, and better understood if they come in closer than expected. If you are a person of high credibility, then you will be more liked if you stand close while low-credibility persons will not. Distance will also make a difference in how to punish someone: while giving negative feedback you will be better liked if you stay farther away than expected, and people feel threatened at a greater distance by a punishing source than by a rewarding source.[30]

Territoriality

People, like animals, have the tendency to own space, a tendency which is called "territoriality." Territoriality acts as a sort of extension of personal space. Cars are very much an extension of the self; your house, your desk, and sometimes your chair become extensions of yourself. You may get irritated if someone else enters your territory uninvited. Somehow you "just know" when someone is "too close" or "too far," and you may not really be sure how you came to know it. Yet the distance "feels" right, or it does not.

Territoriality is usually defined culturally.[31] Territoriality most of the time provides an advantage to the owner of the territory. Playing a home game is somehow easier than playing in the competing team's home field or court. You may feel more at ease and comfortable on your own grounds, and the other person is at a slight disadvantage. The question "My place or yours?" is a loaded one. If a supervisor calls you to his or her office to discuss some business matters, there is a certain advantage for the supervisor associated with that territory. If, on the other hand, your supervisor meets you in your office, on your turf, then you have a subtle but real psychological advantage. Some territories are considered neutral.

Territoriality represents an extension of your personal space and helps define communication relationships with others. *(© Peter Menzel/ Stock, Boston)*

For examples, hallways, lobbies, public places, cafeterias, etc., belong to everyone. Communication which takes place in such neutral places takes on certain characteristics.[32]

Observe, for example, your communicative behavior with one of your teachers. You may meet him or her in a hallway and exchange some pleasant small talk, an appropriate "hallway conversation." However, should you switch the topic and mention that you would like to discuss an upcoming assignment, chances are your teacher will suggest that you both meet in his or her office—no longer neutral territory. The teacher, deliberately or not, reestablishes authority in the relationship (becomes one-up) by getting back into the superior position, one which will give greater control of the situation. The advantage may be a subtle one, yet it matters. It matters a great deal in diplomatic relations, where the location of peace talks or negotiations is indeed crucial. Such negotiations are invariably held in neutral territory where neither party has an undue psychological or logistical advantage over the other. If you are in a dominant position with someone and wish to change to a more equal relationship, then you may choose to communicate on grounds other than your own to compensate for your superior position. You may hold the conversation in the other person's territory or in a neutral place.

Physical arrangements   Special elements other than interpersonal distances also affect you. The arrangement of a room, the shape of a meeting table, or the size of a classroom in relation to the number of students occupying it all influence the development of interpersonal communication.

Researchers have found, for example, that communication is distributed more evenly among people sitting at a *round* table than among people sitting at a *rectangular* table. At a rectangular table, people sitting at the ends are more likely to be talked to and to talk than the other group members. Researchers have made extensive studies of seating arrangements and their influence on people's perceptions of competition, cooperation, and togetherness.[33]

Figure 9-1 describes three basic arrangements. Sitting face to face across a table, for example, is likely to be perceived as competition. Most competitive games, in fact, are played face to face. When you sit face to face on the other side of someone's desk, you may tend to perceive the situation in competitive or adversary terms. A cooperative seating arrangement is more likely to be diagonal or side by side. In fact, we talk about being "on the same side" in arguments or discussions. In diagonal seating, close contact can be maintained, although the corner of the table or desk provides some safety from unwanted intrusions into your personal space. Working together on the same project, particularly if you must manipulate objects together, is enhanced by side-by-side seating.

Observe desk and chair arrangements in your teacher's office, for example. Does the teacher move out from behind the desk to talk with you? Is there a chair available at a diagonal angle? Are the chairs set on the other side of the desk, inviting a face-to-face seating? Do you ever sit side by side when you and the teacher work on your schedule or when you discuss a grade you received on a term paper?

Although the seating arrangement is not the only factor involved in maintaining control or producing competition or cooperation, these nonverbal factors do not happen randomly, by accident. People choose how they arrange their offices, at least within the structural limitations imposed by the shape and size of the room and the organizational constraints of how many chairs they own. People choose, to some extent, how they position themselves in relation to others. These moves have great communicative value.

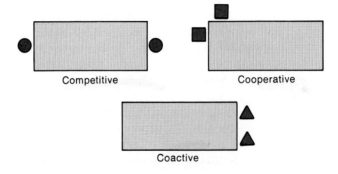

Competitive   Cooperative

Coactive

FIGURE 9-1
Seating arrangements.

> ### BOX 9-11. Nonverbal in the Classroom
>
> Many researchers suggest that there is a definite relationship between the nonverbal messages in a classroom and the kind of learning which takes place.* Having studied the writings of commentators on nonverbal messages and applied those principles to the classroom setting, they report that students develop confidence in teachers' honesty and authenticity by watching for nonverbal cues. They also conclude that "the student who possesses less verbal facility, who has learning disabilities, and who is culturally disadvantaged relies even more heavily on nonverbal communication in the classroom." They go on to say that this student not only checks on the reliability of the communicator, but also expects to get clarification of verbal material by watching the nonverbal system. Such an exchange places great responsibility on a teacher to be aware of and honest in nonverbal communication.
>
> * D. M. Brooks and A. E. Woolfolk, "The Effects of Students' Nonverbal Behavior on Teachers," *The Elementary School Journal,* vol. 88, September 1987, p. 50. E. Babad, F. Bernieri, and R. Rosenthal, "Nonverbal Communication and Leakage in the Behavior of Biased and Unbiased Teachers," *Journal of Personality and Social Psychology,* vol. 56, January 1989, p. 89. A. A. Badini and R. Rosenthal, "Visual Cues, Student Sex, Material Taught, and the Magnitude of Teacher Expectancy Effects," *Communication Education,* vol. 38, April 1989, p. 162. P. V. Lewis and Z. Page, "Educational Implications of Nonverbal Communication," *ETC: A Review of General Semantics,* vol. 31, no. 4, December 1974, pp. 371–375.

SUMMARY: CHARACTERISTICS OF NONVERBAL COMMUNICATION

The Impossibility of Not Communicating

You cannot not communicate. The nature of human communication is such that it is unavoidable. As we pointed out earlier, you can refrain from communication with words but you cannot escape nonverbal communication. To say nothing and remain silent is in itself a form of communication. You cannot stop from moving and expressing yourself with your gestures and facial expressions. Whatever you do or do not do communicates something about yourself. Interpersonal communication is inevitable when people are in each other's presence, because all observed behavior has some message value.

Interpersonal communication may not be conscious or intentional, or successful, but it takes place. Unless you know this principle and try to understand the communicative value of other people's behavior and your own, the potential for interpersonal problems looms large.

The Expression of Feelings and Emotions

Nonverbal communication is your primary mode of communicating feelings and emotions. You usually communicate about content and tasks through verbal communication. Verbal language is your primary mode of communicating cognitive information and dealing with the business at hand. Nonverbal communication, however, is your mode of sharing feelings with one another and dealing with the process of human relationships. Words usually carry *content information;* nonverbal communication expresses *affective information.* From the way you look at someone you may communicate love, hate, dislike, interest, trust, sexual desire, admiration, acceptance, scorn, etc.—a full range of human emotions which you do not always express verbally. Gestures such as tapping your fingers or your foot can communicate impatience, boredom, or nervousness. Your face has innumerable ways of expressing likes and dislikes, approval and disapproval.

Information about Content and Relationship

Nonverbal communication usually includes information about the content of a verbal message. Nonverbal communication gives you the clues that you need to interpret the verbal messages that you hear. The same words (same content) said in different tones of voice should probably be interpreted differently. The tone of voice, among other nonverbal messages, is a clue as to which interpretation to make.

Nonverbal communication also gives you information about credibility, intelligence, commitment, and the nature of the relationship between you and those with whom you communicate.[34]

Reliability of Nonverbal Messages

In some interpersonal situations the content of a spoken message does not fit the affective information about that message you get from other signals—primarily nonverbal. A friend says, "I love you . . ." but somehow the tone of voice, body stance, or touching, or any other nonverbal signals may deny the words just spoken. Someone assures you she trusts you, but her behavior toward you consistently denies that assertion. What are you to believe in these cases, the words you think you heard or the nonverbal signals you believe you picked up?

Not everyone agrees with a previously strongly held notion that words can equivocate or lie more than can the nonverbal system. You may believe intuitively that words alone are not enough to convince you about the authenticity of a message—you look for some confirmation or denial in the nonverbal system.

According to one side of the reliability argument,

> The best way to protect ourselves against deceptive communication is to increase one's sensitivity to the subtle cues which are part of multichannel communication. We have a good deal of conscious control over the meanings we communicate verbally or facially but much less over our use of gestures or what have been identified . . . as psychophysiological responses (blushing, sighing, etc.). The communicative cues over which we have little control provide the receiver with the most information as to our true intentions. Most often these cues are nonverbal and when such cues reveal information about a communicator which he is trying to conceal they are called "leakage" cues. Our best protection against deceptive communication is our ability to read leakage cues accurately.[35]

Other researchers take issue with the practice of dividing verbal and nonverbal into separate channels or systems when studying deception or inaccuracies:

> A major assumption of the "separate channels" model is that the nonverbal channel is less well controlled, so that while people may be able to lie verbally, they will either "leak" the truth nonverbally or manifest nonverbal deception clues. Because we doubt that the verbal aspects of a message are under different and better control than the nonverbal aspects, we do not believe that the nonverbal reveals what the verbal conceals. Specifically, we propose that the nonverbal aspects of a message do not "leak truth"; they are just as capable of lying (or equivocating) as are the verbal aspects.[36]

Incongruent or equivocal messages have a disruptive effect on your interpersonal communication when you expect congruency or directness. The people you most trust are those whose verbal/nonverbal messages seem to fit together. When accurate or truthful communication does not happen, it is less likely caused by the dishonest qualities of a person than by the difficult situation in which people find themselves.[37] While that knowledge may not change your expectations or hopes for verbal and nonverbal communication to be clear and congruent, it can help you to a better perspective about mixed signals. You can focus on both the words and nonverbal signals to identify difficult choices others have to make, rather than simply deciding they are liars or mean and sneaky people.

END NOTES

[1] J. A. DeVito, "Silence and Paralanguage as Communication," *ETC: A Review of General Semantics,* vol. 46, Summer 1989, p. 153.

[2] M. L. McLaughlin and M. J. Cody, "Awkward Silences: Behavioral Antecedents and Consequences of the Conversational Lapse," *Human Communication Research,* vol. 8, no. 4, Summer 1982, p. 299.

[3] McLaughlin and Cody, op. cit., p. 314. See also J. Cappella and S. Planalp, "Talk and Silence Sequences in Informal Conversation," *Human Communication Research,* vol. 7, no. 3, Spring 1981, pp. 117–132. Also W. B. Stiles, "Verbal Response Modes and Dimensions of Interpersonal Roles," *Journal of Personality and Social Psychology,* vol. 36, 1978, pp. 693–703.

[4] J. K. Burgoon and J. L. Hale, "Nonverbal Expectancy Violations: Model Elaboration and Application to Immediacy Behaviors," *Communication Monographs,* vol. 55, March 1988, p. 58.

[5] S. L. Kitch, "Gender and Language: Dialect, Silence, and the Disruption of Discourse," *Women's Studies,* vol. 14, July 1987, p. 55. N. M. Henley, *Body Politic: Power, Sex, and Nonverbal Communication,* Simon and Schuster, New York, 1986. "Big Girls Don't Frown, Big Boys Don't Cry: Gender Differences of Professional Actors in Communicating Emotion via Facial Expression," *Journal of Nonverbal Behavior,* vol. 12, Summer 1988, p. 106. M. W. Isenhart, "An Investigation of the Relationship of Sex and Sex Role to the Ability to Decode Nonverbal Cues," *Human Communication Research,* vol. 6, no. 4, Summer 1980, pp. 309–318. R. Buck, "A Test of Nonverbal Receiving Ability: Preliminary Studies," *Human Communication Research,* vol. 2, no. 2, Winter 1976, pp. 162–171.

[6] M. A. DeTurck and G. R. Miller, "Training Observers to Detect Deception," *Human Communication Research,* vol. 16, no. 4, Summer 1990, p. 603. H. D. O'Hair, M. J. Cody, and M. L. McLaughlin, "Prepared Lies, Spontaneous Lies, Machiavellianism, and Nonverbal Communication," *Human Communication Research,* vol. 7, no. 4, Summer 1981, pp. 325–339. G. J. Keiser and I. Altman, "Relationship of Nonverbal Behavior to the Social Penetration Process," *Human Communication Research,* vol. 2, no. 2, Winter 1976, pp. 147–161.

[7] A. Mehrabian, *Silent Messages,* Wadsworth, Belmont, CA, 1971. See also by same author and publisher, *Nonverbal Communication,* 1977.

[8] D. Leathers, *Nonverbal Communication Systems,* Allyn and Bacon, Boston, 1976, pp. 21–36. See also by the same author, *Successful Nonverbal Communication: Principles and Applications,* Macmillan, New York, 1986.

[9] R. L. Birdwhistell, *Kinesics and Context,* University of Pennsylvania Press, Philadelphia, 1970, p. 192.

[10] Ibid., p. 173.

[11] Ibid., p. 99.

[12] Ibid., p. 8.

[13] "Facial Clues to Deceptive Behavior," *USA Today,* vol. 118, Sept. 1, 1989, p. 8. A. E. Scheflen, *Body Language and Social Order,* Prentice-Hall, Englewood Cliffs, NJ, 1972. P. Ekman, W. V. Friesen, and P. Ellsworth, *Emotion in the Human Face,* Pergamon Press, New York, 1972. M. Konner, "The Enigmatic Smile," *Psychology Today,* vol. 21, March 1987, p. 42. For a bibliography and test of the feedback hypothesis, F. Strack, S. Stepper, and L. L. Martin, "Inhibiting and Facilitating Conditions of the Human Smile," *Journal of Personality and Social Psychology,* vol. 54, May 1988, p. 768.

[14] B. S. Friedman, T. L. Mertz, and M. R. DiMatteo, "Perceived Bias in the Facial Expressions of Television News Broadcasters," *Journal of Communication,* vol. 30, no. 4, Autumn 1980, pp. 103–111.

[15] J. F. Dovidio, C. F. Keathing, K. Heltman, S. L. Ellyson, and C. E. Brown, "The Relationship of Social Power to Visual Displays of Dominance between Men and Women," *Journal of Personality and Social Psychology,* vol. 54, February 1988, p. 233. J. A. Task, "Seeing Her Looking at You: Acquaintance and Variation in the Judgment of Gaze Depth," *American Journal of Psychology,* vol. 101, Summer 1988, p. 239.

[16] M. Harris and M. Coltheart, "Gaze Patterns in Spontaneous Speech," *Journal of Reading,* vol. 31, November 1987, p. 175.

[17] R. Friedman, "Hand Jive" (research on interpreting gesture), *Psychology Today,* vol. 22, June 1988, p. 10.

[18] Scheflen, op. cit.

[19] See Mehrabian (1971), Leathers (1976), and Scheflen (1972) cited above.

[20] A. Montagu, *Touching: The Human Significance of the Skin,* Harper & Row, New York, 1978.

[21] Ibid., p. 35.

[22] Leathers, op. cit., p. 96.

[23] A. Galin and B. Benoliel, "Does the Way You Dress Affect Your Performance

Rating?'' *Personnel,* vol. 67, August 1990, p. 49. P. S. Satran, *Dress Smart: The Thinking Woman's Guide to Style,* Doubleday, New York, 1989. L. Fenton and E. Olcott, *Dress for Excellence: The Executive Guide for Looking Like a Leader,* Rawson Associates, New York, 1986. J. T. Molloy, *Dress for Success,* Warner Books, New York, 1976. N. J. Golden, *Dress Right for Business,* McGraw-Hill, New York, 1986. A. Femer and S. Bruss, *Dress Smart,* Fairchild Publishers, New York, 1988. K. Gibbins, ''Communication Aspects of Women's Clothes and Their Relation to Fashionability,'' *British Journal of Social and Clinical Psychology,* vol. 8, 1969, pp. 306–307. E. Fox-Genovese, ''The Empress's New Clothes: The Politics of Fashion,'' *Socialist Review,* vol. 17, January–February 1987, p. 6.

[24] J. Wallace, *Dress to Fit Your Personality,* Fleming H. Revell, Old Tappan, NJ, 1989. E. M. Love, *Dress Up,* Dorchester Publishing, New York, 1988. L. Rosch, ''The Professional Image Report: What Matters, What Doesn't,'' *Working Woman,* vol. 13, October 1988, p. 109. S. L. Baylor, ''To Command Respect, Dress Professionally,'' *The Vocational Educational Journal,* vol. 63, January–February 1988, p. 14. D. Kazanjian, ''The Art of Presentation'' (visit with an image consultant), *Vogue,* vol. 179, September 1989, p. 304.

[25] E. T. Hall, *The Silent Language,* Doubleday, Garden City, NY, 1966. See also by Hall, *Dance of Life: The Other Dimension of Time,* Doubleday, Garden City, NJ, 1984.

[26] Edward T. Hall, *The Hidden Dimension,* Doubleday, Garden City, NJ, 1973. (Reprint edition issued by Greenwood Press, Westport, CT, 1980.)

[27] Ibid., p. 121.

[28] Ibid., p. 123.

[29] Ibid., p. 107 et seq.

[30] A. Rustemli, ''The Effects of Personal Space Invasion on Impressions and Decisions,'' *The Journal of Psychology,* vol. 122, March 1988, p. 113. J. K. Burgoon and S. B. Jones, ''Toward a Theory of Personal Space Expectation and Their Violations,'' *Human Communication Research,* vol. 2, no. 2, Winter 1976, pp. 131–146. J. K. Burgoon and L. Abo, ''Field Experiments on the Effects of Violations of Conversational Distance,'' *Communication Monographs,* vol. 49, no. 2, June 1982, pp. 71–88.

[31] Barnlund, op. cit., see chap. III.

[32] J. L. Krotz, ''A Room of One's Own,'' *Working Woman,* vol. 13, September 1988, p. 130.

[33] R. Sommer, *Personal Space,* Prentice-Hall, Englewood Cliffs, NJ, 1969, pp. 58–75.

[34] J. K. Burgoon, T. Burke, and M. Pfau, ''Nonverbal Behaviors, Persuasion and Credibility,'' *Human Communication Research,* vol. 17, no. 1, Fall 1990, p. 140. See also Henley, op. cit.; Barnlund, op. cit., p. 126; and Leathers (1976), p. 245.

[35] Leathers, op. cit., p. 245.

[36] J. B. Bavelas, A. Black, N. Chovil, J. Mullett, *Equivocal Communication,* Sage Series in Interpersonal Communication, no. 11, Sage Publications, Newbury Park, CA, 1990, p. 180.

[37] Ibid., chap. 3.

CHAPTER
10

RELATIONSHIPS, ROLES, AND TRUST: LIVING WITH OTHERS

OBJECTIVES

When you have completed this chapter, you should be able to do the following:

1. Define the term "relationships" compared and contrasted with the term "transactions."
2. List five stages of relationships, giving characteristics of each stage and how they might be recognized in two different kinds of settings (such as in family, friendships, workplace, college, etc.).
3. Define the term "roles" in relation to behaviors.
4. List seven different kinds of role expectancies which you may experience, and give an original example of each.
5. Discuss how defining roles relates to your communication behaviors.
6. Repeat the story of Jackson as an example of complex role relationships, and explain the boxes and the clouds over the heads of Jackson and his "circle."
7. List at least two possible outcomes of your relationships if the "pictures in their heads" of people in interaction are not congruent or have major discrepancies.

8. Explain the three situations which Rossiter and Pearce assert are necessary to experience trust, and give an original example of each.

9. Discuss the statement: "It is easy to lose trust but difficult to gain it."

INTRODUCTION

In this textbook we have frequently used the terms "interpersonal" and "transactions" to refer to what happens when you communicate with others.

For our broadest study of communication dynamics, let's agree that *"interpersonal" does not mean only "intimate."* For our purposes, interpersonal refers to those situations in which you want to speak or listen or somehow interact with others whether they are strangers or dearest friends.

"Transactions" should have a similarly broad definition. As the basic unit of communication, transactions give us a way of looking at human exchanges of information or feelings. Your transactions may occur in very casual or temporary situations, as well as those of great significance or permanence.

RELATIONSHIPS

"In everyday usage, we use the term close personal relationship to refer to lovers, marriage partners, best friends, and persons who work closely together."[1] The list in that quotation might cover most of what you normally expect to have as significant relationships in your life. Other writers have proposed more finely divided classifications, for example, putting best friends of the same sex in a different category from best friends of the opposite sex, and having a group of "acquaintances" in each sex.

You don't usually consider as "relationships" those casual instances and contacts of very short duration, or any transactions which are of little interest or lasting consequence to you. These are, however, clearly relationships in the most inclusive sense, even though you and others may hesitate to class them as *real* relationships. You go to the post office to buy stamps and the person in the window engages in a business transaction with you, without your necessarily considering it a "relationship." To you it may just be stamps for a letter. To the post office authorities, however, that transaction is important in terms of your patronage, your pleasure, and your continued support, so they spend millions annually on training their personnel in what they call "human relationships."

On the other hand, much of what we do in this high-tech society is done without immediate human interchange—there are machines to sell you stamps, to handle banking transactions, to check out at a grocery counter, to sign up for classes, to put gasoline in your car, to sell you airline or theater tickets.

RELATIONSHIPS DEFINED

Most people are both seriously involved in and fascinated by the relationships they develop. They can usually tell you when they are in a relationship, although developing a scientific definition for purposes of study and measurement may not be so easy. A somewhat traditional list of characteristics which has been used to define relationships includes these twelve items which partners in a relation generally use to define their having a relationship.[2] (This list also serves as a checklist for the widest range of kinds of verbal and nonverbal communication messages the "relators" might exchange.) The characteristics or "themes" are: (1) dominance-submission, (2) emotional arousal, (3) composure-noncomposure, (4) similarity-dissimilarity, (5) formality-informality, (6) task versus social orientation, (7) intimacy, (8) depth or familiarity, (9) affection, which includes attraction and liking, (10) inclusion-exclusion, (11) trust, and (12) intensity of involvement.

While those very inclusive characteristics are helpful in scientifically measuring relationships and in research, we propose here a less rigorous and more informal set of components which you might use in determining whether or not a relationship exists. Remember again, these describe only those relationships which are easily recognized as the deepest ones, and the most important to you—not the casual, nonrecurring, brief, transient, or passing relational transactions.[3]

1. Relationships are *relatively long-lasting;* they involve more than buying stamps at a post office window or seeing someone drive by. Defining a precise length of time that people need to be together to qualify as a "relationship" is not a useful activity, but at least the persons involved need to see themselves as interacting over a period of time.
2. Persons in a relationship *spend time together and do things together.* Such "spending time" must be mutually acknowledged as being together on purpose and not just waiting at the same bus stop, or being next to each other in a cafeteria line.[4] However romantic one may feel about the accident of meeting a charming other, such accidental meetings may be a prelude to a relationship but not the real thing until some purposive mutual activities develop.
3. Persons in a relationship *share an important environment* or setting. In living accommodations this may be dormitory roommates, married persons, families, or couples of the same or different sex sharing an apartment. In work settings, relationships can develop among people whose job assignments bring them together frequently or for long periods of time, in conferences, in meetings, or at adjacent desks.
4. Relationships encourage, if not require, the *exchange of personal information and reports of feelings.* Levels of disclosing are high, and members in a relationship get involved in conversation both about work and about more intimate concerns. Variety of discourse is re-

Relationships occur between friends. (© Alan Carey/The Image Works)

Relationships occur between professionals and in work settings. (© Barbara Rios/ Photo Researchers)

Relationships occur in families. (© Hugh Rogers/ Monkmeyer)

quested, and occasions of "let's not talk shop" effectively encourage a different kind of personal talk beyond business data exchange.

5. Relationships are also defined by those involved when *they see them-selves "relating" and are seen by others* that same way. In this way a relationship grows when the participants acknowledge either covertly or overtly that they are associated and behave in ways which make it evident to others.

Where Relationships Occur

Relationships may occur between friends of either sex, in families, in the work setting, in classrooms, or in any places where people see themselves linked to others for common purposes over time. "Marriage" is a term we use when a romantic attachment between two people reaches a certain stage and the two people want to formalize their relationship by either legal or religious rituals. Is the term "divorce" used to describe the end of the "marriage" relationship, or is it another form of relationship by itself? "Socialization" is a term used in corporations to describe the process by which a relationship gets established between an employee and the company rather than between people in the organization. How does taking the same class with another person qualify as a relationship?

What is important to remember, however, is that even if we assert that communication is purposeful, we do not mean only that you communicate to sell a product, get your way, or inform the uninformed. We mean that one very important purpose can be the relationship itself. You may communicate for no other reason than to develop, or sustain, or disengage a relationship.

STAGES OF RELATIONSHIPS

As you know, some relationships hardly get off the ground, while others sustain themselves at a highly involved level over a period of time. Many writers and researchers have set up various lists of stages. Some start at zero, and some start after a first meaningful contact; some take people to a positive conclusion, and others describe a roller coaster of stages which go from casual acquaintanceship through intimacy to a complete breakup and dissolution of the relationship.[5]

We will suggest the following stages as a way of looking at the movement from the first encounter or transactions. Be aware, however, of three problems with this set of stages which may be inherent in any attempt to take a dynamic process and chop it up into identifiable steps.

First, relationships are always changing, and this listing of stages may give you the wrong impression that when you reach one stage, you're set. In the give and take of communication, in the flow of motives and

---

BOX 10-1. Every Transaction Is Not a Relationship

Some years ago a movie titled *Bob and Carol and Ted and Alice,* as a satire on sensitivity group training, included an episode where Carol with the others in a restaurant tried to engage a waiter in a "meaningful relationship." The waiter did not want to get involved with these diners beyond taking their orders. Many transactions can, and should, occur in our lives without becoming fully functioning relationships.

behaviors, in the constant display of new reactions to new or old forces, persons involved in a relationship may respond sometimes in an unexpected or unpredicted way to each other and to the situations that develop. Much as you might like another to be the "same" all the time, experience tells you that it is not going to be that way. You must accustom yourself to expect change, and develop some ways to handle it when change inevitably comes.

Second, these stages may not occur in a nicely arranged order or sequence. Stages also do not usually appear in their pure form—you may spend some of your communication energy going back over a previous stage to reinforce a behavior there, or you may skip ahead from time to time to another stage. Nor should you consider these the only possibilities of relationships—we have already suggested that transactions, as units of relationships, may take unique or interesting directions in your contacts with others.

Third, these stages are not prescriptions on how you should develop and grow with relations. We do not place a particular value on moving from stage 1 in a direct or linear fashion through the subsequent stages. In fact, your relationships may very honestly move in any direction at any time.

Stage 1: Contacting

As the opening stage for relationships, this is sometimes called "initiating," "auditioning" (referring to the "tryout" nature of the activities), "sampling," or "circling." In this stage you first begin to decide whether or not you want more of a relationship. Does the other person seem to have traits, interests, ideals, values, habits, personality, or resources (including such items as a new Porsche, or an A average in math) which fit your needs or values? Does the other person seem interested in more transactions with you—doesn't everyone appreciate some encouragement before going on in a relationship?[6] Among today's popular how-to-do-it books are guides for both sexes which tell you how to "pick up" a person of the opposite sex, mostly dealing with how to go well beyond the most casual opening transactions. One aim at this stage is to find out if the person is interested, and is interesting.

Malinowski's "phatic communion,"[7] or small talk, as a preparation for more serious talk, occurs at this stage whether you are sitting next to a person in class, meet someone in a bar, encounter a new person in a nearby office or workstation, or meet a visitor to the family. "Small talk," so characteristic of this "contacting" stage, is really not "small" at all, as you can find out a great deal about each other without either of you risking too much by disclosing highly personal data. If you find the person appealing and willing to continue beyond this stage, you will continue the relationship. If not, you can shut off the relationship quickly with little cost to you.

Stage 2: Evaluating

At this second stage you balance your rewards from the relationship with the costs and decide how much of yourself to invest. Going often to the library with another student may mean giving up other friends or missing your favorite television programs, but that activity may lead to a valuable exchange of study time and personal pleasure. At work you may want to see a peer frequently to exchange both emotional and informational material about the job, but in so doing you have to be away from your desk or change the pattern of who you see for coffee breaks or lunch. This stage is often referred to as "bargaining," "exploring," "involvement," "trials," or "mutuality." Dating another person may have economic costs for either men or women (tickets, meals, transportation, special attire or equipment as for jogging or skiing, etc.) as well as emotional costs, and you must decide if the payoff to you and the future relationship is enough to continue. Remember that entering this stage does not mean that the "contacting" is over—you likely will continue to test, as you did in the beginning, new areas of interest and attitudes to help you evaluate the relationship.

Stage 3: Committing

This stage is characterized by intensifying relationships leading often to signing a contract of some kind—in business or in marriage, agreeing to go to the same college, getting "pinned," joining the same club, opening a joint account, making major purchases together. You may ask each other to narrow your associations to the primary one in your life. While some analysts consider two separate stages as operating here, the com-

Dating relationships may have economic and personal costs to either men or women. (© Joel Gordon)

Communication stage. Marriage is a traditional form of male-female relationship reaching a commitment stage. (© *Thomas Craig/The Picture Cube*)

binations are often referred to as "intensifying," "revising," "linking," or "major interaction," and then "bonding," "institutionalizing," "intimacy," "coupling," or "stable exchange."

Within this stage, negative judgments about the other person are at a minimum. You overlook the other person's faults, and you concentrate on the joy of associating; you begin to restrict your interactions with others in favor of this relationship. "Going steady" is an early symptom of this stage, and the term "starry-eyed" is often used to describe the behaviors. Even in relationships not so closely identified with affection or intimacy, as in the work setting or in classrooms, you may develop a set of "in" jokes, perhaps a personal language of terms whose meaning is special between you, unknown to others, and a further indication of the desire to exclude others from your relations.

For classmates or friends, you decide to change your major, to car-pool, to sign up for a class you had no previous interest in, or to request a double room in the dorm to accommodate you and the other. For lovers this is the "our own desert island" stage where you would like to completely escape from the rest of humanity and to be with each other every moment, in what subconsciously may be a very predictive and poignant attempt to protect the newly developed rapture from change or potential disintegration. The most identifiable and usual form of commitment in male-female relationships is, of course, marriage or living together.

Stage 4: Doubting   While the previous stage concentrated on the "good qualities" of the other person, in this stage you begin to see more of the "bad." Some writers call this stage the stage of "intolerance," "differentiating," "deterioration," "stagnating," or "conflict development." The habits or attitudes once considered acceptable, or even lovable, are now a source of annoyance. Partners share less and make less effort to please each other. Sometimes a "take me as I am" attitude challenges the other person to stop finding fault. Even if you argue more, you also find more things you are not supposed to talk about—taboo subjects.

If you are classmates, you don't share lecture notes as helpfully as before, and you find that you can't agree on how awful that last test was. Roommates may assert territory rights like "keep your things off my desk," or increase their use of terms like "always" and "never" with each other: "How come you *always* turn on the faucet to brush your teeth when I'm in the shower—I get scalded."

At work you discover reasons to criticize the efforts of the other; you doubt that person is going to make it in the company; you find yourself not returning phone calls or being too busy to have coffee or lunch.

In a marriage, you may revert to "small talk" about your work, the children, the people you see: "How was your day?" "Okay, yours?" You may not initiate conversation as much as before, especially about intimate or personal things or ideas. You may begin the first steps to "disengage" from each other by focusing your attention, while together, on television shows or the family pet or the children—most anything which is outside the paired relationship.[8]

We call this the "return to the first person singular" stage. During the "committing" stage your use of pronouns had been mostly "ours," "we," and "us," but in this "doubting" period your language may revert to the "contacting" stage when your commonest pronouns were "I," "mine," and "me."

Stage 5: Disengaging   A stage of "avoiding," "ending," "dissolving," or "terminating" may be either rapid or slow. An example of a quick disengagement is breaking off an engagement suddenly, or moving out of a dorm room in midterm, or getting an overnight transfer to another job assignment. Friends who want to disengage will change their habits of when they shop or whom they spend time with so as to avoid contact. Divorce, a very common way for ending a marriage relationship, can happen very slowly or very precipitously.

Disengagement may also be *complete* (divorce, death, moving away, complete disconfirmation, reverting to the precontacting stage), or it may be *incomplete* or partial. Even when physical separation is not possible, a psychological or emotional separation may occur.[9] Disengagement of married couples may occur in fact (when members of a marriage behave singly or apart) although the legal dissolution of the marriage may not

Disengagement stage. "I used to think you were a Renaissance man, Michael, but now I think you're a Neanderthal." *(Drawing by Koren; © 1977 The New Yorker Magazine, Inc.)*

take place because of economics, children, religion, convenience, or some external reason.

Other relationships, less dramatically evident, may also defer total disengagement even after the value of the relationship to either partner has diminished to nothing. Roommates may continue to occupy the same room of a residence hall, but avoid being there at the same time. Co-workers have a very difficult time if they continue to be employed at the same place, as the demands of common effort may force them to interact. Business and working situations have traditionally been one of the most fertile places to develop multilevel relationships (personal and professional), and at the same time one of the least outwardly accepting of personal or emotional alliances. (See Box 10-6, p. 255.)

ROLES

In Chapter 1 we introduced you to the term "transactions" to indicate that communication should be looked at as an ongoing activity between people who (1) take each other into account, (2) work out their respective *roles,* and (3) conduct their interactions by a set of principles which can be analyzed and predicted.

In order to better understand how you behave in "relationships" we need to look at roles and how they affect what happens between you and others (the transactions as defined earlier).

Roles are patterns of behavior which you decide are appropriate for specific situations. Relationships then are affected by each person taking certain roles which fit or do not fit expectations of others. If you are a student some of the time, you fit that role by going to class, reading books, listening to lectures, writing papers, and so on. You might also be a mother, or you might be a waiter. Certain behaviors are expected from mothers,

BOX 10-2. Watching Others Relate

When you see a married couple coming down the street, the one who is two or three steps ahead is the one that's mad.

Helen Rowland

When people are angry with each other—and not only married couples—they make a point of indicating their feelings, usually nonverbally. In this brief satirical quotation you can see not only that people have feelings but also that they have some very predictable ways of showing their feelings; and further, they are very anxious to make sure the other person (and maybe the rest of the world) knows something is wrong. How do people in love walk down the street together? How would you know if two people walking together were new acquaintances? Were casual friends? Were in stage 1 of "contacting" or in stage 5 of "disengaging"? Could you tell something about those stages by watching people walk together?

students, or waiters, and they are not defined in isolation but in relation to complementary sets of behaviors, other roles. You are not a mother without a child to mother; or a student without a teacher to learn from; or a waiter without someone to wait on.

Very often we relate to each other in respect to roles rather than considering the person who is occupying that role. This is a form of behavioral shortcut which makes it simpler sometimes to get on with the business of living. This is the basis of stereotypes, as described in Chapter 7. How do you feel about a person filling the role of police officer? How much do you believe a person in the role of politician? Do you feel the same when you are in the role of student in class as when you are in the role of family member?

Negotiating Your Roles

Because role is likely to be one of the first items you bring up in the "contacting" stage of relationships, you will always face the issue of "role relationship negotiation." Do you ask the other person, "Are you a student here?" to break the ice? And then whichever answer you get—"yes" or "no"—you will frame your next transaction. "Where do you work?" is a question about your role, not so much about your physical location of expending your labors. "He's a frat guy," "She's married," "He's a senior" are role labels to give you a clue of what you may expect in the way of behaviors from "those" people. For that reason, if you have a choice of how to be judged by others, you will determine which role you want to be known for and negotiate for it. Relationships will depend a great deal on how your roles meet the expectations of others.[10]

BOX 10-3. Television and Role Development

Much criticism has been leveled at television for its part in developing roles for people. Learning our social roles from the shows on television can be both a good and a bad experience. Some television characters may not be the best role models for us to follow—such as the aggressive bully who gets away with intimidating others, or the dishonest person who is not caught in the act or punished, or the generally disagreeable character whose language and behaviors are not socially acceptable. Television may portray to young children (as well as to adults, who also may be affected by role models on television) family behaviors which vary from their own experience. Research has shown that shows about family life depict the least amount of violence and aggression and the most amount of cooperative and affiliative behaviors. Children may actually see a better form of family life on television than they see in their own experience. If children believe that family life should be "like that" in real life, then the influence of television, in this instance, may be helpful in developing healthy family roles. Learning consumer behavior is also related to media viewing habits and family communication patterns. The process of learning from television is itself less significant than the influence parents exert over their children to watch programs that ensure healthy role development.*

In other kinds of activities, role development may be just as strongly influenced by television. A study of the driving habits of television characters shows a relationship to attitudes of viewers about their own driving. The conclusions suggest that some driving-age viewers accept irregular driving behavior (such as "burning rubber" and screeching brakes) as "normal." They believe that speeding is all right and that most speeders don't get caught, that seat belts are unnecessary, and that dangerous driving will not have serious consequences. They also believe that the proper roles are for males to drive and females to be passengers; that young people (in their twenties) do more irregular driving than others; and that vans, trucks, and sports cars are the most likely vehicles to drive in a dangerous or irregular way.†

Television may deserve its reputation as a generator of roles for regular viewers. With so many types of programs available, there is no shortage of models, or examples, for us to pattern our lives after.

* H. Gray, "Television, Black Americans, and the American Dream," *Critical Studies in Mass Communication*, vol. 6, December 1989, p. 376; C. Schine, "Three Popular Shows Offer Motherhood Role Models" (*thirtysomething, Roseanne*, and *The Donna Reed Show*), *Vogue*, vol. 79, November 1989, p. 262; N. L. Buerkel-Rothfuss, B. S. Greenberg, C. K. Atkin, and K. Nuendorf, "Learning about the Family from Television," *Journal of Communication*, vol. 32, Summer 1982, p. 191; R. L. Moore and G. P. Moschis, "The Role of Family Communication in Consumer Learning", *Journal of Communication*, vol. 31, Autumn 1981, p. 42.
† B. S. Greenberg and C. K. Atkin, "The Portrayal of Driving on Television, 1975–1980," *Journal of Communication*, vol. 33, Spring 1983, p. 44.

Role expectations:
Intimacy

You define your relationships partly in terms of how close you feel to another person. How you expect to act, and others to act toward you, will be affected by your "tacit agreement" about intimacy. This quality is difficult to put into words, and so you usually depend on an unspoken understanding. That makes it easy to violate and difficult to anticipate. "Jill, please type this letter," "Jill, honey, would you type this letter," and "Miss Smith, type this letter" imply different degrees of closeness and informality. Information about intimacy is usually transmitted by nonverbal cues—you use a special tone of voice; you stand close; you look into his or her eyes; you touch; you may sigh or snarl. You know people whose tone of voice, demeanor, stance, or gaze habits indicate to you that they prefer distance and formality. You know people from whom you expect more intimate and affectionate behaviors. You also know that the setting, suggested below, will have an effect on how intimately you can act.

Role expectations:
Authority

Differences in authority will dictate how you act with another person. Teacher-student, father-child, doctor-patient, boss-subordinate—all are relationships which imply that communication will take place along dominant-submissive lines. Some relationships are culturally and socially defined as those just mentioned; others may develop dominance-submission by meeting the expectations and needs of the participants. For example, in most marriages one partner tends to be dominant about selected affairs, usually with the tacit agreement of the other partner. Divorce may occur when authority expectations are not consistently met over time. Some relationships are based on an equal authority pattern, as between friends, colleagues, fellow students, or members of your same club or team. If you play soccer and consistently fail to pass the ball to a teammate, that person cannot force you to change your behavior since he or she lacks authority, but the coach could influence your playing tactics quite easily. "Jill, type this letter" gets the response "Right away, Mrs. Jones," and you can recognize that an authority relationship exists and also that both people understand the relationship and will act on it.

Role expectations:
Situation

Because it is possible for you to select among several roles at different times, the situation or the context of your transactions may be crucial in helping you determine what role you choose at any given time. You are expected to behave differently in the library than you would at a sporting event—your role of studious researcher will not work well in the cheering section of a football game. Your role of class clown may be more effective with peers than with professors. Intimate roles are reserved for secluded places and quiet moods.

Role expectations:
Professions and
occupations

Roles are often tied to professional labels as well as to who is boss—"my son, the doctor," "so you're a mechanic," "excuse my language, Reverend." You tend to figure out how the other person will behave by the occupational or professional label.[11] You also have a clue about how you

---

**BOX 10-4. Authority Expectations:
A Cross-Cultural View**

The term in Japanese *danson-johi* refers to the idea that men are superior to women and have authority over them. It sets up and confirms traditional family roles of a husband-as-breadwinner and wife-as-housekeeper. Confucianism condemned any mixed company in public places or any changes of roles for the two sexes in society. Consequent lack of social interaction between young men and women has been blamed for a present lack of understanding between sexes. Equality of sexes was not established in Japan until after World War II, in spite of some feminist movements in the early part of the twentieth century.

"The Fourteenth Article of the Constitution of Japan, enacted in 1947, provides that sex discrimination must be abolished, but sexism still exists today especially in the business world. . . ."*

* B. Hoffer and N. Honna, *An English Dictionary of Japanese Culture,* Yuhikaku Publishing, Tokyo, 1986, p. 34.

---

should behave toward that psychiatrist, that lawyer, that janitor, that professor, that farmer, that police officer. In other words, your relationship not only starts but may continue for a while based mainly on how you see the other person's role in relation to experiences you have had with that role before. If you hate classical music, you will not likely develop a strong or lasting relationship with a symphony violinist. If you enjoy little children, you may find friends among parents or kindergarten teachers, or decide to become a parent or a teacher yourself.

**Role expectations:
Age roles**

You have ideas of how people at various ages should act. A tantrum by a 3-year-old does not "mean" the same thing as a tantrum by a 50-year-old. Do you address your parents' friends the same way you talk to your peers? Do you talk about the same things? Do you engage in the same activities with people many years younger or older than you are? You as a teenager or a young adult or a middle-aged person are given certain role limits by society. If you violate those limits, others may have trouble relating to you unless they are so attached to you that they will tolerate your aberrations (as in the "committing" stage of a relationship). As the median age of the American population increases, new attitudes and role expectations seem to be forming about "old folks" who run marathons, drive sports cars, and engage in sex or politics.

**Role expectations:
Family relations**

Changing also, if however slowly, are the expectations of family relations. The once "nuclear family" and the "extended family" ideas are being challenged by changing social norms and circumstances. The number of

Role expectations. You usually have clues about how to behave toward others based on occupational or professional labels. *(© Sepp Seitz/Woodfin Camp)*

single-parent families, the frequency of divorce, and the growing acceptance of care for the aged outside the family are only a few such items. There is close affiliation implied by "blood relations," as you are likely to accept behaviors from relatives which you will not tolerate from "strangers."[12] You keep in touch with parents, cousins, or siblings long after your interests may have become very different. Sons or daughters of the owners of a business enterprise sometimes appear to have advantages not enjoyed by just any employee. On the other hand, offspring of prominent families may be unfairly pressured to sustain family prominence or to become outstanding themselves.

Role expectations: Gender

Another important source of role expectations involves gender differences. In spite of attempts to challenge sex role stereotyping, you may still expect that boys don't cry, girls play with dolls, boys become engineers and doctors, girls become secretaries and nurses. The same behaviors in men and women may be interpreted quite differently simply because of gender difference—behavior in a man that is characterized as "ambitious" and "go-getting" may be seen in a woman as "pushy" and "aggressive."

Nowhere has this ambiguous role of women been displayed more clearly than in the "how to be successful" books for women. Authors disagree on how to measure success for a woman (and some don't even try but leave that up to the individual woman to decide for herself); they give varying advice on how to reach this undefined "success." Buying one of those career books, however, the woman does get a set of role assumptions about how the society will treat her—a clear indication of the impact of role differentiation by sex. Programs to train executives to

---

BOX 10-5.   Relations and the Goals of Education

In commenting on marriage and the changing intimate relationships for the American adults, the distinguished psychotherapist Carl Rogers writes this about the isolation being fostered by the educational system:

> One of the elements which stands out for me, in so many . . . marriages I have known, is that young people start out without the foggiest notion of how to live in human, personal interaction—literally without any experience in real interpersonal sharing communication with persons. . . . I wonder if [our educational system] would be willing not only to believe but to prove by their actions that one goal of education is to assist the young person to live as a person with other persons.*

* C. Rogers, *Becoming Partners: Marriage and Its Alternatives*, Delacorte Press, New York, 1972, p. 214.

---

relate to women executives are becoming more common and are based on historically derived and strongly held assumptions about gender roles (see Box 10-6). There is some evidence that the communication patterns of men and women may be more alike, in more ways, than our folk wisdom or our superficial guesses have led us to believe. In marriage as well as in the workplace, researchers are finding a complex variation of communication styles between men and women. They also find that when men talk only to men, or women only to women, their communication patterns are more different than when they are in mixed groups. In other words, both men and women seem to communicate more like each other when talking with persons of the other sex.[13]

Consequences of Defining Roles

Once you figure out what role you need to take and what role the other person is likely to take, you have a great deal of information about what behavior is expected of you, and what you can expect from the other person. Increase in pedictability helps all parties in both setting up and maintaining a relationship.

Roles spell out how you will dress (in a uniform, far-out, demure, revealing, gaudy, etc.); how you will speak or be spoken to (profanity, slang, formal speech, address forms such as "Yes, ma'am," "Doctor," etc.); what kinds of rights and privileges you are entitled to (having a key to the executive washroom, touching, sitting together, standing at attention, raising a hand to speak, sharing a shower, having your own parking space, etc.).

If you are a college student, you will talk to other students much of the time, to professors less often, to a dean seldom, to a college president rarely, and to a trustee probably never. If you are a trustee of a college,

---

BOX 10-6.   Gender Relations at Work

As more women move into management and into corporate leadership positions, new uncertainties and some discomforts are experienced by both male and female executives. A study reported in early 1987 by Catalyst, a nonprofit research and advisory organization in New York,* discovered that male executives of any age may be unaware of the sexual biases which govern their decisions, hence relationships, with female executives. Older men, in more senior positions, appear to have the greatest difficulty coping with women executives, summarized by the statement: "They really can't understand why a woman would want to be the chief financial officer of a company when she could be home with her children." Images of romantic relationships occur in the minds of both men and women, the report says, and one specific difficulty occurs when a woman executive is expected to entertain a male executive; and some males say that they hesitate to offer criticism to women because they assume that the woman will cry and they cannot cope with tears, or they don't send women executives on the road because they assume that women do not like to travel.

Representatives of the Catalyst company, offering training to reduce male-female relationship problems in the management setting, say that there is no chance that the gender-related tensions will disappear from the work setting. They are optimistic, however, about the increasing numbers of management personnel, female as well as male, who are openly and directly facing the problems and trying to adjust to new relationship dynamics.

* G. Collins, *The New York Times,* January 30, 1987; F. Fejes (ed.), "Gender Studies and Communication," *Critical Studies in Mass Communication,* vol. 6, June 1989, p. 195.

---

you will speak to other trustees much of the time, to the president often, to deans sometimes, to professors seldom, and very rarely to a student.

Roles also influence the content of your communication. As a student, you will talk to a professor about the course or exams; even if you see this same professor at the supermarket, you will likely talk about class. "Not mixing business with pleasure" is an expression used when executives interact with employees—their communication is about business-related items and rarely about personal matters. Although a boss may ask, "How's the wife?" the employee would not ask the boss that question. It is possible, therefore, for the superior in many settings to ask more personal questions than are permitted of a subordinate. Teachers may inquire about areas of a student's life which the student does not feel free to ask the teacher about (television viewing habits, sleep hours, friendship patterns, problems at home, etc.). In the family setting, parents may ask

Roles influence the content of
your communication. (©
Michael McGovern/The
Picture Cube) ·

questions of a more penetrating (or nosy?) nature than the children are
permitted to, recognizing a role difference. Older people seem to get away
with asking questions of younger people that would not be acceptable
the other way around. Designated roles such as police officer, judge,
doctor, lawyer, give those professionals an upper hand in setting the
content of discourse—you are expected to answer any questions asked
by them and are limited in what you may ask in return.

A Story of One Man's Roles: Jackson, a Man in the Middle

To illustrate the complexities of roles and role taking, this story is told in
seminars and workshops. It is merely partial, because it focuses only on
Jackson himself—not on the many reflected roles of the others in his
world. Each time Jackson takes a role, there is evidence that someone
else (a boss, a wife, a child, a fellow golfer) has a reciprocal role. Such
reciprocity makes relationships.

Both the *quality* and *duration* of those relationships depend on how
Jackson sees himself in the available roles, and how others' roles respond
to him. If you want the challenge, imagine what the diagram would be
like if the "others" in Jackson's life had their own diagrams of relationships
drawn here also.

As we go through the circle of Jackson's immediate "others," can you speculate on what *stage* each relationship may be in at this moment? Can you also speculate on how the *role expectations* each person has will influence the progress of the relations?[14]

Jackson and a few selected others

In Figure 10-1 you see Jackson in the center, surrounded by some of the people with whom he interacts frequently. Let's focus on Jackson in this exercise—his roles in relation to these few relationships, which could be designated as work, family, friends, marriage, etc.

Jackson is a real, living, human being who breathes, eats, goes to work, shares a personal and perhaps a professional family life, and plays golf or jogs with his friends. He is, for any purpose, a sufficiently identifiable set of features, so that his friends would notice his picture in the paper or be able to pick him out of a crowd.

Pictures in their heads

In the course of a day Jackson talks to many people—only a few of whom are shown here. Each person he talks to has a picture of Jackson; how

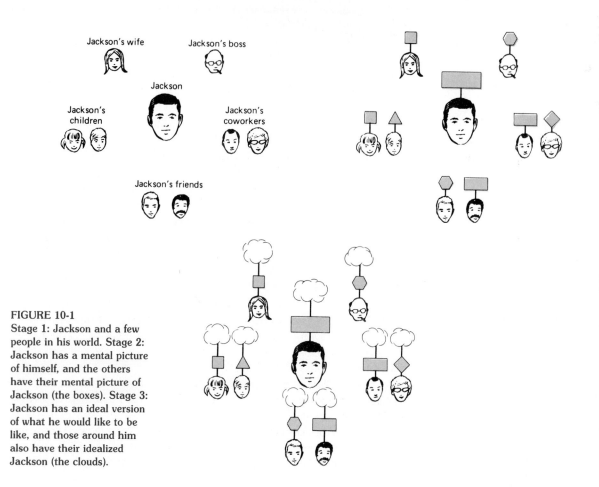

FIGURE 10-1
Stage 1: Jackson and a few people in his world. Stage 2: Jackson has a mental picture of himself, and the others have their mental picture of Jackson (the boxes). Stage 3: Jackson has an ideal version of what he would like to be like, and those around him also have their idealized Jackson (the clouds).

honest, how smart, how important, how good looking, how articulate, etc. Talking to the men and women in his circle, Jackson has his picture of himself, and they have theirs of him (they also have their own pictures of themselves, but we said we were not going to make this complicated).

It is most likely that the transactions involve primarily Jackson's picture talking to their pictures of him. What these people hear from Jackson will depend on how they see him, and how effective Jackson is will depend on how well he guesses what those pictures look like above the heads of the others. As each role relationship comes along, Jackson may have to adjust his own picture if he finds some difficulty talking to the pictures of the others.

Who is Jackson?

Is Jackson the picture in his head? Is he the guy walking down the street? Is he the person in the heads of his circle of people? Which one? Is he none of these entirely, but possibly part of all of them? Is there a "real" Jackson? By getting feedback from others he finds out what kind of Jackson they see; he makes choices on what he wants to be, and as we saw in Chapter 3, *he finds out who he is.*

Consider also the question of who is talking to whom? Do you think that these people are talking to some "real" Jackson, or is it likely that Jackson's picture is talking to their pictures? Does our communication consist of pictures in our heads talking to each other?

The idealized Jackson

Above the picture (the box) Jackson has of himself in the lower diagram is added a cloudlike, ethereal, ideal self—what Jackson would really like to be. This is more of a self-wish than a self-concept. Ideally Jackson would like to behave in some ways he may actually not achieve. He knows that he should be a better father, a better golfer, a better employee, a better friend, a better husband. The clouds represent the ideal "shoulds."

Of course there are clouds of "shoulds" or "idealizations" above the images other people have of Jackson. If the picture of Jackson as seen by coworkers is grouchy and mean, they would ideally like to have Jackson thoughtful and kind. The clouds above the ideal Jackson in that respect may not match the box of how they see Jackson.

Jackson behaves in relation to others

In many situations Jackson can guess what the others expect of him in the way of behaviors. It is up to him to decide whether or not to live up to their expectations, and so he has choices to make. He will also know that whatever choices he makes and however he acts, those others will judge him on the basis of (1) how they want him to act, the clouds, and (2) how they expect him to act, the pictures. That makes his behaviors very complex events.

A number of conclusions about role taking are developed from this oversimplified example of Jackson. They are listed in Box 10-7 and can form guidelines for your looking at your own roles and relationships.

BOX 10-7. Principles behind Roles of Jackson

1. The greater the discrepancy between the pictures you have of yourself and the pictures others have of you, the greater the chance for misunderstanding and ambiguous feedback.
2. The greater the discrepancy between your picture of yourself and your ideal self, the greater will be your dissatisfaction with your communicative behaviors.
3. The greater the discrepancy between the pictures others have of you and their idealizations of what you should be like, the less chance there is for satisfactory relationships to develop.
4. Your pictures of yourself and the pictures others have of you are the result of behaviors toward each other.
   a. You find out what you are like by having people respond to you, that is, from the feedback you get from them.
   b. Others find out what you are like by collecting their reactions to your behaviors toward them.
5. Your idealization of yourself is related to your value system, and the expectations of others toward you are likewise related to theirs.
   a. The role you play has much to do with your idealization of how a person in that role should act.
   b. You depend on feedback from others to tell you not only how they perceive you (their pictures), but also how they would like you to behave (idealization).

Behind Your Relationships

If you are like Jackson, you would like to communicate with others with some mutual understanding and not to botch it up. You may know people who will sometimes deliberately mislead you, but it is our optimistic assumption in this book that you and most everyone else want mutually satisfying relationships.

In later chapters we suggest some approaches to improve your communication, to resolve the conflicts and defensiveness you may experience in yourself and others. There are, however, no ten easy steps to communication effectiveness; no simple cookbook approach, and no communication pill you can take for instant recovery from interpersonal ailments. This is particularly true in respect to *trust* and the risks involved in that part of your interpersonal transactions.

THE ART OF TRUSTING

What does it mean to trust? How does trust relate to interpersonal communication? Whom and when do you trust? How do you demonstrate that you can be trusted? These are important questions, and they do not have simple answers. In this section we consider trust on the basis of a provocative and sensitive analysis by Rossiter and Pearce.[15]

The Situation Context of Trust

According to Rossiter and Pearce, you can experience trust only when your relationship with another person is characterized by *contingency, predictability,* and *alternative options.*

"Contingency" refers to a situation in which the outcomes of another person's actions significantly affect you. If what somebody does has no effect on you, there is no need for you to trust that person.

"Predictability" refers to the degree of confidence you have in what the other person will do. You guess about the other person's behavior or intentions. In situations where predictability is low, you cannot have much confidence that the other person will behave in a certain way. You may have hope but no trust.

Finally, "alternative options" implies that you are free to do something else beside trust. Trust is present only by choice.

If any one of these three characteristics is missing, we cannot speak of trust. When the three characteristics are present, trust *may* develop. The word "may" is deliberately emphasized here because, as we will discuss, trust is an option and is never automatic. If what happens to you depends on another person's behavior, if you have some basis for predicting how the other person will behave, and if you have a choice about your own behavior, then you are in a situation in which trust *may occur.* This is usually the case in a manager-subordinate, husband-wife, or roommate relationship. The other person's behavior may affect you significantly, you have some basis for determining whether your predictions about the other person are accurate, and at least some of the time you have options about what to do. Table 10-1 gives examples of situations in which you must decide to trust or not to trust.

The Belief Basis for Trust

When you trust another person, you take a risk, or at least you increase your vulnerability to that other person. Trusting means that you will let the other person's behavior affect you. To do so you must believe that the other person is both willing and able to behave in ways that will not hurt you.

In other words, you trust another person when you believe that person won't hurt you. Intentions are not enough. Abilities are crucial. Is the other person able or competent to perform the action you predict will take place? After all, a friend who is not a qualified brain surgeon may be very well intentioned and may never wish to hurt you, and yet you may not "trust" him or her to perform brain surgery on you. The reverse is equally true. Although you may perceive somebody as quite competent, if you also perceive that person's intentions to be devious or self-serving, you are not likely to trust.

How Do You Develop Trusting Relationships?

Being trusted by others does not happen by magic or by mechanically following a technical manual which specifies the steps to be taken to "make others trust you." In fact there is no sure way to make other people

TABLE 10-1.
Situations for Trust

Characteristic, and how to check on whether it is present	A clerk in a store is showing you a bicycle you want to buy.	A friend offers to meet you at 6 P.M. and give you a ride home.	Driving in traffic, you stop at a red light and wait for it to turn green.
Contingency—Does it make any difference to me what the other person does?	You want the bicycle to be as advertised; you will have to live with your own decision to get it or not.	Accepting the offer will save you both time and worry about how to get home; you will depend on the ride.	The effect of stopping is not getting into a collision. You have to trust that those behind you will stop as you do and that those in the cross lanes will only go when their light is green.
Predictability—Can I count on the other person?	Check out the reputation of the store; think about your own experiences with clerks; consider how bicycles generally hold up after you take them on the street.	Is your friend known to be punctual? Does the friend's car work all right? Are there other factors which could keep the friend away?	Most drivers obey the stop signals. Although the yellow light is dangerous to run through, red and green are usually predictable.
Alternative options— Can I personally do anything about trusting or not?	Check out what you can see about the bicycle; get a guarantee on all parts. If you are not satisfied that a trust situation is possible, then don't buy the bike.	Walk; take a bus; ask another friend to back up the offer; phone the friend just before 6 P.M. to check.	Don't drive; take a bus. If you do drive you are very dependent on other drivers to obey the signals and not run into you, especially after the light turns green for your lane.

trust you. While trusting other people only *sometimes* encourages them to trust you, distrusting them *almost always* will make them distrust you.

You cannot make someone trust you. If someone is bent on misunderstanding you and refuses to perceive you as either well intentioned or competent, there is very little you can do to change that person's interpretations of what you are like. Anything you do can always be misinterpreted, and everything you say can always be held against you, and taken as further "proof" of that person's original conception of you.

Trust is built through risks mutually taken one by one in a given relationship. For example, if you make yourself vulnerable to another person—that is, accept the fact that his or her actions may affect you adversely—and if the other person accepts your initial move by not hurting you and by making himself or herself vulnerable to you, then mutual trust building is started. You may then make yourself a little more vulnerable, and so may the other person. And the process goes on as you work together, taking more risks.

Rossiter and Pearce contend that for a trusting relationship to be established, three factors must be present: (1) You must trust even though you are not sure that the other will reciprocate. (2) You and the other

When you trust another person you increase your vulnerability to that other person. (© *Janice Fullman/ The Picture Cube*)

person must be willing to trust, that is, (a) not follow impulses to exploit the other and (b) interpret the other person's behavior as trustworthy rather than foolish. (3) You must both be willing to negotiate the process through incremental steps, a little trust at a time.

You cannot force trust on other people. If they are intent on distrusting you, they will always find something to support their belief that you are not trustworthy. Ultimately all that you can do is trust in the hope that the other can and will respond in kind. Of course there is no guarantee that this will happen; and as you take risks in making yourself vulnerable, there is always the possibility that the other person will see you as a fool and will take advantage of you. You must, therefore, always decide whether the risks are worth taking and whether you can afford to take them. In a sense, this implies that to have others trust you, you must actively take some initiative and not simply wait for others to make the first move. If you want to be trusted, you have to make the first gesture, and the opening gambit always involves some amount of risk.

Developing trust in others is not simple. It depends on both your behavior and the ability of the other person to trust and to take risks. You have little control over another person's ability to take risks. However, you do have some control sometimes over the degree of risk involved for the other person, should he or she trust you.

If you are reliable in the messages you send—if most of the time you do what you say, your actions match your words, and your nonverbal messages fit your verbal ones—others can develop the ability to predict your actions and thus minimize their chances of guessing wrong about what you will do.

You can sometimes have some degree of control over the outcomes of risk-taking behavior. How you respond to people who take risks and make a mistake may affect to a large extent their decision to take risks again. You may tell an employee, for example, to go ahead with a project on his or her own and that you will support whatever he or she comes up with. If you bawl out the employee when the product is not exactly as you would have wished, you make it unlikely that the person will believe that you meant what you said. Parents who encourage children to tell the truth about some matter may then punish them for the behavior they confess. It's likely that those children will learn to withhold the truth or tell lies because the risk of being truthful did not pay off.

Deciding to Trust

There are times when you know that you'd better not trust somebody. Get-rich-quick schemes which require you to do almost nothing smack of deceit. If a person you don't know well appears very trusting toward you, there is no sure way to know if that person is really trying to develop an honestly trusting relationship or possibly setting you up for a con game.

Thus, you are faced with decisions: trusting when you should not, or not trusting when you should. If you prefer to err in the direction of trusting when you should not, then you may be seen by some people as warm, compassionate, and nice, but by others as gullible and stupid. If you choose to err in the direction of *not* trusting when you should, you may be perceived by some as worldly wise, hard-nosed, and shrewd, but by others as distant and cynically suspicious.

Do you lend a fellow student your class notes to take away for a weekend? Is your car available to others whenever a hard-luck story is told to you? If you supervise others, do you let them off early or forgive their showing up late when they give you excuses? Do you invest in financial ventures proposed by friends of friends? Do others know better than to ask you to borrow money or some personal item? Can you keep a secret and do you have a reputation of being trusted with confidences?

There is no easy answer to trusting, but as a friend, a parent, a classmate, a manager, a sibling, an employee, a student, or a teacher, you have to come to terms with this issue as an essential part of your relationships.

SUMMARY

Relationships form one of the most important aspects of human communication, and may be defined as longer-lasting than casual encounters;

they occur when people spend time together and do things together, share an environment or setting, exchange personal information and feelings, and also see themselves as relating and are seen that way by others.

Relationships may occur between friends of the same or opposite sex, in a family group, at work, or in any of a number of settings or pairings. A relationship may exist as an end in itself, and have no other purpose between people.

Because relationships are dynamic and changing, it is important to look at them from a process view—a series of recognizable stages which may occur in a variety of sequences. Stages progress from a first encounter ("contacting"), to a more serious stage of looking each other over ("evaluating"), to the point of becoming more serious about the relationship ("committing"). Then more negative considerations may occur ("doubting"), which if sufficiently negative may result in an end to the relationship ("disengaging").

Roles are patterns of behavior which you adopt for specific situations. Others help you decide your roles, and role negotiation occurs among people over the issues of intimacy, authority, situations, professions and occupations, age, family relations, and gender. How you adopt roles will affect both the content and the style of your communication with others. An extended example of one person's (Jackson's) roles demonstrates the complexity of role relationships and develops some conclusions about how they affect communication.

Trusting relationships develop when you are affected by another person's actions (contingency), when you have confidence that the other person will act in a dependable way (predictability), and when you have other options than trusting (alternatives). Trust is more difficult to establish than it is to lose, and is contingent on your taking risks and negotiating trust usually a little at a time.

END NOTES

[1] H. H. Kelley, *Personal Relationships: Their Structures and Processes,* Lawrence Erlbaum, Hillsdale, NJ, 1979, p. 1.

[2] J. K. Burgoon and J. J. Hale, "Validation and Measurement of the Fundamental Themes of Relational Communication," *Communication Monographs,* vol. 54, March 1987, p. 19. And by the same authors, "The Fundamental Topoi of Relational Communication," *Communication Monographs,* vol. 51, June 1984, p. 193.

[3] It should be noted that mostly these same definitions or criteria are used in the study of *group dynamics* to define a "group" as opposed to a "simple collection of people," as expressed by R. Bales, *Interaction Process Analysis,* Addison Wesley Press, Cambridge, MA, 1950, p. 33, and in D. Crech, R. S. Crutchfield, and E. L. Belachy, *Individual in Society,* McGraw-Hill, New York, 1962, pp. 383–384.

[4] M. I. Hallinan and S. S. Smith, "Classroom Characteristics and Student Friendship Cliques," *Social Forces,* vol. 87, June 1989, p. 898.

[5] For a detailed discussion of stages see M. L. Knapp, *Interpeᵣ cation and Human Relationship,* Allyn and Bacon, Newton, MA, which appeared originally as *Social Intercourse: From Greeting tᵣ the same author and publisher, 1978; or see K. L. Villard and ᵢ ...nipple, *Beginnings in Relational Communication,* John Wiley & Sons, New York, 1976; H. H. Kelley and J. W. Thibaut, *Interpersonal Relations: A Theory of Interdependence,* John Wiley & Sons, New York, 1978; and a pioneering descriptive work by F. Heider, *The Psychology of Interpersonal Relations,* John Wiley & Sons, New York, 1958.

[6] C. A. Langston and N. Cantor, "Social Anxiety and Social Restraint: When Making Friends Is Hard," *Journal of Personality and Social Psychology,* vol. 56, April 1989, p. 849.

[7] B. Malinowski, "The Problem of Meaning in Primitive Languages," in C. K. Ogden and I. A. Richards (eds.), *The Meaning of Meaning,* Harcourt, Brace, 1965, p. 315.

[8] D. Vaughn, "The Long Goodbye: Secrecy and Cover-Up in Failing Relationships Often Hide the Problems Until It Is Too Late to Solve Them," *Psychology Today,* vol. 21, July 1987, p. 86.

[9] L. Yarrow, "How Kids Make Friends: They Make Up and Break Up before They Learn How to Establish Bonds of Friendship," *Parents Magazine,* vol. 84, October 1989, p. 95.

[10] L. A. King and D. W. King, "Role Conflict and Role Ambiguity: A Critical Assessment of Construct Validity," *Psychological Bulletin,* vol. 107, January 1990, p. 48.

[11] T. Li-Ping, "Effects of Work Ethic and Task Labels on Task Preference," *The Journal of Psychology,* vol. 123, September 1989, p. 429.

[12] D. Bjorklund and B. Bjorklund, "The Heroes We Know" (family members as heroes), *Parents Magazine,* vol. 84, September 1989, p. 203.

[13] C. S. Burggraf and A. L. Sillars, "A Critical Examination of Sex Differences in Marital Communication," *Communication Monographs,* vol. 54, September 1987, p. 276. A. Mulac, J. M. Wiemann, S. J. Widenmann, and T. W. Gibson, "Male/ Female Language Differences and Effects in Same-Sex and Mixed-Sex Dyads: The Gender-Linked Language Effect," *Communication Monographs,* vol. 55, December 1988, p. 315. K. Alfie, "Girl Talk, Guy Talk: Do Men and Women Really Have Distinctive Communication Styles?" *Psychology Today,* vol. 22, February 1988, p. 65. For another classic study of gender language see B. L. Dubois and I. Crouch (eds.), "The Sociology of the Languages of American Women" published as *Papers in Southwest English (PISE IV),* Bates Hoffer (ed.), Trinity University, San Antonio, TX, 1976.

[14] S. Coverman, "Role Overload, Role Conflict, and Stress: Addressing Consequences of Multiple Role Demands," *Social Forces,* vol. 67, June 1989, p. 985.

[15] C. M. Rossiter and W. B. Pearce, *Communicating Personally,* Bobbs-Merrill, Indianapolis, IN, 1975, p. 119.

CHAPTER
11

MANAGING INTERPERSONAL TENSIONS

OBJECTIVES

When you have completed this chapter, you should be able to:

1. Compare and contrast the traditional view and the more recent way of looking at conflict.
2. List and give original examples of three potentially negative outcomes of unmanaged conflict.
3. List and give original examples of three potentially positive outcomes of conflict when properly managed.
4. Discuss the differences among the personal, interpersonal, and organizational levels of conflict.
5. Identify from your own experience two examples of avoidance strategy for managing conflict.
6. Identify from your own experience two examples of defusion strategy for managing conflict.
7. Identify from your own experience an original example of each of the three kinds of confrontation strategies.
8. Argue for the use of "principled negotiation" as opposed to the more familiar form of "positional negotiation."

9. Describe the four areas of the Johari window in relation to giving and receiving feedback and disclosing.
10. Explain and give examples for the principles of how to focus your feedback, including:
    a. Focus on behaviors
    b. Focus on observations
    c. Focus on description
    d. Focus on sharing information
    e. Focus on the effect on the receiver
11. Define ''feedforward'' and give an example of how it works.
12. Explain when it might be appropriate to self-disclose and when this might not be an appropriate behavior in relation to both the timing and the content.

INTRODUCTION

Tensions arise when people communicate. In previous discussion of relationships, we often referred to potential difficulties between you and others. Even in the closest friendships or families you may not all think alike on all issues. It would be hard to imagine such a perfect relationship that everyone agreed all the time about everything. The transactional nature of human communication strongly suggests that there are individual differences among people—differences which must be resolved some way if people are to understand each other and get things done together.

When we use the term ''tensions,'' we refer to the wide range of reactions people may have to each other, ranging from very quiet, orderly disagreement all the way to open, aggressive, and overt battling. Such tensions directly involve the twin notions of ''conflict'' and ''negotiation,'' and another pair of closely related behaviors we call ''feedback'' and ''disclosure.''

CONFLICT AND NEGOTIATION

Have you ever heard people boast about how well everybody in their group gets along—their family, their dorm, their class, their club, their office, or their neighborhood? They may go so far as to claim that nobody ever disagrees, nobody argues—''just one big happy family.'' When you hear those claims, are you inclined to (1) doubt their honesty or (2) doubt their awareness of what is going on in their world? A completely trouble-free, conflict-less group would be hard to find among people who have normal human instincts of self-interest and commitment, and have a reasonable level of alertness and vitality.

A Traditional View of Conflict

Historically people have viewed conflict as evil, something to be avoided or to be hidden from others, something to be ashamed of. Traditional assumptions about conflict implied that conflict was bad, was avoidable, and usually was caused by some few undesirable troublemakers. Conflict was associated with anger, aggressiveness, physical and verbal fights, and violence—all basically negative feelings and behaviors. "Nice people don't fight," "It's better to get along," "Don't argue in front of the children," "Now you just shake hands and forget it," "If you loved me you wouldn't disagree" are all very familiar messages which teach that conflict is basically a bad thing, and only bad people get into conflicts.

Of course, there are very real possible negative effects from some conflict. On a grand scale, wars among nations are conflict at its worst. On a smaller scale, but still painful to the participants, are divorces, separations, firings, resignations, verbal confrontations, a punch in the nose, or other embattled and embittered relationships.

Even though much of the world treats conflict as a negative transaction, a new view is emerging. Communication analysts now suggest that the old negative view of conflict is often inaccurate and, at best, limited.

A Contemporary View of Conflict

More and more communication writers are describing a new set of assumptions about conflict—and hence about negotiation—which have an effect on our personal lives, our business lives, or international affairs.[1] These newer approaches are based on the ideas that (1) conflict is inevitable, (2) conflict is often determined by the structural factors or situation as well as by people, (3) conflict is often predictable and understandable, and (4) managed properly, conflict can be a very useful part of the process of change and growth in both relationships and larger affairs of humankind.

Conflict is a natural part of any communication relationship. It is also transactional, by the definition we used earlier. By that we mean that an interpersonal conflict cannot occur unless both parties see it—you are about as likely to have a one-person conflict as you are to have a one-handed hand clap. Unless the conditions are seen as conflict by you and the others involved, there is no conflict, and of course no negotiation.

However compatible you may feel with another person or group, there will come a time when your respective needs, your motives, your thoughts, your values, your actions, or your ownership of belongings will not exactly match. *Result:* Conflict!

"Living happily ever after" is the stuff of fairy tales; no two people, no two groups, can ever be so alike that if they are interacting they must always behave identically. Living happily *with conflict* is the stuff of mature, interpersonally sophisticated, realistic, and skillfully managed communication relationships.

Positive and Negative Outcomes of Conflict

Not all conflicts have the same outcomes; some will lead to destructive ends or to constructive ones. How conflicts are managed or completed will depend on a number of factors, and your negotiations may lead to resolutions of various kinds or to further trouble.

It would be wonderful if all your problems could be solved as easily as they are in television situation shows. Most programs are half an hour long, and in that time the people in your favorite show get into trouble and conflict ensues, but by the end of the thirty minutes, everything is worked out just fine. Solutions to conflict come even more quickly in the television *commercials* than in the programs. As the commercial starts, some unfortunate person has dingy teeth, "ring around the collar," water spots on the dishes, or a pet who will not eat what is offered. One quick application of the advertiser's product and the conflict is removed in less than half a minute—a successful love affair has followed pearly white teeth, a husband's admiration for your laundering ability replaces shame, a successful dinner party for mother-in-law features sparkling dishes, and your pet is greedily consuming the advertised pet food and loving you instead of hating you. Advertisers know that your worst fears in facing conflict are that you may lose the material goods you prize or the friends you prize even more. You have learned from an early age that conflict has only bad outcomes, except when you can assure success using an advertised product and regain power, position, friends, romance, or happy pets.

On the minus side

Among the negative outcomes of unmanaged conflict are "making enemies" of people or hurting those you need to or want to be with. Constant bickering and frequent bitter disagreements tend to wear you out, and make it hard for you to commit yourself to a relationship. You use up a great deal of energy in conflict which could be used productively. You may, in anger, withhold information potentially useful to another person. You may be so afraid of getting into conflict that you and your group engage in extreme conservatism, conformity, and massive unreasoned agreement—the "groupthink" phenomenon described in studies of group dynamics.

With that recitation of possible negative outcomes, it is easy to see why people try to avoid or suppress conflict. Yet it may have some benefits.

On the plus side

Tension and conflict often give people more energy or motivation. You may thrive on competition, a controlled form of conflict. As such, conflict is a strong mobilizer of energies which otherwise might not be tapped or available. Conflict and tension can lead to innovation, creativity, and change. When conflict is suppressed for the sake of conformity or security—"we don't want any disagreement"—then groups tend to stagnate, to freeze up, to play it safe, to kill any new ideas, instead of taking on challenges and opportunities. Often the self-expression from conflict helps people toward greater commitment and better decisions. Open and free disagreement may lead to a very healthy exploration of values, attitudes, and feelings—cementing relationships rather than tearing them apart.

Conflict can help clear up reasons why people differ; it can help find areas of similarity. From conflict you may end up learning more about yourself, about others, and about your mutual relationship. Each time a conflict is approached, admitted, worked on, and perhaps even negotiated, you can learn more about how to handle the next one—how to manage your relationships; how your communication seems to influence the conflict positively, or what seems to make it worse.

Types of Conflict

While conflict used to be seen as coming from the personal quirks or the tricks of troublemakers, more recent studies of conflict seem to attribute it to other factors. Three identified types of conflict are (1) personal, (2) interpersonal, and (3) group. These three are summarized graphically in Table 11-1.

Personal conflicts

This type of conflict may occur when you experience (1) conflicting desires, needs, or values; (2) competing ways to satisfy a given need or want; (3) frustration from blocks getting in your way of satisfying a need; and (4) roles that do not match.

1. CONFLICTING DESIRES

Even if these are sometimes described as conflicts going on inside you, they will have an effect on your relationships with others. One form of this conflict is an attempt to "have your cake and eat it"—or to select from two favorable outcomes. Should you go to a movie or play cards with friends? Should you buy that hi-fi or save up for a VCR? Will you spend your time studying for the calculus test or the history test? Are you asked to choose between two quite equally attractive friends who both want to spend time with you? (Psychologists call this "approach-approach" conflict.) One way of getting out of this conflict is to redefine the

Approach-approach conflict involves choices from among equally attractive options. (© *Toni Michaels/The Image Works)*

TABLE 11-1.
Types of Conflict

Type	Common sources	Examples
Personal	Conflicting needs	Study or go out on a date (Approach-approach: You need or want to do both but can't.)
		Dull job but it pays well (Approach-avoidance: Both a good and a bad consequence are available.)
		Cheat or flunk an exam (Avoidance-avoidance: Neither option is desirable.)
	Competing ways of satisfying a need or want	Different ways to arrive at a goal (Do you try to get a good grade point average by concentrating on a few of your tougher courses, or give all your courses an equal amount of work?)
	Frustration from blocks in the way	A person or circumstance keeps you from getting a promotion.
	Roles which do not match	Your church expects you to behave in one way, and your friends do not act that way or want you to.
Interpersonal	Individual differences	"Generation gap" problems, cultural patterns, gender distinctions
	Limited resources	How to slice the pie equally (Who gets the car tonight? Whom does your best friend spend time with?)
	Role balance	Can you order another person around? (Who waits for phone calls from the other? Who decides which movies to go to? Do you ask for permission to go somewhere?)

alternatives; are they really competing opposites, or is there some way both can be accommodated? Backing up and taking another look at what *appears to be* a conflict may help you see options—you can buy a less expensive hi-fi and begin to save for the VCR; you can organize your time differently so that you can study both history and calculus.

Sometimes your alternatives are between what you *want to do* and what you *have to do;* this is referred to as an "approach-avoidance" type of conflict. Go to the movie, or go to the library? Take a trip skiing, or spend the money for some necessities? Finish the term paper and not see your girlfriend or boyfriend tonight? Do you tell the professor she made a mistake and run the risk of making her angry? Much of what we describe as "stress" in people's daily lives has its roots in this kind of personal conflict.

TABLE 11-1.
Types of Conflict *(continued)*

Type	Common sources	Examples
Group	Structure and levels	Do people in the group or organization rank themselves above some of the others? (Do your club officers act on matters without consulting the membership? Does a professor give you very sudden and arbitrary exams or assignments?)
	Functions and goals	What titles and official status of people around you have an effect on their behaviors? (Does an office in the college treat students as if they were a bother even though its purpose is to serve students? Does your club avoid contact with other individuals or groups you consider "outsiders"?)
	Resources (goods, funds, power, authority, responsibility)	Resources in an academic world include time, money, needed items for your pursuit of an education, authority, responsibility, etc. (Only a limited amount of time for conferences with a professor; a limited number of top grades on a "curve"; hours the library is open; the time a student can cash a check at the business office; or the number of catalogs or course schedules printed and available.)

There are also situations in which you don't like either alternative. You hate the course, hate the teacher, but can't drop out because you need the credit for graduation. If you are a strong advocate about "right to life," do you continue to associate with a friend who had an abortion? If you can't stand smoking, do you let your smoking friends ride on a long trip in your car without telling them to quit? Would you tell a friend whom you saw shoplifting to put the merchandise back? One of our favorite ways out of this "avoidance-avoidance" dilemma is to do nothing but to hope it will not come up again or will somehow go away.

2. COMPETING WAYS

As you set your goals, you may find that there are many ways to achieve them. Are there class schedules you can arrange which give you work time as well as study time? If you want to make money, have a satisfying job, and perform a service to society, what profession would you choose? Do you spend more time on a course you have trouble with or a course you are enjoying? Which friends or clubs do you spend your time with, and do they help you achieve your goals for enjoyment and prestige? If you maintain a clear idea of your goals and needs, you will make better choices for yourself among the available options.

3. FRUSTRATION FROM BLOCKS

Personal conflict may occur when something or someone gets in your way of reaching a goal. Have you ever been in class with a teacher who seems intent on keeping you from doing your best? Are you just short of enough money to buy a car and your other expenses are going up? Is the person you are most interested in romantically also very interested in a friend of yours? Is the job you want dependent on your passing a qualifying test or perhaps on the class schedule you can arrange? Is the class you need for graduation not being offered until next year? Many people respond to frustration by taking it out on others—"kicking the dog," it is called. Blaming others for your predicament is easier than (a) changing your goals when you discover too many blocks or (b) locating another way to approach the problem other than direct, fixed, or sometimes stubborn confrontation.

4. ROLE DISCREPANCIES

As we mentioned in Chapter 10, role conflict is a common experience for people who belong to several different groups and relate to a variety of others. You may be expected to behave in certain ways in one group and to hold values consistent with that same group. When all your "others" have the same values and behave very much alike, you have no problem. But if you belong to a conservative political party and want to promote some individual liberal cause, you experience personal conflict. Can you maintain relationships with your classmates and be a favorite of the professor? Can you meet the role expectations of your parents and your peers at the same time? Among working women, striving to be wives-mothers-workers, this kind of conflict is described as one of the most difficult to manage—often complicated by being female in some historically oriented male world like manufacturing, transportation, investments, or medicine.

Interpersonal conflicts

Not all relationships proceed along a smooth course forever. From time to time conflicts occur. It has been estimated by most writers on the subject that generally the causes of interpersonal conflict can be attributed to (1) individual differences between people, (2) limited resources to be shared in a relationship, or (3) different roles or role expectations (see Chapter 10 for a review of role expectations).

1. INDIVIDUAL DIFFERENCES

You are different in many ways from some others around you, including your size, age, attitudes, experience, skills, intellect, training, etc. Some differences may not make a difference; some may make a lot of difference to you.[2] Gender is an important difference if a woman wants to try out for a men's athletic team, but not for the woman who wants to get a driver's license. Have you ever tried to play a game like Trivial Pursuit or charades with a person from a foreign culture, or a game such as tennis against a beginner when you are a very good player? Is the so-called generation gap a clear example of individual age differences? Do people from rural areas see the world as urban dwellers do? Do you know a couple who are so different from one another that you cannot understand how they can possibly get along, and the only way you explain it is to say "opposites attract"? (Or it may be the case that whatever similarities they find in each other are more important to them than the differences you see.)

2. LIMITED RESOURCES
No family, friendship, group, or organization has all the resources it wants or needs. Time, money, authority, attention, feelings, material things—all are defined as "resources" to be shared in relationships. Choices have to be made about allocating those resources—handing out the goodies is not to be taken lightly. Competition is essentially a built-in part of the system. Each person or side competes for a share of what can be given out. The smaller the pie to be divided, the greater the competition among those who want a piece of it. Lovers who have to spend much of their time at work or in other places become very possessive about the time they spend with each other. Roommates share a bath and other space only by accommodating to each other's needs and habits. Grading on a curve is one way professors have for allocating the resources known as grades. In a society where time is treated as a commodity, as in America, your use of meetings, appointments, dates, schedules, and conferences can give you daily conflicts when your scarce time resource is doled out to the competing relationships.

3. ROLE BALANCE
Conflict between people occurs frequently not because there is disagreement about *what to do* but because people don't agree about who is in control, who receives credit, who can make demands on the other. In our earlier discussions on roles, it was emphasized that *mutual* discovery and acceptance of roles is important for relationships.[3] A professor trying to be too much a "buddy" to students may cause role problems; students expect role differences in that relationship. A friend telling you how you should behave is taking on an advisor or parent role you may not accept. Do you resent a lover trying to limit whom you can and cannot see, or how you spend your time? "Bring me my dictionary" said to different people may get different responses: "Get it yourself" from a sibling, "Say

'please'" or "I'm busy" or "Here, catch!" from a friend. The request sounds the same, but different roles are stated in the different responses you get.

Group conflicts

In many cases, potential conflict comes from the structure of the group or organization itself. As organizations get bigger and more complex, they inevitably develop functions and roles which simply build in the possibility of conflict.

Not all group structures fit everyone involved in them. In a college, the president does not see things the way students do. In a very large club, as compared with a two-person dormitory suite, the things which need to be done to keep the club active can involve many more behaviors. Even in a single classroom, as a group example, the seating, testing, reciting, and discussing create levels of interaction giving rise to possible conflict. In a large company or institution, the many levels may not know or appreciate each other, and it is easier to fight against those you don't know. The impersonal "they" to describe faculty groups, student groups, Greeks, athletes, represents some different and distant, and often competing, roles.

As your class, your company, your club, your family, tries to meet its goals, you compete to get your things done, to meet your own needs. Is there a limited library "reserve list" for class readings? Can faculty check out books which students may not? How many seats that you prefer are there in the classroom—by the window, at the back, in the front, etc.? Does your club have privileges given to officers but not to members? Are the pledges given the same rights as actives? Are you permitted to park on campus? Can freshmen live off campus, or only seniors? Who registers first for classes: returning students, or new students, or seniors, or those whose last name begins with "A"? Family members compete for television viewing, for the family car, or for the contents of the cookie jar.

Uneven distribution of power and authority in groups makes it almost impossible to avoid conflict. All persons in the group will have feelings about how fairly they are treated. People are sensitive about how privileges, rewards, and sanctions are handed out. If parents or teachers or administrators play favorites—or even are *perceived* to play favorites—there is a great chance for conflict.

Conflict Management Strategies

A persistent point we are trying to make is that conflict is a reality of life. Conflict can be of great value when it prevents stagnation or thoughtless conformity, and when it stimulates exploration of new ideas and procedures, new relationships, and healthy acceptance and adjustment to change. Conflict and the airing of differences can permit problems to be revealed, discussed, and solved.

Rigid behaviors or structures which suppress the "reality" of conflict by ignoring it can provoke even more violent types of conflict. If you are more flexible and open and you allow for expression of differences, you are more likely to head off the most violent conflicts. Conflict which you face and handle appropriately can be quite beneficial. Thus it's important for you to know how to handle conflict—to know the strategies that are available to you.

We have summarized from a variety of sources[4] three general categories of conflict management strategies. They are (1) avoidance, (2) defusion, and (3) confrontation. These three classic types are further summarized in Table 11-2.

Avoidance

Many people feel uncomfortable with conflict. Avoiding conflict or potential conflict is a common behavior. When you do this, it is with the hope that if you don't see it, it will go away. You seem to believe in magic or deliverance. But pretending not to see a problem seldom makes the problem disappear.

Specific techniques you may use to avoid dealing with conflict include denial, withdrawal, suppression, or smoothing over. You can leave the situation by walking out of the room, cutting class, quitting a job, falling asleep at a meeting, running away from home, filing your fingernails, staring out a window, doodling, whispering to someone next to you, or simply daydreaming. You can change the subject any time a potential disagreement looms. You can tell jokes to break the tension. You can distract others in a number of ways and get their minds off the possible conflict.

Accommodation to the problem is also considered a strategy for avoiding conflict or not breaking things up.

Avoidance strategies are used whenever people feel threatened by potential conflict and are afraid they may not be able to handle it effectively. Avoiding the situation is not likely to solve it. Conflict may simply come back in another, and sometimes more extreme, form.

Defusion

If you are involved in a conflict and would like to stall until tempers have time to cool off, you may be using defusion strategies.

One way is to try to get agreement on smaller issues, or on side issues, or minor points, and thus avoid taking on the bigger problems until things quiet down, until you get more information, or while you try to have people see things in a different way. Defusion strategies permit some small agreement, but the bigger issues remain unsettled.

Confrontation

Three substrategies are suggested as possibilities under this heading. Various authors and researchers have suggested these kinds of outcomes, all possible under confrontations. With the classic idea that conflict is war, you might assume there are winners and losers. To set up the substrate-

TABLE 11-2.
Conflict Management Strategies

Type	How to recognize the strategies
Avoidance	Withdrawal, denial, suppression, smoothing over, not facing reality of conflict, walking out, quitting a job, making jokes, "let's not argue," "we want to run a happy ship," "busy people don't gripe," "can't we just have a good time and not fight . . ."
	Consequence likely: Conflict will reappear in some other form, possibly more violent or vicious; it is not likely to go away just by wishing.
Defusion	"Let's come back to this later . . ."; calling for a short recess in discussions; asking to have someone go after (1) more data, (2) more experts, (3) more coffee and sandwiches.
	Consequence likely: You may get some small agreements, but the big issues will remain unsolved; at best you can get angry participants to cool off or rigid debaters to reconsider their frozen positions; at worst it will be a form of avoidance—see above.
Confrontation Win-lose or power strategies	"I am the boss (or your parent) and I say so"; pulling rank; railroading a vote; intimidation; not to be confused with the athletic competitions or poker games; imposing rules; going by the book; hiding behind regulations and policies to enforce your way. Voting is the most common and widely accepted strategy.
	Consequence likely: Any creative problem solving is stifled; there is bitterness and resentment by losers, who wait their turn for vicious retaliation if power shifts.
Lose-lose or concession strategies	Settling for a middle ground which neither party wants just to make sure the other doesn't get any advantage; doing anything to keep the other from winning: "If you won't let me bat, I won't play."
	Consequences likely: A short-run concession may get to be a habit, so the two parties never take turns or negotiate their differences; both parties come up short of what they could have obtained together.
Win-win or integration strategies	When negotiators indicate that (1) conflict is a symptom of a problem to be solved, not a fight to be won, and (2) nobody has to lose completely. Face-to-face open negotiation is possible if the point is to solve a problem, not to determine who is right. Time is spent defining the specified and unspecified differences, working at alternatives which will meet common interests. You look for ways in which positions are alike, not just opposed. You work from a "we," not a "we-they," orientation.
	Consequence likely: This is not a cure-all, but it provides an interesting and little-used option to the power plays and compromise we are accustomed to. At worst you can develop more ways of looking at each others' positions without solving the problem or gaining more understanding of why the other parties believe as they do. At best you can come out with a better solution than either party started with, greater trust, understanding, and respect, and a commitment to live up to the agreement. It takes time, but it may be time well spent for all participants.

gies, then, it seems reasonable to start with the most familiar to us—we have been taught it since childhood—somebody wins and the other loses. A less familiar form occurs when each side loses in a deliberate effort to keep the opponent from winning or everybody concedes more than makes them happy. A third form (the only option left) occurs when both sides win, which, given our basic assumption about conflict, must at first appear to be impossible.

WIN-LOSE: POWER STRATEGIES

The most common ways of confronting conflict, these strategies are based on the idea that for a conflict to be solved, one person must win; furthermore, winning is not possible unless the other side loses. I get the top bunk; you have to take the bottom one. You want to go to a Chinese restaurant; I hold out for pizza. There are many situations in which winning and losing are part of the competitive contract—football games, poker, politics, and horse races, to name a few. You run for office in the student government, hoping to beat out the other candidates. But to treat all conflict as win-lose is to miss opportunities for making compromises and developing goodwill. Mother drags the 3-year-old from the store to the car; she's bigger and has the authority (but wait fifteen years and see how the authority shifts). One of the characteristics of this power-based win-lose option is that the losers never forget, and may wait a long time before they can get even when a power base shifts.

"Majority rules," which results in ballots or voting procedures is a very popular and widely applied win-lose strategy to settle many kinds of conflict. If agreed to and supported, it is an effective method.

LOSE-LOSE: CONCESSION STRATEGIES

Outcomes where everyone loses don't seem to be particularly useful ways of resolving conflict. But this strategy occurs, particularly when scarce resources are involved. You may agree to your roommate's smoking in the room but insist on having the windows open to the bothersome noise and drafts from outside. Nobody in your club wants to give up other time, and so the only meeting hour is for breakfast once a week and hardly anybody shows up, and the members who do meet are surly with each other. Concessions may be of temporary value, but seldom constitute a long-term resolution to a conflict. New concessions are constantly being worked out, and each side has a clear "statement of accounts" on how much they have given up in the past and how much you owe them on the next one.

WIN-WIN: INTEGRATION STRATEGIES

Very seldom used by most of us, this type of strategy is becoming more accepted and recommended. It is not our habitual way of approaching conflict management; and it appears at first to take more time and effort than the other strategies. Win-win is based on the twin ideas that (1) conflict is a symptom of a problem to be solved rather than a fight to be won, and (2) conflict can be managed so that nobody has to lose completely. Resolving differences this way means that both parties have to define a common ground rather than aggressively stating and stubbornly holding to opposing positions. Look at the conflict in terms of "us together" rather than "me versus you." Mutual concerns need to be expressed openly; and if both sides do not have the same information, they need to find or share it. Disagreement is not a disaster in this strategy; it is a critical way of stating openly and frankly the possible differences. Compromise is often an *effective* outcome of this strategy.

PRACTICING THE WIN-WIN STRATEGY

When you use the win-win strategy, you often will (1) come up with a better mutual solution than either of the parties would come up with by themselves and (2) develop greater trust, understanding, and respect among those involved. Naturally, problem solving by this method takes time, and you do not want to adopt it for trivial or inconsequential conflicts that may not be worth your time. However, the more you try this method, the more proficient you become at it, and the more often you will begin to think about finding solutions to problems rather than fighting battles. Rather than battling an imaginary enemy, you practice approaching a shared problem with an associate. Much creative energy is freed in the process.

The key to practicing win-win strategies is your *attitude* or *orientation* toward conflict and confrontation. First, you should be convinced that conflict is a normal part of relationships, not a sinful or dreaded threat to your personal security or happiness. Second, you should consider both *what* you are disagreeing about and the *person* you are disagreeing with; you need to care about the people in the transaction as well as the issues; you need to be sensitive about people's feelings. Third, you need to recognize that using win-win will take time and effort and that conflicts may not be solved all at once, but by careful increments of several different transactions. Fourth, you need to stay open and flexible about exploring new options, about trying new approaches, about looking at the problem in new ways rather than staying rigidly fixed to your arguing position.

This win-win approach to conflict management works toward a solution which can satisfy, at least to some extent, all the parties involved. With goodwill, a little creativity, a commitment to refrain from imposing too narrow a solution too soon, and the patience and time to keep working, the positive negotiation of conflict is possible. Some further considerations of negotiation that follow are based on acceptance of win-win as one significant way of confronting conflict.

Conflict Management and Negotiation

Conflict is a reality of both public and personal life. How you view conflict will determine how you negotiate the management of your conflicts, and how successful your negotiating outcomes will be. If you think conflict is always something bad and to be avoided at all costs, then you will respond by negotiating in a defensive or aggressive way. You may miss much of the richness of interpersonal problem solving if you believe that conflict does not or should not occur. Conflict and happiness are not necessarily polar opposites.

If you admit that conflict happens, but you don't want any part of it—defusion strategy—you may be simply unwilling or unable to negotiate effectively. You may have the hope that if you take on a few small issues related to the bigger conflict that maybe the big one will get better. It rarely does. You may settle for a partial or short-run solution which can develop into an even bigger problem in the longer run.

Our suggestion, therefore, is to make use of enlightened negotiation skills to confront conflict. You will not solve every conflict every time to everyone's total satisfaction, but you can successfully manage many more of your personal and professional conflicts than you ever imagined you could.[5]

Negotiation and communication

Conflict management skills and negotiation skills are basically communication skills. They include (1) diagnosing the nature of the conflict, (2) initiating a confrontation, (3) listening, and (4) problem solving. A brief review of how those skills are related to communication follows.[6]

In *diagnosing the nature of a conflict* you may want to consider this prayer, credited to Reinhold Niebuhr and adopted by Alcoholics Anonymous:

> God grant me the strength to change the things I can, the patience to accept the things I cannot change, and the wisdom to know the difference.

These words seem most appropriate for a discussion of conflict negotiation. When you encounter potential conflict, you should ask yourself whether (1) this issue is one which affects you and has enough significant consequences for you to be concerned about it, (2) this conflict is caused by personal or value differences for which some objective solutions can be found, and (3) the other parties are willing and able to enter into a negotiated agreement—that is, a win-win problem-solving sequence.

Some problems may simply not affect you directly. If you dislike smoking and no one in your environment is a smoker, then you may not be particularly dedicated to carrying on a strong antismoking campaign. On the other hand, if your roommate or closest friend chain-smokes in your apartment or car and the lack of ventilation is a contributing factor, there may be both a *reason for* and a *possibility of* change.

It is difficult to change another person's value system or deep-seated beliefs. It may also not be necessary for you to change another's values in order to settle disputes. Your friend is always late. You value punctuality. It may be as useless to try to change your friend's value about being on time as it would be for your friend to change yours. To confront such a conflict you should "operationalize" the conflict and spell out carefully what *behaviors* you would like to see changed on what occasions. "I know you are not as interested as I am in arriving on time; but they close the doors of the theater promptly at 8:15, and if you are not in the lobby with me before then, I will go in without you and meet you at the first intermission."

Essentially you can do something only about *your own behavior,* not the behavior or values of others. The often-used expression "Behave yourself" is a redundancy—you cannot behave anyone else.

In other words, look at the causes of the conflict and make sure there is some reason to take on a negotiation. Don't fight battles when there are no reasons to fight—if you are not involved directly or have no confidence that any change will result. Make sure the sources of conflict are identifiable, real, and negotiable.

Timing is of great importance in confrontations. If your teacher is swamped, obviously worried about a lot of problems, and in a big rush, that is not the time to expect a leisurely discussion of a less immediate problem. Also, when you negotiate, you must state clearly and specifically (1) what the other party does and how it affects you tangibly, and (2) what you would like to have happen at the end of the negotiation or what you would like the other person to do.

If those items are not clear to either of you, then it is important to begin exploring the problem together. Don't command your smoking friend to stop. You may assert that the smoking bothers you and tell how. You may ask that both of you work out some way to minimize the difficulty to you and continue to permit your friend to maintain a habit which is evidently important. Taking time to talk about the problem even before you demand some solution is another way to be sensitive to timing.

Listening as a collaborative act is important. Truly effective communication, and therefore negotiation, does not take place without taking into account what another party has to say.

Pay attention to the feelings expressed as well as the words. Empathic or active listening has an important place in negotiating conflict. You have a difficult time listening when you are emotionally involved in an issue, and you will be tempted to argue your point of view rather than paying attention to the other person's arguments. Yet negotiation will depend on the airing of both points of view.

Problem solving is the win-win approach to negotiation. You can gain

BOX 11-1. Principled Negotiation

Many writers and researchers are at work on the subject of negotiation. Workshops are available, seminars are taught, short courses are provided to people in corporations and professions. The Harvard Negotiation Project has become known as a group which "deals continually with all levels of conflict from domestic to business to international disputes." Two members of the project, Roger Fisher and William Ury, have written a best-selling paperback on the subject of negotiation.*

Their message is that the old-fashioned, and often unsuccessful, negotiating system concentrated on bargaining over *position*. They claim that the more people argue over position, the more locked in they will get; the more they defend and get committed, the more impossible it is to ever reach a negotiated agreement. "As more attention is paid to positions, less attention is devoted to meeting the underlying concerns of the parties."†

People negotiate *to obtain satisfaction* more than to obtain goods or services. Taking notice of the internal motivations of parties can be a most rewarding and successful method of reaching agreement. Fisher and Ury have named their proposed system "principled negotiation" or "negotiation on the merits" to distinguish it from what they have called the less effective "positional bargaining."

They propose four parts to their method: (1) separate the people from the problem, (2) focus on interests, not on positions, (3) invent options for mutual gain, and (4) insist on using objective criteria. Negotiators following this set of steps can see the similarity to problem solving as the basic approach to negotiation: treat the conflict as a problem to be solved by competing parties, not as a battle to be won at the expense of the losing side.

* R. Fisher and W. Ury, *Getting to Yes*, Penguin Books, New York, 1983, originally published by Houghton Mifflin, Boston, 1981; the quotation is from the promotional back page.
† Ibid, p. 5.

much if you can treat conflict as a problem to be solved rather than a fight to be won or lost. Negotiation can occur in an atmosphere of mutual concern for getting to the root of a problem and managing the differences.

Negotiation: Content and process

Most literature on negotiation refers to the "mixed-motive" nature of negotiation, whether in international relations or in domestic situations. By that it is meant that parties to a dispute must reach goals which benefit them all, but which seem to be inconsistent, even competing and opposite at times. What we know is that people enter negotiation with some goals and that they conduct their communication by a set of rules which will have some effect on the outcome.

Content of negotiation is what parties talk about, what their respective ideas are, what their demands and issues are, what they stand to gain or lose in the interaction. Important as these content issues are, they are only part of the negotiation.

Process is the relational dimension by which people negotiate, their styles, their procedures, their tendencies to attack or withdraw, the rules by which they exchange information about the content.[7]

The outcome of some negotiations can be predicted by looking at how the participants behave (their power strategies) in relation to their prenegotiation expectations. Those factors appear to have an important effect on successful negotiating.[8] Your success in negotiating gives you an attitude about succeeding in the next set of negotiations.

Reciprocity in negotiation is a typical concern of parties engaged in conflict which calls for resolution. Do you take a negative reciprocity attitude ("an eye for an eye and a tooth for a tooth") or a positive one ("do unto others as you would have them do unto you") in approaching negotiation? Both of these attitudes are found in human interaction.

For example, the choices of attacking or defending as basic strategies were studied to find out if the actions of one side affected the actions of the other.[9] Not surprisingly, the researchers determined that there is a tendency to answer an attacking strategy with an attack of your own. They further discovered that in power situations, it is likely that (1) if you have more to give away than the others, you will act in a defensive way, and (2) if you have less power and are bargaining for more service, more money, more favors, more time, or a higher grade, you will take the offensive. More simply stated (and not surprising) the "haves" tend to defend, while the "have nots" tend to attack. If you have favors to give, the negotiation will place you in a more defensive, or even passive, stance. When all the negotiation principles and strategies are considered, we discover that most people negotiate to obtain satisfaction.

INTERPERSONAL EXCHANGE

Negotiation and conflict management depend on adequate sharing of interpersonal information, both about content and process. A central theme of this book has been that communication is the means toward achieving satisfactory human relationships. How you give information to others, and how you get information from them, is the subject of this final part of the book.

In Chapter 1 we discussed models for looking at communication. Here again we will present a model for your study. This model is a familiar one to communicators, used to demonstrate information exchange along two very significant dimensions: (1) giving and getting feedback, and (2) disclosing to others.

The Johari Window

You disclose to others through your verbal and nonverbal behaviors; others give you feedback about their reactions to you and thus you find out how you are doing.

In this respect, the Johari window is a useful way to look at the transactional process of disclosure, feedback, and information and feeling exchange.[10] The transactional nature of your communication is demonstrated by the Johari window, where a change in any of the four quadrants (or "panes" of the "window") will mean a change in another. (See Figure 11-1.)

The term "Johari window," exotic as it may sound, simply honors the first names of the originators of the now-classic model, Joseph Luft and Harrington Ingram. The window represents a way to look at your self and your knowing, and others' knowing. There are things you know about yourself, and things you don't know. There are things other people know about you and things they don't know. Information, shared or unknown, becomes an integral part of this model.

Area 1, the area of free activity (I know, others know) represents your public self, the shared knowledge about who you are and what you generally stand for. Basic information is in this quadrant which includes your physical appearance, how you dress and talk, as well as many things you are sure other people know about you which you also know.

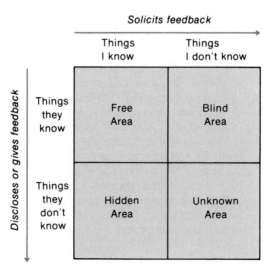

FIGURE 11-1
Luft and Ingram's Johari window.

Area 2, the blind area (others know, I don't know) includes information others have about you which you do not have. Some mannerisms, how your voice sounds, a reputation you have among peers which nobody has expressed to you, and how others expect you to behave which might really surprise you if you knew.

Area 3, the hidden area (I know, others don't know) represents all the things you are not willing to share easily with others. In your interpersonal negotiations, you hold back some data to maintain a more firm position. You do not share your fantasies, motives, thoughts, or behaviors you are ashamed of, things you feel are personal and are nobody else's business.

Area 4, the unknown area (I don't know, others don't know) includes those things about yourself which have not yet penetrated your consciousness. This may remain hidden from you and from others, but there is some curiosity about it as it may represent your deep-seated needs, expectations, unconscious fears, your internal physical condition, etc.

This model shows the dynamics of interpersonal transactions. Through disclosure, you can shrink the hidden area, thus opening up the area of free activity to share more of your ideas, arguments, beliefs, goals, expectations, as they become common ground to work with others. Through feedback, others can help you shrink your blind area by giving

---

BOX 11-2. We All Do Windows

You will have different "windows" for different relationships, and need to be careful to apply each window to only the one it was intended for. The four quadrants tell you something about how free you are to interact with others on the basis of what they know about you and you about yourself, but only for that particular relationship.

Draw for yourself the window you may have with a new acquaintance—some "stranger" you sat next to in class. Draw another window to represent you as you see yourself in relation to your best friend of the *same sex*. Would it be different from a window of your best friend of the *opposite sex*? What does the window look like for one of your parents? And is the window the same this year for a parent as it was ten years ago? Has a friend's window changed over the years?

Your windows are subject to change: (1) they change from one relationship to another, (2) they change from one time to the next in a single relationship, (3) and they change because of changes in either you or the other person.

you data only they have, further opening the area of common transactions for you and them.

Most new relationships (meeting people for the first time, joining a club or a different work situation) present a small area of free activity. You seldom trust strangers at first sight and share intimate things with them, or give away much of your own ideas or arguments quickly. Conversation centers around the weather, movies, jokes—items not included in your self or the issue you may be working on if you are negotiating. At the beginning of a relationship, you may protect your "real self" from dangerous exposure. Others seem also to withhold feedback which might be useful to you, except in safe areas—"You are sure tall," "You look like you're a student here."

As relationships mature, as your interaction moves along favorably, as negotiations proceed, the area of free activity may expand as you disclose more of yourself and the others give you more defined feedback. There seems to be a tendency in most people to want to get closer to others, be it in a casual setting or in a serious negotiation. Most people seem to prefer getting and giving more data—using feedback and disclosing—rather than staying in a shell of a rigidly restricted and small "free area" on the window.

To help open the free area, you may follow the arrows in the Johari model and (1) solicit accurate feedback from others to open the blind area, and (2) disclose appropriately to others to reduce the hidden area.

FEEDBACK, FEEDFORWARD, AND SELF-DISCLOSURE

Tensions in transactions are reduced when you and others develop more predictable interpersonal behaviors. Whether you are involved in a casual encounter or in a significant negotiation, obtaining more information from others can be a great help.

Feedback is an integral part of your transactions as it represents verbal or nonverbal indications of how you are doing in the estimation of others. You generally want, and often need, to have some responses to your behaviors so you can adjust them if you choose, or can understand better how you are doing, and the effects you are having on others.

Feedforward is a specific anticipatory device to let others know something about how you expect, or hope, the rest of the conversation, debate, or negotiation is likely to go. It helps set some "rules" in advance about the limits of your interactions.

Disclosure generally describes what passes between you and another, such as personal data or invitations to share such data. Just as giving and receiving feedback has some advantages and some disadvantages, depending on how you behave, so does the process called *self-disclosure*

BOX 11-3. Feedback

1. Feedback is the kind of information needed to check out whether the actual results of your communication are the same as your intended results.
2. Feedback is absolutely necessary for survival and for growth.
3. Feedback at best is a nonevaluative process of sharing data with another person while respecting that person's right and freedom to accept or reject it, to act on it or not act on it.
4. Feedback is not the kind of gang bombardment pictured in some television stereotypes of groups. It is not sharpshooting, sniping, or blasting.
5. Feedback is not forcing another person into your preconceived mold or expectations.
6. Feedback is not just a request for change in behavior. In human relationships, it may well be the beginning of the process of mutual acceptance.

---

have a strong effect on transactions, all the way from intimate or casual up to public confrontations.

Learning to Give and Receive Feedback

An integral part of reducing barriers in communication is making optimum use of feedback, in both giving and receiving it. You need to practice giving a clear indication of how much a message sent to you is actually received and also train your senses to observe clearly how your messages are responded to by others.

To start, let us say that all human beings need the contact of relationships and that organizations and the people in them do not operate in a vacuum. Even a hermit, living in a cave in a mountainside, has contacts with the environment which make it essential to respond. When hermits are hungry, they must find food, responding to the message from their stomachs. When they feel the cold wind blow, they respond by seeking shelter or putting on protective clothing. Although hermits may have little verbal communication, they still must be involved in sensing feedback and adjusting their moves to what happens to them in their surroundings.

Because few of you are hermits, you need to adjust not just to the cold or to hunger, but to the constant stream of messages you get from others in the course of a day. The number of messages you send or receive may vary, just as your ability to react appropriately may vary from

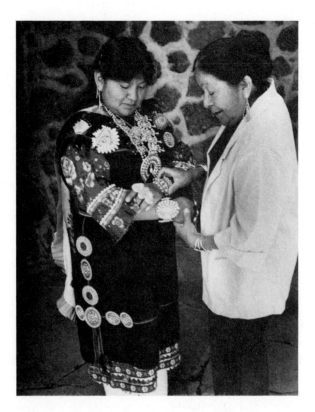

Giving and receiving feedback are important parts of an effective relationship. (© *Joel Gordon*)

one person to another. In this way you begin to identify those who can give clear instructions, those who can do what they are asked, those who can understand complex information, those who have difficulty in grasping new ideas. Much of the ability to perform well in assignments is related to the ability to give and receive feedback.[11] The sensitive person can pick up the cues offered by another who does not understand instructions—maybe it is the professor responding to a quizzical look on the face of a student by asking, "What is not clear in what I have been saying?" The sensitive person also can predict what parts of a message may be subject to confusion, and restate or clarify those parts without even being asked, simply because he or she has anticipated the hearer's confusion.

In communication, people need to share meanings of words and messages. It is important for them to know that communication is transactional—that is, it takes place between people under rules which they agree to follow. One of the rules is that if someone looks angrily at you after you have made a remark, you need to figure out what it was you said to make that person angry. Another rule is that if the listener smiles and nods, you are thereby permitted to continue with that kind of message. So your transactions are affected by the kinds of feedback you receive—whether negative, which pulls you up short, or positive, which encourages you to go ahead. In Chapter 8 we discussed meanings of words. If the meanings for words vary from person to person, so do your emotions vary. It is important in your communication transactions to be aware of both content and emotion.

There is a tendency in all of you to sometimes pretend you understand when you really do not. It is not considered intelligent to ask, "What do you mean by . . . ?" and you may try to avoid looking stupid. As a result, you may miss some important messages by pretending and may give the other person feedback which is false. Two factors are important here: first, that you try to give more honest feedback about your depth of understanding, and second, that you make it easy for the other person to say he or she does not understand. If you can reduce the other person's anxiety about asking questions by suggesting in advance that you may not be making your message clear, you may receive more honest feedback. On the other hand, you may have to swallow your pride and admit that you do not understand, and thus provide more honest feedback to the other person's message.

More than content

We mentioned above that not only content but also emotion is involved in the feedback process. Your attention to feedback will help you verify *who you are* in relation to others, as well as *what is said.* Keep in mind that you discover who you are by watching the reactions of others. By developing the ability to give and receive feedback, you also may better meet your interpersonal needs. Some of these needs are implied in the following suggestions based on workshop experiences.

In workshops where training has been conducted on giving and receiving feedback, it has been shown that your "guesses" about how others see you have been significantly improved when you are given feedback.[12] Just having feedback available, however, is not enough. You need to know how to handle it—that is, how to give it appropriately and how to receive it intelligently. Some suggestions for giving and receiving feedback follow.

Focus feedback on behaviors rather than the person

You generally can look more objectively on what you do than on what somebody says you are. Your behaviors, or actions, are only a momentary part of you, and therefore you feel more comfortable about being challenged to change them. If someone calls you "dishonest," it sounds quite different from saying that you acted "dishonestly" in a given situation. You cannot tolerate very well an attack on "you," which is what much criticism sounds like. If someone is critical of your *behavior,* you can more easily accept responsibility for that action, rather than tell yourself you are a product of your genetic inheritance and for that reason cannot possibly be blamed—or think of changing.[13]

1. To describe behaviors you use adverbs—e.g., "loudly," "kindly," "happily," "grumpily," or "sincerely."
2. Avoid the use of adjectives relating to the qualities of the person, to personality—e.g., "bigmouth," "kind," "happy," "sorehead," or "sincere."
3. Behaviors include those things a person does well as much as the things done badly. In describing behaviors you tend to concentrate on those which need improvement, but a person can often learn much from feedback about those actions which facilitate, support, or improve communication. Descriptions of behaviors should not be evaluative or selective, but should comment on what went on.

Focus feedback on observations rather than inferences

1. Observations are those things which could be seen or heard by anyone, but inferences are your own interpretations or conclusions about what went on. If you spice your observations with inferences, you tend to obscure feedback, and so you must be careful to differentiate when you are making inferences, or extensions of your observations.
2. Observations involve what is going on, not what happened at some previous time or some persistent characteristic you have noticed over a long period. In training groups, the term "here and now" is used to keep participants involved in what is happening and hence more concentrated on observations public to everyone. Research has shown that feedback given as soon as appropriate after observation will be more specific, more concrete, and generally more accurately reported.[14]
3. Observations should be reported in terms of degrees of more or less, not as black-and-white, either-or dichotomies. This helps you keep in mind the "quality" of the behavior rather than a category which is too frequently judgmental and subjective. Behaviors are very active, alive, and related to other behaviors in a more-or-less continuum rather than in a static good-or-bad polarization.[15]

Focus feedback on description rather than judgment

1. As in the case of focusing on behaviors, to use description is to avoid evaluation of the other person or of his or her actions. Description attempts to remain neutral, but judgment takes sides.
2. Concentrate on the "what" rather than the "why." Again, the "what" of the behavior is observable by others and therefore can be checked for accuracy. The "why" of a person's behavior is inferred and leads you into the dangerous area of "intentions" and "motives" and the

emotionalism which goes with it. It may be useful at times to explore the "why" of behaviors, but this should be done with the help and consent of the person being discussed.

3. Most of you enjoy playing "shrink" to all your friends, but you should realize that your analysis of the other persons' behaviors may be more subject to your own aberrations than to theirs. If you concentrate on the "why," you may miss much of the very useful "what" of feedback.

Focus feedback on sharing of ideas and information rather than giving advice

1. You need to feel a joint responsibility for the outcome of the feedback encounter and be ready to assist others rather than direct their responses.

2. Telling others what to do with the information you give does not leave them free to determine the appropriate course of action *for them.* Giving advice is a poor attempt at problem solving which does not give other people leeway to make their own choices.

3. Explore alternatives rather than provide solutions. If you concentrate on a variety of available responses, you can help move toward a more satisfactory answer. Too often you have ready at hand a list of solutions waiting for the problems to come along which might fit. When you offer a solution, ready-made from your own experience, it may not be useful to others, because their experiences are different or because the problem may not be exactly as you saw it.

Focus feedback on what it may do to the person who receives it

1. If giving feedback is only making *you* feel good, you may not be helping as much as you are imposing.

2. Be aware of how much feedback another person can handle at one time. Avoid the long recitation "and then you did . . ." after the recipient has given you some feedback that he or she is full to the brim. After that time you are only satisfying your own need, and not the other person's need.

3. Emotional reactions may result when feedback is given at the wrong time or place. This is particularly true in the more sensitive and personal areas of human behavior. Even if you have some worthwhile points to make, they should be presented with the recipient in mind.

Feedforward

Preparing the way for a message has been called "feedforward"[16] for an obvious reason—it sets up the possibility of getting feedback. Making use of appropriate feedforward lets the person you are speaking to know something of what you expect the conversation to be about, and in some instances how much you already know. You may precede a statement to another person with a feedforward phrase like "If you have no plans for tonight . . ." or "Let's talk about next week's assignment . . ." or "About that ten bucks you owe me . . ." Those phrases give a cue to your listener that you expect a response and what direction you want the discussion to take.

Feedforward is an integral part of much listening behavior and should not be mistakenly considered the opposite of feedback, but is a special part of the total feedback system. Feedforward helps you and others to anticipate actions. It may be an interpersonal plan for "What will I do if . . . ?" or "I hope the chair next to Sally is empty because I want to tell her something . . ." or "If Dad says no when I ask for the car, my next argument will be . . ." Two strangers sitting next to each other on an airplane will make some moves to test whether or not the other is willing to talk and to find out what they can talk about. In this kind of conversation, a related behavior which has been labeled "candidate statements" or "model statements"[17] serves a purpose of asking for information exchange, at the same time limiting the kinds of answers you are after. "On your way back to college somewhere . . . ?" means the asker has observed something about you which indicates you might be a college student, and is seeking confirmation of that observation as well as setting up some future conversation about your major, year, interests.

Similar features of traditional feedforward and the information-seeking strategies of Pomerantz's[18] "candidate answers" include: in both, the respondent is told what kind of answer will satisfy the purpose for asking; both let the other know how little or how much is needed in the response; both let the asker show off what is known about the situation (as the inference that the fellow passenger is a college student); both may let a speaker show an open or inquiring attitude about the other, thus indicating expectation of limited or extensive future dialog.

Feeding forward in your conversations will often result in more appropriate responses, less time spent in clearing the air, and a more efficiently derived set of "contracts" under which you will carry on your communication with others.

Self-Disclosure

How easy is it for you to tell others about yourself? What information will you tell others easily? Will others disclose personal information to you easily—are you considered a keeper of intimate secrets, or a shoulder to cry on? Can you be comfortable exchanging quite personal ideas or thoughts with others? How long do you have to know another person before you can easily tell him or her how you feel about your religion, your fantasies, your secret fears? What does it take for you to risk revealing some of your inner thoughts?[19]

Revealing yourself can take many forms. You can share those reactions you are immediately experiencing about an event, the other person, or whatever you and the other person are engaged in. You can also share your thoughts and feelings about things in general: your views on politics, religion, education, etc. You can share values and things that are important to you or that you believe in very much: what you would die for, what you wish to become, what kind of person you wish to be. You can also share those things about you that you like very much and that you are proud of: your accomplishments, your skills, your special talents. You can also share things that you do not like about yourself and perhaps would like to change.

Self-disclosure is usually one of the bases for healthy relationships. When you hide things from another person, your concealment can damage the relationship. In addition, hiding or masking what you are for fear the other person may not like you or may hurt you often leads to loneliness.

There are some interesting ideas about self-disclosure. The more you self-disclose to another person, the more likely that person will like you. The amount of sharing you do will determine the amount of sharing the other person will do. The more you share, the more the other person shares.

Researchers in social psychology have given us a better understanding of disclosure. It has been demonstrated that disclosure is an activity closely

Self-disclosure is easier between people who have developed a long-standing relationship than between strangers. (© *Susan Lapides/ Design Conceptions*)

related to interaction—not some inborn or stubbornly acquired trait of character which people have or don't have. The dynamics of disclosure are being studied by scholars who look at the relation between the way you disclose, how that depends on who starts, what kinds of information you will disclose early or late in a relationship and in what sequence, and how quickly disclosure patterns develop between people. For example, too much disclosure too soon is viewed as somewhat aberrated, while not disclosing at all is seen as a snub. Personal attraction appears to be related to disclosure—you disclose more to people you like. Other studies suggest that we may also "come to like those to whom we disclose most."[20] It has been suggested that under some conditions intimate disclosure can lead to more attraction between experimental subjects than nonintimate disclosure does. In your own experience, do you think you like people better—and they like you better—when you can talk easily with them about very private matters?

Research on self-disclosure also shows that if you are the kind of person who self-discloses willingly, then you are probably competent, open, and socially extroverted, and you probably feel a need to interact with other people. You are also probably flexible and adaptive, and you may be a bit more intelligent than those people who are not as willing to self-disclose. You also tend to view people as generally good rather than basically evil. These statements, of course, are generalizations, and, as such, they may not hold true for every person who is willing to self-disclose.

Being self-disclosing means that you are open, willing to let other people know who you are, as you are, without masks, fronts, or other protective covers. Self-disclosure is based on honest, genuine interaction with others, and this is why it is such a prerequisite for the building of meaningful relationships. In addition to being open to others, you are also willing to be receptive to the self-disclosures of others. You are interested in other people, willing to hear them, and interested in how they feel and think. This need not mean that you will pry uninvited into their lives; you may be simply willing to listen.

When is self-disclosure appropriate?

Self-disclosure is not always appropriate. There are times and situations when self-disclosing too much too fast or with the wrong persons may have negative consequences for you. It is important that you be sensitive to those situations in which self-disclosure is appropriate and those in which it is not. If you self-disclose when you should not, then you are likely to scare people off and get hurt in the process. Once you have told another person very intimate things about yourself, or shared some inner secrets, that person "owns" a bit of information which carries some responsibility with it. Here are some guidelines you might want to use in determining when self-disclosure is appropriate—remembering that you must decide for yourself when and what to disclose and under what conditions. You may want to disclose:

1. When you have an already developed relationship, and disclosing is not simply an isolated incident, unrelated to your future or past.
2. When the other person is willing to disclose also.
3. When self-disclosure is about what is going on in the present between you and the other person. (Avoid historical references in a relationship, or saving up concerns, slights, worries, or other feelings or thoughts so you can "dump them" on the other at some later time.)
4. When self-disclosure is about positive rather than negative things. (Very often the person who discloses too much negative information about self is considered "poorly adjusted.")
5. When self-disclosure leads to improving your relationship.
6. When you are sensitive to what effects self-disclosure will have on the other person. (Do not make others responsible for all your troubles without making sure they want to be, for example.)
7. When self-disclosure is gradual, a little at a time. (Don't "dump on" the other person by giving him or her too much to handle.)
8. Self-disclose when you trust the other person, and you are confident the other person trusts you. (Both of you should be willing to take the risks associated with self-disclosure.)

What will you disclose?

What kinds of things are you willing to disclose to another? An answer to that question will depend on many factors. One factor is how intimately you know the other person. Another factor is the purpose of your disclosing, and still another is your own feelings about taking risks. The level of your disclosing therefore is related to the sensitivity of the information you intend to share, any cultural norms you have between you, the feelings you have about the other person and your perception of the relationship, and the amount of risk you want to take for yourself. Table 11-3 gives you an idea of the range of material or information you might want to disclose and the conditions under which you might disclose.

What do you gain from self-disclosure?

We suggest that self-disclosure, appropriately done, can be helpful to your communication. The payoffs include these: (1) Improving accuracy of communication, and adding thoughts and feelings to the already public material you share with another. *Example:* "I just saw that movie, and it was depressing to me." (2) Getting to know more about another person in a more intimate way. *Example:* Learning from the other what depth of feeling you may share on some issues and thus increasing the predictability of your communication. (3) Getting to know more about yourself. *Ex-*

TABLE 11-3.
Levels of Disclosing

Content to be disclosed	Risk level	Conditions of disclosing	Examples
Information available to you and the other; of a general and public nature.	Minimal. Just let the other know you know.	Can be done between persons who are strangers as well as close friends.	Basic neutral data or data of little consequence to the participants: "I just saw that movie." "The President is on television tonight." While the content may be neither very revealing nor very significant *of and by itself*, it may prepare the way for more sensitive disclosing later.
Preferences you have; likes and dislikes.	Some risk.	Used if you want to get your own way or want to avoid doing something you dislike.	"I'd prefer a beer." "Let's play tennis instead of swimming." "Can you shut the door more quietly?" "I'd rather watch the football game on television."
Thoughts or ideas you have about public issues such as politics, books, and movies.	More risk.	Individual differences are likely to occur in ideas, and so people may react negatively to what you think.	"I really hated that movie." "My course in history represented a very global view and liberal ideas." "The President is not helping the poor."
Feelings, emotions, your own values, internal reactions, faith, judgments.	Most risk.	You may be able to argue from data about such matters, but your feelings are so personal that it is most difficult to share them with others.	"What faith do you have?" "I believe that students are less moral today than they used to be." "I'm opposed to drinking any alcoholic beverages." "The thought of dying frightens me."

ample: As the other person mirrors your feelings and whatever impressions your own behavior creates, you gain new insights into yourself.

Self-disclosure is an important element in developing close relationships with others and in knowing yourself. However, you must be sensitive to your needs as well as the needs of others. When you are able to self-disclose in a sensitive manner, you have made a giant step toward warding off loneliness, and toward developing high predictability about how you and others will act in a great variety of situations. You are your own tool in learning how to belong, how to care, how to share, and how to communicate your own needs appropriately in relation to those of others.

Another way of looking at the outcomes of self-disclosure is by focusing on what it does to the "self," putting aside any effects on others. First, you are giving of yourself. Second, you learn to recognize more of yourself. And third, you learn to evaluate your "self" more accurately and more predictably.

SUMMARY

Interpersonal communication has great potential to make you more productive, more effective both in your professional and personal relationships. As in any activity, communication may produce tensions which have to be resolved in some way in order for you to continue interacting with others. Negotiating to manage conflicts, seeking and giving accurate feedback, and appropriate self-disclosure are all presented here as the means of managing the inevitable tensions which arise among dynamic people.

Traditionally conflict was viewed as bad and avoidable. People who took part in conflicts were considered deviants, troublemakers, and a problem for those in authority, whether parents, teachers, managers, or club officers. More recently we have come to view conflict as both inevitable and potentially good. Some conflict can be functional and helpful and may spur growth and positive change.

Types of conflict include personal, interpersonal, and group, depending on the central place of involvement. Strategies for dealing with conflict include avoiding, defusing, and confronting. Confrontations occur in any of three ways, which we call win-lose, or the most common and traditional competitive means of managing conflict; lose-lose, or a system of giving concessions in which all parties appear to come up short of being satisfied with an outcome, and win-win, a seldom applied system for mutual problem solving and principled negotiating.

Experienced negotiators manage conflict with understanding and deliberate attention to both the content needs (what the argument, disagreement, or discussion is about) and the process needs (how the participants treat each other during the confrontations).

The Johari window is a classic model which describes your relationship with persons or groups around you in terms of how much you and they know and are willing to share in an ultimate effort to reduce ambiguity, misunderstandings, and tensions. The two important strategies proposed by this model are (1) giving and receiving accurate and timely feedback from others about your behaviors, and (2) disclosing data appropriately to others which will help their working with you and understanding you better.

Feedback is a way of improving the accuracy and dependability of your interpersonal transactions. Five suggestions are offered on how to make your feedback to others more effective by focusing (1) on behaviors rather than the person, (2) on observations rather than on inferences, (3) on descriptions rather than on judgments, (4) on sharing of ideas rather than on giving advice, and (5) on what your feedback may do to the person who is receiving it more than on your own needs to speak out.

Feedforward is a special kind of anticipatory communication which helps establish with another person the range of your discussion and the directions it might take.

Self-disclosure as it relates to giving data and feedback to others is very risky, but often rewarding communication behavior when carried out according to some "rules" which you and others will follow. Knowing what and when and how much to disclose is a refined skill, and some suggestions are offered on how you may evaluate your own disclosing tendencies and behaviors.

END NOTES

[1] J. Z. Rubin, "Some Wise and Mistaken Assumptions about Conflict and Negotiations," *Journal of Social Issues,* vol. 45, Summer 1989, p. 195. B. Gordon, "Settling Conflicts among Your Workers," *Nation's Business,* March 1988, p. 70. C. H. Coombs, "The Structure of Conflict," *The American Psychologist,* vol. 42, April 1987, p. 355. D. D. Cahn, "Conflict Communication: Intimate Relationships, 1986–1990," Speech Association of America, Annandale, VA, 1990 (an updated version of sources on conflict resolution). F. Jandt, *Win-Win Negotiating: Turning Conflict into Agreement,* John Wiley & Sons, New York, 1985. J. P. Folger and M. S. Poole, *Working through Conflict: A Communication Perspective,* Scott, Foresman, Glenview, IL, 1984.

[2] D. Druckman, B. J. Broome, and S. H. Korper, "Value Differences and Conflict Resolution: Facilitation or Delinking?" *Journal of Conflict Resolution,* vol. 32, September 1988, p. 489. R. A. Emmons and L. A. King, "Conflict among Personal Strivings," *Journal of Personality and Social Psychology,* vol. 54, June 1988, p. 1040.

[3] D. Elkind, "Power Struggles," *Parents' Magazine,* vol. 64, October 1989, p. 239. D. M. Buss, "Conflict between the Sexes: Strategic Interference and Evocation of Anger and Upset," *Journal of Personality and Social Psychology,* vol. 55, May 1989, p. 735. E. Jones and C. Gallois, "Spouses' Impressions of Rules for Communication in Public and Private Marital Conflicts," *Journal of Marriage and the Family,* vol. 51, November 1989, p. 957. M. A. Rahim and G. F. Buntzman, "Supervisory Power Bases: Styles of Handling Conflict with Subordinates," *The Journal of Psychology,* vol. 123, March 1989, p. 196.

[4] Jandt, op. cit.; Folger and Poole, op. cit.; R. Blake, H. Shepherd, and J. S. Mouton, *Managing Intergroup Conflict in Industry,* Gulf Publishing, Houston, TX, 1984; A. C. Filley, R. J. House, and S. Kerr, *Managerial Process and Organizational Behavior,* 2d ed., Scott, Foresman, Glenview IL, 1976; Student Manual, "Workshop in Constructive Conflict Resolution," Bureau of Training, Communication, and Office Skills Training Center, Washington, DC, 1977. Although the author of this following piece uses a taxonomy of five ways of managing conflicts, they represent the same grouping as our three including the confrontation subgroups: D. H. Stamatis, "Conflict: You've Got to Accentuate the Positive," *Personnel,* vol. 64, December 1987, p. 47.

[5] W. Mastenbraek, *Negotiate,* Basil Blackwell, Cambridge, MA, 1989. J. F. Byrnes, "Negotiating: Master the Ethics," *Personnel Journal,* vol. 66, June 1987, p. 97. T. C. Kaiser, "Negotiating with a Customer You Can't Afford to Lose," *Harvard Business Review,* vol. 66, November–December 1988, p. 30. E. J. Belzer, "The Negotiator's Art," *Working Woman,* vol. 15, April 1990, p. 98. J. M. Brett, S. B. Goldberg, and W. L. Ury, "Designing Systems for Resolving Disputes in Organizations," *The American Psychologist,* vol. 45, February 1990, p. 162.

[6] C. Legette, "How to Improve Your Negotiation Skills," *Black Enterprise,* vol. 20, October 1989, p. 106. R. W. Henkel, "Americans Don't Have a Good Understanding of the Way the Japanese Do Business: Partly Because of This, Only 1 in 25 U.S.-Japanese Negotiations Succeeds," *Electronics,* vol. 60, April 30, 1987, p. 8 (an editorial). M. Schatzki and W. R. Coffey, *Negotiation: The Art of Getting What You Want,* New American Library, New York, 1981. H. Margolis and K. J. Tewel, "Resolving Conflict with Parents," *NASSP Bulletin,* vol. 72, March 1989, p. 1. M. S. Koch, "Resolving Disputes: Students Can Do It Better," *NASSP Bulletin,* vol. 72, March 1988, p. 16. R. Greene, "Seven Steps to Winning a Fight," *Forbes,* vol. 42, July 25, 1988.

[7] F. E. Jandt, *Conflict Resolution through Communication,* Harper & Row, New York, 1973. Also by Jandt, *Win-Win Negotiating: Turning Conflict into Agreement,* John Wiley & Sons, New York, 1985. G. I. Nierenberg, (senior editor), *The Art of Negotiating Newsletter,* Negotiation Institute, Inc., New York, published eight times a year. R. J. Laser, "Practical Negotiating Skills," program developed and reported in Laser, *Build a Better You,* Showcase Publishing, San Mateo, CA, 1980. W. A. Donahue, "Development of a Model of Rule Use in Negotiation Interaction," *Communication Monographs,* vol. 48, July 1981, p. 106.

[8] W. A. Donahue, "An Empirical Framework for Examining Negotiation Processes and Outcomes," *Communication Monographs,* vol. 45, August 1978, p. 247. In this paper, the researcher studied the interaction of the components of situation, social power, expectation, and personality. R. L. Pinkley, "Dimensions of Conflict Frame: Disputant Interpretations of Conflict," *Journal of Applied Psychology,* vol. 75, April 1990, p. 117; this research uncovered and defined how disputants interpreted conflict on a cognitive level.

[9] D. M. Dobson, "Resolving Interpersonal Conflicts: An Analysis of Stylistic Consistency," *Journal of Personality and Social Psychology,* vol. 52, April 1987, p. 794. D. D. Cahn (ed.), *Intimates in Conflict: A Communication Perspective,* Lawrence Erlbaum, Hillsdale, NJ, 1990. L. L. Putnam and T. S. Jones, "Reciprocity in Negotiations: An Analysis of Bargaining Interaction," *Communication Monographs,* vol. 49, September 1982, p. 171; the authors also tested the differences between male and female bargainers to study the effect of gender on the outcome of the bargaining sessions and the results seemed to contradict the earlier "claims that female bargainers were too cooperative for the art of confrontation" (p. 190).

[10] J. Luft, *Of Human Interaction,* National Press Books, Palo Alto, CA, 1969.

[11] D. R. Ilgen and C. F. Moore, "Types and Choices of Performance Feedback," *Journal of Applied Psychology,* vol. 12, August 1987, p. 401.

[12] G. E. Myers, M. T. Myers, A. A. Goldberg, and C. E. Welch, "Effects of Feedback on Interpersonal Sensitivity in Laboratory Training Groups," *Journal of Applied*

Behavioral Science, vol. 5, no. 2, 1969, p. 175. See also, C. A. O'Reilly and J. C. Anderson, "Trust and Communication of Performance Appraisal Information," *Human Communication Research,* vol. 6, Summer 1980, p. 290.

[13] P. L. Hunsaker and A. J. Alessandra, "Giving—and Getting—Feedback," *Working Woman,* vol. 12, April 1987, p. 30.

[14] D. B. Fedor, M. R. Buckley, and R. W. Eder, "Measuring Subordinate Perceptions of Supervisor Feedback Intentions," *Educational and Psychological Measurement,* vol. 50, Spring 1990, p. 73.

[15] G. W. Chilcoat, "Developing Student Achievement with Verbal Feedback," *NASSP Bulletin,* vol. 72, April 1988, p. 8.

[16] B. Sondel, *Power Steering with Words,* Follett, Chicago, 1964.

[17] A. Pomerantz, "Offering a Candidate Answer: An Information Seeking Strategy," *Communication Monographs,* vol. 55, December 1988, p. 360.

[18] Pomerantz, ibid., p. 372.

[19] K. J. Corcoran, "The Relationship of Interpersonal Trust to Self-Disclosure When Confidentiality Is Assured," *The Journal of Psychology,* vol. 22, March 1988, p. 183.

[20] J. H. Berg and R. L. Archer, "The Disclosure-Liking Relationship," *Human Communication Research,* vol. 10, no. 2, Winter 1983, p. 279.

LABORATORY MANUAL

INTRODUCTION TO THE LABORATORY MANUAL

If I hear, I forget.
If I see, I remember.
If I do, I know.
          Chinese proverb

GENERAL COMMENTS

You will find this laboratory manual, as well as the accompanying text, somewhat different from others you may have been used to. Other books tend to be full of information for you to acquire. The accompanying text material in this book provides a *method* for you to practice, as well as some information for you to acquire. The method of the text and the course is based on the simple premise that *people tend to learn better by discovering for themselves than they do by just being told.*

In communication study, particularly, we feel that it is important for students to experience their own communication and the communication of others. You need to watch communication going on around you. A laboratory situation is a relatively safe place to experience human communication, and it can be an interesting place to observe the limitations of human communication.

Another reason we believe experiences with communication can be valuable is that there is only one person who can do anything about your communication—you. No one can change your com-

303

munication habits for you. In the laboratory situation you can try out new communication behaviors if you want to, or you can refine the behaviors you feel are your successful ones. Only you can make the exciting discoveries of your own communication strengths and weaknesses, and only you can decide to change if you like.

WHY A COMMUNICATION LABORATORY?

Laboratory learning is, of course, not new. Any biology or chemistry student has put in hours of work in a lab. Although laboratories are somewhat newer in the social sciences, the applications are growing for laboratory learning in our educational settings. In communication laboratories there are no test tubes or microscopes. The apparatus is our language and paralanguage, and the experimenters are you—the students—and your instructor. In the process of laboratory learning you will be both the observer and the observed. You will learn about communication by practicing it with others in a protected environment where you will be able to see and analyze the consequences of your behaviors. In the laboratory you will hear yourself and others talk. You will raise questions about identity, alienation, relating, and caring. You will discuss roles, norms, games, values, strategies we hide behind, and masks we wear to protect ourselves. You will have the opportunity to examine your communication value system and how it affects you.

Finally, we hope you will discover that your communication is so involved with your attitudes that communication is much more a state of mind than it is a garble of words.

SELF-PACING LABORATORY EXERCISES

If you are taking this class with a group of students in an organized course, the instructor will assign exercises and assignments for you to complete and group actions for you to assist with. It is possible to experience many of the same insights if you are studying this text alone. Although the group activities are difficult for the solitary student to manage, there may be some groups available to you and willing to take part in the games and activities. Certainly most assignments are possible to work on by yourself, as they are primarily designed to be accomplished outside of class time anyway.

One of the advantages of this laboratory approach over most other texts is the set of questions related to the exercises. From these questions you, the student, can develop, whether in a group discussion or alone, the major insights of the exercises.

DISCUSSION QUESTIONS

A unique feature of this laboratory manual is the elaborate set of questions for discussion and the probes designed to assist class discussion. They call your attention to the principles brought out by the exercises and help you relate the experience to theories and to your own life outside the classroom.

One of the major problems we have found in experiential learning settings is that games are played, exercises worked out, activities performed, and puzzles solved, but the main purpose of these experiences is often neglected—the transfer of learning from the experience into the actual behaviors of the student. This part of the class takes time; discussion should be detailed, involving, and extended. It should bring out the reactions of the students to the exercise and not just the instructor's knowledge. After all, the instructor knows these things about communication and is helping you, the student, discover them. Such discovery takes time; it develops in the discussion periods following the games and exercises.

Other questions and comments will be generated besides those provided by the authors; certainly the curious students will ask their own questions. In processing the experience for the class, a great emphasis should be placed on the discussion questions.

Even if you do not use all the exercises (as is very likely, since many more are provided than there is class time for), you might be interested in reading the rules or procedures of the exercise and then going over the questions in the discussion section. There are many chances for clarifying your own relations to communication as you work on the exercises. They will be magnified in their value if you spend time on the discussion and not simply on the game or the case or exercise.

CLASS ACTIVITIES AND EXERCISES

Only by getting together to talk about things or getting on your feet to report to others can you begin to feel the impact of oral communication. The dynamic quality of human communication cannot be felt by simply sitting and reading this book or any other book; nor can it be felt by writing reports in the solitude of your room to be read by a teacher in the solitude of an office. Interaction is important to demonstrate dynamic communication and to learn about it.

Emphasis in these laboratory exercises is, therefore, on an exchange of ideas and impressions between students or between the students and the instructor. Some time ago, many of these activities were given the label "GOYF" by some of our students. They coined the term as an abbreviation, an acronym, for "getting-on-your-feet" exercises. When we announced that the intention of this game or this activity was to get the class members on their feet to think and speak (in that order), the students responded by providing this label. Some attempt was made to establish the expression "TOYF," for "thinking on your feet," but it never gained the support it deserved.

Recommended activities are grouped according to the subject matter of the chapters of the text. Some exercises, naturally, will demonstrate several different principles of communication, and so it must be admitted that the arrangement of the exercises is somewhat arbitrary. In addition to the activities for which you have worksheets in this book, your instructor may add other projects or class exercises from time to time.

The thrust of activity groups, again, is to have you thinking and speaking at various levels of communication abstractness. Oral communication activity is always encouraged, so that you can learn how to think and speak by doing it.

Feedback Blanks

Feedback blanks are provided in each of the following chapters. They are designed to give you another means of interacting with one another and with the course. Honestly given, the laboratory feedback can reflect a growing awareness of communication maturity for the class.

A collation or a frequent report back to the class is important if the maximum effect is to be obtained from the feedback blanks. Although it is fun to be able to comment on the class anonymously—nobody knows who did it—we would urge you to resist the temptation to cut and slash your friends by verbal abuse in the feedbacks. A faithful, unedited version of the feedback blanks as they were turned in is important to the success of the project. If students take advantage of secrecy and lash out or become profane or otherwise act indiscriminately, then the feedbacks ought to be curtailed. Answer the questions thoughtfully, and the results will be surprising to you.

Cases for Discussion

In most chapters of the textbook, anecdotes were cited which serve the purpose of illustrating the principles of communication. A case is an extended anecdote. Cases are designed to give you some experience in solving other people's communication problems so that you can perhaps do something about your own.

Cases can be discussed in small groups (this is usually recommended in the laboratory sections) or can be discussed by a forum in front of the class. Some instructions on how to conduct a forum discussion are included below. Also included are some reflections on how groups tend to solve problems which come to them as cases. One such examination involves the stages a group tends to go through in arriving at a solution. Another examination, "Notes on Discussing Cases," should be helpful as your group gets together to conduct a case discussion.

Forum Discussion

The forum discussion may be "leaderless," leader-oriented, or some combination of the two. Avoid having each member make a pleasant, pat little speech and then lapse into silence. Try for interaction of ideas; try involving the audience and other members of the forum. Do not discuss the topic so thoroughly in your planning session that you lose spontaneity in your performance. Planning time should concentrate on selecting the topic and getting some kind of agreement on the terms to be used in your discussion. One person may introduce the topic to the audience, explaining the limits your group has set on the key words used. You may want a moderator to open the speaking and review it at the end, making sure to stay within your time limit. The idea is to stimulate thought and discussion, not necessarily to reach conclusions or obtain group agreement. In fact, your discussion may have to end at the most heated moment or before all questions are answered. Good topics include personal experiences: "how we handled a communication difficulty in the office or classroom," "children should be taught honesty in the home"—something based on your own communication experience. Family, campus, civic, church, or classroom problems are much more real to most of us than international issues.

Notes on Discussing Cases

1. Case discussion begins with the following areas:
   a. Details of the case and their relationships
   b. Inferences that are drawn by the participants in the discussion concerning why the event occurred; also, inferences about the motivations of the people involved in the case itself
   c. Illustrations and examples from personal experiences, as brought up by participants in the discussion
   d. Expressions of feelings about the actions and assertions in the case
2. What can be analyzed in a case:
   a. *The content of the sender's message*
      What was said? Do we have all that was said?

b. *The kind of message that was sent*
   Was it written, oral, or both? Was it simple, clear, or ambiguous? What made it simple, clear, or ambiguous? What does this have to do with the way the situation developed?

c. *The setting of the communication situation*
   Where did the incident take place—office or home; over the telephone or face to face? What kind of situation was it? Were people tense or relaxed, formal or informal?

d. *The sender*
   What status does the sender have, and does this affect the communication? If so, how? What assumptions does the sender have toward the situation? What attitudes, opinions, or feelings? What kind of person is the sender?

e. *The receiver*
   Same questions as those asked about the sender. In addition, what is the receiver's response to the sender's message, and how does this affect the communication?

f. *Outside pressures*
   Did the situation occur in an environment which provided certain rules and regulations that governed the sender and the receiver? Was the message sent directly, or was it received through intermediaries?

Role-Playing Cases or Incidents

Many of the cases in this laboratory section can be performed as skits or dramas, either in small groups by themselves or in front of the class. Often a point can be made more clearly by a dramatization of the incident than by simply talking about it. If your class has a number of members who enjoy "acting" or doing skits, these exercises will lend themselves to such role-playing activities. There need be no elaborate props or staging. Much of the success of this kind of role playing depends on its spontaneity rather than on its polish—and so no rehearsals are needed for most "shows." It helps to clarify who the actors are and what the situation is—then let the actors go.

Both the instructor and the students may want to enter into the decision about which exercises should be role-played, how long the skits will last, and whether the role playing will take place in small groups (several groups doing the same skits at the same time is called "multiple role playing") or by one or more groups in front of the class. Some technical hints on conducting a role-playing exercise follow.

Warm-up (planning time) should concentrate on establishing a problem situation and assigning roles. Performance is more spontaneous if each actor understands the "character" and liberates his or her emotions through that character. A "stage manager" may set the scene and identify the characters for the audience. More than one act may show a problem, its developments, and possible solutions. Try using techniques such as these:

Alter ego (a person stands behind an actor, and speaks his or her thoughts, interrupting by placing a hand on the actor's shoulder).

Soliloquy (this time the actor speaks the thoughts in asides to the audience, by changing his or her voice, or by some other sign to indicate that silent thoughts are being expressed).

Extensions (as with alter egos. several players stand behind the actor to represent different times of life or different points of view: a woman as she is this year or last year; a man as a father, a boss, a lodge member, etc.).

BOX INTRO-1.   How Groups Solve Case Problems*

A group will generally tend to go through several stages to arrive at a satisfactory solution in discussing a case.

Stage 1: The stage of condemnation and aggressive evaluation

Participants take sides; they tend to put the blame for the communication breakdowns on one person or another, usually reflecting their own biases about the kind of people involved in the case. The tendency at this stage is to oversimplify the situation by blaming.

Stage 2: The stage of frustration and rejection

Participants complain that they do not have enough data to solve the problem. They do not feel that they are given enough information to come to a solution. The discovery that we all must make decisions most of our lives on the basis of fragmentary or incomplete evidence is an important experience.

Stage 3: The stage of widening perceptions

Participants will begin to ask more probing questions and try to discover how the people in the case view the situation.
Analysis is made of past history and of other pressures acting on the people in the case.

Stage 4: The stage of alternative solutions and resolutions

Participants come up with thoughtful considerations of possible solutions.
Solutions grow out of the complexities of the situation and are proposed with a feeling for the consequences of actions growing out of the case.

* Eugene Rebstock, "General Semantics Training through Case Analysis," *ETC: A Review of General Semantics,* vol. 20, no. 3, 1963.

Interaction Observers

To help foster class discussion, you may be assigned an observer's role to cover groups in their discussions or to watch other situations in the class. Observers are usually appointed by the instructor for a specific activity or group project. You may be asked to report to the whole class or to certain groups. But how you make and report your observations should help the learning of all participants.

Observers have an advantage in not being directly involved in the discussion preparation; they therefore have time to observe interactions and communication behaviors. It helps to compare functioning of groups with functioning during other meetings of the class. Improvements should be noted. The observer role is meant to provide the audience (the entire class or the small group) with information and insights not available to everyone. Interaction during the planning session is very important—but consider also the effect of the group's efforts on the audience, the appropriateness of the problem chosen to demonstrate a principle, the development of the problem, the solutions offered, the clarity of the views expressed, and the communication behaviors of the group members (loudness, language, flexibility of delivery during preparation time and performance, tension in voices, nonverbal cues fitting the verbal ones, and other emotional responses to audience or situation). Observe not only the oral input, but the "feeling level" of communication as well. Your report to the class should be brief (avoid the dull and pointless repetition of "then he said to her" and "she said to him," etc.).

"Goldfish Bowl" Observing

One special kind of observing occurs when a group sits in a circle or around a table and is observed by another group arranged outside it in another circle. The name given to this arrangement is "goldfish bowl," to describe the visibility of the inner group's activities.

Some of the group discussions call for this arrangement so that the persons observed can get feedback on their behaviors. This is carried out in a "pairing" arrangement—each person in the inner group is observed by a partner in the outer group. The feedback is given in dyads, usually personal kinds of observations. By swapping locations, the inner group then becomes the observer or outer group, and the former observers become the actors to be observed.

Another arrangement is the general observation system, where the entire inner group is observed and commented on by the entire outer group. One of the disadvantages of this system is that only part of the interaction is concentrated on by all observers and many individual actions go by unnoticed in the attempt to follow the most exciting "action."

The goldfish bowl system has great potential for developing understanding of behaviors as they are reported by observers in a relatively safe atmosphere. It has a disadvantage in that often the inner group engages in "role playing" for the observers rather than interacting normally. After a short while, participants tend to forget the observers, however, and usually carry on their discussion easily.

Videotape Playback Observing

While the cases and discussion situations in this laboratory manual will not refer specifically to use of videotape recording, it is a very useful and exciting way to support group observations and to provide accurate and timely feedback.

Videotaping is effective in recording the actions of a group or of performers in discussion settings—in role playing and in individual presentations to the class. Immediacy of the playback gives a very dramatic view of behaviors and supports class discussion of the events or exercises.

One method we have used involves having the class discuss an interaction (an exercise or event) which has been videotaped; but to carry on part of the discussion *before seeing any playback*. In that way the playback is used to (1) bring the incident back to life, (2) reinforce or check on observations already asserted by the members, and (3) provide opportunity for additional insights or observations which may have been missed during the "live" production, much like an instant replay to analyze more behaviors than can be seen in "real time."

Videotape and playback equipment or facilities are usually available from audiovisual or library departments or from an academic department, and many individuals in a course may have access to camcorders or other videotape reproduction technologies. Occasional use of this technology brings amazing insights which may be only partially developed by human observers watching the behaviors of others and making their reports to the class.

ASSIGNMENTS AND PROJECTS

Besides the activities you will have during class time, there are many other opportunities to explore human communication through a variety of assignments and outside class projects. Your instructor will assign those which are most appropriate with respect to the time involved and the interests of the class. In addition to the assignments suggested in this manual, the instructor may add tests or other assignments which do not appear.

Journal

The instructor may assign you the project of maintaining a journal of communication happenings. These will become a collection of your own observations of communication around you. Although the assignments for journal entries do not appear in every chapter of the laboratory manual, it might be useful to continually keep a "communication diary" of the things you notice about the communicative behaviors of yourself and others.

Scrapbook

A collection of newspaper clippings, notes, letters, printed ads, and other published or written materials will help you analyze the communication habits of the people who make news and who suffer from the same communicative difficulties as the rest of us. (Whereas the journal makes a record of your own private life and observations, the scrapbook will tend to be more sweeping in its scope and more distant in its relation to your personal life.)

Although there may be many individual and different ways to make a scrapbook, we suggest that you use a loose-leaf notebook as the basic part of your scrapbook. Then you can add pages (punched to fit the rings) as you add clippings. Trimming the clippings neatly will make your book easier to compile and to read. Instead of just putting the clippings together, we suggest that you paste them on standard-size paper so that pages of your scrapbook will be the same size. This also provides you with space to write comments on the clippings. From time to time the instructor may ask you to turn in the scrapbook or to share your latest collection of clippings by discussing some of them in class.

Communication Case

Another kind of outside assignment is the case which you construct from your own experience or the experience of others. Purpose of this assignment is to have you describe and analyze a communication problem or incident. The case should present a relatively complex problem which is still largely unsolved. If the problem is too simple and uncomplicated, all we have is an illustration which can be read with interest but which leaves little room for creative analysis. For that reason, the case should contain a record of misevaluations and errors amenable to analysis with the principles and concepts presented in this course.

It should consist of three distinct parts:

1. *The description of the problem.* This part should be sufficiently detailed that it can be role-played. The case does not have to be of monumental importance to the future of the world, but it can represent the tragedies which befall us in our relations with others through faulty communication— as observed over a period of time. Deal with something you know about firsthand—the everyday

kind of mess we often make of our interpersonal communication. This is an objective report. Treat it as a third-party story, even if it happened to you. Try to minimize personal judgments, slant, and inferences. This first section is only a description of events: what happened to whom, when, and where. It may be written as a narrative or a dialog, or in any form you wish.

2. *The analysis.* In this part you will analyze communication difficulties from the point of view of the behaviors described in this course and text. Include if you like some recommendations about how the behaviors you report could have been improved by applying some of the principles discussed in class. If you want at this point to propose solutions and inject your personal feelings about the case, you may do so.

3. *Your reactions.* Report the reactions you noted in yourself in carrying this assignment through from its inception (perhaps when you first read these instructions) to the completion of your paper. You are asked for your reactions to the assignment at this point, not your reactions to the case itself or the people in it.

Personal Improvement Blanks

At the end of each set of assignments you will find a personal improvement blank (PIB) which asks you some questions about your communication behaviors and the behaviors of those around you. It is designed to have you look at your communication as everyday life and not just as what goes on in class. Over the years students have reported that these exercises have provided them with a way of watching their own communication development (hence, "improvement") in a realistic way. As we wrote earlier, you are the only one who can do anything about your communicating. If that is so, then you must have some means of monitoring your changing behaviors or your attempts to try out new behaviors and the results of those attempts.

Other Assignments

Each section has related assignments: writing, making lists, studying outside sources, etc. Some of these will be assigned by the instructor as a way of giving you outside contacts with the material from the text itself.

You will notice that the assignments focus on the application of the theories and writings in the text. They are an attempt to get you to think in terms of communication as the dynamic process it is—affecting all you do and all you are.

FEEDBACK BLANK

EXERCISES

ASSIGNMENTS

PERSONAL IMPROVEMENT BLANK

FEEDBACK BLANK (Chapter 1)   DO NOT SIGN

1. Rate the productivity of this week's (session's) work for you. (Circle one number.)

    1   2   3   4   5   ⑥   7   8   9   10

    Not productive   Highly productive

2. Rate how you think the rest of the class felt about this week's (session's) productivity.

    1   2   3   4   5   6   7   ⑧   9   10

    Not productive   Highly productive

    Comments:

3. Comment on your contribution in the small group or in the class exercises. Did you speak too much? Too little?

    I felt that I did contribute to the discussion. The teacher regulated people's participation. I probably could have participated more.

4. Comment on the class activities this week (session). What did you like, dislike? What was helpful to you and why?

    I like the discussion on why we communicate. I felt it highlighted the major issues of the course.

5. Add other comments, criticisms, questions, suggestions, etc.

EXERCISES:

EXERCISE 1-1
WHAT IS COMMUNICATION? (Discussion)

List all the things you can think of which are communication. First do this by yourself and then get together with others in a group to compare lists and to draw up a composite list to read or present to the class. (Your list will include such items as "speaking," "waving," "touching," "clothing.")

Discussion

A. When the lists are compared, the groups or the class can discuss the common elements in the items which make them "communication."
B. Classify the items by writing them on the chalkboard or on a chart for the class to see in two categories: (1) content, (2) process communication. Can some communication items be classified in both categories?
C. Discuss the axiom "You cannot *not* communicate" in relation to the list of items you consider communication.

EXERCISE 1-2
COMMUNICATION STRENGTHS AND WEAKNESSES (Discussion)

Write down a list of at least five behaviors, habits, or tendencies you have which are communication strengths. Then write down three or more of your communication weaknesses.

In a small group of four or five, share your lists of strengths. An effective way to do this is to take turns: each person lists one strength, and then a list representing the group is compiled. (Duplicates should be noted and reported because any group should recognize the strengths shared by several members.)

Follow the same procedure with the communication weaknesses—sharing the list, or as much of it as you feel comfortable about. A composite group list of weaknesses can be compiled.

Discussion

A. What similarities do you find among different groups' lists of strengths and weaknesses?
B. Can most of you identify those communication habits and behaviors which are helps or hindrances to you?
C. Did the items as they were listed come as a surprise to any members of the groups? Did anyone have difficulty listing strengths and talking about them with the rest of the group? Was there any disagreement about whether someone's listed weakness was actually a weakness?
D. How many of the listed strengths depend solely on the "owner"? Do many of them also depend on a relationship with others?
E. How many of the listed weaknesses are possible to change or alter in some way to either neutralize them or turn them into strengths?

EXERCISE 1-3
WHO KNOWS WHAT? (Group Project)

Form small groups of four to seven members. The purpose of this exercise is to find out which member of the group can be counted on to know certain things or to be able to do certain things—in other words, to locate the talents, abilities, and interests in the group. For each of the following situations, ask group members to volunteer information about their own abilities to take part in the activity suggested. How do group members feel about taking part in those activities?

1. A group to plan a party and a dance
2. A group to solve a complex mathematics problem
3. A group to write and perform a one-act play for the class
4. A group to make drawings or illustrations of this group's behaviors toward each other
5. A group to arrange for a lecturer to visit the campus and meet some classes

Discussion

A. The communication needs of each of the five groups are somewhat different. Which seem to require greater cognitive or content skills (digital communicative behaviors), and which seem to require more relational or interpersonal skills (analogic communication)?
B. How would you rank the five activities if you were given a choice of which to participate in? Pick the one you would like best; then the least; then second best; then next to last; and finally the middle one. How many of the class members selected each group activity as their first choice? As their last choice?

EXERCISE 1-4
ACQUAINTANCE QUESTIONNAIRE[1] (Discussion)

Your instructor will read aloud each of the following incomplete statements. You will be allowed a moment to complete each statement. Write spontaneously. Don't think about the statements too much.

1. I am a _____
2. I am happy when I _____
3. Ten years from now I want to _____
4. This school is a _____
5. Next Saturday night I want to _____
6. My three heroes or heroines are

   (a) _____
   (b) _____
   (c) _____

[1] Adapted from Elwood Murray et al., *Speech: Science-Art*, Bobbs-Merrill, Indianapolis, IN, 1969, p. 74. By permission of the authors and the publishers.

Discussion

A. In a small group discuss how you answered the incomplete statements. Expand on your "first-impulse" completions by talking with others in the group about why you gave the answer you did.

B. After fifteen minutes in the small groups, the entire class can discuss the kind of information which is exchanged by the responses you made. Did you learn more about the items (the future, the school, heroes, etc.), or did you learn more about the persons making the completed statements? Does this suggest that you always talk about yourself even when you are talking about other things?

EXERCISE 1-5
GIVING INSTRUCTIONS (Group Project)

1. Break up into small groups of five or six students. For every group formed there is an assigned "order taker" who does not participate in the group planning and must be out of the room or segregated from the planning session.

2. You are to develop instructions for performing a very common task: you will instruct a person from outside your group, the order taker, on *how to put on his or her coat.* In the preparation time (ten minutes) your group should develop a series of instructions to be given orally to your order taker. You will assume that this order taker has never seen a coat, does not know anything about coats or what they are for, and will not understand any of the words used to name parts of the garment. The order taker will just rely on what you will tell him or her to do—nothing more, nothing less.

3. After your group feels that it knows just what to say to the order taker to make him or her complete the task successfully, you will call the order taker and begin the actual order giving. The order taker will stand beside a chair. A coat is hung over the back of the chair. Start telling him or her what to do . . .

4. Variations on this exercise include the following:

    a. Using a set of Tinker Toys, your group will instruct the order taker on how to assemble a relatively complex item that you have worked out and sketched so that you can give directions orally but without showing the drawing to your order taker.

    b. Give the order taker a sheet of paper and have him or her draw a figure (preferably not a very simple one) just from your oral instructions; or have each member of your group give one part of the instructions and not repeat them.

    c. Tell the order taker how to sit down in a chair. Again, this person must assume no knowledge of the words used or the actions to be performed, but must follow directions exactly.

    d. Explain to the order taker how to print the word "cat" from the moment that person picks up the pencil, pen, or chalk; include instructions on how to hold the instrument.

Discussion

A. When you start to give orders or simple instructions to another person, what assumptions do you make about how much others already know? What assumptions do you make about how much of your language is easy to misinterpret? What assumptions do you make about how clearly you yourselves understand the process?

B. If a person deliberately wants *not* to understand, or wants to make errors, do the English language and ordinary social attitudes permit him or her great opportunities to miscommunicate?

C. Do you realize how much of your behaviors and your information have come to you by imitation of nonverbal as well as verbal instructions?

D. When things don't go right in giving or receiving instructions, what is a very predictable reaction in the people involved? What does that do to communication?

EXERCISE 1-6
TO SPEAK OR NOT TO SPEAK (Discussion)

List three situations in which you *want* to speak (communicate) with others (for example, asking a salesperson for help in locating the right size clothing).

1. _____

2. _____

3. _____

List three situations in which you *do not want* to speak (communicate) with others (for example, being called on in class when you don't know the answer).

1. _____

2. _____

3. _____

When you have listed those six items, be prepared to discuss how you would act in each situation. (For example, when you need help finding clothes of the right size, you will first try to find out who the salesperson is so that you won't ask another customer; then you get the salesperson's attention; then you tell him or her what you are looking for; and then you give him or her a chance to answer you or to direct you to the right part of the store.)

Are there certain things you usually do in situations like these? Do you make use of the same physical moves and language? Do your strategies (the ways you handle yourself) vary with different kinds of situations? Can you predict how you are going to act?

ASSIGNMENTS:

ASSIGNMENT 1-1
WORDS TO LIVE BY
In folklore and collections of "wise sayings" there are many maxims or epigrams about communication. "Silence is golden" is one such maxim. "Children should be seen and not heard" is another. Many of the most popular sayings have opposites. For example: "Speech is God's gift to humankind" opposes the idea that "Silence is golden," just as "Truth comes out of the mouths of babes" says something quite different from "Children should be seen and not heard."

1. From any sources available to you (collections, interviewing others, etc.), find a list of at least five maxims or wise sayings about communication.
2. Find out whether there are also *opposites* of those sayings in folk wisdom and submit the list along with the five maxims from item 1.
3. Continue to collect communication maxims—especially those which have popular opposites.
4. Write a brief essay on why you think these folk sayings or epigrams may have opposites.

ASSIGNMENT 1-2
EAVESDROPPING
Listen to some conversations between other people (family members at dinner, strangers on a bus, etc.). Without identifying the people whom you have listened to, give a brief summary of one conversation which did not directly include you and analyze it for the principle of chicken and egg. How did you become interested in the sequence of statements? What did you hear and what did you miss in the flow of the conversation? Speculate on what other items of information were exchanged and how they might have affected the outcome of the conversation.

   As another part of the analysis of this overheard conversation, try to estimate the relationship of the communication pattern in relation to speakers as equals or nonequals.

ASSIGNMENT 1-3
JOURNAL, DIARY, SCRAPBOOK
This is an excellent project to carry out over the term. Now is a good time to begin collecting a written record of your thoughts and reactions, and those of relevant others or those of a public nature.

1. A *journal* (as described in the introduction to this laboratory manual) is a collection of your personal observations of communication around you. It may be about the class or your outside contacts. It consists of brief notes or even essays on your response to communication in your environment.
2. A *diary* may be different from a journal, listing more specifically daily communication encounters of any kind which made an impression on you for some reason. It may have a more factual approach than the journal and might well include your extensive recitation of reactions to communications and your subjective analyses.
3. A *scrapbook* collects the impressions of others and the communication habits of others. Cartoons, newspaper clippings, posters, etc., all may be used to record the communication activities of

famous people in the news, or of less famous people whose communication actions contribute to the news or to a record of human interaction.

ASSIGNMENT 1-4
AN ESTIMATE OF MYSELF AS A COMMUNICATOR

Your own communication experiences have provided you with a wealth of information about yourself in your relationships with others. How you see yourself in your communication with others has a strong effect on what you do. For this assignment you are asked to answer three questions:

1. How effective am I as a communicator in a one-to-many situation (having to talk to fifteen or more people, as in the "A-personal" range, below)?

DIAGRAM 1-1
Scope and Levels of Communication

	Levels		
Scope	**Intellectual level**	**Skills level**	**Emotional level**
Intrapersonal range	Reading, listening, watching Sensory inputs processed Vocabulary recognitions Language acquisitions Data gathering Data storage in brain Planning, worrying	Overcoming accents Training memory Pronunciation practice Organizing data and arguments Solving puzzles Ear and eye training Problem definitions	Self-image development Acquisition of values Expression of needs Artistic listening and watching Concepts of self and others Worrying Anticipating pleasures

Interpersonal range	Giving instructions
	Reporting observations
	Taking orders
	Telling data
	Logical persuading
	Debating, arguing
	Listening to data
		Conversational skills
		Listening skills
		Interviewing
		Leading groups or
		    organizations
		Selling products
		Movements and gestures
		Adapting behavior to feedback
			Sharing feelings
			Persuasion concerning values
			Discussions of artistic
			    expressions
			Playing music, reading
			    together
			High-pressure selling
			Reporting inferences

A-personal public communication (mass communication— sociocultural range)	Public reports
	Judicial proceedings
	Parliamentary practices
	News reporting
	Law making
	Documentary productions
	Nonfiction writing
		Political speaking
		Public addresses
		Organization of data by
		    speakers and listeners
		Debating, open forum,
		    discussion techniques
		Reports, digests, etc.
			Mob actions
			Panic situations
			Mass movements in society
			Artistic performances in music,
			    drama, movies, etc.
			Art exhibits
			Oral interpretation

This diagram shows behaviors on different levels of communication related to the range of their influence. There are many more examples that you could add to these. Human communication activity can be identified by level and by range for the sake of study, but the reader should be cautioned that some activities will naturally involve several of the levels and will, in their application to real-life communication, cross many of the ranges. You should remember the *process* nature of communication and assume that this diagram is for the sake of "stopping the process to look at it." These communication acts are not likely to occur in this carefully defined system except in textbooks and diagrams.

2. How effective am I as a communicator in small groups (committees, work groups, buzz sessions, etc.)?

3. How effective am I as a communicator in a one-to-one situation (talking to one other person)?

   Note   It is essential that you write from your own point of view how you see yourself and not how you think other people see you. You do not need to ask others for their estimates of your effectiveness. However, you should be prepared to have class members read your paper.

   Allow yourself enough time to do some thinking about the three questions before you write anything down on paper. Use the diagram below to study your behaviors in relation to the three ranges and three levels.

   You should be prepared to read some of what you wrote in a presentation to the class; or the instructor may ask you to make an oral summary of your answers to these three questions in a few minutes of speaking in front of the class.

PERSONAL IMPROVEMENT BLANK (Chapter 1)

1. Write a brief report about a time when you tried to communicate with someone. What was the result? My Mother asked me what I wanted to order from some catalog. I tried to tell her which I wanted. However, she already had a preconceived idea of which I wanted. No matter how I tried to contradict her opinion she was convinced she knew best. Finally, I just gave up

2. List two relationships you have developed with others which are
   a. Equal; describe how they are equal: Julie & I have a very equal friendship. We both have times at which we are the primary speaker + at times are the listener. We are pretty balanced. I know that when I need someone to listen she will be there.

   b. Unequal; describe how they are unequal: My parents & I have an unequal relationship. They do most & sometimes all the talking. With them, I am the primary listener. I don't have very much input.

3. Are you aware of situations in which you have to start from somewhere in your communication relations (the chicken-and-egg question)? Give a brief example. (When you go to report a car accident, how far back in the history of the car and the drivers do you begin the story? In your relations with someone else, what was the latest communication behavior which had an influence on you? Etc.) When you introduce someone, how much information do you give? Do you tell how you met them? or Do you give info about your relationship? or About their special qualities?

Your name _Liz Rothenberg_

Perception: The Eye
of the Beholder

FEEDBACK BLANK

EXERCISES

ASSIGNMENTS

PERSONAL IMPROVEMENT BLANK

FEEDBACK BLANK (Chapter 2)   DO NOT SIGN

1. Rate the productivity of this session's work for you.

   1   2   3   4   5   6   7   (8)   9   10

   Not productive   Highly productive

2. Rate how you think the rest of the class felt about this session's productivity.

   1   2   3   4   5   6   7   (8)   9   10

   Not productive   Highly productive

   Comments:

3. At this point, how comfortable or at ease do you feel in this class? Why?

   I feel very comfortable in the class.

4. If you do not feel comfortable, can you isolate the reasons why?

5. Did you feel left out in any of the activities this week, in your groups or during any of the exercises? If you did, do you think anyone noticed?

EXERCISES:

EXERCISE 2-1
THE ACCIDENT CASE (Discussion)
John Howell had been waiting at the corner to catch the bus for work. As he was standing there, a light-blue car driven by a young man of 19 was involved in an accident with a white car driven by a 26-year-old mother of two. John arrived at work and described the accident to Harry, a coworker.

"I was standing there at the corner waiting for the bus when I saw a blue car coming down the street at a fairly fast rate. At least it looked as though the car was going fairly fast. The driver was a young fellow about 19 or so who attends the university. He was on his way to class. Anyway, he must not have been paying much attention to what he was doing because he hit a car in the intersection. He hit the car at the rear, and the rear door was dented pretty badly. The college fellow was not injured; but the woman was shaken up, and one of her children lost a tooth. It wasn't a bad accident, but it sure shows you can't be too careful."

Harry went home that night and told his wife that John had seen an accident.

"John saw a bad accident this morning. He was waiting for the bus when a crazy college kid came roaring down the street. John said he was doing 90 and nothing. He must have been late for class, and he was not paying attention to what he was doing. He was probably listening to the radio or something. A woman was waiting at the intersection, and this guy just plowed into her. He did not even hit his brakes. The woman was hysterical. One of her children was all bloody and lost one tooth. They should take the guy's license away from him. If anybody can't drive better than that, he doesn't deserve a license."

What will Harry's wife think when she reads about the accident in the paper saying that the woman was given a citation for making a dangerous turn and failing to yield the right of way?

Discuss the implications of the story.

Discussion
A. For the person who did not see the event (this accident) is it possible to make up, or to imagine, details which were not part of the event?
B. When you report incidents to others, do you have more purposes than simply exchanging information? Do you, for instance, want to make a point about the way others drive or what college kids are like, or do you want to shock others with bloody and gory details?
C. How would you characterize the objectivity of perceptions shown by: (1) how John told Harry about what he actually witnessed on the spot, (2) how Harry told his wife about what John had reported to him, and (3) what appeared in the newspaper long after the event had been evaluated and judged by officers of the law and witnesses and a reporter?
D. If you are an insurance investigator for either of the parties involved, what set of perceptions will you need to rely on?

EXERCISE 2-2
AGREE-DISAGREE LIST ON PERCEPTION (Group Project)
1. Indicate whether you agree or disagree with the statements in the table on the following page. Mark A if you agree, D if you disagree, on the left-hand side of the table.

Individual (A)	(D)		Group consensus (A)	(D)
_____	_____	1. The perception of a physical object depends more upon the object than upon the mind of the observer.	_____	_____
_____	_____	2. Perception is primarily an interpersonal phenomenon.	_____	_____
_____	_____	3. The fact that hallucinations and dreams are as vivid as waking perceptions indicates that perception depends very little upon external reality.	_____	_____
_____	_____	4. The reaction we have to what we see generally depends on learning and culture.	_____	_____
_____	_____	5. We tend to see what we wish to see or are expecting to see regardless of reality.	_____	_____
_____	_____	6. Given the undependable nature of perception, we can never tell the "true" nature of reality.	_____	_____
_____	_____	7. Though there may be reality "out there," we can never really know it.	_____	_____
_____	_____	8. We may eliminate the undependable in our perception by careful, scientific observation.	_____	_____
_____	_____	9. Scientific instruments, though they extend the limits of human perception, do not make perception any more real.	_____	_____
_____	_____	10. What we perceive is no more than a metaphor of what is.	_____	_____
_____	_____	11. Perception is a physical response to a physical reality. It is only when we begin talking about our perceptions that we begin to distort them.	_____	_____
_____	_____	12. If we are careful, we can see the world as it really is.	_____	_____
_____	_____	13. We react to our environment on the basis of what we perceive that environment to be like and not what the environment is really like.	_____	_____

2. Form groups of six or seven students and reach a consensus for each of the statements in the above table. Record the group consensus on the right-hand side of the table.

Discussion

A. If you do not agree on the items, what does that say about your ability to speak to each other about what you "see" or "hear" beyond the very obvious fact that you may stand in different places or communicate with different people? Do your basic attitudes about perception, then, have an effect on what and how you perceive?

B. Had you thought about all these ideas on perception before you began making out your "agrees" and "disagrees"? What new ideas came to you while you worked on the list?

C. Because you had written down your A or D before the group got together, did you find it difficult to give up your answer? Would it have been easier for you to discuss these items without bias and objectively if you had not first written down your own ideas? In other words, do you go into your real-life groups with some ideas already firmly established? What happens to objective discussion if many of the people in the group already have a firm commitment to some idea?

When people enter groups with a preset or preconceived idea of what should be done, this is often referred to as their "hidden agenda."

D. How did the group arrange to come to agreement? Did you understand what is meant by "consensus"? What does it mean? How does a group approach it?

EXERCISE 2-3
COMMUNICATION AND THE CRIMINAL MIND (Case)

Case of the Telephone Page
When Robert Charles heard his name paged at the San Francisco International Airport, he made his way to the nearest telephone just as he had been instructed by the paging message.

At the telephone two airport police officers arrested him. Mr. Charles had a few hours earlier escaped from a prison work farm in San Jose, California, and was planning to make his way out of the country. Acting on a tip, the FBI had arranged the phone-call trap. It was never clear who Mr. Charles was expecting a phone call from.

Discussion
A. What assumptions about human nature and the desire to communicate did the FBI agents make when they set this trap? Did they know Mr. Charles would respond this way? Why could they be so sure?

B. Are there other communication traps we fall into? Do salespersons use tricks to get you into a buying mood? Have strangers ever "forced" you to talk to them when you didn't want to? Would you answer a ringing telephone or a paged message over a public address system even if you did not expect anyone to call you?

Case of the Telltale Holdup Note
A man in Orlando, Florida, who wrote a holdup message on the back of his own probation-parole card and then left it behind, was arrested as he prepared to board a bus.

Police reported that the suspect, Terry Wilson, stepped up to a Sun Bank teller and passed the teller a note saying "Give me all your money or else I'll shoot you. Bang." So the teller handed over some money and the man fled, leaving the note, written on the back of his probation-parole card, with the teller.

Mr. Wilson was identified by the parole card, and police arrested him a few minutes later at the bus station next door to the police station and a few blocks from the bank. A police investigator commented: "He wasn't real sharp."

Discussion
A. Did this man perceive the note as simply an extortion message and not his own parole card? How did the perception of that piece of paper change once he had handed it to the teller?

B. Once the message was delivered, do you suppose the holdup man perceived the situation as completed? Is that why he could expect to simply walk to the bus station and leave town?

C. What perception did the police have of this criminal? Do you think they had an accurate estimate of the person's abilities?

EXERCISE 2-4
HOW MANY SQUARES? (Group Project)

Working by yourself, count how many squares there are in Figure 2-1. After your estimate is recorded in the space at the left and below the diagram, get together with some other members of the class and compare the totals you came up with. After you have had time to discuss any differences, put in the space on the lower right the number you agree on with the others in your group.

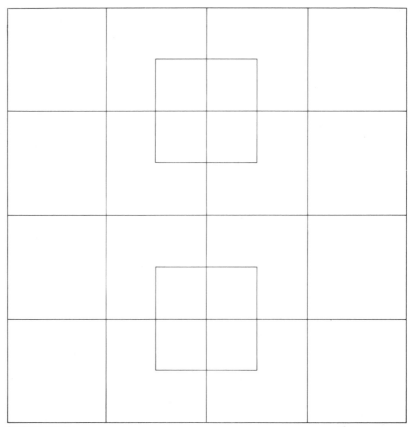

Student's answer   Group consensus

FIGURE 2-1
How many squares?

Discussion

A. If everyone did not come up with the same number, how do you account for the differences? Do people make different assumptions about squares, or do we simply see the same objects a little differently?

B. If you count the squares only once, do you come up with the same number as if you count them again? What happens when you take more time interacting with a problem, a puzzle, an event, an incident, or another person? Do you tend to see more completely, more deeply? What does this say about your first impressions of others or about your quick reactions to behaviors of others?

C. Is there some difference of opinion on how to define "squares"? Does that difference account for how many you can count? Do definitions affect your perceptions?

ASSIGNMENTS:

ASSIGNMENT 2-1
NEWSPAPER CLIPPINGS

Examine the newspaper accounts of a recent controversial event. Examine also the various reports of the investigation commissions if any commissions were formed and if those reports are available. From your investigation of these sources, identify the communication barriers and breakdowns which were involved in the situation.

Be prepared to discuss your clipping with the class. One variation of this assignment is to find clippings on lawsuits, investigations by Congress, contested elections, etc., and to take sides and explain how you gathered the information on which you are basing your arguments.

ASSIGNMENT 2-2
INTERVIEW

Do *either* 1 *or* 2 below:
1. Arrange an interview with a professional artist (painter, sculptor, musician, etc.) to discover his or her views on "art as communication." Report the results of your interview.
2. Talk to a public school teacher to find out how he or she views the communication role of the teacher in the classroom. Report the result of your interview.

Reports of these interviews may be written or oral. You may be asked to tell the class about the interview and to describe the setting in which you found the artist or teacher. Was the place where you interviewed the person a factor in the kinds of responses you received?

ASSIGNMENT 2-3
PERCEPTION INCIDENT

Think about what happened to you this past week—trivial and important things, happy and sad things. Were any of the unsatisfactory events of the week due to inadequate communication? If so, were any of the communication difficulties traceable to differences in perception between the people involved or to distortions in what was perceived which caused subsequent difficulties?

Write a brief summary of such an instance and analyze its consequences on you and the people around you.

Be prepared to talk about this instance in class. You may be asked to get together with another student and to work out a brief oral report on one of your "cases" or incidents, or to lead a class discussion about your case.

PERSONAL IMPROVEMENT BLANK (Chapter 2)

1. Recount briefly an event which occurred to you recently in which faulty perception caused a disagreement or misunderstanding. The event can be rather trivial. It is in trying to cope with disagreements at all levels of your life, not only the most important events, that you develop bad feelings.

Kim + I both were mad over the same argument. However, we both perceived that different things had been said & perceived the situation.

2. If you recognize that a difference in perception is causing some problem between you and another person (or group), how can you go about trying to get others to understand that the problem may be one of *perceptions*? Be specific.

I tried to explain to her that we had both different versions of the argument. We had each taken what we wanted to hear

3. Cite a recent incident in which you were perceived unfairly. What was the result of the error in perception? Did it come out all right?

In the past at a certain conference, Hamilton has been known for partying hard. One of the advisors assumed since we were from Hamilton, we were drunks with no interest in doing well. We showed him + everyone else who doubted us by doing an excellent job as well as having a good time

Your name *Liz Rothenberg*

CHAPTER
3

Self-Concept: Who Am I?

FEEDBACK BLANK

EXERCISES

ASSIGNMENTS

PERSONAL IMPROVEMENT BLANK

FEEDBACK BLANK (Chapter 3)   DO NOT SIGN

1. Rate the productivity of this session's work for you.

    1   2   3   4   5   6   7   8   9   10

Not productive   Very productive

2. Rate how you think the rest of the class felt about the productivity of this session's work.

    1   2   3   4   5   6   7   8   9   10

Not productive   Very productive

Comments:

3. In relation to this session's subject matter, were you assigned a role you did not like in any group activity? If people assign "identities" to you, what effect does this have on your reactions?

4. Did you enjoy working with your group? Why or why not?

5. Add other comments, criticisms, questions, suggestions, etc.

EXERCISES:

EXERCISE 3-1
SELF-ESTEEM: CALIFORNIA STYLE (Discussion)

The state legislature of California created a twenty-five-person panel to investigate whether the state should do more to promote self-esteem among Californians, especially young people.

After years of battling skeptical colleagues in the state legislature, John Vasconcellos, a Democratic assemblyman and a national leader of what is called "The New Age Movement," pulled together enough support for the passage of the bill, which was supported by "human potential" groups.

Proponents argued that insufficient self-esteem may be at the root of many problems ranging from a high dropout rate in high schools to teen pregnancies to alcoholism, drug abuse, and crime. The panel is called "Task Force to Promote Self-Esteem, Personal and Social Responsibility" and was given the assignment to recommend steps the state of California can take to enhance the self-esteem of its citizens.

Discussion

A. If you were selected to be on such a panel, how would you want to begin?
B. Do you think the argument is valid that self-esteem has anything to do with those social factors cited by the assemblyman?
C. If the panel should find conclusive evidence that there is a relationship between self-esteem and the problems of California young people, how might the panel go about tackling the self-esteem problem?
D. Formation of the "task force" was the subject of derision by a number of commentators, including the cartoonist Garry Trudeau, creator of "Doonesbury." Do you think people should make fun of this kind of statewide effort? How would you answer critics of the efforts?

EXERCISE 3-2
WHAT IF YOU WERE . . . ? (Role Playing)

This is an exercise in assuming a role different from the ones you usually play. Here is a chance for you to act like some other person, and to demonstrate that people are really quite conscious of how roles are developed and what is expected of a person in any given situation or relationship. Pick one of these situations and role-play it (act out the dialog) for the class:

1. The President of the United States greets the prime minister of a foreign nation in the Rose Garden of the White House. (One person should be the President, and the visitor's role may be either imagined or played by another member of the class.)
2. You have been elected Miss Universe, and you step forward to the microphones to deliver your acceptance speech.
3. You are a famous novelist autographing your books at a local department store. You have been asked to talk to the store employees about how you came to write the best-selling book.
4. *This is a role-playing situation for two or more persons.* A parent has just discovered that his or her 12-year-old child must undergo a very delicate and dangerous eye operation. The parent

has elected to talk to the child about the impending operation, rather than having the doctor do it.

5. You have been selected to meet the governor of your state at the airport and act as official escort to the annual Chamber of Commerce dinner. (Select someone in the class to act as the governor you are escorting.)

6. You are to introduce the governor's speech at the dinner.

7. You are a famous baseball (or football) player and have returned to your old high school to talk to the graduating class.

8. *This is a role-playing situation for two persons.* You are the dean of students confronting a student leader in an attempt to get help in finding out who has been responsible for recent vandalism on the campus.

9. As a famous composer you have been invited to conduct the local symphony orchestra in one of your major works. Role-play your first session with the orchestra.

10. *This is a role-playing situation for two persons.* One student plays a local attorney who has decided to run for the office of city prosecutor, and the other plays a local news broadcaster who is doing an interview for the five-o'clock news.

Discussion

A. The class should decide how accurately the portrayal of any of these roles fits the expectations of most of the class members. Discuss your ideas of how you might have played a role differently from the person who did it. Why are there some similarities? Why are there some differences?

B. Where do you get your ideas of how that role should be played? Did you feel comfortable in trying out that role? In watching others?

C. Identify some roles you play every day and determine where you got practice in them. How do you know when to change your "act"?

EXERCISE 3-3
AGREE-DISAGREE LIST ON BEHAVIORS (Discussion)

For each of the items in the table on the next page, working alone first, write an A or a D in the space below "Individual" to represent whether you mostly agree or mostly disagree with the statement. When you have completed the list, you should get together in a small group and try to reach consensus on the items. Record the group consensus on the right-hand side of the table.

Individual			Group consensus	
(A)	**(D)**		**(A)**	**(D)**
_____	_____	1. Behaviors, although only a portion of you at any one time, are still yours. They are your responsibility. You invented them, and must take the consequences of them because they belong to you.	_____	_____
_____	_____	2. Behaviors may not always be the same but may vary as your relationships vary.	_____	_____
_____	_____	3. Behaviors demonstrate habits which may encourage others to label you in ways you may think unfair or that you may not like.	_____	_____
_____	_____	4. You use your behaviors as a way to test others (i.e., patience, loyalty, love, etc.).	_____	_____
_____	_____	5. Others may judge you based on your behaviors.	_____	_____
_____	_____	6. Your behaviors are an overt expression of your intentions, real or subconscious.	_____	_____
_____	_____	7. You may change your behaviors at your will or at the will of others.	_____	_____
_____	_____	8. You can learn more about yourself if you pay attention to the feedback you get about your behaviors.	_____	_____

Discussion

A. Even if you did not entirely agree (or disagree) with each item, did you have a strong enough feeling about it so you were leaning more toward one or the other: Agree or Disagree?

B. Were you surprised when someone disagreed with your belief?

C. How did the group manage to talk out its differences? Could you reach a consensus?

D. Which items seemed to give you the most trouble in trying to reach a consensus? Why do you suppose they did?

ASSIGNMENTS:

ASSIGNMENT 3-1
ROLES YOU TAKE

List as many items as you can think of concerning what is expected of you in the role of a *student*. How did you find out what a student should be like—the role of a student? How do you find out, on the basis of the role you play, whether you are succeeding or not succeeding in that role? How do you feel about the kind of data you have to rely on to make your judgment on how you are doing?

Select another role you have (besides that of "student") and list as many items as you can which are expected of you in that role. If that role is a voluntary one, tell why you chose it. If it was thrust on you, analyze the forces which put you in that role.

ASSIGNMENT 3-2
SELF-ESTEEM AND PERSONAL FACTORS

A study at Boston University reported that your degree of happiness correlates positively with your degree of self-esteem. That study also reported that there was no evident difference in basic self-esteem between blue-collar workers and professionals—the key to higher self-esteem seemed to be how *well* you perform your work rather than what your work is. Research at the University of Massachusetts and Germany's Marburg University demonstrated that a person's self-esteem strongly affects the way that person regards how others feel about him or her. If you lack self-esteem, the study said, you consistently believe that people are putting you down, even when such slights were not intended. These items were reported in *Family Weekly* magazine along with many other items related to self-esteem. Can you find other such reports of self-concept and self-appraisal in the popular magazines or newspapers? Look for stories which cite their sources, or which quote experts with impressive credentials. Clip any such articles and be prepared to share them with the class or turn them in.

ASSIGNMENT 3-3
LITERARY REFERENCES

Find the original story of Pygmalion and Galatea on which George Bernard Shaw based his play *Pygmalion*. Read excerpts from the Shaw play, and compare them with similar parts of the successful musical *My Fair Lady*, which uses the same story. It is of particular importance to a class in communication to note that the character Professor Higgins was a teacher of phonetics who elevated a poor girl into high society primarily by making a change in linguistic patterns. "Language makes the person," this story seems to say. Does it also say that you can become what you believe you are? Discuss in class the meaning of the "Pygmalion effect" and how it relates to other behaviors you can anticipate.

ASSIGNMENT 3-4
CHANGING ROLES

Write a short essay on your own experience in trying to change a role you were cast in and decided not to follow. (A classic example with college-age people is the role in which parents tend to try to keep their "child," and the efforts a maturing student home from college is involved in to get the family to accept the new role.) Describe the role you intended to take, the former role, which may not have been as effective for you, and how you went about making the change. How successful were you in making the role change?

ASSIGNMENT 3-5
TELEVISION ROLES

Write a brief report on a television show you have seen recently, analyzing the following: (1) What behaviors did the characters show in order to make you like them, dislike them, believe in them, or oppose them? (2) Did the characters employ nonverbal as well as verbal behaviors to establish a role? (3) How do television writers help establish a character in a brief period of time?

PERSONAL IMPROVEMENT BLANK (Chapter 3)

1. Record briefly here something which you have found out about yourself in the very recent past and how it came to you. Was it as a result of getting feedback on some behavior of yours?

2. Is there something you would like to tell someone in this class about his or her behaviors which you are sure that person does not know? Without telling what it is, or telling who the person is, can you suggest some way of letting that person know this item?

3. Has your motivation in this class changed in the past few weeks since the term began? Has it become higher or lower? What could be done to improve a person's motivation to perform well in a class like this?

Your name _____

FEEDBACK BLANK

EXERCISES

ASSIGNMENTS

PERSONAL IMPROVEMENT BLANK

FEEDBACK BLANK (Chapter 4) DO NOT SIGN
1. Rate the productivity of this session's work for you.

    1   2   3   4   5   6   7   8   9   10

Not productive   Very productive

2. Rate how you think the class felt about the productivity of this session's work.

    1   2   3   4   5   6   7   8   9   10

Not productive   Very productive

Comments:

3. List those members of the class or of your group with whom communication is easy for you. Can you speculate why?

4. List those members of the class or of your group with whom you find it difficult to communicate. Why?

5. At this point, how comfortable or at ease do you feel in this class?

EXERCISES:

EXERCISE 4-1
DESCRIBE THE STYLES (Role Playing)

This is a role-playing exercise for at least two persons at a time; pick a partner with whom you can work out a believable "script" to fit the styles described in the text.

Situation   You and a friend are discussing the possibility of taking a summer vacation together. While you are very much interested in the outdoors, your friend is much more interested in historical events and would like nothing better than to go to museums, tour battlefields, and visit library collections of historical significance. Role-play the conversation you would have if your friend were to act in a consistent way in each of the following styles:

Blaming or aggressive

Placating or nonassertive

Computing or intellectual

Distracting or manipulative

Leveling or assertive

EXERCISE 4-2
LEVELING OR ASSERTIVE STYLES (Role Playing; Discussion)

This is an exercise in examining the ways in which four unhealthy styles can be replaced by a more healthy one. The text lists the following styles as categories on which to base responses to communicative incidents: (1) blaming or aggressive, (2) placating or nonassertive, (3) computing or intellectual, (4) distracting or manipulative, and (5) leveling or assertive. Of these, the last seems to be most effective.

Working in small groups, make up cases of threatening communication (which normally would result in a defensive response from the person involved) or situations in which you would normally respond defensively. Role-play in two acts. The first act should show one of the ways most people respond to such a communication—aggressive, computing, placating, or distracting. The second act should demonstrate how the leveling or assertive response might be more appropriate.

If the groups do not have time to develop skits or role-playing situations in two acts, they may simply carry on a group discussion of the various responses which would be appropriate for the situation. (One situation that might be used is a teacher telling the class that because two students are suspected of cheating on the last exam, the entire class will have to take the exam over. If that is an aggressive approach, how would a placating approach handle the same situation, or a leveling approach? In another example, a friend asks to borrow your car, although he or she has not been very careful with it in the past. How do you respond? Why? Is that the only response available to you?)

Discussion

A. When you are confronted with opportunities to react to communication situations, do you tend to react much the same way most of the time? In other words, are there patterns you have adopted which you depend on? Are they always appropriate? Do you become known as a certain kind of "responder"? Do people expect you to act a certain why? Does that in turn affect how you react? (Remember how much of your behavior is related to others' expectations of you.)

B. In the situations you worked out, were some styles of response more effective than others? Why?

C. Is it easy to work out ways in which a leveling or assertive response can replace the less desirable options? Does that response take longer? Does it involve more thought?

EXERCISE 4-3
AGREE-DISAGREE LIST ON ASSERTIVENESS (Discussion)

Working by yourself read the items and write down in the column at the left whether you agree (A) or disagree (D) with the statement as it appears. If you have reservations about any item, you should still write one or the other choice with the understanding that you may qualify it later in discussion. When you have completed all the items, you may check your choices with others in a group and discuss reasons you may differ, and share the reasons you may agree and write down the group attitude in the spaces on the right. Did any of your choices change after discussion with others? Did anyone else change to agree with yours? Do you think everyone understood the principles of assertive behavior equally well?

Working alone (A)	(D)		Working in a group (A)	(D)
____	____	1. Assertiveness is very much like aggressiveness except done in a nicer tone of voice.	____	____
____	____	2. If you let people walk all over you, you get what you deserve.	____	____
____	____	3. Women don't behave as assertively as men do.	____	____
____	____	4. Assertiveness is a personality trait, and as such cannot be changed or taught.	____	____
____	____	5. Only minority people need to be assertive in their behavior.	____	____
____	____	6. There is way too much emphasis today being put on assertiveness in books and magazines.	____	____

EXERCISE 4-4
GIVING COMPLIMENTS (Group Activity; Discussion)

Each person in class is responsible for saying something nice about some other person. They may either stay at their seats and address a compliment to anyone in the room—making sure that each person has a chance to speak and to be spoken about. Or you may organize the exercise to have pairs of students stand in front of the class and give a compliment to each other.

In either activity, do not anticipate by prior discussion any of the responses—save discussion until after all members who want to participate have had the opportunity.

When each person has taken part, the class will begin a discussion about what happened in relation to these questions (or additional ones which may surface during the discussion):

1. How did you feel having to say something nice about another person (a) if you knew the person well, or (b) did not know the person well?
2. What other factors might have made you more easy or more self-conscious about giving a compliment?
3. How did you feel when you were *receiving* a compliment from someone else?
4. Did you observe differences in the class in how some persons reacted to compliments? Consider the following items as having an *effect* on how you receive compliments: (a) not all of us receive compliments the same way, (b) who is giving the compliment has some effect as well as your receiving behaviors, (c) the situation you are in—for instance, a public display—may affect how you respond, (d) paralanguage, or tone of voice, may have an effect as well as what is being said, (e) the opportunity to reciprocate, to compliment back to the other, has some effect on how comfortable you are, and (f) what else?
5. Can you identify some giving or receiving behaviors in this exercise which you would like to adopt for your own? Be specific about what they were and who did them.

EXERCISE 4-5
WHICH COMES FIRST (Discussion)
One of the principles of "behavior modification" involves the order in which changes may occur—it is predicted that a change in behavior will precede (and maybe effect) a change in attitude.

Are you prepared to support that claim, or would you argue that a change in attitude will more likely produce a change in behavior?

A. Organize a class discussion about the issue of which comes first, basing your arguments on your own observations or those of a larger sphere (such as the attempts to legislate "equality" for minorities and how those efforts relate to changed attitudes).
B. Organize a more formal class discussion—perhaps even in a debate format—to which selected or volunteer students should bring research data or other outside sources and references as the basis of their arguments. The topics such as "behavior modification," "behavior therapy," and "change agent" may be appropriate for reference search.

ASSIGNMENTS:

ASSIGNMENT 4-1
WHICH STYLES DO YOU RECOGNIZE AROUND YOU?
For a week, watch the people around you as they interact in their normal ways. Identify (probably without using the names of the people you are observing) two or more instances of each of the five styles from the text. Note the situations in which the styles were employed, the outcome of the use of the styles, and if the styles were appropriate or not for the situations. (*Remember:* All styles can be appropriate under some conditions; all are useful in our communication for some purposes.) Make notes and be prepared to discuss them in class, or write a short paper describing the instances you noticed and your assessment of the effectiveness of each style use.

ASSIGNMENT 4-2
HOW THEY GIVE COMPLIMENTS
Observe how people on television shows give compliments, and make notes on your observations to share with the class.

1. Watch a talk show, or an interview show which has hosts or hostesses and guests. How much of the time is spent in complimenting each other or making supportive statements to or about the guest? Is that a particularly important part of the start of such a show? How does the guest react to the compliments and to this positive attention? Do these shows seem to have a predictable pattern for their interview format and dialog?
2. Watch a situation comedy to observe the way people give compliments to each other. What is the usual form of behavior when someone is complimented? "I deserved that . . ." "Aw, shucks, it wasn't nothin' . . ." "You are wonderful, too . . ." Do people in your experience adopt any of those responses for their own in receiving compliments? Why is humor an acceptable way to receive (or turn off) a compliment?

ASSIGNMENT 4-3
COMMUNICATION STYLES FROM LITERATURE
From readings you may already by familiar with, or in new readings of either classical or popular literature, can you identify characters who are represented by habitual use of one or more of the styles in this chapter (aggression, assertion, etc.)? Write a brief report on this character and identify the style used, the consequences of that habit, how that style moves the story along, and if there are any style changes by that character as the story progresses.

ASSIGNMENT 4-4
LOOKING FOR THE IFD
From your own experience can you identify one or more situations in which you or someone you know suffered from the IFD disease as described by Wendell Johnson? Write a brief description of

the person's idealization—what was it that this person wanted to have happen?—and include your own estimate of why this might have been an unrealistic ideal, or one which existed only in the verbal world. Then add what kinds of frustrations were encountered by the person. Finally trace the demoralization and its consequences. You may want to offer a corrective for this situation or one like it.

ASSIGNMENT 4-5
TELEVISION ASSERTIVENESS

After viewing some situation dramas on television, write a short essay or a few analytical paragraphs which respond to the following questions or comments about communication styles. You may pick any one of these items for the basis of your essay.

1. List some of the ways (how they behave) people are shown to be aggressive and assertive. Is there a pattern to those behaviors which are intended to show an aggressive person, or an assertive one? What does the writer have people do or say which quickly gives you an idea of the kind of person this is?
2. In order to have a character behave consistently, do his or her actions always take on the same style? In the short time a television show is on, how is it possible for you to get a clear picture of the personality traits of any one character? Are there extremes of behavior used; are there stereotypes used?
3. Which styles (aggressive, nonassertive, intellectual, manipulating, or assertive) seem to be displayed most of the time by the characters you are supposed to be most sympathetic to? Do the writers of situation dramas intend for you to identify with one or more characters most closely? What traits do they want you to be most in tune with, to empathize with? Do those represent a value in society at large, or in some selected groups?

PERSONAL IMPROVEMENT BLANK (Chapter 4)

1. Have you an identifiable style which you seem to like to use on most occasions? Describe it, and tell at least one instance of your using it effectively; then tell one instance when it was not as effective.

2. How do you generally act when you get compliments? Does it depend on such things as the source, the setting, your own sense of competence in that incident, etc?

Your name _____

CHAPTER
5

Needs, Attitudes, Beliefs, Values:
How Did I Get This Way?

FEEDBACK BLANK (Chapter 5)   DO NOT SIGN

1. Rate the productivity of this session's work for you.

      1   2   3   4   5   6   7   8   9   10

Not productive   Very productive

2. Rate how you think the rest of the class felt about this session's productivity.

      1   2   3   4   5   6   7   8   9   10

Not productive   Very productive

Comments:

3. Did you observe people who were silent in your group? How many people? Was anything done to bring them out and encourage them to participate more?

4. How useful is this feedback for you? Can it be made more useful to you? How?

5. As you work in a group, do you become comfortable with others and not want to change? How would you feel about having the same people work together in the same small groups all the time in this course?

EXERCISES:

EXERCISE 5-1
VALUES; RHETORIC; BEHAVIOR (Role Playing)

In a small group (five or six people) make up a short skit or drama to perform for the class in which you demonstrate how someone's values, rhetoric, and behavior may not all be consistent. (For example, a father may tell his son never to cheat and also boast how much he beat the Internal Revenue Service out of on his latest income tax return.) You may want to make a drama in two acts, the first setting the stage for the inconsistent behavior or statements which show up in the second act. The drama may be taken from your own experience or from some public event.

Discussion
A. Is it hard to identify the actual values people hold when they talk and act as if the values were something else?
B. Even though you can see the inconsistencies of other people, is it easy to see your own? When you act differently from how you talk or believe, is it possible to reduce the dissonance of these inconsistencies for yourselves? Can you explain them to others? What does the term "rationalization" mean in this context?
C. In your drama did the class recognize the inconsistencies easily? Did they see things you missed as you prepared the skit? Are you sufficiently familiar with incongruencies among values, rhetoric, and behavior to see them before they become fully developed? Can you, in other words, anticipate situations in which they are likely to appear? Does that help your ability to predict what other people may do or say in relation to those events? Do others also predict your behaviors?

EXERCISE 5-2
YOU'RE THE EXPERT IN MOTIVATION (Discussion)

In the following cases, a need to motivate another person is evident. If you have some means available to you for motivating the individual, how can you go about it? Do you first decide what theory of motivation may be the most applicable (Maslow, etc.) and then proceed to solve the case? What does the person *need* in order to be motivated?

Case 1   Sally has been coming to work late mornings. Because other men and women in the office depend on her to assign their work, her lateness holds up the functioning of several people. You as her supervisor have found out that Sally received a good raise just six months ago in recognition of the fact that she had been a good worker for three years in the office. You want to have her become more punctual, to arrive at least on time with the others in her section. What do you say to her? (You may want to discuss this case in a small group session or plan to role-play it with others in the class.)

Case 2   Harry is clerking in the sports department of the store where you are a personnel counselor. You have received a complaint from the billing office that recently Harry's charge slips have been made out incorrectly, causing losses of money and time for the store. Harry also was accused by a customer of "not paying any attention" when asked questions about exercise bicycles, and the head of the sports department took over when Harry simply disappeared from the floor and ignored the customer. You are talking to Harry about his performance and hope to retain him, since he's been a very productive employee for six years.

Case 3   You are a news editor on a daily afternoon paper with six reporters assigned to you. They range in age from a person nearing retirement to a very new graduate of a journalism school. All six are bright and quick to locate new sources and to write their material when given assignments. In the past few weeks, however, the oldest member of your staff has failed to find time to cover the assignments and has not produced even reasonably good stories on his own. He is near retirement but would like to continue to free-lance for other publications after he retires in eighteen months. In the meantime, he has been most valuable to you and has been helpful in training the new people. You want to maintain his efforts both for his sake and for the sake of your successful news operation.

To make matters worse, the new reporter, a bright young woman named Jill, has also suddenly become uninterested in following up assignments and has turned in very sloppy copy. Although she fit in very well when she started with the paper just over a year ago, her production has decreased so much that you are left with only four of your six regular reporters to handle all the work.

Are these problems related? In order to motivate these two different individuals you must first determine what happened to their drive and interest. What approaches do you make to motivate their renewed efforts?

Discussion

A. If you discuss these cases in small groups in class, do all groups come up with the same solutions or recommendations? Are there different ways of motivating people? Are there different circumstances which require different treatments?

B. Compare the recommendations by class members to see if some general agreement can be reached on which approaches would be most effective.

C. As you discuss these cases and your recommendations, consider how much of what you propose is based on stereotypes of how workers ought to be treated and what people are really like in the jobs described. Lacking more specific data, for example, do you fall back on a stereotypical picture of the aging reporter as perhaps drinking too much, or the young woman reporter as being put down by her colleagues? Do you sometimes make motivational decisions in real life as much on the basis of stereotypes as on the basis of obtainable data? Do you tend to put people into "typical" roles and thus treat a person as a role and not as an individual?

EXERCISE 5-3
WILL YOU FIGHT FOR IT? (Discussion)
To check the saliency of an attitude or a value (how important it is to you), work with a group of five or six people on this activity. Try to develop one or two issues which you agree would elicit each of the following reactions:

1. You would become curious about what was being said when you heard others talking about this particular topic or person or concept, and you would begin to listen more closely.

2. You would become mildly annoyed when someone spoke against this thing which you believe or hold as a value.
3. You would argue pretty strongly and might act rather upset when this topic was discussed.
4. You would become quite angry and either verbally attack the speaker or withdraw from argument when someone said something you did not like about this topic.
5. You would fight physically as well as verbally; you would come to blows over this issue or value.
6. You would risk your life, or be willing to die, for this cause.

Discussion

A. Since this was a group project, did you find difficulty agreeing on items which were equally important to all of you?
B. Which classes of items are you as a group inclined to agree on—those that elicit the most serious reactions or those that elicit the mildest reactions? Why?
C. Does this range of reactions describe most of your ways of reacting to attack on your beliefs or values? Do you hear comments about things in which you have no interest? How do you react then?
D. Are there values in society which have no interest at all for you? What would it take to get you interested?
E. How much of your reaction to these items is directly related to other people who would hold similar views? Were you affected in the group discussion by the weight of who else held those views?

EXERCISE 5-4
CONSULTANT ON RACE RELATIONS (Group Project)

You have been appointed to a national committee on race relations. Your assignment is to advise the President of the United States on how to go about reducing racial tension in all parts of the country—particularly that part closest to you and most affected by your potential influence. You meet with four or five others of the committee and prepare a report for the President which you will give to the class in oral form. Considering that you are all involved citizens, interested in having your views heard, you should develop as broad a plan as possible. As your group develops the plan to present to the class, try to reach agreement on why you are recommending certain actions and what their consequences might be. When each group has made its recommendations to the class, you can analyze the various reports to see which values or behaviors are most commonly brought up by the different groups.

Discussion

A. What values of the society do your recommendations support or attack?
B. Is there some evidence that values are not entirely represented by the rhetoric (what many people say) or by the behaviors of those directly involved with the issue of race relations? Are there unpopular things to say? Are there unpopular and even illegal things to do? How much change in values has been represented by any changes in rhetoric or behaviors?
C. As you advise the President, are you realistic about how much influence he may have on the actual implementation of your ideas? What will the message (rhetoric) be from the President when he gets your plan? What will actually be done (behaviors)?

EXERCISE 5-5
STEREOTYPING—DEVELOPMENT OF ATTITUDES (Forum)

Earlier the idea was developed that stereotypes are useful to you in your attempts to evaluate things on the basis of a few common characteristics which they share with a larger category. You react, not on the basis of what you know or feel about them individually, but mainly on the basis of what you know or feel about each category. In this way stereotypes become a shortcut to thinking, a way to react without having to work too hard to make decisions about people or events. Can you see the relationship between stereotypes and the development of attitudes? Do you depend on those basic attitudes to give you your ways of behaving? It has been said that a stereotype is a "frozen attitude."

For the class exercise, assign a group of four or six students one of the following topics to use as a basis for a panel presentation to the rest of the class. The format could be to seat the discussion group in front of the class and give each panel member a few minutes to make a statement about his or her ideas on the subject; then the discussion could be opened to the other panel members and eventually to questions from the class.

1. How is the grading system most widely used in today's schools related to stereotyping? How do you react to such statements as "She is an A student" and "He is a D student"? What do they mean? What are the consequences of such statements?
2. Think of a specific stereotype that you may have about a particular group (e.g., religious, ethnic, or political). Try to explain how the stereotype developed and how it influences your behavior toward the members of the group. Be specific in describing the effects of the stereotype on your behavior.
3. Is it possible to treat an individual as an individual regardless of classification? Defend your answer. Use examples from your experience if possible.
4. List some attitudes you have held, or still hold, which you now consider to be stereotypes. How were they formed? Why? What has made you perceive them as stereotypes?

Discussion

A. Is it hard to admit to having stereotypes? Do you avoid talking about things in which you may be accused of having biases or prejudices based on stereotypes?
B. Is it easier for you to talk about grading systems than about religious issues? Why?
C. How did the presence of the class affect your participation in the discussion with others on the panel?

ASSIGNMENTS:

ASSIGNMENT 5-1
WISE SAYINGS AND FOLKLORE

Write down as long a list as you can of sayings which comment on inconsistent behaviors or differences between speaking and acting. Some examples are "Do as I say, not as I do" and "He always talks a good fight." Another example is characterization of the states where liquor has traditionally been prohibited as "voting dry and drinking wet."

Your list should be handed in to the instructor and should include an indication of what kind of inconsistency is represented—that is, rhetoric not representing values, etc.

ASSIGNMENT 5-2
THEIR ATTITUDES AND OUR ATTITUDES

Write a description of the values and attitudes of a particular group of people you are familiar with which differs from a group you identify with or belong to.

Analyze the differences in attitudes and make some guesses about where they came from. If the other group (which believes a different way from the way you do) grew up in another part of the world or came from a different state, from a different size family, from a different ethnic background, etc., does that begin to explain something about the origins of your attitudes and beliefs? Be prepared to describe your own values and attitudes orally, comparing them with those of another group you can identify.

ASSIGNMENT 5-3
MOTIVATION IN THE NEWS

Look in the popular press or in specialized magazines or newspapers (such as *The Wall Street Journal, Nation's Business, Forbes, Money*) for articles or editorials on the subject of motivation of people either in the workplace or in other phases of their lives (including, of course, classrooms). Based on the material you find, complete any one of the assignments below:

1. Make a scrapbook of the items you find, organizing them in a way to make a point about or commentary on present trends in motivation.
2. Write an original essay on the subject of changing attitudes (in management or society in general) concerning motivation as shown in the writings you discovered.
3. Write an original essay on the subject of techniques being employed (either classic or innovative) to motivate people for some purposes, again based on what the recent writings show.

PERSONAL IMPROVEMENT BLANK (Chapter 5)

1. Have you been confronted recently with any situation in which you altered your opinion of a friend or acquaintance on the basis of what that person said about one of your personal values or beliefs? Briefly recall that example.

2. If you had a question about whether or not a casual or distant friend believed as you do about something, how would you go about finding out an answer?

3. What does the term "hypocrite" mean to you?

Your name _____

Listening: Is Anybody Out There?

FEEDBACK BLANK

EXERCISES

6-1. Listening   Role Playing
6-2. Listening Behaviors   Discussion; Group
                                                     Activity
6-3. Listening for Feelings   Role Playing

ASSIGNMENTS

6-1. Looking at Listening
6-2. Type IV Listening: Are We Changed?
6-3. What Should a Listening Course Look Like?

PERSONAL IMPROVEMENT BLANK

FEEDBACK BLANK (Chapter 6)   DO NOT SIGN
This feedback blank is designed to provide you with an opportunity to evaluate the course up to this point in the term.

1. Rate on a ten-point scale how productive this course has been for you so far.

    1   2   3   4   5   6   7   8   9   10

Unproductive   Very productive

Comments:

2. What aspects of the class have seemed of *most* value to you? Why?

3. What aspects of the class have seemed of *least* value to you? Why?

4. Have you usually felt free to participate in class? Why or why not?

5. Have you felt that the class has been interesting and challenging? Why or why not?

EXERCISES:

EXERCISE 6-1
LISTENING (Role Playing)
In a small group prepare a role-playing situation in which one actor is designated to listen to the following: (1) an elderly person, (2) a child, (3) a very attractive person of the opposite sex, and (4) a very important person.

Play the skit for the class. Use any topic of discussion for content. The content itself is less important than the interaction.

Discussion
A. Was there a distinct difference in listening with the different speakers? Were there similarities?
B. What generalization can you draw from the way most groups presented their actors in these settings?
C. How would you feel about the "listener" if you were each of the various persons doing the talking? Can you put yourself in the place of that speaker when you are such a listener?
D. What techniques did the listener use to indicate the degree of listening which was going on? Were the techniques discernible to the speaker? Did the speaker adjust to take those signals into account?
E. In the acts as presented, was there an emphasis on both verbal and nonverbal behaviors? Which seemed most effective in giving information to the other person? To the class? Are there nearly universal behaviors in listening?

EXERCISE 6-2
LISTENING BEHAVIORS (Discussion; Group Activity)
The exercise of repeating what the other person said before you can make your own statement is a technique developed by Dr. Carl Rogers and has produced many an hour of frustration for the participants. It is not easy to repeat statements others make, even when you put them in your own words. When group members make long speeches, it becomes nearly impossible to synthesize the speech and its meaning. You are really not accustomed to repeating the statements of others, and for that reason a referee is suggested to help remind you that the rules of the game call for getting approval of a repeated statement before you can make your own contribution to the discussion.

Instructions to Participants
Your task consists of discussing any one of the topics for discussion listed below. However, you must follow these rules:

1. Each group member must first summarize, *in his or her own words* and without notes, what the member who spoke just previously has said and must do it to that member's satisfaction.
2. If the summary is felt to be incorrect or incomplete by anyone in the group, the referee will help clear up any misunderstanding.
3. When someone else summarizes what you have said, do not be too easily satisfied just for the sake of moving the discussion along.

Instructions to Referees

1. Read the instructions to participants and find out what topic your group will discuss.
2. Your job is to make sure that members stick to the rules throughout their discussion. They cannot speak unless they have summarized what the previous speaker has said to that speaker's satisfaction.
3. If you think that the summary is incorrect or incomplete, you must interrupt and help clear up the misunderstanding.

Topics for Discussion

Group A

Sports programs are of great value to a college.

Group B

Premarital sex relations—acceptable or not?

Group C

Grades should be totally eliminated in college. Why or why not? What other alternatives do we have to evaluate students' work?

Discussion

A. How easy was it to stick to the rules and repeat everything before starting your own statements?
B. Did it get others upset? How did they show it?
C. Was there a tendency for participants to learn to make shorter speeches and to become more clear in their statements?
D. What other changes did you notice in the way people talked in this situation compared with the normal kind of give-and-take conversations? Does that say anything about whether or not we are really listening to each other in the "normal" situations?
E. Are there any features of this exercise which you might want to adopt for your own behaviors? Would you like to tell some special others about doing this exercise? Are you interested in reforming their listening habits? What about their wanting to reform yours?

EXERCISE 6-3
LISTENING FOR FEELINGS (Role Playing)

In Chapter 3, the topic of "confirming" behavior is related to what you do in your listening. When you do not listen to others, you do not hear their words; you also—and this is very important—tell them something of your attitude about them as persons. Role-play the following situations in which you make up dialog and action to suit what you think would happen. Concentrate as you do this on the effect your listening behavior would have on the feelings the other persons might have about themselves, about you, and about how you value each other as persons—not only on how you hear the words spoken.

Situation   Three people are discussing a movie. Select a movie which all members of the group have seen. One person should attempt to fill in the plot, cast of characters, etc., while another listens and helps. The third person should pay no attention to the "data" or information being presented but should only watch for errors in grammar, vocalized pauses, mispronunciations, or other personal slips by the speakers—including just plain ignoring the topic, mentioning people passing by, or relating other events outside the topic of the movie. (At the end of the role playing, ask the class and members of the group to react to how they feel about the "disconfirmer." What should have been done to make a more effective communication situation?)

Situation   A family is having dinner—two parents, three children. All the children attend school. The youngest wants to tell about something that happened today. None of the others pay attention but instead interrupt to have food passed or to laugh at a joke they heard on television, somehow managing to keep the speaker from ever getting reinforcement to tell the story.

Situation   A planning group in class is getting ready to speak on an assigned topic. One member continually makes suggestions which "plop" or never get acknowledged by the others. Later, when another member suggests the same thing, it may get picked up. Indicate in the role playing how silence toward a participant can make such a person give up membership in the group. Listening can be a supportive activity on a personal level, or it can be a device to extinguish another person in a group.

Situation   A lecturer in front of an audience is met by a variety of listening behaviors. Role-play the kinds of listening which can take place and make use of "alter egos" (or persons speaking for the actors as if they were speaking their thoughts) to show what is happening in the listener and how that shows up in overt behavior.

Discussion
A. Use the situations above to develop some understanding of how listening behaviors affect others.
B. People too often think that the only time they are really letting others know much about them is when they talk. After these exercises, do you have a better understanding of how you affect people even when you are in the supposedly passive role of listener? Are you aware of the extent of this influence?

ASSIGNMENTS:

ASSIGNMENT 6-1
LOOKING AT LISTENING

1. Are there special times when you pay more attention to your listening than others? Has anything happened recently which made you aware of your own listening habits or the habits of others. As if you were making a diary entry, recount an incident in which you observed either very good or very bad listening behavior in yourself or others.

2. Write down the names of several people you know well and have quite frequent interaction with. After each name put down the kind of listening they usually do—appropriate, effective, sensitive, or other modifiers. Are they all alike? What features do they seem to have in common? How are they different? How does that affect your interest in conversing with them? Share your list (perhaps by disguising the names) with the class.

3. Based on your estimates of listening abilities and habitual behaviors among your friends, fill in the blanks below:

My Two Best Listeners   **Their Good Habits**

1. _____   _____

                                      _____

2. _____   _____

                                      _____

My Two Worst Listeners   **Their Bad Habits**

1. _____   _____

                                      _____

2. _____   _____

                                      _____

ASSIGNMENT 6-2
TYPE IV LISTENING: ARE WE CHANGED?

From any source you want to use (personal experience, literature, popular myths, family activities, movies, television, etc.) find an example where someone was changed by listening. It may be a persuasive communication situation, or a conversion from one kind of attitude to another, or some action induced or prevented. Write in a few paragraphs your own evaluation of what factors were involved which made a change important to someone, how the change was directly related to someone's listening with real introspection, and what outcomes were prevented or altered by the listening behaviors.

Oater Example   In the classic early western movie the lynch mob, carrying guns and torches (since this always happened at night), headed for the jail to break out the prisoner and hang him. Sworn to uphold law and order, the sheriff had to stand alone, facing this angry, bloodthirsty mob. One gun against their many. As the citizens snarled at him and told him to get out of the way or get killed, the sheriff had to convince them, without getting himself shot, to disperse. What happens in this case if the mob does not listen? But somebody always yells for the rest to pay attention, and the sheriff by rhetoric more than by his handy sawed-off double-barreled shotgun gets the mob to go home. A clear and corny case of complete conversion by the forces of introspective listening.

ASSIGNMENT 6-3
WHAT SHOULD A LISTENING COURSE LOOK LIKE?

Many people have suggested that a regular course in listening be introduced into the educational process. At the present time this seems to be primarily taught to people on the job, long after they have finished their formal schooling. Based on the idea that somewhere in the curriculum from kindergarten through college there ought to be a course in listening, write a proposal based on one of the following scenarios.

Include answers to these questions at a minimum: What would you include as content or basic material in such a program? How should the course be set up as in frequency of meetings, credit, teacher certification or experience, etc.? What techniques or system for teaching it would you recommend?

1. A listening course should be included in the early grades of school so the students can have the advantage of good listening habits for most of their educational lives.
2. High school is the best time for a listening course since the students already have developed other communication skills and are ready to sharpen their listening. (Additional option: It should be combined with speaking as an oral communication requirement.)
3. College is the appropriate time to teach listening since the curriculum is already so open for new developments. Among the skills to be given the incoming first-year students, listening should be a primary consideration.

PERSONAL IMPROVEMENT BLANK (Chapter 6)

1. Find a person who has had a course in listening—either as part of a curriculum or in business—and ask that person:

    a. What the course consisted of

    b. What the person thought it accomplished

2. Write below an example of a poor listening behavior you observed recently and how it affected you or some other person.

Your name _____

FEEDBACK BLANK

EXERCISES

ASSIGNMENTS

PERSONAL IMPROVEMENT BLANK

FEEDBACK BLANK (Chapter 7)   DO NOT SIGN
1. Rate the productivity of this session's work for you.
       1   2   3   4   5   6   7   8   9   10
    Not productive   Very productive

2. Rate how you think the rest of the class felt about the productivity of this session's work.
       1   2   3   4   5   6   7   8   9   10
    Not productive   Very productive

    Comments:

3. Did anything you remember interfere with good communication in your group? Was there anything which held back understanding or prevented your working with each other effectively?

4. Did you observe anyone in your group who was silent (or nearly so)?

5. Can you give any examples of communication difficulties created by different use of the same words by different group members?

EXERCISES:

EXERCISE 7-1
KEEPING A LANGUAGE PURE—ADD SPANGLISH TO FRANGLAIS
(Discussion)

Most people are familiar with the historical efforts of the French to keep their language pure through the efforts of the French Academy fighting against what has become known as "Franglais," a combination of French and English. Every year about fifteen government ministries in France publish a list of foreign (mostly English) words that are then banned from use in official communications—supplying an acceptable French equivalent to the banned English terms. Now a private group called "Agulf," an acronym for the General Association for the Users of the French Language, has begun to sue those companies which use the forbidden terms in advertising, a practice which is banned by a 1975 French law. Agulf forced Trans World Airlines to pay a $500 fine for distributing boarding passes in English at Charles de Gaulle Airport; it brought the bottled water company Evian to court for calling a new product "le fast drink des Alpes." A furniture maker was accused by Agulf of using forbidden language when he advertised a "showroom" of furniture instead of a "salle d'exposition." He sued back and won against Agulf, but their efforts continue.

Less well known is the North American Academy of the Spanish Language which claims that "Spanglish," the combination of Spanish and English, does not exist. They say there are merely people who speak both languages badly. The academy is one of twenty-two in the world and the latest since King Philip V established the Royal Spanish Academy in 1713 to "cultivate and to set standards for the purity and elegance of the Castilian tongue." The academy objects to such expressions as "vacunar la carpeta," which to Hispanic New Yorkers would mean to vacuum the carpet, but to many Latin Americans using a standard dictionary would mean "to vaccinate the portfolio." When there are current and clearly defined words already available in Spanish, the academy suggests that they be used instead of borrowing English terms.

A study by a professor of marketing at Texas Tech University found a number of embarrassing translations when English-oriented companies advertised their products or services in Spanish. A beer company used the term *sueltese,* intending to say "turn it loose," and found out that Spanish-speaking consumers would read the message "Our beer causes diarrhea." A pet food manufacturer tried to be humorous by showing a cat which had died eight times and, if it did not have this advertised pet food, would surely die for its ninth and final time; no problem with the language, but what the ad agency did not realize is that in Latin folk culture, the felines have only seven lives, and so the ad was nonsense.

A chicken company had its sales slogan translated literally, and it went from the English version, "It takes a tough man to make a tender chicken," to the Spanish interpretation, "It takes a sexually excited man to make a chick sensual." A cigarette advertiser claimed its smoke had "less asphalt" instead of less tar. Car manufacturers have found out that they cannot simply transfer the names of their cars to Spanish, as the Chevrolet "Nova" becomes *no va,* or "it doesn't go."

Discussion

A. Why should a nation want to preserve the language in its historical form? Does a language remain static over time, or does it change as new ideas and products come into public attention?

B. Is American English a pure form, or is it a combination of many different languages? Which languages seem to have been some of the strongest influences on English?

C. If you were in charge of an advertising campaign in France or in a Spanish-speaking nation, what steps would you take to make sure the language used in your messages was appropriate? Is the Spanish of Spain the same as the Spanish of Mexico or Puerto Rico, or does one language have influences the other does not?

D. Can you find or recall other instances of messages suffering when translated into another language?

EXERCISE 7-2
WHAT'S IN A NAME: LITERARY DIVISION (Discussion)

The following quotation, taken from a play by Shakespeare, represents a common situation in literature. The names of families or of countries take on such a symbolic importance that enemies spend their lives in vengeful conflict. In a small group (five to seven members), analyze the dramatic impact of this situation. What happens later in the play as a result of the family names? Make a list of three or four such situations in literature. Then make a list of three or four such situations in real life which you know about. Select a few of the most dramatic ones to share with the class during a general discussion.

Juliet, of the Capulet family, addresses Romeo:

'Tis but thy name that is my enemy.
Thou art thyself though, not a Montague.
What's Montague? It is nor hand, nor foot,
Nor arm, nor face, nor any other part
Belonging to a man. Oh, be some other name!
What's in a name? That which we call a rose
By any other name would smell as sweet;
So Romeo would, were he not Romeo call'd,
Retain that dear perfection which he owes
Without that title.

Discussion

A. Although many word-oriented prejudices may not result in death to the major characters, they make life miserable for those involved. Of the examples given by the groups, are any of life-and-death significance? Are any of the examples more subtle or more low-key?

B. Why does a story like the tragedy of Romeo and Juliet appeal to so many different periods of history and types of people? (Was *West Side Story* a simple remake of *Romeo and Juliet*?) Do you all understand how people can be so hooked on symbols that they do not act rationally?

EXERCISE 7-3
WHAT'S IN A NAME: FINANCIAL DIVISION (Discussion)

When Humble Oil changed its name to Exxon, the company had to consider not only the 26,000 service stations with about 50 printed items each but also files, forms, tankers, oil-well signs, and billing forms. More than 300 million pieces of printed material had to be changed. The company felt that the expense was justified by the impact the new name would have on the competitive market.

A small college in Columbia, Missouri, changed its name from Christian College to Columbia College because it felt that the very restrictive connotation of the name "Christian" was a deterrent to some students and donors and that the new name indicated a more academic tone. A few years before that change, the college advertised in national newspapers that it would be renamed after anyone who donated $5 million to it. There were no takers, however.

Before being absorbed by the University of Denver, an institution that had been known as Colorado Women's College was given the legal title to an estimated $25 million shopping center by a man named Temple Buell. The trustees renamed the college Temple Buell College as a condition of the gift. Not many years later, the name was changed back again, and the title to the gift was returned so that the college would be free to make other major fund-raising efforts.

Discussion

A. What makes names so important that companies will spend millions of dollars to change them? Are they recognizable to an intended audience? Are they a "property" that the company needs to own? What things make names important?

B. Would you change your name? For what reasons? Every year, a large number of people (besides women who get married) change their names legally. How does a change of name change the person? What does your name tell others about you? Should women change their names when they marry?

C. Have all the members of the class say their names at once and then have each person say his or her name individually. Then ask whether the class members formed a different impression of others because of the way they said their own names.

EXERCISE 7-4
WHAT RULES SHOULD YOU FOLLOW IN SPEAKING? (Role Playing)

An official of the Airways Facilities Sector (AFS) in southern Texas sent a letter to all employees saying: "It has come to my attention that a language other than English is being used during official duty hours. This language has been used in the presence of persons or officials who speak only English, and this practice has caused some concern and misunderstanding among those who do not understand the language."

Some employees complained to the Federal Aviation Administration about the letter, and that agency promised an investigation to make sure there were no infringements on anybody's right to speak to others during informal conversations or while not engaged in official activities.

Discussion

A. Have a group in the class discuss the kinds of situations in which such a letter might have become necessary. Did the AFS official have a responsibility to write this kind of letter to all employees? What started this chain of events, which ended up with an official writing a letter? Who complained in the first place? Was that complaint reasonable?

B. Have a group in the class discuss the reactions that the employees who spoke "a language other than English" might have had when they received this letter. Why did the official letter not refer to the language by name? Are there different reactions to the names for the Spanish language in that region—names like Mexican, Tex-Mex, or Chicano? Does the letter imply a patronizing attitude toward those who speak another language?

C. Role-play situations in which speaking a different language would be upsetting to those around you who did not understand it. You might want to role-play the situation just described, or select another situation in which official business is being conducted, and there is also informal conversation going on among employees.

EXERCISE 7-5
OVERHEARD ON A BUS (Discussion)
On a bus in Hawaii, a woman of Oriental extraction made this remark when she was pushed aside by another woman for a seat.

"You high fo lookin Potagee hoa, you no fit be on bus. You push folk roun an you git trouble. Think you big cuz hapa haole."

The other woman replied in a nasty tone: "You pau now Pakay bag, or do I send you head up puka in roof?"

Discussion
A. Although Hawaii is supposed to be a melting pot and a symbol of the ability of diverse groups to mingle with ease and lack of prejudice, there are times when cultural and racial differences seem to cause friction. A common language is spoken, which a Mainlander would find difficult to follow. Can you interpret the exchange above, which contains some Hawaiian words and some words that are spelled as they might sound to a listener?

B. Would you expect either speaker to use another language with her own family or friends that would be different from this pidgin English?

C. Is this a substandard language? Is it a dialect? Do you think both women managed to convey their emotions to each other and exchange a message? Would you be likely to use this language (or dialect) at the university when analyzing literature or chemical compounds? Would students use it in the coffee shop? Would roommates use it?

EXERCISE 7-6
LEGISLATING LANGUAGE (Discussion)
For nearly 150 years the Belgian government has disagreed over the problem of which language is to be spoken in which parts of the country. Belgium was founded in 1830 and has debated ever since that time whether its citizens should speak French, Flemish, or German dialects. Both French and Flemish are spoken in Brussels, the capital. In mid-1972 the government was forced to resign over an issue involving some 6,000 farmers in eastern Belgium living in six villages where residents speak a mixture of French, Flemish, and Walloon, but seem to prefer French. The Flemish-speaking parliament members, however, say that these villagers have been assigned the Flemish language. This debate has been going on for many years, as one government after another has tried to make an acceptable linguistic decision.

Discussion

A. How would you feel if a government said you had to stop speaking the language you grew up with and adopt another one? Has that happened with Native Americans in reservation schools? With Chicano children in the southwest? With ghetto black children?

B. What are the arguments, do you think, for imposing a language on one section of a country? Is there an "official" language in the United States? Is it possible for a nation (or a state or a district) to have one written language and several spoken ones?

C. Why do people feel strongly about their language? Is it more than just sounds or squiggles on paper? Does it represent a culture? A way of looking at the world? A familiar force binding people together?

ASSIGNMENTS:

ASSIGNMENT 7-1
WORDS AND WHAT THEY DO TO YOU

If a word were to be written on the chalkboard in your class, do you think you would have any reaction to it? Are words neutral? Are they without power to make us feel some kind of emotion? Write in the blanks below the words that would make you react in each way described, and turn your answers in to the instructor.

What is the most beautiful word you know? _____

What is the softest or gentlest word? _____

What is the ugliest word? _____

What is the most frightening? _____

What is the harshest or sharpest? _____

What word makes you feel lonely? _____

What word makes you feel angry? _____

What is the most overused or trite word? _____

What word makes you happiest? _____

ASSIGNMENT 7-2
DEFINITION

1. Scientists use the concept of "operational definitions" in their work. What is the difference between an operational definition and a dictionary definition?
2. Make up a list of words and see if you can find operational definitions and dictionary definitions for each. How do the definitions differ? What types of words have the greatest differences in definitions?
3. Try writing an operational definition for some nonsense word. Then, try to use the word in its various forms in sentences. Make a variety of sentences.
4. In class try out your different definitions orally on other students. Is it harder to define a word by writing it or by speaking the definition?

PERSONAL IMPROVEMENT BLANK (Chapter 7)

1. Can you think about things for which there are no words? Give examples of something you can think about for which there are no words.

2. Different words mean different things to different people. Give an example of a word which would have very different meaning to someone else from what it means to you.

3. Do you think you speak a dialect? Do you consider your speech "standard" or "nonstandard"?

Your name _____

FEEDBACK BLANK

EXERCISES

ASSIGNMENTS

PERSONAL IMPROVEMENT BLANK

FEEDBACK BLANK (Chapter 8) DO NOT SIGN

1. Rate on a ten-point scale how productive this session was for you.

    1   2   3   4   5   6   7   8   9   10

Unproductive   Productive

Comments:

2. What did you learn about your own use of language that will be helpful to you in communicating with others?

3. Did you learn anything about how people may abuse the language in ways they may not even be aware of? Examples?

4. How do you feel when others use polluted language on you?

EXERCISES:

EXERCISE 8-1
LANGUAGE POLLUTION (Discussion; Reporting)

The historic words of some admirals have come down to us as famous sayings. Following the invasion of the island of Grenada in October of 1983, Admiral Wesley L. McDonald told the Pentagon, "We were not micromanaging Grenada intelligencewise until about that time frame." Bruce L. Felkner, director of yearbooks for *Encyclopaedia Britannica,* suggested that statements by earlier admirals could be translated into this form of language pollution, which has also been made famous by a former secretary of state, Alexander Haig:

John Paul Jones said, "I have not yet begun to fight." A polluted translation might be: "Combatwise, the time frame is upcoming."

Oliver Hazard Perry said, "We have met the enemy and they are ours." Today it could be: "Area accessed in combat mode; mission finished."

David Farragut said, "Damn the torpedoes. Go (full speed) ahead." This could be translated as: "Disregard anticipated structural damage. Continue as programmed."

George Dewey ordered: "You may fire when ready, Gridley." Today he might order his gunnery officer: "Implementation of aggressive action approved; time frame to be selected by fire control officer."

Either individually or in a small group, recall some famous statements of history similar to the ones attributed to great naval heroes. Then rephrase them into polluted form or into political gobbledygook. (An example might be to take Horace Greeley's statement "Go West, young man" and distort it. Recall an advertising slogan you heard on television or read in the paper and see how it can be changed.) After you have made your list of a few expressions, either recite them to the class or put them on the board and ask other class members to identify the original quotation.

EXERCISE 8-2
IRREGULAR CONJUGATION—THE CONJUGATION OF ADJECTIVES (Group Project)

Bertrand Russell, on a British Broadcasting Company radio program called *Brain Trust,* gave the following "conjugation of adjectives."

I am firm.

You are obstinate.

He is pig-headed.

The *New Statesman and Nation,* quoting the above as a model, offered prizes to readers who sent in the best conjugated adjectives of this kind. Here are some of the published entries:

I am sparkling. You are unusually attractive. He is drunk.

I am righteously indignant. You are annoyed. He is making a fuss about nothing.

I am fastidious. You are fussy. He is an old woman.

I am a creative writer. You have a journalistic flair. He is a prosperous hack.

I am beautiful. You have quite good features. She is not bad-looking, if you like that type.

I daydream. You are an escapist. He ought to see a psychiatrist.

I have about me something of the subtle, haunting, mysterious fragrance of the Orient. You rather overdo it, dear. She stinks.

In a small group complete the following statements or make up some of your own to share with the rest of the class.

I am stocky.   _____   _____

I am slender.   _____   _____

I love music.   _____   _____

I don't believe in excessive savings.   _____   _____

I believe in the new morality.   _____   _____

I am imaginative.   _____   _____

I need plenty of sleep.   _____   _____

I believe that honesty is the best policy.   _____   _____

I am a casual housekeeper.   _____   _____

Discussion

A. What does this exercise reveal about the way you talk about yourselves as compared with how you talk about others? You would like your own behaviors and attitudes to be considered positive while those same characteristics in others might be questionable.

B. When speaking to another person, is it easier to be charitable than when you are speaking about a third party or an absent person? Face-to-face conversation is likely to make your evaluations less critical than if you are speaking about someone not present.

C. When you use the word "is" to describe someone, does that speak about behaviors or about some static condition or invariable quality? Does the static verb "to be" in all its forms limit your views of other people and their characters? Do you settle for one or a few characteristics when you use "is," and put blinders on your relationship by pretending you have adequately described another person?

D. Would a conjugation of verbs (describing actions rather than permanent and owned qualities) or even of adverbs be a more true-to-fact assessment of your friends and acquaintances?

EXERCISE 8-3
WHO SPEAKS ANOTHER LANGUAGE? (Goldfish Bowl; Forum)

Besides the variety of dialects in the United States, many people here are bilingual—that is, speak some foreign language as well as English. As your own experience will tell you if you have studied a foreign language, there are word traps which can catch you in some humorous, serious, or embarrassing incidents. Most travelers to a foreign country who have trouble with the native language will report such incidents. Even those who apparently speak the "same" language such as people in England and the United States may have trouble with those many examples of unfamiliar words such as "lift" for "elevator," or "lorry" for "truck".

In your class find out whether there are students whose native language is not English. If there are no naturally bilingual students, call on those students who are studying a foreign language or who have had a recent experience in a culture where a foreign language is spoken. Develop a goldfish bowl setting in which the bilingual students are in the center. They are to respond to questions from other students in a circle around them. Students in the center should be ready to compare experiences and reactions to reinforce the items of discussion.

Discussion

A. Begin the discussions by asking the foreign-speaking students to cite some example of language problems caused by mistaken meanings. (This may be especially true of slang or modernisms.)

B. Are there basic differences in cultures based on language use which can be identified by the foreign-language speakers? How does the native speaker of an Eastern language such as Chinese or Japanese address different members of the family? How does the speaker of French know when to use *tu* and when *vous* in addressing other people? Are there rules which you never break, or have you developed some exceptions to them? How does the speaker of Spanish explain to the English-speaking person that there are two forms of "to be" in Spanish whereas there is only one form in English? Can these two forms be explained in terms of different states of existence, permanent and temporary? Is that complicated for the English-speaking person to understand and difficult to adopt automatically? Do all these different ways of using language have an effect on how people think in those languages?

C. Do the students in the center of the goldfish bowl have any feelings about their language differences? Do students who speak only English have any feelings about speaking another language?

D. Is learning to speak another language simply a matter of finding a direct translation of one word for another? Are there different grammatical or logical constructions which must also be learned? What does this say about computer-generated translations?

E. Ask the bilingual students what their most difficult task was in learning English. What characteristics did they notice about those who speak English which may not be noticeable to those persons themselves? What was easiest about learning English? What characteristics of speakers of English made it rewarding to learn the language?

EXERCISE 8-4
WILL YOUR MOTHER UNDERSTAND YOU? (Group Task)

The University of Iowa chapter of the Society of Sigma Xi adopted a program to encourage graduate students doing research to make their reporting of their work more understandable. They offered cash awards and established a series of public research lectures that would enable students to present their findings. The following criterion for basic clarity was suggested: "If you can't explain your research to your mother, you may not understand it yourself." The advantage of being able to explain research at that level was, according to the chapter, that it would help bridge the understanding gap between the scientific world and the general public on matters which really have some relationship to the public.

Discussion

A. Have you ever tried to explain to your parents just what it is you are studying in one of your courses? Have you ever tried to explain snow skiing to a native of Florida who may never have seen snow, or to tell a child how to tell time, or to describe to a friend who knows nothing about a computer what a floppy disk does?

B. Form a group and work out among you a subject which you know about and you are sure most of the others in the class do not—this might be (1) what the principle of AM stereo is, (2) how to sail a small boat, (3) how to keep statistics at a football game, (4) how to drive from the campus to an out-of-the-way restaurant, (5) what the differences are among snow, sleet, hail, and rain, (6) how tennis is scored, (7) how *jai alai* is played, (8) how to test the acid level in a swimming pool, or (9) how to train a hunting dog. As you consider what you want to tell others, do you have to know something about how much information they already have? Do you need to know what words will make sense to them and what words may not? What order would you use in describing?

C. After you have worked out a presentation, try it out on the class or on another group. Make a note of the language problems and try to figure out why they occurred.

EXERCISE 8-5
THE UNCRITICAL INFERENCE TEST[1] (Game)

Instructions

This test is designed to determine your ability to think *accurately* and *carefully*. Since it is very probable that you have never taken *this type* of test before, failure to read the instructions *extremely carefully* may lower your score.

1. You will read a brief story. Assume that all the information presented in the story is definitely *accurate and true*. Read the story carefully. You may refer back to the story whenever you wish.
2. You will then read statements about the story. Answer them in numerical order. *Do not go back* to fill in answers or change answers. This will only distort your test score.
3. After you read each statement carefully, determine whether the statement is:
   a. T—On the basis of the information presented in the story, the statement is *definitely true*.
   b. F—On the basis of the information presented in the story, the statement is *definitely false*.
   c. ?—The statement may be true or false, but on the basis of the information presented in the story you cannot be certain. If any part of a statement is doubtful, mark the statement "?".
   d. Indicate your answer by circling either T, F, or ? opposite the statement.

[1] Reproduced by permission from W. Haney, *Communication and Organizational Behavior,* rev. ed., Richard D. Irwin, Homewood, IL, 1967, pp. 185–186.

Sample Test—The Story

The only car parked in front of 619 Oak Street is a black one. The words "James M. Curley, M.D." are spelled in small gold letters across the front left door of that car.

Sample Test—Statements about the Story

1. The color of the car in front of 619 Oak Street is black.   (T) F ?
2. There is no lettering on the left front door of the car parked in front of 619 Oak Street.   T F ?
3. Someone is ill at 619 Oak Street.   T F (?)
4. The black car parked in front of 619 Oak Street belongs to James M. Curley.   T F (?)

Remember Answer *only* on the basis of the information presented in the story. Refrain from answering as you think it *might* have happened. Answer each statement in numerical order. Do not go back to fill in or change answers.

The Story

A businessman had just turned off the lights in the store when a man appeared and demanded money. The owner opened the cash register. The contents of the cash register were scooped up, and the man sped away. A member of the police force was notified promptly.

Statements about the Story

1. A man appeared after the owner had turned off his store lights.   T F ?
2. The robber was a man.   T F ?
3. The man who appeared did not demand money.   T F ?
4. The man who opened the cash register was the owner.   T F ?
5. The store owner scooped up the contents of the cash register and ran away.   T F ?
6. Someone opened a cash register.   T F ?
7. After the man who demanded money scooped up the contents of the cash register, he ran away.   T F ?
8. While the cash register contained money, the story does not state how much.   T F ?
9. The robber demanded money of the owner.   T F ?
10. The robber opened the cash register.   T F ?
11. After the store lights were turned off, a man appeared.   T F ?
12. The robber did not take the money with him.   T F ?
13. The robber did not demand money of the owner.   T F ?
14. The owner opened the cash register.   T F ?
15. The age of the store owner was not revealed in the story.   T F ?
16. Taking the contents of the cash register with him, the man ran out of the store.   T F ?
17. The story concerns a series of events in which only three persons are referred to: the owner of the store, a man who demanded money, and a member of the police force.   T F ?

18. The following events were included in the story:
someone demanded money, a cash register was opened, its contents were
scooped up, and a man dashed out of the store.   T F ?

Discussion

A. Be prepared to inspect your own stereotypes, assumptions, and inferences as they relate to the way you answered the questions.
B. Do you argue harder for your own answers when you have "declared" your stand?
C. Is this only a "tricky" kind of situation where you are asked to make definite statements about an event, or does something like this happen in your daily lives? Compare this example with the one in the text about whether or not the post office is open.

EXERCISE 8-6
WHAT'S HER NAME? (Game)
Try to untangle the following riddle:

A man went for a walk one day and met a friend whom he had not seen, heard from, or heard of in ten years. After an exchange of greetings, the man said, "Is this your little girl?" and the friend replied, "Yes, I got married about six years ago."

The man then asked the child, "What is your name?" and the little girl replied, "Same as my mommy's."

"Oh," said the man, "then it must be Margaret."

If the man did not know whom his friend had married, how could he know the child's name?

Discussion

A. There are many riddles like this one which are simply based on some assumption or inference which continually leads the respondent down blind alleys in an attempt to solve them. Do you have a favorite riddle which depends on inferences falsely applied for its success? [*Example:* The child's riddle "What's black and white and re(a)d all over?" depends on the hearer's mistaking the word "read," past tense of "read," for the word "red." Most riddles are better spoken than printed. The old answer to that riddle used to be "a newspaper" but the more sophisticated child now expects the answer "an embarrassed zebra."]
B. Are you more successful in solving this riddle by being able to talk with others—such as in a group project—than by working alone? Why?
C. Can you make a case for childhood riddles being an effective force in helping the child become conscious of wrongly applied inferences, thus suggesting a survival value in developing linguistic acculturation? Or are riddles just so much childish fun?

ASSIGNMENTS:

ASSIGNMENT 8-1
CREATING APHORISMS
Witty and quotable statements, called "aphorisms," are possible for anyone to create. At the University of Iowa, Professor David Hamilton has been, for the past several years, assigning the writing of aphorisms to his students. These make use of twists of meaning, language imagery, turns of definitions and meaning, vivid and brief statements, plays on words, and other games related to our language. See if you can create some aphorisms (or epigrams) of your own, being conscious of what linguistic tricks are being played in each and what purpose each is to serve—to amuse, inspire, instruct, etc. Below are some samples created by Professor Hamilton's students:

Taste makes waist. (*Play on words—pun*)

I think, therefore I must be around here somewhere. (*Satire*)

When you row the other fellow across the stream, you get there yourself. (*Inspiration*)

Put your money in taxes; they'll surely go up. (*Amusement*)

You've got to kiss a lot of frogs before you find your prince. (*Humorous advice*)

Nothing in the world is so powerful as a terrorism whose time has come; all ideas melt in its presence— even its own. (*Philosophical commentary*)

ASSIGNMENT 8-2
WORDS TO CONCEAL MORE THAN THEY TELL
In many of our interactions with others we use words as much to avoid giving information as to actually tell others something. Words which conceal more than they tell are used when we don't know how to answer, or when we actually intend to misinform, or when an answer at that moment would not be to our best advantage. Make a list of words which tend to be used by people who want to conceal something—find special words for each of the following situations (a few samples will help you develop your own list).

Family Situations

"Soon" as an answer to "When can we go?"

"Early" as an answer to "When are you coming home?"

"We'll see—" as an answer to "Can we have a dog?"

Buying or Selling

"To be perfectly honest . . ."—and you suspect that person is not.

"By the way. . ."—and you know here comes the hook. "Tell you what I'm going to do for you . . ." Look out; here comes the hook again.

In the Office

"Incidentally. . ." The request that follows will not be a very incidental one.

"Frankly. . ." Here comes bad news.

"It's up to you . . ." Not really; it's more of a command.

In the Classroom

"That's a good question."—And I haven't got a good answer ready just yet.

"Research has shown . . ." The items listed are all borrowed from . . .

ASSIGNMENT 8-3
TOO MUCH HONESTY MAY NOT BE GOOD FOR US

In the columns devoted to giving advice to people about how to handle their affairs with others, Dr. Joyce Brothers suggested the following solution to a person's problem of being too honest.

A person wrote to Dr. Brothers recounting that a friend had walked out of that person's office saying "I don't know why you have to be so honest," evidently hurt by something that was said. The writer then went on to say that, being an honest person, it seemed important always to give honest answers or statements and others respect that.

Advice given by Dr. Brothers suggested that although people may ask for honesty, they don't necessarily want to hear the whole truth, and often people who insist on telling the truth can be abrasive and sometimes needlessly cruel. She also suggested that it may be a sign of smugness to boast about how honest you always are, and that giving an opinion should be understood to be just that—opinion—by both the speaker and hearer. Also, she added, it seems that many people prefer sensitivity and tact to total honesty.

Discussion

A. How do you feel about being absolutely honest with others in all things? Are there ever any occasions when you might be less than 100 percent truthful about something with someone? Make a list of the kinds of situations in which you consider it appropriate to not be absolutely honest, but to engage in equivocation or "strategic ambiguity."

B. If there has been an emphasis in the past fifteen years on openness and honesty—taking off our masks and being clearly expressive to others about our feelings and ideas—is that a useful way to be? Where do you think the emphasis on "being open" comes from? Can you write a short paragraph either for or against that behavior?

C. Can you determine which people you are close to who will respect you more if you are absolutely honest? Are there people close to you who would not feel so strongly about your insisting on absolute honesty in all interactions? List those who expect you to be honest all the time in everything, and in another column list those among your acquaintances and friends who would not be so critical if you were not always absolutely honest.

PERSONAL IMPROVEMENT BLANK (Chapter 8)

1. In a recent news story about a political candidate or a member of the government, can you find any examples of language pollution which represent these levels of polluted meaning:

   a. Confusion

   b. Ambiguity

   c. Deception

2. As you observe the language of people around you, do you find that some of your friends are aware of the potential for confusion from polluted language, or do they seem to accept most statements at their face value? Give examples of polluted statements you heard used on you or your friends when you had a tendency to overlook the confusion they caused.

Your name _____

Nonverbal and Silences:
Communicating without Words

FEEDBACK BLANK

EXERCISES

ASSIGNMENTS

PERSONAL IMPROVEMENT BLANK

FEEDBACK BLANK (Chapter 9)

This feedback blank is somewhat different from the previous ones. Please read the directions before filling out the form.

Directions

Below are two sets of statements. You are to rank and order the items in each set from 1 (most like the meeting) to 10 (least like the meeting). Use this procedure; rank 1 first, then 10, then 2, then 9, alternating toward the middle.

The session was like this

_____ There was much warmth and friendliness.

_____ There was a lot of aggressive behavior.

_____ People were uninterested and uninvolved.

_____ People tried to dominate and take over.

_____ We were in need of help.

_____ Much of the conversation was irrelevant.

_____ We were strictly task-oriented.

_____ The members of the group were very polite.

_____ There was a lot of underlying irritation.

_____ We worked on our process problems.

My behavior was like this

_____ I was warm and friendly to some.

_____ I did not participate much.

_____ I concentrated on the job.

_____ I tried to get everyone involved.

_____ I took over the leadership.

_____ I was polite to all group members.

_____ My suggestions were frequently off the point.

_____ I was a follower.

_____ I was irritated.

_____ I was eager and aggressive.

EXERCISES:

EXERCISE 9-1
PARALANGUAGE—MEANINGS IN CONTEXT (On Your Feet)

The class should study the list of phrases or sentences below and imagine how they can be said differently to mean different things. Ask for two volunteers who want to say these lines to each other. When the two are on their feet in front of the class, they can take turns reading lines. After each reading, the class should guess (1) what the character of the message was intended to be (being playful or joking, being authoritarian, giving orders, asking help, etc.) and (2) what the implied relationship is between the two people—the one who speaks and the one spoken to.

After two people have finished their dialog and the class has guessed about the relationships and the "meanings," ask for two other students to read the lines and repeat the experience in a different way. A third pair of students could probably invent another set of relationships to demonstrate with tones and inflections which indicate what is being asked or ordered.

Sample statements follow (or you can make up some of your own):

"Get out of here."

"Come back."

"Are you busy?"

"What's that for?"

"Read it to me."

Discussion
A. Do you use a different tone of voice with people above you in status and those below you? Do you use a different tone of voice in relation to what you want to have done—like asking a favor, or giving an order to be carried out?
B. Not only does your tone of voice tell what you intend to have happen, but it tells the relationship between you and others. Was it hard to identify the roles being taken by the speakers? Where did you learn those specific ways of speaking to other people? If you listen to little children playing, are they imitating their parents' ways of speaking to each other?
C. If some of the relationships were difficult to guess, was it possibly because they were not very well defined? If two people are very much on the same level of authority, do they give orders to each other in a severe way?

EXERCISE 9-2
FIRST MEETING (Role Playing)

Role-play a first meeting between two people. Ask for pairs of students from the class to act out a situation in which two people are encountering one another for the first time. Ask the class to observe carefully the nonverbal as well as the verbal exchanges. Ask the actors to pay particular attention to their nonverbal behaviors, so that they can discuss it later with the class.

Some sample situations: (1) Two students are assigned to be roommates in the residence hall.

(2) Two parents of students who share a dormitory room meet in the room on the school visiting night. The roommates have described each other to their parents, but the parents have never met before. (3) A boy and a girl sit next to each other on a cross-country bus; or two men sit together on a cross-country bus; or two women sit together on an airplane. (4) You and another person are the only ones in a doctor's waiting room. (5) You are in the market for a new car. You enter the showroom of a local car dealer and are met by a salesperson.

Discussion

A. How much of the information about each other was exchanged by verbal as compared with nonverbal channels? What information was available to each person about the other? Did the performers seem to pay attention to the nonverbal cues?

B. When the encounter is over, what does each person report about the other? Does it take more than a few minutes to begin to draw conclusions about another person? How accurate are the first impressions? Are they more accurate if you draw your impressions from what you see as well as what you hear? Is the balance of verbal and nonverbal information more important than either by itself?

C. If you receive contradictory nonverbal and verbal information about the other person, do you tend to believe the nonverbal rather than the verbal information? Which channel (verbal or nonverbal) seems to you to be more reliable? Is that always true? Are there situations in which the opposite may be true?

EXERCISE 9-3
SHAKING HANDS (Game)

Each member of the class is asked to shake hands with another person, demonstrating the following:

1. A firm confident handshake
2. A limp, "dead-fish" handshake
3. A very active, pump-handle shake
4. A delicate, fingertip handshake
5. The "bruiser," or bone-crusher

Discussion

A. Did you have any trouble demonstrating these different styles of shaking hands? Have you had experience with them?

B. What other behaviors, nonverbal and verbal, would you expect to go with each kind of handshake? Did you adopt a "role" when you attempted each kind of handshake—a role that seemed appropriate for the kind of hand clasping being attempted? Is there more to a handshake than simply the hands of two people grasping each other? Are there postures, head positions, facial expressions, and verbal reinforcements for the handshakes?

C. Taking each of the five different handshakes in turn, have the class demonstrate the other nonverbal and verbal signals which would logically (for the majority of the class) accompany each handshake. Where did you learn to do that? Are your estimates of the person doing those things consistently accurate? Is a handshake one of the first contacts we may have with others?

D. Does American culture make as much use of handshaking as other cultures? At one time in our history the expression "We shook hands on it" implied a binding contract. What kind of handshake accompanies that kind of deal?

E. Another historical item: When asked if he knew a certain person, a rural American man said, "We've howdied, but we ain't shook." What level of acquaintance was signified by that response? Is that expression clear to you?

EXERCISE 9-4
HOW FAR AWAY TO SIT? (Game)

Using chairs set up in front of the class, have two or more students locate them in relation to each other according to the suggested situations. (You may want to develop some sample situations of your own.) As the class observes, the "actors" adjust the arrangement of the chairs to fit the following cases:

1. There are four chairs available. Two people who don't know each other come into the waiting room of a dentist.
2. Two good friends come into the same waiting room.
3. A mother and her worried 10-year-old child come into the same waiting room.
4. There are six stools at the counter of an eating establishment. Four people come in and take their places at the counter. Two strangers, a woman and a man, enter first. Then two people enter together who are obviously friends going to have lunch together.
5. A boss has called in a secretary to complain about consistently smudged and crooked letters. Arrange the two chairs in relation to a desk showing where each would sit.
6. A boss has called in a shipping clerk to say that the last few orders were very carefully dispatched and the customers have already telephoned compliments. There are four available seats and a desk in the room; arrange the furniture.
7. You have asked for an appointment with your boss in order to request a transfer to another department. When you enter the room the boss is at the desk and invites you to sit anywhere. There are three chairs available to you. Locate them for distance and direction.

Discussion

A. As the actors adjust the chairs, the audience may be consulted and some consensus developed on the placement of the persons in relation to one another. At the end of each skit the audience should be asked to comment on the location of the actors and their furniture, and also to comment on the reason for any lack of agreement with the actors' arrangements.

B. Status has some effect on where people sit. Does placement confer status, or do people of status take over a group from any position? A Scottish chieftain—Macdonald—was attending a dinner at a lord's castle and was asked, "Don't you want to sit at the head of the table?" To which he replied, "Wherever Macdonald sits, there is the head of the table."

C. Even in public places do you feel strongly about how you are seated? Is this a cultural factor as well as a personal matter? Do some cultures encourage closer seating at public events?

D. Where did you learn how far away to sit from someone else? How do you know what others are telling you by their location when they are talking to you? Are there predictable distances and arrangements? Do you see them yourself, or do you just have them used on you?

EXERCISE 9-5
HOW CLOSE SHOULD YOU STAND? (Game; Role Playing)

This exercise can be done by pairs of students acting out the situations and reporting to each other their feelings and experiences. It also should be demonstrated by one pair of students in front of the class so that the advice of all the class members can be used in establishing distances.

Dyads: Working in pairs   At a signal from the instructor the members of each pair stand up and place themselves at a distance which both can agree is comfortable to meet the assignment. If you and your partner cannot agree, make a specific note of which parts of the exercise caused the most difficulty in agreeing.

Simulate the following situations:

1. You want to tell the other person a secret. How close do you get?
2. You want the other person to check a list of items for you; no talk is needed.
3. You want to ask the other person to help you decide which necktie or scarf to wear.
4. The purpose of this exercise is to imagine what it is like to be a small child in a world of adults. Each dyad consists of an "adult" and a "child." The adults stand on chairs or in some other way elevate themselves about 1½ feet above the children. The children ask permission to have a friend over to dinner, or to go to the movies, or to buy some popcorn. The children try their best to be heard and to politely get what they want. After a few minutes, the members of the dyads exchange roles and repeat the exercise.

Demonstration in front of the class   Two persons from the class should be selected to role-play the appropriate distances for the situations listed below and for others suggested by class members. When the pair is ready to perform, the class members can call out their ideas.

Sample situations follow:

1. A boy and girl talking about class assignments
2. A boy and girl deciding where to go to eat
3. A boy and girl with a secret between them
4. Two women talking business
5. Two men talking sports
6. Two men conspiring to get another man fired
7. Two women who are doctor and patient talking
8. A man patient and a woman doctor talking

If the distance is not agreed on by the class members, ask the actors what they think. Clarification of the relationships, and additional data about the content of what is being exchanged, may affect the distance.

Discussion

A. Ask the dyads to tell how they feel when another person is encroaching on their space. Were any of the situations difficult to understand?

B. How did the "child" feel when trying to talk with the "adults"?

C. When dyads disagree about how far apart to stand in any of the sample situations, ask the class to guess why the differences exist. Do the dyad members come from different cultures? Is there a predictable difference between men and women? Does content make the most difference? (In other words, does what people are talking about establish how far apart they should be?)

EXERCISE 9-5
NONVERBAL ON VIDEOCASSETTE (Discussion; Role Playing)

A company called Transvision sells a videocassette called *Body Language.* Promotional material in catalogs look like this:

SHARPEN YOUR COMMUNICATION SKILLS!!

Knowledge of body language is a powerful tool that can help you in both your professional and personal life. Learn how to recognize over 100 different body signals, how to see what others are thinking, and much more. FREE: audiocassette and booklet with your order.

1. For class discussion of that advertising message, (a) see how many of the "100 body signals" you can imagine might be included, and (b) for each one you can list, ask someone else in the class to speculate on how being able to recognize that "body signal" might achieve the advertised goal of letting you ". . . see what others are thinking . . ."

2. Role-play the scene in a video store where the salesperson is attempting to explain to the potential customer how owning this videocassette will enhance both the personal and professional life of the purchaser. After two sets of role play, ask the class to define which of the arguments have some validity and which are based on nonverbal myth.

ASSIGNMENTS:

ASSIGNMENT 9-1
ADJUST YOUR TELEVISION SET

A. Watch a television show with the sound turned down. Are you able to follow much of what is happening? If you are watching a comedy, do most of the gags depend on sight rather than sound? Write a paragraph about your reactions to this experience, and estimate what percentage of the meaning of the program you were able to understand by only seeing it.

B. Try the opposite experience. With the sound turned on normally, either close your eyes or turn your back on the television set. Besides the content of the show, with the information provided by your hearing, are there elements of paralanguage which help you interpret the action? Write another paragraph about your reactions to this experience, and estimate what percentage of the meaning of the program you were able to get by only hearing it.

C. In a final paragraph, speculate on how the two systems of seeing and hearing reinforce each other. Are there instances in which they do not? (One classic example is the play-by-play narration of a football game which accompanies the television action. The announcers may not be accurately describing what is happening, and the same narration on radio has no picture to be compared with.)

ASSIGNMENT 9-2
LOGGING SILENCES

During the course of a day keep a record of the times when you experienced silence. Arrange the incidents by these categories:

1. Silences which occurred because nobody was around to talk to
2. Silences which represented indecision—not knowing what to say
3. Silences which were deliberate retreats into privacy
4. Silences of some emotion—sadness, awe, etc.
5. Silences of difficult thinking, or problem solving
6. Other categories

Write your reactions to these various silences. Were you aware before this exercise how much time was spent in silence? Or how little? Are silences useful to you? Do you enjoy them? Do they bother you?

ASSIGNMENT 9-3
SPACE DESIGN

How may the way a house is designed affect the nature of family relationships? Use examples from your own experience to answer this question.

ASSIGNMENT 9-4
GROUP OBSERVATION

Select any small group (not more than twelve members) on the campus holding its regular meeting. Secure permission to attend the meeting and observe the group. Make a chart representing the seating arrangement and observe only the nonverbal behavior of the group members. Observe their postures, facial expressions, who they look at, how they look at each other, etc. Take notes, and later summarize your findings in a short paper or an oral report to the class.

ASSIGNMENT 9-5
INTERVIEW

If you are able to meet one or more architects, interview them and ask them how they see spatial relationships, space design, and the effects of design on communicative behavior. Use the notes you take during your interview to make a report.

ASSIGNMENT 9-6
YOUR OWN NONVERBAL SIGNALS

Make a list of the gestures, moves, actions, etc., which you use to communicate with others (nodding your head to encourage someone to speak more, waving your arms to attract attention) in your everyday speaking encounters. Ask the class members, or other people who know you, if they have noticed these moves and if the moves meant anything to them.

Write a description of your nonverbal moves as you have observed them and had them checked by someone else. Analyze the moves to determine which are so characteristic of you that they may be considered a trademark, or a means of identifying you to your friends. Speculate on why people develop characteristic moves or nonverbal devices. Speculate on how communication effectiveness relates to use of nonverbal behaviors.

ASSIGNMENT 9-7
HOW ASSOCIATED PRESS TELLS YOU ABOUT RELATIONSHIPS

Reports from Manila during a crisis in the government headed by President Corazon Aquino gave reporters many opportunities to portray relationships by describing interactions which might not be typical if the chief executive were not a woman. One such story described the meeting between President Aquino and her Defense Minister, Juan Ponce Enrile, and it said she smiled and patted his hand but he wore an angry expression and looked away.

Discussion
A. Find reports in the newspapers where stereotypes of behaviors are cited as nonverbal expressions of relationships. Does a reporter's observation that someone "looked angry" or "turned away" give you important data on the interaction and how to interpret the news story?
B. Words used in the most objective news stories are supposed to be nouns and verbs with a minimum of colorful modifiers. In the stories you see, how many adverbs and adjectives are used

to describe features which cannot be described as either clear actions or clearly attributable quotations? Do most of those modifiers refer to nonverbal messages?

ASSIGNMENT 9-8
INTERIOR DECORATION ON SITCOMS

Television critics tell us that we feel comfortable with television programs which give us settings which are familiar—the living room for our favorite situation comedy, the kitchen where so much action has always taken place in family-comedy shows. The intimacy of repetition is very important for viewers, critics say, and if the furniture or decoration of your favorite situation comedy changes, it makes you uneasy and you may not know why. Long-running programs like *Dallas* even become identified with the "real ranch" in Texas which is used in establishing shots of SouthFork, and people drive past it expecting to see the Ewing family or other *Dallas* characters driving in and out and behaving just as they might on the fictional program.

Discussion

A. As you watch one of your favorite television shows, make notes on the room in which most action takes place. What features about it make you feel comfortable, and does the interior decoration seem to fit (1) the kinds of characters and (2) the kind of action you expect them to perform?

B. Compare the room most often presented in a comedy series with the similar room presented in a dramatic series. What differences do you see? Compare the furnishings in rooms of homes of the very wealthy (as in *Dallas*) with scenes in homes of poor or less affluent families. Do those furnishings seem effective in clearly depicting the correct socioeconomic levels?

C. As you see reruns of old programs, do you feel disturbed by the furniture and the design of the rooms? Are the interior decorations as much a part of "dating" the show as the style of clothing worn by the actors?

PERSONAL IMPROVEMENT BLANK (Chapter 9)

1. Watch a group sitting together some distance from you in a restaurant, a waiting room, a committee room, or some other place. Describe what behaviors you noticed and—because you were not listening to what was said but were only observing the nonverbal—tell why you think the group members were together. Did they work well together? What was their general mood?

2. As you watch others' nonverbal behavior, do you pay more attention to the (a) head signals, (b) moves of the body, or (c) actions of the arms and legs? Is it possible to isolate each part and its messages? Do you make better evaluations of the messages when you watch for the total context of nonverbal messages as they combine to form a total picture?

3. What have you learned in this unit on nonverbal communication and silences which will be of immediate use to you in your communication? Be specific.

Your name _____

FEEDBACK BLANK

EXERCISES

ASSIGNMENTS

PERSONAL IMPROVEMENT BLANK

FEEDBACK BLANK (Chapter 10) DO NOT SIGN

1. Rate the productivity of this session's work for you.

   1   2   3   4   5   6   7   8   9   10

   Not productive   Very productive

2. Rate how you think the rest of the class felt about the productivity of this session's work.

   1   2   3   4   5   6   7   8   9   10

   Not productive   Very productive

   Comments:

3. In relation to this chapter, were you assigned a role you did not like in your day-to-day activity? If people assign "identities" to you, what effect does this have on your reactions?

4. Add other comments, criticisms, questions, suggestions, etc.

EXERCISES:

EXERCISE 10-1
CHARACTERISTICS OF MEN AND WOMEN (Group Project)

This exercise is based on a number of studies which have investigated the attitudes of American society about men and women and their roles. It can provide an interesting study of sex stereotyping if the class members can remain open-minded and avoid having their feelings hurt by what must inevitably be sexist statements or categories.

Divide the class into groups, men on one side and women on the other. Ask each group, working independently of the other, to make lists of: (1) the chief characteristics of men in our society and (2) the chief characteristics of women in our society. When both groups have finished, members of the groups should put all four lists of characteristics on the chalkboard or write them with felt markers on large sheets of paper in big letters.

Each group will be allowed three additions and three subtractions as peremptory challenges if either group feels that the other group's lists have particularly unfairly characterized that sex. For example, the women may insist that a total of three items be removed from the men's lists and that a total of three items be included on the men's lists.

After this period of adjustment, have the students compare lists. Lead a discussion on the implications for roles and communication.

Discussion

A. In comparing the lists, ask if the men see their own characteristics better than they see those of women. Ask if the women are more perceptive about men's characteristics or their own. Ask for specific comparisons of those lists to make sure there is a careful examination for accuracy.

B. Select those items in each of the four lists which are positive in their relation to the society's values and those which are negative. Some items on the lists may be neutral or may so depend on circumstances that their positive or negative value cannot be determined in the abstract. Are there more positive items about men than about women? What implications does that have for self-concept and for assuming roles?

C. What kinds of items did the women and the men ask to have either removed from or added to the opposite group's list? Was there a pattern to those objections? How did the participants feel when they were challenged by the other group? Was there any reason given for the omission or the inclusion of these objectionable items?

D. Ask each group to rank its characteristics by selecting the five most important characteristics from the lists. (Each sex group may use any of the items from any of the lists.) The women will select those five items they most prize as characteristics for women; men will select the five most prized items for men. This should be done individually, unless there is a substantial amount of time for the segregated groups to spend in reaching an agreement on the top five characteristics. After all individuals have ranked their choices, ask for a discussion on what prevents all persons of the same sex from agreeing on items. Would you think that the opposite sexes would agree on items?

EXERCISE 10-2
CASES; TRUST AND DEFENSIVENESS (Role Playing)
Select people from the class to take various roles.

Situation   A new plan for city revenue has just been proposed by the city council in the city your college is in. The plan involves taxing students for use of the city streets; it will apply only to those students who do not live in the city, and therefore it sounds like an equitable way to get "transients" to help pay for the upkeep of the streets they use. A special ordinance will require each college or university in the city to assist in the fee collection by reporting all registered automobiles owned or operated by students. Local automobiles will, of course, not be taxed, as it is assumed that the people owning them are already supporting the local government's projects by paying some taxes. (If there are other items of concern to the actors, make up some reasonable extensions of this ordinance.) The scene is a meeting of the city council where various witnesses and other interested people are in attendance. The mayor is presiding and has asked certain people to speak (they will be so indicated in the cast of characters); others may want to be heard and will volunteer. The parts to be played include:

The mayor (who is in favor of the ordinance)

A city council member who is in favor of the issue

A city council member who is against the issue

The president of one of the local colleges (invited by the mayor, even though he or she is opposed to the ordinance)

A student from out of town

A student from within the city

Observers   Several observers should be appointed. Watch for the signs of defensiveness, and mark them down to report later. Other observers should watch for the ways in which defensive communication was either avoided or introduced and what effect it seemed to have on the flow of communication. Still other observers should watch for signs of developing trust, or for symptoms that trust did not develop.

EXERCISE 10-3
WIN AS MUCH AS YOU CAN[1] (Game)
The instructor will give details on how the game is to be played. The class is divided into groups of eight. Students not finding a place in a group will be assigned roles of observers and help monitor the activities. Groups of eight will be known as "clusters." Each group of eight, or cluster, will be further divided into dyads.

Each round is directed by the instructor. Time for working on a choice will be monitored, and

---

[1] Adapted from an exercise developed by William Gellerman. In J. William Pfeiffer and John E. Jones (eds.), *A Handbook of Structured Experiences for Human Relations Training,* vol. 3 (rev.), Universities Associates, La Jolla, CA, 1974.

payoff scoring will be quickly entered in the tally form (Table 10-1). When the round specifies that all the group (or cluster) will talk, it is possible for all members to talk with one another by teams. Otherwise only partners will discuss their strategies, as indicated. Strategies are shown in Table 10-2.

Discussion

A. If this is an exercise in conflict, how do participants deal with the choices of win-win and win-lose?

B. In the title "Win as Much as You Can," who is the "you" referred to? The entire group? A set of partners?

C. In developing strategies, did communication within the cluster have any advantage? When only partners were talking together, did you want to add the others to your conversation?

D. This is also an exercise in trust. What happened when the issue of integrity and honesty came up in the cluster communication?

E. How much could a cluster (the group of eight students) win if it were to maximize its wins and minimize its losses as a cluster? Did any groups come close to the maximum? Why not? Trace the negotiating efforts of those groups which had the highest scores—not just partners, but the entire cluster—to see whether there is anything special in what they did.

F. Would more frequent communication have been an advantage?

EXERCISE 10-4
WHEN TO TRUST AND WHEN NOT TO TRUST (Role Playing)

Remember the picture of a political candidate and the legend under it which asked "Would you buy a used car from this man?" If that means we judge a person at least somewhat by physical appearance, what other factors do we also use to make sure we can trust someone?

TABLE 10-1
Tally Sheet

Directions. **For ten successive rounds, you and your partner will choose either an X or a Y. The payoff for each round is dependent upon the pattern of choices made in your cluster:**

4 X's:	Lose $1 each
3 X's 1 Y:	Win $1 each Lose $3
2 X's 2 Y's:	Win $2 each Lose $2 each
1 X: 3 Y's:	Win $3 Lose $1 each
4 Y's:	Win $1 each

TABLE 10-2
Strategy

Directions. You are to confer with your partner on each round and make a joint decision. Before rounds 5, 8, and 10, confer with the other dyads in your cluster.

| Round | Strategy | | Choice | $ Won | $ Lost | $ Balance |
	Time allowed	Confer with				
1	2 min.	Partner				
2	1 min.	Partner				
3	1 min.	Partner				
4	1 min.	Partner				
5	3 min. + 1 min.	Cluster Partner				Bonus round: Payoff is multiplied by 3
6	1 min.	Partner				
7	1 min.	Partner				
8	3 min. + 1 min.	Cluster Partner				Bonus round: Payoff is multiplied by 5
9	1 min.	Partner				
10	3 min. + 1 min.	Cluster Partner				Bonus round: Payoff is multiplied by 10

In a small group develop a skit or drama of a communication situation in which the question of trust is central. The situation may be personal or general, and it may be quite trivial or of larger significance. The best kinds of role-playing material come from the experiences of the students themselves, but newspapers provide a wealth of examples. (The famous "pigeon drop" swindle is a classic, and reports of that con game appear almost weekly in the newspapers. In this trick, the victim is offered a part of money which was "found in an envelope." But to establish "good faith" the victim must put up some personal funds, usually placing them in an envelope with the original money. The victim even gets to hold the envelope while the con artists go to check just one more time on who lost the envelope. They never come back. The victim soon discovers the envelopes have been switched so the original money and the victim's "good faith" funds have gone off with the con artists and all the victim has left is an envelope of cut-up paper. This is a recurring example of greed balanced against trust.)

It must be emphasized that you can trust others with your feelings as well as with material goods. Your role-playing situation can make use of the fact that people can develop trust by words, looks, actions, and a past history of comparing those. Husband and wife, child and parent, teacher and student, customer and salesperson are all relationships in which development of trust is important. These are only a few suggestions for the role-playing situation you will plan and produce.

At the end of your skit, ask the class whether or not the people in the drama should have trusted each other. Ask the class to estimate what would be the outcome of the situation.

Discussion

A. Besides the questions you ask the class after the skit is finished, there are some general ideas which can be developed. For example, are people more careless about the smaller items of trust than the larger ones?

B. In looking back on the skits, discuss which kinds of information—verbal, nonverbal, etc.—were most influential in establishing trust. Do you believe what you hear or see or ''know'' from past experience? Which trust-producing devices did the actors use? Are they familiar ones to you in your real life?

C. If there are differing opinions in the class on the outcome of the skits and on who should have trusted whom, how do you account for the differences? Do you start out to trust or not to trust at a different level from others in the class? Where did you learn about trust? Do you rely primarily upon your own experience? Do the media and literature influence you also?

EXERCISE 10-5
THE CITIZEN OF THE YEAR (Role Playing)

"Well, friends," said the chairperson of the Community Club, "that does it! We've selected our 'Citizen of the Year.'"

"And a close race it was, too," said Al Martin. "People were saying it was going to be close, but I never figured . . ."

"By the way, Al," the committee chairperson broke in, "I want to see that all three candidates are at the Community Club dinner Thursday night. I don't care how you get them there, but they all should come."

"You mean you want all three candidates rather than just the winner?"

"That's right, Al. I've been thinking. With the selection being as close as it was, I really think we ought to mention all three candidates—even though, of course, only one will receive the award." The other committee members nodded in agreement. "We've never done this before, but it will be good to have a change in format."

The committee began to break up, and Al sighed. Well, he would see what he could do.

Al's job is to see each candidate and convince each to be in attendance without telling which one is to be the Citizen of the Year. The candidates are Jim Farnsworth, Frank Siciliano, and Anne Rollins. Al has a note in his pocket from the committee listing the name of the winner. He knows the winner's name but must not disclose it. In a role-playing skit, Al will talk to each candidate and after the skit is completed, the class will be asked to guess which of the three was elected. Al will then share the note with the entire class.

One by one, Al approaches the candidates and tries to convince them that they should be present as finalists. None of the candidates, however, is anxious to come to that dinner and be presented only as a "runner-up." The candidates want to find out as much as possible about their chance of being the winner before agreeing to be there. The actor selected for Al's role should be persuasive but able to keep a secret without ever lying—a difficult combination.

Al may choose to see the three candidates together (more difficult) or one by one in a series of short scenes; use no more than five minutes each if possible.

Discussion

A. Watch especially for the devices used by the three candidates to get information out of Al without directly pinning him down. How does he avoid answering their questions? Are these familiar devices to you?

B. How would each of the candidates feel about going to the dinner after having the conversation with Al? How high would each person's expectations be about receiving the award? When the announcement comes, are all the candidates going to be preparing to rise and be recognized?

C. What does Al risk in disclosing too much? In disclosing too little?

D. What do the candidates risk in demanding to know too much? In not knowing enough?

E. How can trust be maintained between Al and his committee if he lets the candidates know which is to be given the award, and then the runners-up do not appear at the dinner? How can Al maintain the trust of the candidates when they ask him about their chances of receiving the award? What would you do in Al's position?

ASSIGNMENTS:

ASSIGNMENT 10-1
RELATIONSHIPS

Everyone is talking about "relationships." Young people are accused of jumping into relationships irresponsibly. What is a "relationship"? What role does communication play in building a relationship? How do you avoid a breakdown in communication which ultimately jeopardizes a relationship? Do you and those with whom you share a relationship play by rules? If so, what are some of the rules? Do you have "relationships" with friends?

Keeping your answers to the above questions in mind, what do you think are the differences in your relationships with the following people?

1. A fellow student of the opposite sex
2. A fellow student of the same sex
3. A male professor
4. A female professor
5. A dean
6. The kids you went to high school with who do not go to college
7. Your parents
8. Your rich aunt or uncle (or some other rich relative, or a rich friend of the family)
9. Your drinking aunt or uncle (or some other relative)
10. The man or woman who interviews you for a job

Why are there these differences? Can you generalize about "relationships" from these ideas? Write a brief essay on what you think is the central consideration in relationships.

ASSIGNMENT 10-2
TEACHER EVALUATION

1. What would you like your instructor to know about you in order to evaluate you fairly? Write a list.
2. Look at what you just wrote, and try to figure out how much of it you said because you thought your instructor would want to read it, or because it would look good, and how much of it represents a real and honest expression of what you believe is important for the instructor to know in order to evaluate you fairly.

In class get together with another student or two to compare lists. Make an oral summary of results from your dyad or triad after you have picked out the important features you would like known. Consider how those characteristics would affect the evaluation you would get from an instructor. The instructor may comment on what must be known about students in order to give them accurate evaluations. Do the lists seem alike?

ASSIGNMENT 10-3
REFERENCE GROUPS

Reference groups help us determine whether or not we are performing our roles successfully. Can you give examples from your own experience that would support this statement?

Make a list of the reference groups you can identify that have an influence on you. After you have made the list, rank the groups in order of their importance to you. After the most important ones write a brief comment on (1) why the group is important to you and (2) how much time or energy you spend in keeping a relationship going with that reference group.

As a class exercise, it is interesting to compare lists of highest-ranking reference groups for the entire class. Are there consistent patterns among the students which indicate a similarity of role relationships?

PERSONAL IMPROVEMENT BLANK (Chapter 10)

1. On the basis of material in this chapter, identify briefly a relationship you have with a person whom you consider to be in a role very much like yours. Without using names, describe how you act toward each other. What is your communication like?

2. Identify a relationship you have with someone whose role you consider very different from yours. Without using names, describe how you talk and act toward each other.

3. Briefly list a recent example of "developing trust" which you either experienced or observed.

Your name _____

FEEDBACK BLANK

EXERCISES

ASSIGNMENTS

PERSONAL IMPROVEMENT BLANK

FEEDBACK BLANK (Chapter 11)   DO NOT SIGN

1. Rate the productivity of this session's work for you.

     1   2   3   4   5   6   7   8   9   10
   Not productive   Very productive

2. Rate how you think the class felt about the productivity of this session's work.

     1   2   3   4   5   6   7   8   9   10
   Not productive   Very productive

   Comments:

3. Are there signs of conflict in this class? If so, can you speculate on the causes?

4. Do you find it easy to give feedback to others in this class about their behaviors? Are you comfortable giving feedback to the instructor? What would make it easier for you in either case if you have difficulty at present?

EXERCISES:

EXERCISE 11-1
THE FAIR HOUSING CASE (Discussion)

The Problem

You are the local community advisory and investigatory board which determines whether or not a specific case involving alleged racial discrimination should be brought to court under the Fair Housing Act in your state. The board employs its own investigator.

The section of the act with which you are presently concerned reads: "It shall be an unlawful discriminatory practice . . . for any person to . . . refuse to sell, transfer, assign, rent, lease, sublease, finance, or otherwise deny or withhold commercial housing from any person because of race, color, religion, ancestry, or national origin of any prospective owner, occupant, or user of such commercial housing."

Greg Stephen and John Moore have filed a case with your board alleging that Mr. Genove has unlawfully discriminated against them. They state that they are students at the university. They are black. They arranged by telephone, answering an ad in the local paper, to rent an apartment owned by Mr. Genove. The apartment is part of a four-unit apartment house. They sent a check for the first month's rent on an upstairs apartment. The check was cashed by Mr. Genove. He wrote them a letter which stated they could rent the apartment for a full year if they so desired. Mr. Genove did not know that the men were black.

The men stated that they arrived at the university on the day before registration for the fall semester. They called Mr. Genove, and he delivered the keys to the apartment. Mr. Genove seemed "surprised" that the men were black. He gave them the keys, however, and stated at the time that he hoped they would find the apartment comfortable and that they would "decide to stay."

One week later, the men were served notice by registered mail that Mr. Genove was starting eviction proceedings and that they had two weeks to vacate the apartment. They phoned Mr. Genove to ask him why they were being evicted. Mr. Genove replied, "My attorney advised me not to discuss the case."

Additional Information

The board's investigation disclosed the following:

1. Mr. Genove and his attorney, in conference with the board, claimed that there was absolutely no discrimination involved in asking the men to move.
2. Mr. Genove showed the board a note from one of his renters in the apartment units, complaining that the men had staged a "wild party the night they moved in, with people tramping up and down the stairs until 3 A.M. and noise like a wild orgy or something."

In talking with the men, the board discovered:

1. They claim not to have had a "wild" or noisy party. They state that on the night in question, they had asked two of their friends over and that they had watched television and played cards until 12:30 A.M.
2. The men claim that while they were moving in, they overhead the complaining renter say to another occupant: "I am going to do something about them."
3. The complaining renter refused to talk to the board, stating that he did not want to be bothered by a lot of "silly" questions.
4. The only other occupant of the building who was home on the night in question stated that she had heard the men "laughing" late in the evening but did not consider it "excessive noise."
5. Mr. Genove has stated that the complaining renter was an old, retired man who had been renting from Mr. Genove for fourteen years.

What should the board do? One very effective way of analyzing this case is to divide the class into small groups and ask them to come up with a consensus on what the board should do.

Discussion
A. In analyzing the possible actions by the board, it would be useful to apply the principles of Chapter 11 of the text. First, try to analyze the types of conflict involved: personal, needs, etc. Identification of the basic nature of the conflict will be helpful in determining the course of action for the board.
B. Conflict among the participants must be managed either by directive of the board or by some other means. How possible do you think it is for the board to impress on the participants the need to manage their conflict?
   1. Should the board attempt to have participants avoid the conflict?
   2. Should the board attempt to defuse conflict by its own actions?
   3. If the board attempts to confront the conflict, should it work from the basic situations of win-lose, lose-lose, and win-win?
   4. Is it too idealistic to anticipate that the participants (as well as those who are not directly involved but who add to the conflict) will integrate their conflict rather than be subject to power or compromise? What are the possibilities?
C. If all the class were to be divided into separate small groups and each group given the responsibility for deciding what to do, would all groups come up with the same answers? What does that say about negotiating conflict? Is it always subject to the same "one right and correct answer"? On what do the various answers depend?

EXERCISE 11-2
ALLOCATION OF RESOURCES AND FAVORS (Role Playing)
Role-play some of the situations below to demonstrate how conflict arises from the scarcity of some commodity—whether a real thing like dollars, or a subjective concept like love or attention. It might be interesting to have small groups in the class work out role-playing skits from these items and

present them in two acts: the first act to set the scene for the problem and the second act to present a potential solution or resolution of the conflict.

1. A roommate borrows your sweater very often and has begun to use it even without asking. You go to the closet for the sweater; it's not there. You wait, ready to start an argument as soon as your roommate comes in.
2. A brother and sister both want to use the car on the same night. Should they settle the conflict with or without parental help? Look at it both ways.
3. You want to buy a motorbike. Your father wants you to save the money for college.
4. A new word processor is purchased for the office where you work. You and two other employees have old models, and each hopes to get the new machine. The boss has said that the three of you must decide who gets it. The boss refuses to participate in the discussion.
5. Four members of the history department are up for promotion to full professor from associate professor. Only one can be awarded that promotion this year. The other six members of the department are given the responsibility of deciding which member of the department gets promoted.

Hint Managing conflict in these situations may involve avoiding, defusing, or confronting. Try some solutions from each of these options to see which may be most dramatic to role-play for the class. Identify the kind of conflict management you are working with. Ask the class for comments on that method of handling the conflict.

Discussion

A. In applying the skills recommended in the chapter did you tend to get stopped at the stage of identifying the nature of the conflict? Do you find it easy to just sit and blame each other?
B. The steps recommended in the chapter have a certain logic to them and a recommended sequence. Did you have difficulty following the sequence? Was it hard to stay on the topic of conflict management?
C. Does this set of role-playing skits demonstrate why we are insisting on the terminology "management of conflict" instead of "avoidance"?
D. Can you identify the types of conflict you are dealing with? Personal conflict? Interpersonal conflict? Organizational conflict? Why is it useful to identify the type? Is it important therefore to understand that not all conflict is the same in its origin, and therefore that not all conflict may be amenable to the same kinds of solutions or management?

EXERCISE 11-3
TAKING RISKS (Discussion)

In a small group (four to six persons) develop a list of disclosure situations or communication occasions for which you believe there is a risk involved (talking to a salesperson, asking support for a political candidate, discussing your religious views, asking for a date, etc.). Be prepared to write these on the chalkboard or on large sheets of paper for a discussion by the class.

When you have set up your list, ask group members to speculate on what would be the most serious thing that could happen in the situation. In other words, when people say they are taking a risk, what is it they are risking? If disclosing yourselves to others is a risky business, then what would be the worst consequences?

Add the list of consequences of taking risks to the list of risky situations, and discuss, either in small groups or in class session, the relationship between disclosing and risking.

Discussion

A. If self-disclosure means taking risks, just what kind of risks are involved? Is disclosing worth the risks involved? Can you get hurt physically or emotionally?

B. Was it easy to find a list of occasions on which disclosing would possibly involve some risk? Do you find yourself in those situations very often? How do you deal with them?

C. If you avoid situations of disclosure, how do you manage that? Are your patterns different from those of the person who actively seeks situations for self-disclosure?

D. In the class discussion were there some situations which everyone seems to be involved in? Some which were very unusual? Do coping patterns differ?

EXERCISE 11-4
WHERE THE MONEY GOES (Discussion; Role Playing)

You are the chairperson for a committee to allocate funds among several agencies in the community. You have been given $100,000 to distribute among the organizations which community donors have given funds to support. Only a small amount of the money is specifically earmarked for an agency: Mr. Mintner gave $1,500 to the general fund with the clear commitment that it would all go to the cancer center; another anonymous donor gave a sum of $1,000 only if it would go to the child abuse council. Other funds are not earmarked. You and your committee have only this one meeting to decide how to allocate the total amount. Agencies making their appeals, together with the amounts they are requesting, are listed below. Notice that they are asking for many thousands more than you have available to distribute.

Child abuse council

This council assists in the detection, prevention, and education of parents who abuse children, and provides medical aid for abused children. Asking for $36,000.

Cancer center

This center works with detection of cancer and referral to treatment centers, but does no treatment itself. Asking for $30,000.

Boy Scouts

Local chapters active in all city areas including the inner city. Asking for $16,000.

Girl Scouts

As with the Boy Scouts, all areas of the city appear to be served by this organization. Asking for $14,000.

Symphony society

Membership drives have recently not produced enough funds to keep its best musicians employed. Asking for $20,000.

Drug center

This agency is a center for advice and referral for addicts and for education of citizens of all ages and school centers. It distributes some medications but is primarily a referral center. Asking for $20,000.

Crisis center

This telephone system for advice and counseling for persons who are in trouble or are emotionally disturbed serves as suicide prevention and psychological referral center. Asking for $15,000.

Aid to the aged

This agency is an information center for elderly citizens, giving advice about their legal rights and pensions. It would like to expand its service to include recreation. Asking for $22,000.

1. First, working alone, make up a list of the amounts you would personally award to any of the agencies. Be ready to defend your allocations.
2. Working in a small group, try to reach a consensus on how much to allocate to the agencies. When you have reached a general conclusion, the class should meet so that individual groups can report on how they allocated the funds.
3. A role-playing situation can be developed from the different allocations by asking for a small panel of class members (four to six) to act as the allocating committee and hear the arguments from the appealing agencies. In turn, each pair of class members can approach the committee to ask why their request was not granted, or why their allocation was the size it was. By approaching the committee as a pair of pleaders for the agency, you will reinforce each other's arguments and resolve to get straight answers from the committee.
4. After the role playing is finished, ask the class to vote again on allocations. Determine whether the opinions of any class members were changed by the appeals of the agency representatives as they confronted the committee.

Discussion
A. How easy was it for you to make the allocations to these different agencies? Were there some which were your sentimental favorites? Did your social conscience dictate your choices? Could you defend your choices?

B. In the group discussion was it easy for you to stick up for your own allocations? Were there some agencies about which you knew so little that it didn't matter to you what they received? Would you have argued less if you had not written down your answers before joining the group discussion?

C. If there were several groups reporting, did they all come up with the same allocations? Why might there be differences? What does that say about committees or other groups who are given the responsibility of allocating scarce resources?

D. As the result of the role-playing part of the exercise, did any opinions change? Were you in favor of those changes? How were the changes brought about? By good argument? By majority impact? By logic? By emotional appeal?

EXERCISE 11-5
JOHARI WINDOW (Dyad; On Your Feet)

(See diagram and discussion in Chapter 11.) Begin this exercise by yourself. Write down a list for each of the following:

"Five things I know about me that I'm sure others also know" *(Free area)*

"Five things I'd like others to know about me, but I'm pretty sure they don't"

"Five things I'd like to know about me which I suspect others may know but I don't"

After you have done that, find another person in the class and compare lists. Each of you should pick one item which is very important to you in each category. Ask (and answer) this question:

"What can I do to help others know about me and to learn about myself?"

Be specific in the reply to that question. Help each other develop ways in which an exchange of communication can be useful in getting others to know about you or helping you know more about yourself.

If there is time, it would be interesting for each pair of discussants to present *one of their items* to the entire class. First, list the kind of item (such as: something I want others to know about me) and then explain how you would go about letting it happen, or helping it to happen. Asking the class for their reactions to the information and how you can manage it is also a useful part of this exercise.

Discussion

A. In reviewing the quadrants of the Johari window, it should be emphasized that these vary with different relationships or situations. Your window is a different shape with different people depending on the maturity of your relationship.

B. Check the "free area" statements to find out *how* members of the class know whether or not others know those things about them. Then check with each other to see whether the "unknowns" are really unknown. How accurate are your pictures of how much others know about you?

C. In diagnosing the means of getting others to know about you, what communication systems or devices are available to you? How about when you want to know more about yourself and try to get others to tell you? Are there societal norms about giving honest feedback on *disagreeable* matters which may inhibit this exchange? Do you also have some difficulty *complimenting* one another?

D. If you poll the class on how much members know about each other, can you expect to get a wide variation of responses from your classmates? Do some know more things about you than others? Do some know more intimate things than others? Do some know almost nothing about you?

E. What relationships do you hope can be better developed by looking at how much is known between you and one other person? Is it easier to interact with your friends after you've shared many experiences? Explore reasons for different levels of interaction between you and specific others.

EXERCISE 11-6
THE BOB LEE CASE (Discussion)

Bob Lee was taking a difficult, required course during his junior year at Strivemore University. Bob needed a B average to keep his scholarship, but no matter how hard he studied, he could only get C's and D's on the weekly tests that would form the major part of his grade in the course. The professor curved the grades of the thirty students in the class, and Bob just could not seem to come out on the top of the curve.

After the fourth test, Bob was complaining about the situation to a fraternity brother who also was in the class. The brother sized him up and decided that since Bob was a good guy and part of the group, he'd give him the inside dope on the course. He swore Bob to secrecy and then told him the whole story. It seemed that the professor didn't correct her own papers but used a graduate student grader. The grader had found a new way to work his way through college. He had arranged, through a star football player in the class, to provide cram sessions before each test based on the key the professor gave him. He "tutored" nine of Bob's classmates at the rate of $5 per test or $10 if the student wanted the answers to memorize. For just "five or ten bucks" a week, Bob could join the group, and his problem would be solved.

Bob had a little money from his summer job, but he wasn't immediately ready to invest it in an A. Wasn't the whole thing unethical? Shouldn't the professor be told? But then again, what if his fraternity brother or the football player were expelled? Still, what about the students at the bottom of the curve?

All these questions and more went through Bob's mind. He had to decide soon, or it would be too late to save his grade.

If you were Bob, what would you do? Why? Try to get a consensus from your group. Have one member report your decision to the rest of the class.

Discussion

A. If more than one group in the class came to a consensus, did all groups come up with the same answer? What are the implications of that?

B. Was there a role conflict as well as a question of ethics? What did Bob want to be? How did he see himself? Which of many roles did he give a priority to?

C. In your analysis of the case, you placed yourself in Bob's role and made some assumptions about how you would act. Were you also conscious of the role you play as a member of a group discussing this case? Did the others in the group you are with have an effect on how you responded to Bob's dilemma? What are the implications of belonging to different groups who can influence you in different ways, even on a single issue?

EXERCISE 11-7
ENCOURAGING OTHERS TO TELL THE TRUTH (Role Playing; Discussion)

Asking someone to tell you the truth implies that you do not believe what is going on, or that you are sure the truth is important. The situation also has some risk for the truth-teller. The child whose father asks who broke the window is in a position of risk in the relationship. If there is an error in a set of accounting books, the question "Did you check these carefully?" is more than a simple request for data; it includes an indictment of the work and hence the worker.

In a small group develop some situations similar to the above examples in which a question is being asked with the intention of probing for a truthful answer. Either role-play the situations or discuss in the group the potential consequences of responding in various ways.

Is it possible to develop a "sandwich" situation by asking questions about the involvement of others? You give some information and at the same time take some, making layers of data.

Some additional suggestions for role playing: (1) The honor system of the military academies has come under fire in relation to the other norms of society which say that one doesn't tell on one's friends. (2) A child who breaks a lamp is promised no punishment for telling the truth, but then has privileges taken away. (3) A teacher asks a student if he or she received help on a paper, and then gives a failing grade when the student confesses.

Discussion

A. Do you make a contract with others when you ask them to tell the truth even if it is damaging to them? What immunity can be assured? In the courts of law "deals" are made in which testimony is given in exchange for a light sentence. How do you feel about such arrangements?

B. Have you ever been in a school or situation where the "honor" system was the approved way of managing relationships? How did it work? What was the reaction to it by those in authority? By those on whom the "honor system" was imposed or who pledged to follow it? That statement has been made about "honor systems": "In a college with the honor system, the faculty has the honor and the students have the system." Comment.

C. In the role playing, were you conscious of the nonverbal messages which were very much a part of the verbal communication? Do you pay attention to all the available data when you are in trusting or risking situations? Are you more attuned to what is happening than in everyday situations of simple information exchange among your friends?

ASSIGNMENTS:

ASSIGNMENT 11-1
HOW TO BEHAVE

Find some passages in a book of etiquette or a manual of manners which tell you how you should behave in a certain situation. Does this advice fit all occasions? If your etiquette book is not up to date, maybe the advice is not too good. Copy down and hand in:

1. A brief passage giving advice on how to behave which you believe would help a reader reduce role ambiguity or role conflict.
2. A brief passage which gives advice which would make you feel out of place rather than helping to reduce your role ambiguity.

ASSIGNMENT 11-2
A WEEK OF CONFLICTS

A. Keep a diary for a week on the conflicts you experience, whether they are trivial or of grave importance. At the end of the week categorize each conflict as "personal," "interpersonal," or "organizational." Speculate in a brief paragraph on which category seems to be most prevalent and why.
B. From the same list, put the conflicts into three time categories: (1) already taken care of, no carry-over, (2) being worked on and capable of imminent solution, and (3) very long term and possibly insoluble. How do you feel about each of those categories? Which take most of your time each day?
C. Place each conflict in one of the following categories: (1) conflicts you have avoided or will attempt to avoid, (2) conflicts you have defused or are attempting to defuse, and (3) conflicts you have confronted or will confront.
D. Finally, estimate how many of your conflicts could have been treated or managed with the skills of conflict management discussed in Chapter 11.

ASSIGNMENT 11-3
LOVERS' QUARREL

You have just had a serious quarrel with your boyfriend or girlfriend. As a result, you won't be having your usual date this weekend. The quarrel was over the amount of control that your parents exert over your relationship; specific gripes were exchanged about your parents' involvement in your affairs.

You are now faced with explaining this situation to the people around you, who will probably ask why you will not be having your usual date this weekend. How will you explain the situation to:

1. Your best friend
2. His or her best friend
3. Your roommate
4. Your parents
5. Your meddling aunt or uncle

Can you make some generalizations about the levels of disclosure that you will use in your explanations to these different people? With which people do you use the most abstract language? The least abstract language? Why?

Write up your sample dialogs with the various people listed above, answering the questions in this assignment in a summary of the differences you would put into your conversations with the different people.

PERSONAL IMPROVEMENT BLANK (Chapter 11)

1. Recount briefly here a recent conflict situation in which you won, lost, or came out even. What contributed to the outcome? Did you have any control over the outcome? Could you have applied the skills suggested in this chapter?

2. Write out a recent case or incident that required conflict management over the allocation of scarce resources. Describe the parties who were contending for the resources, their methods of confronting, and the outcome.

Your name _____

AUTHOR INDEX

* Numbers in italics indicate citations in footnotes or in chapter end notes.

SUBJECT INDEX